The International Law Dictionary

THE INTERNATIONAL LAW DICTIONARY

Robert L. Bledsoe
University of Central Florida

Boleslaw A. Boczek
Kent State University

ABC-CLIO

Santa Barbara, California
Oxford, England

Library of Congress Cataloging in Publications Data

Bledsoe, Robert L.
  The international law dictionary.

  (Clio dictionaries in political science)
  Includes index.
  1. International law—Dictionaries. I. Boczek,
Boleslaw Adam. II. Title. III. Series.
JX1226.B57 1987   341'.03'21   86-32060
ISBN 0–87436–406–X (alk. paper)
ISBN 0–87436–489–2 (pbk. : alk. paper)

10 9 8 7 6 5 4 3 2 1 (Cloth)
10 9 8 7 6 5 4 3   (Paper)

ABC-Clio, Inc.
130 Cremona
P.O. Box 1911
Santa Barbara, California 93116-1911

Clio, Press Ltd.
55 St. Thomas' Street
Oxford, OX1 1JG, England

This book is printed on acid-free paper ∞.
Manufactured in the United States of America

Clio Dictionaries in Political Science

SERIES STATEMENT

Language precision is the primary tool of every scientific discipline. That aphorism serves as the guideline for this series of political dictionaries. Although each book in the series relates to a specific topical or regional area in the discipline of political science, entries in the dictionaries also emphasize history, geography, economics, sociology, philosophy, and religion.

This dictionary series incorporates special features designed to help the reader overcome any language barriers that may impede a full understanding of the subject matter. For example, the concepts included in each volume were selected to complement the subject matter found in existing texts and other books. All but one volume utilize a subject-matter chapter arrangement that is most useful for classroom and study purposes.

Entries in all volumes include an up-to-date definition plus a paragraph of *Significance* in which the authors discuss and analyze the term's historical and current relevance. Most entries are also cross-referenced to give the reader the opportunity to seek additional information related to the subject of inquiry. A comprehensive index, found in both hardcover and paperback editions, allows the reader to locate major entries and other concepts, events, and institutions discussed within these entries.

The political and social sciences suffer more than most disciplines from semantic confusion. This is attributable, *inter alia,* to the popularization of the language, and to the focus on many diverse foreign political and social systems. This dictionary series is dedicated to overcoming some of this confusion through careful writing of thorough, accurate definitions for the central concepts, institutions, and events that comprise the basic knowledge of each of the subject fields. New titles in the series will be issued periodically, including some in related social science disciplines.

— Jack C. Plano
Series Editor

CONTENTS

A NOTE ON HOW TO USE THIS BOOK

The International Law Dictionary is organized so that entries and supplementary data relating to a particular topic are arranged alphabetically within subject-matter chapters. Entries pertaining to flag-state jurisdiction, the Law of the Sea Convention (1982), and the International Law of Marine Pollution, for example, can be found in the chapter entitled "The Law of the Sea." When doubtful about which chapter to consult, refer to the general index. Entry numbers for the definitions appear in the index in heavy black type; subsidiary concepts discussed within entries can be found in the index identified by entry numbers in regular type. For study purposes, numerous entries have also been subsumed under major topical headings in the index, giving the student access to broad classes of related information.

The authors have continued to follow the format of this dictionary series so as to offer the student a unique means of gathering information about the numerous areas pertaining to international law. This framework provides not only definitions of terms but also additional information highlighting the significance of each of the entries. Such a format makes the dictionary a versatile tool useful in a variety of ways, including (1) as a *dictionary* and *reference guide;* (2) as a *study guide* for courses in international law, international organization, and international relations; (3) as a *supplement* to international law textbooks or casebooks; (4) as a *source of review material* for the student enrolled in advanced courses in the field; and (5) as a *cognate-course aid* in various law-related courses, such as international business or public policy courses.

PREFACE

The Clio Dictionaries in Political Science Series is founded upon the premise that precise language is a basic tool of every intellectual discipline. This is particularly true in the field of law. Legal terms and concepts have specific meanings that are critical to an understanding of such a complex and changing subject. Yet it is difficult to create a reference source that will serve both the undergraduate student and the law practitioner or scholar. Should the definitions be general in nature in order to satisfy the needs of the student being introduced to international law for the first time, or should they be more technical and detailed for those already acquainted with this branch of law? We have attempted to meet the needs of both clienteles, the result being a unique reference source for those interested in public international law.

The three hundred and sixty-eight entries of this dictionary are grouped by subject matter into twelve chapters, the outline of the book corresponding to the latest developments in the theory and practice of international law. It begins with a general introduction to international law, its basic concepts and sources, and publicists important to its development. Subsequent chapters deal with states as subjects of international law; individuals, human rights, and international organizations; jurisdiction and jurisdictional immunities; the treatment of aliens; the spatial context (land, air and outer space, and the oceans); treaties; peaceful methods of settling disputes; use of force and war; and the laws of war and neutrality. The dictionary is a joint product of the coauthors in both its outline and selection of entries; but in general R. L. Bledsoe wrote Chapters 1–6 while B. A. Boczek authored Chapters 7–12, and substantively reviewed the contents of the volume. R. L. Bledsoe also thoroughly went through the text and drafted the Index.

In keeping with the format developed by Series Editor Jack C. Plano, each entry is defined, its basic features described, and is then followed by a *Significance* section in which an analytical, historical, and interpretative treatment of the entry is presented along with illustrative examples. This provides the reader with a greater understanding of the importance and meaning of the term, concept, or institution within its contemporary context.

We are indebted to a number of people whose contributions in various capacities have aided immensely in the fruition of this undertaking. We owe a particular debt to Professor Jack C. Plano who not only encouraged us to undertake the project but also devoted much time to critical reading of the manuscript in all its stages. Cecelia A. Albert, our ABC-CLIO editor responsible for shepherding us through the project to its conclusion, was a model of understanding and support as deadlines kept slipping by. We cannot say enough about the professional word processing skill, efficiency, and patience of Karen Lynette as she worked through numerous drafts, catching errors that we overlooked. Finally, the only way in which we can thank our families for their tolerance and understanding of the disruption of family life such a project entails is to point to the dictionary and hope that its use by students and others will foster a greater commitment to international law and a safer and more peaceful world for themselves and their families as well as ours.

In a work of this length and complexity there is ample opportunity for errors of commission and omission. For such, the authors claim sole responsibility and encourage the readers to alert them to any that they discover.

— Robert L. Bledsoe
University of Central Florida

— Boleslaw A. Boczek
Kent State University

The International Law Dictionary

1. International Law in General

Act of State Doctrine (1)

The rule that a state's executive, legislative, or judicial acts—having effect within that state's territory—are not subject to judicial inquiry by other states. The act of state doctrine has a long history of support in the United States, with perhaps its clearest expression set forth by the Supreme Court in *Underhill v. Hernández*, 168 U.S. 250 (1897): "Every sovereign state is bound to respect the independence of every other sovereign state, and the courts of one country will not sit in judgment on the acts of the government of another done within its own territory." While the doctrine is not universally accepted, it is founded upon the principle of state sovereignty and the assumption that a state is better able to determine the validity of its acts vis-à-vis its own laws than is the court of another state. In American courts, the doctrine is viewed more as a matter of constitutional law than of international law, with courts generally exercising judicial restraint vis-à-vis the executive branch in matters of foreign policy. *See also* SOVEREIGNTY, 75.

Significance   The act of state doctrine is widely supported by both Anglo-American law countries (the British refer to it as the sovereign act doctrine) and communist states, while many noncommunist civil law countries prefer to deal with such issues through conflict of laws (private international law). The act of state doctrine raises several sets of issues, particularly those in which acts may be contrary to international law or where they are contrary to the public policy of another state affected by such acts. U.S. courts have held that the act of state doctrine is applicable in those instances when foreign actions are contrary to U.S. policy. In the controversial Supreme Court case of *Banco Nacional de Cuba v. Sabbatino*, 376 U.S. 398 (1964), the Court was not willing to apply the doctrine in those instances where the issue is an alleged violation of international law. The controversy evoked by the *Sabbatino* decision prompted the Congress in 1964 to pass an amendment to the Foreign Assistance Act of 1961, the so-called "Hickenlooper Amendment," which forbids U.S. courts to decline to rule on grounds of the act of state doctrine in cases involving expropriation of American property in violation of international law. Despite the Hickenlooper Amendment, American courts have generally viewed acts of state as political rather than legal issues. Therefore, the initial determination of a course of action is left to the executive branch before ruling on the merits of the case, since foreign policy is mainly in that branch's domain. Some foreign courts, however, have been more willing to rule on the legality of acts of state such as in the case of *Anglo-Iranian Oil Co., Ltd. v. Jaffrate* (Aden Supreme Court, 1953), in which the Court held the Iranian Nationalization Act of 1951 to be contrary to international law.

Austinianism   (2)
A theoretical school of jurisprudence that holds that law exists only when it emanates from a superior authority and can be enforced by punitive sanction. Austinianism is named after the English author and jurist John Austin (1790–1859) who, in his *Lectures on Jurisprudence*, argued that law is the command of a sovereign enforced by the threat or use of force (police action). To Austin and his followers, international law is at best international "positive" morality. Any international norms to which a state subscribes are voluntary and inferior to domestic law. The Austinian school is sometimes referred to as the "analytical" school. *See also* AUTOLIMITATION, DOCTRINE OF, 3; TRANSFORMATION, DOCTRINE OF, 44.

Significance   Austinianism holds that international law is not true law because there is no superior authority above the state to enforce international legal norms and to punish transgressors. To the followers of Austin's thinking, only when an authority superior to the state is created with the power to enforce the observance of international norms will international law be true law. Despite such arguments by the Austinian school, the constitutions of many states contain explicit statements attesting to the existence of and subscription to international law, and international practice universally recognizes the legal nature of this system of law. Nevertheless, the decision (as well as the means) to sanction violators of international law remains largely that of states rather than of regional or global agencies.

Autolimitation, Doctrine of (3)

A school of thought on the nature of international law which suggests that, since a state can create binding domestic (municipal) law, it can also create binding international law. However, the autolimitation school goes on to say that since the state voluntarily creates such laws, the state may also unilaterally terminate them. This doctrine of self-limitation was popularized by Georg Jellinek in his *Die rechtliche Natur der Staatsverträge* (The Legal Nature of Treaties, 1880) and *Allgemeine Rechtslehre* (General Jurisprudence 3d ed, 1914). *See also* AUSTINIANISM, 2; MONISTS, 23.

Significance   The autolimitation school approaches the debate over the nature of international law by rejecting the assertion of the Austinans that international law is not law at all. At the same time, autolimitationists resemble Austinians in the weak and untenable position in which they place international law vis-à-vis the state. This is the case because of the central role accorded states in creating legal norms. Since the state alone creates the norms and voluntarily abides by them, states may also unilaterally terminate them. This position is sometimes referred to as inverted monism, since it argues for supremacy of municipal law over international law in a hierarchical legal system.

Codification and Progressive Development of (4) International Law

A systematic organization and statement of the international legal norms pertinent to a specific topic. This can be (1) "codification," that is, a more precise formulation and systematization of rules in fields where there already has been extensive state practice, precedent, and criteria; or (2) "progressive development," meaning the preparation of draft conventions on subjects that have not yet been sufficiently developed in the practice of states. *See also* INTERNATIONAL LAW COMMISSION, 16; TREATY, 279.

Significance   Codification efforts have dominated the twentieth century in the evolution of international law, beginning with the landmark Hague Conventions of 1899 and 1907, resulting from the conferences of the same years, and the League of Nations–sponsored Codification Conference of 1930. In the post–World War II era, much of the codification of international law has been the result of the work of the International Law Commission created by the United Nations General Assembly in 1947 in response to Article 13 of the United Nations Charter enjoining the Assembly to encourage the progressive development of international law and its codification. The four 1958 Geneva conventions dealing with various aspects of the ocean regime, the 1961 Vienna Convention on Diplomatic Relations, and the 1969 Vienna Convention on the Law of Treaties are only a few examples of codification efforts of the International Law Commission. Other codification of international law has been undertaken by the United Nations itself—the United Nations Convention on the Law of the Sea (1982) is an outstanding example. Other international organizations, both public and private—nongovernmental organizations or NGOs; for example, the International Committee of the Red Cross—have also been engaged in codification work in their particular spheres of interest.

Comity   (5)

Friendly gestures or courtesies extended to one state by another without legal obligation. Comity (*comitas gentium*) is based upon the concept of the equality of states and is normally reciprocal. Extended and widespread usage of such practices may eventually lead to their becoming part of customary international law, but such gestures are not in the strictest sense part of the law of nations. *See also* SOURCES OF INTERNATIONAL LAW: CUSTOM, 39.

Significance   Comity aids in promoting and maintaining friendly relations among states. It is apparent in such matters as (1) a public vessel of one state dipping its flag when passing a public vessel of another state, or (2) states reciprocating in not requiring passports or visas when citizens of one country visit the other for short periods of time. While technically not legal norms, such practices can be widely observed and have from time to time evolved into customary practices and/or were codified, thus becoming part of international law. A recent example is the exemption from customs duties of articles for personal use by diplomats (formerly an example of international comity), which is now reflected in the 1961 Vienna Convention on Diplomatic Relations (Article 36).

Communist View of International Law   (6)

To Marxist-Leninist states, international law is that body of norms to which states have given their consent to be bound. Communist states view sovereignty as the key feature of the international system, and it governs their reaction to specific international norms. The communist view of international law claims to be based upon the principles of peaceful coexistence; mutual respect for the territorial integrity and sovereignty of states; nonaggression; noninvolvement in the internal affairs of states; and equality and mutual benefit. In Soviet legal theory, peaceful coexistence is central to the Soviet Union's view of international law and, while initially viewed as only temporary by the People's Republic of China, the Chinese have also accepted it as the foundation of the international legal order in the post–Cultural Revolution period.

Significance   Initially the communist view of international law was that it was only a temporary phenomenon developed by capitalist states and would wither away as states ultimately would, in the Marxist view. The Soviet focus upon peaceful coexistence as the basis of international law gives the international legal order a greater role. In the Soviet view, peaceful coexistence is a means to protect socialist states and keep them apart from capitalist states. Conversely, Western states have assumed that peaceful coexistence is a means of linking states together in a more constructive and positive relationship. In adapting Marxist-Leninist theory to the international legal order, communist states have viewed states as the only subjects of international law, denying individuals standing under any conditions. More recently, they have included international organizations as subjects of international law. To such states, treaties form the basis upon which states accept international legal norms (as they must give their consent to such norms and it is, therefore, an expression of their sovereignty). Norms based upon custom and usage are viewed with caution (although not necessarily rejected), as they are capitalist in origin. The same may be said about general principles of law. At the same time natural law is not rejected, as it is viewed by communist legal theorists as part of the historical dialectic. Soviet theorists have developed a typology of international law, consisting of international law as it applies to dealings between capitalist states, between capitalist and socialist states, and between socialist states, the latter being the highest form of law. Ironically, while sovereignty is the key to the relationships of the first two categories, being the means whereby socialist states protect themselves against capitalist states, it is not so absolute in dealings between socialist states. The Chinese also divide international law into categories—socialist, Western, and Soviet (the latter being inferior to the socialist legal order represented by the People's Republic of China). To the Chinese, a major distinction in their approach to international law in contrast to the Soviet approach is that the latter is reactionary and status quo oriented, while the Chinese hold that international law is progressive and should address the concerns of the Third World.

Conflict of Laws (Private International Law)   (7)

That branch of municipal law which deals with private law situations in which the laws, jurisdiction, or judicial judgments of more than one country are involved. Conflict of laws situations typically involve torts, contracts, inheritances, nationality issues, marriage, and divorce.

Significance   Conflict of laws involves the clash of municipal laws of two or more states as they affect individuals beyond a single state's jurisdiction. It seeks to determine the jurisdiction of national courts in cases involving a foreign element. As a result, there exists a great diversity among the rules of private international law in different countries, often producing hardship for persons concerned. Sometimes states enter into bilateral or multilateral treaties designed to unify their rules of private international law. In such cases, the content of private international law comes to be regulated by public international law in the form of a treaty, and the rules regulating the conflicts of two or more systems of private municipal law become rules of public international law.

Consensual Theory of International Law   (8)

The theory that the basis upon which an international legal norm is binding is the consent of states. The consensual theory holds that a state is not bound by a legal norm to which it has not given its express consent. Conversely, should a state not clearly and openly object to a particular norm, then it can be considered to have given its tacit or implied consent to that norm (e.g., custom and usage). *See also* JUS COGENS, 19; SOURCES OF INTERNATIONAL LAW: CUSTOM, 39; SOURCES OF INTERNATIONAL LAW: TREATIES, 43.

Significance   The consensual theory has a long tradition, as it formed the basis of the historical Western international legal order begun through custom and usage based upon the consent of states. In the modern world of ideological conflict and Third World states, the consensual theory of international law remains appealing to many states because it reinforces their sovereignty and independence of action. Rather than being bound to existing international legal norms by virtue of being accepted into the community of nations, states claim that the need for their consent allows them selectively to bind themselves to specific norms rather than the inclusive body of extant law. At the same time, the consensual theory undermines the predictability and regulatory utility of law by its selective application. The theory also clashes with the concept of *jus cogens* (peremptory norms which bind all states).

Domestic Jurisdiction (9)

Those interests and actions that fall solely within the jurisdiction of the state and are subject to its municipal law. States jealously guard their domestic jurisdiction, as it is an attribute of their sovereign independence and equality. So important is it that Article 2(7) of the United Nations Charter specifically precludes that organization from intervening in matters essentially within the domestic jurisdiction of its members. What constitutes matters that are essentially within a state's domestic jurisdiction is a matter of much dispute (it is not defined in the Charter), but it is suggested by various publicists to include some or all of the following: matters of national government and domestic administration; matters of non-self-governing territories; matters of nationality and immigration; and matters of economic and social structure, including human rights and freedoms. Areas such as these are referred to by some as the state's "reserved domain." *See also* SOVEREIGNTY, 75.

Significance   Domestic jurisdiction is a very real but ill-defined concept in international law. Despite the listing of possible matters essentially within a state's domestic jurisdiction, there is no clear determination of what can be so classified. What is or is not within the domestic jurisdiction of the state is, therefore, a relative question. Clearly, the traditional view that the state is free from outside intervention in its international affairs has been subject to challenge. Issues have arisen over state obligations to provide minimum treatment to aliens, protect diplomatic personnel, prevent counterfeiting of other states' money, refrain from allowing the use of its territory for actions injurious to other states, and the proper treatment of minorities and human rights, to name but a few. Furthermore, extensive or serious abuses of a state's reserved domain give rise to theories of collective intervention, humanitarian intervention, and the abatement of a nuisance. Finally, the reserved domain or domestic jurisdiction of the state is subject to change as the international system and international law change. Increased global interdependence, self-determination movements, greater attention to ecological and pollution issues, and human rights issues are today challenging the reserved domain of state domestic jurisdiction.

Dualists (10)

A theoretical school of thought on the relationship of international law to municipal (domestic) law associated with Heinrich von Triepel, Dionisio Anzilotti, and Francis Lassa Oppenheim. Dualist theory holds that the two types of law function on different levels and represent two separate legal orders, with each dominant in its own sphere. International law regulates the conduct of sovereign entities (states); municipal law regulates the conduct of individuals and other private persons within a sovereign entity. Dualists are sometimes referred to as pluralists, since they argue for two separate legal systems. *See also* INCORPORATION, DOCTRINE OF, 14; MONISTS, 23; TRANSFORMATION, DOCTRINE OF, 44.

Significance   There are several versions of the dualist approach but, in simplest terms, the dualist doctrine holds that international law gains its binding effect upon states by being "transformed" (through statutory enactment), "incorporated," or otherwise specifically adopted into municipal law, just as a municipal norm must be incorporated into international law before it becomes a norm binding upon nations. The sanctity of national sovereignty and the notion that states (rather than individuals) are subjects of international law is central to the dualist school. In any clash between the two legal systems, municipal law is supreme. A major dilemma of the dualist doctrine is that, according to its point of view, should a dispute arise over a conflict between national and international law, the only recourse for redress by the injured state is an international tribunal.

Eclectics   (11)
A major school of thought on the nature of the law of nations, critical to its evolution in the seventeenth through nineteenth centuries. Eclectics, or Grotians as they are alternately referred to after their most famous member, held that the law of nations consists of both natural law and positive law, although in practice they tended to give precedence to natural law. *See also* NATURALISTS, 24; POSITIVISTS, 26; PUBLICISTS: GROTIUS, HUGO, 29; PUBLICISTS: VATTEL, EMERICH DE, 33.

Significance   Eclectics gain their name from drawing upon both natural and positive law as sources of international legal norms, rather than single out one or the other, as did the naturalist and positivist schools. While moderate positivists share some similarities with eclectics, they differ in the legal predominance of natural versus positive law in cases of conflict, eclectics arguing in favor of natural law and moderate positivists for positive law (although publicists' positions have not always been consistent in this regard). Eclectics gained ascendancy over naturalists, only to be overtaken in turn by the positivists in the nineteenth century. One could venture a statement that the twentieth century witnessed a revival of the eclectic school as the Third World focused increasing attention on concepts of equity and general principles of law (reminding one of the natural law idea) and nations grappled with the philosophical and moral issues raised by world wars and genocide.

Enforcement of International Law (12)

International law is enforced through a variety of means, although it is mostly self-enforced through voluntary compliance. Other international enforcement means include diplomatic protests, world opinion, mediation and conciliation, arbitration and adjudication, political settlement, bringing the matter before regional and international organizations and, ultimately, such coercive means as sanctions, including the use of force. *See also* ARBITRATION, 283; CONCILIATION, 285; CONTENTIOUS JURISDICTION OF THE INTERNATIONAL COURT OF JUSTICE, 286; INTERNATIONAL ADJUDICATION, 291; MEDIATION, 294; PACIFIC SETTLEMENT OF INTERNATIONAL DISPUTES, 297.

Significance Enforcement of international law is less developed than is the case with municipal law, which has enforcement agencies and effective sanctions against violators of the law. The present state of the international system, which retains the central feature of state sovereignty, precludes such institutionalized enforcement agencies that would operate independent of the desires of states. The consent of states to particular international legal norms provides the main means of enforcing such norms, as the predictability and mutual benefit from reciprocal observance serve the best interests of states. International law is, therefore, self-enforced out of self-interest. It should be noted that violations of international law do not void the law, even if not enforced.

Ex Aequo et Bono (13)

Basis for a decision by an international tribunal on the grounds of justice and fairness. Article 38 of the Statute of the International Court of Justice cites *ex aequo et bono* as an alternate means of decision making in place of the normally employed legal rules of treaties and custom. A case can be decided *ex aequo et bono* only with the consent of both parties to the dispute before the judicial body, however.

Significance *Ex aequo et bono* is somewhat analogous to but not exactly the same as the Anglo-American legal concept of equity. The former is broader than equity and gives the court greater license than the latter. It allows a court to decide a case on considerations other than legal norms—or even in defiance of those norms—if it is sensed that justice can so be served. Neither the Permanent Court of International

Justice nor its successor, the International Court of Justice, has been called upon to decide a case *ex aequo et bono,* although the principle of equity has been applied (e.g., in the dispute between the Netherlands and Belgium over the diversion of water from the Meuse River, settled by the Permanent Court of International Justice in 1937; also the *North Sea Continental Shelf* cases decided by the International Court of Justice in 1969). *Ex aequo et bono* has been resorted to by international arbitral tribunals in the Cayuga Indians claim in 1926, the Guatemala-Honduras boundary issue in 1933, and the Gran Chaco War between Bolivia and Paraguay in 1938. Its relative lack of use reflects the reluctance of states to grant such a sweeping authority to an international tribunal.

Incorporation, Doctrine of   (14)

The principle that international law is considered to be part of the municipal law and, therefore, is binding upon the state regardless of whether there exist municipal statutes that reflect these norms. *See also* MONISTS, 23; TRANSFORMATION, DOCTRINE OF, 44.

Significance   A state that subscribes to the doctrine of incorporation or general "reception" accepts international legal norms as binding regardless of whether the state had a hand in forging those norms. As was eloquently stated by the United States Supreme Court in the case of *The Paquete Habana; The Lola,* 175 U.S. 677 (1900), "International law is part of our law. . . . For this purpose, where there is no treaty, and no controlling executive or legislative act or judicial decision, resort must be had to the customs and usages of civilized nations." While some states simply subscribe to the doctrine of incorporation as a matter of practice (such as the United States), others go so far as to include the doctrine in their constitutions (such as Austria, Switzerland, and the Federal Republic of Germany). Although under the U.S. Constitution (Article VI, Section 2) treaties are "The supreme law of the land," the constitution of the Federal Republic of Germany, for example, states more inclusively that "The general rules of international law form part of the Federal law. They take precedence over the laws and directly create rights and duties for the inhabitants of the federal territory" (Article XXV). Other states, such as the Netherlands and Luxembourg, go so far as not only to subscribe to the doctrine of incorporation, but also to state clearly that in any conflict between international law and municipal law, international law takes precedence. These latter states are examples of the monist school on the relationship of international law to municipal law.

International Law (15)

The body of legal rules considered binding upon states and other international persons in their mutual relations. International law is founded primarily upon treaties and custom, as well as general principles of law recognized by civilized nations (along with such subsidiary sources as judicial decisions and the works of legal scholars). The term "international" is attributed to the English philosopher Jeremy Bentham, as a translation of the term *jus inter gentes* used by Richard Zouche in his manual on international law. International law is also referred to as the law of nations (*droit des gens*), a more traditional name, or public international law (all of which suggest its scope and subject matter). International law is sometimes separated into *universal, general,* and *particular* international law. Universal international law refers to norms considered to be so fundamental or basic to the community of nations that they are binding upon all states whether or not they have consented to them. An example of this would be the principle of *pacta sunt servanda. General* international law is often used to signify the norms derived from multipartite (law-making) treaties subscribed to by a large number of nations. These tend to encompass all regions of the globe and frequently become virtually universal. *Particular* international law refers to the norms created by treaties among a limited number of states, such norms binding only those states. Although international law is applied by international courts and tribunals it is also frequently applied by national courts. *See also* CUSTOM, 39; GENERAL PRINCIPLES OF LAW, 40; TREATIES, 43.

Significance   International law has a rich history dating back to antiquity. Modern international law is linked to the evolution of the modern territorial state system which emerged in Western Europe in the sixteenth and seventeenth centuries, conveniently but inaccurately dated from the Peace Treaties of Westphalia in 1648. Because of its close ties with the Western state system, international law is viewed as a product of Western values and traditions. Some of its rules, therefore, have selectively come under increasing challenge from the non-Western world, where many independent states emerged in the post–World War II period, as well as from communist states. It must be stressed, however, that both of these categories of states accept and approve in principle the traditional system of international law. A major undertaking of the contemporary international system has been, therefore, the creation and adaptation of legal norms to which the global community can subscribe. This is the logic behind such international conferences as those dealing with diplomatic law, consular law, treaty law, and the law of the sea. While such activities often validate existing norms, new norms and changes in past customary practices are not uncommon. Such has been the case, for example, with the expansion of the width of the territorial sea, the exclusive economic zone, and the creation of the concept of the "common heritage of mankind." This latter concept, however, is subject to many conflicting national interpretations.

International Law Commission   (16)

A subsidiary body of the United Nations General Assembly established in 1947 to initiate studies and make recommendations encouraging the progressive development of international law and its codification. The International Law Commission consists of thirty-four members (originally fifteen until 1956) chosen for five-year terms by the General Assembly on the basis of their recognized expertise in international law as well as reflecting the various geographic regions, political views, and legal traditions of United Nations members. The Statute of the International Law Commission charges the Commission to prepare both draft conventions on subjects not yet considered established international law and to codify international law in areas in which there is international legal precedence and practice.

Significance   The International Law Commission has been very active since its creation. Of the various intergovernmental and private bodies and agencies dealing with the codification and development of international law (such as the Asian-African International Law Commission, the Harvard Research in International Law group, the Institut de Droit International, the International Law Association, and the American Institute of International Law), the International Law Commission has been the most productive. It has created draft conventions on the rights and duties of states, offenses against the peace and security of mankind, the elimination of statelessness, diplomatic relations, consular relations, treaty law, and the law of the sea, among others. Its draft conventions have provided the basis for a number of successful codification conferences, such as the four 1958 Geneva conventions on the law of the sea, the Vienna conventions on diplomatic and consular relations of 1961 and 1963 respectively, and the 1969 Vienna Convention on the Law of Treaties. This is particularly impressive given the diversity of political and legal backgrounds of its membership. At the same time, such diversity has made the distinction between codification of existing law and development of new areas difficult, as both communist and Third World states have often challenged the validity of customary norms of Western origin.

Intertemporal Law (17)

Those principles relating to which evolving legal norms over time are to be applied to a particular case. Intertemporal law was eloquently explained by arbitrator Max Huber in the *Island of Palmas* arbitration (U.S.-Netherlands, 1928) in which he stated that "the same principle which subjects the act creative of a right to the law in force at the time the right arises, demands that the existence of the right, in other words its continued manifestation, shall follow the conditions required by the evolution of law."

Significance Intertemporal law reflects the fact that international law, like all law, is dynamic and not all norms are permanent. The creation of a right does not make it static; rather, the continued existence of that right forces it to accommodate itself to changes in the law. Intertemporal law comes into play in those cases where an international legal norm has undergone change or ceases to remain valid over time.

Jus Civile (18)

The civil law of ancient Rome that applied to Roman citizens. *Jus civile* was distinguished from *jus gentium,* which applied to non-Romans of the Empire, as well as relations between Romans and non-Romans. *See also JUS GENTIUM,* 20; *JUS NATURALE,* 21.

Significance *Jus civile* formed part of the foundation for later national legal systems of Europe and other parts of the world. It also contributed many concepts and principles now embodied in international law, governing, for example, acquisition of title to territory, state liability for actions deleterious to other states, and freedom of the high seas. While *jus civile* was purposely distinguished from *jus gentium* by the Romans, many of the norms of *jus civile* eventually blended with *jus gentium* and the concept of *jus naturale,* providing the substance of the law of nations in the modern system of the European territorial states.

Jus Cogens (19)

A peremptory norm of general international law from which states cannot escape. For a norm to be considered *jus cogens,* it must be accepted and recognized by the international community of states as a whole. *See also* GENERAL PRINCIPLES OF LAW, 40; *JUS NATURALE,* 21.

Significance *Jus cogens* (or peremptory rule of international law) was a popular concept among early writers on international law as natural law was its philosophical base. It fell out of favor with the decline of the doctrine of natural law, however, and has been revitalized only in recent decades. The most explicit expression of *jus cogens* in the contemporary period is Article 53 of the 1969 Vienna Convention on the Law of Treaties, where it is stated that "A treaty is void if, at the time of its conclusion, it conflicts with a peremptory norm of general international law." By this it is meant that a treaty cannot modify or evade a norm of *jus cogens* unless it is done by the international community as a whole. The rules against aggression and genocide are the two peremptory rules of international law enjoying general acceptance.

Jus Gentium (20)

That body of Roman (civil) law that applied to all non-Romans in the Empire as well as dealings between Romans and non-Romans. *Jus gentium* (law of tribes) was based upon the norms and concepts common to the various groups throughout the Roman Empire. *See also* JUS CIVILE, 18; JUS NATURALE, 21; POSITIVISTS, 26.

Significance   Jus gentium came to be viewed by early writers and jurists as universal in applicability, since it consisted of norms common to divergent individuals and social groups who might or might not have had prior contact with one another. Since it governed the relations with and among disparate non-Roman peoples, *jus gentium* has provided international law with many concepts that border on private law, such as contracts, treaties, and property rights and, in the classical legal literature on "the law of nations," acquired the meaning of present-day public international law.

Jus Naturale (21)

Those norms and principles derived from natural law by which man and states are bound. *Jus naturale* (natural law) is the law of reason. Its foundation is traced to Greek Stoic thought of the third century B.C., which held that man was a rational being. Natural law was adapted by the Romans and blended with *jus gentium* to govern the relations of non-Romans in the Roman Empire. *See also* JUS COGENS, 19; JUS GENTIUM, 20; NATURALISTS, 24.

Significance   Jus naturale (believed to be of divine origin), with its emphasis upon order and reason, was influential in the early development of international law through theorists such as Francisco de Vitoria, Francisco Suárez, Alberico Gentili, and Hugo Grotius. In their view, natural law is based upon universal or immutable laws to which all are bound simply by the fact that it is the natural order of things. While eventually displaced by positivist concepts of treaties and customs in the eighteenth and nineteenth centuries, natural law has left its imprint upon international law with such concepts as justice, morality, rationality, and equality under law.

Lex Posterior Derogat Priori (22)

The legal maxim that the subsequent law abrogates the preceding law. The maxim of *lex posterior derogat priori* (or often simply *lex posterior*) suggests that if a law explicitly contravenes a prior treaty, or a treaty contravenes prior law, or a treaty contravenes a prior treaty, the courts will apply the most recent expression of the law. *See also* INCONSISTENT TREATIES, 260.

Significance *Lex posterior derogat priori* is not a universally applicable practice among states in certain circumstances. Clearly, if two or more states sign a treaty contravening a former treaty between or among the same signatories, then the most recent treaty applies on the assumption that they are aware of the existence of the former treaty. The matter becomes more complex when dealing with treaties and municipal legislation that conflict with one another. For states that hold that treaties and international law are superior to municipal law, any governmental action or statute violating the treaty is void. The practice for states that apply *lex posterior,* such as the United States, is for the courts to determine whether the legislature had prior knowledge or clearly intended the legislation to conflict between the two while looking to the executive branch to resolve the problem. If it was the intent of the legislature to contradict the terms of a treaty, then the court will apply the most recent expression.

Monists (23)

Persons subscribing to the theoretical school of thought regarding the relationship of international law to municipal law which upholds the unity of all law, reasoning that both systems are parts of a universal body of legal rules binding states and individuals alike. Monists argue that both international law and municipal law are based upon the same premise—that of regulating human conduct. International law and municipal law are, therefore, two sides of the same coin. In the case of a conflict, however, international law is supreme. *See also* DUALISTS, 10; INCORPORATION, DOCTRINE OF, 14; TRANSFORMATION, DOCTRINE OF, 44.

Significance   The monist theory refutes the separateness of municipal law and international law advocated by the dualists, arguing that
the two systems are closely linked. Most monists hold that municipal
law derives its legitimacy from international law and is, therefore,
inferior to international law. Others argue that international law is an
extension of municipal law and, therefore, governed by the latter. The
position of states varies. Austria, the Netherlands, and Luxembourg,
for example, hold to the supremacy of international law in any instance
where national law contradicts international law.

The practice of the United States is less conclusive, consisting of the
following guidelines: (1) customary international law is the law of the
land, but the courts may give effect to congressional or presidential acts
without regard to customary international law; (2) a treaty takes precedence over prior conflicting legislation if the treaty is self-executing,
i.e., requires no ancillary legislation and operates of itself; (3) legislation adopted subsequent to a treaty that contradicts the treaty is only
binding upon the courts if the Congress clearly expresses the purpose
of abrogating the treaty; and (4) courts and other agencies of government try to minimize or avoid the clash between a municipal and an
international norm when it is possible to do so, on the assumption that
the Congress would not intentionally contravene an international legal
norm (see *MacLeod v. U.S.*, 229 U.S. 434 [1913]). However, in cases
where the two are irreconcilable and municipal law is applied by the
domestic court in conflict with international law, this does not absolve
the United States (nor any other state for that matter) of its responsibility internationally, regardless of domestic legislation.

Naturalists   (24)

Followers of the school of thought related to the nature and origin of
international law that was popular in the classical period of the law of
nations through the eighteenth century. Naturalists emphasized the
supreme position of natural law with regard to the origin of norms by
which states were bound. *See also* ECLECTICS, 11; *JUS GENTIUM*, 20; *JUS
NATURALE*, 21; PUFENDORF, SAMUEL VON, 31.

Significance   Naturalists rejected the idea of positive international
law (man-made law). Naturalists held that international law derived
from natural law, which was the law of reason. The unfortunate product of such reasoning was that no human institutions, such as legislatures or international conferences and organizations, could create
binding norms for the international community. Only the state could
determine what was natural and based upon reason. Such selective

commitment to metaphysical norms ran counter to a definable international order, and the naturalist school lost ground to the positivist and the eclectic (Grotian) schools in subsequent centuries.

New States and International Law (25)

To the newly independent members of the post–World War II international community, treaties constitute the primary source of international law. Customs are only selectively accepted as norms to which states must comply, and general principles are an ambivalent notion. International law is viable as a standard of conduct among nations, but only so long as it does not stifle the social and economic progress of developing states.

Significance   The late arrival of many Third World nations into the international community has meant that, for the most part, they had no role in shaping the legal norms to which they are expected to conform. To the nations of the Third World, some norms of international law embody the ideas of Western civilization, its historical experiences, and its legal systems. Although in principle Third World countries endorse the system of international law, they are reluctant to accept some customary norms that they equate with preservation of the status quo. The assessment of the role of general principles of law is more perplexing for Third World nations. On the one hand, the concept is founded upon the principles common to "civilized nations" (i.e., historically Western states); but, on the other hand, general principles can be a vehicle for Third World nations to create new legal norms. The desire by Third World nations for social, economic, and political change is hampered, in their view, by an international legal system that benefits Western states, particularly in those areas dealing with property rights, ownership of resources, and the global economic system. Thus, they have used United Nations–sponsored conferences and other methods in their efforts to codify and redefine the legal norms of the international community in a way that would promote the objective of a "new international economic order."

Positivists (26)

Followers of the school of thought on the nature and origin of international law which maintains that international law consists of those norms states have agreed to obey. The emphasis of the positivist school is upon treaties and customary practices to which states have consented to be bound. Also called the historical school, positivism prevailed over

naturalism in the eighteenth and nineteenth centuries. *See also* ECLEC-
TICS, 11; *JUS GENTIUM*, 20; *JUS NATURALE*, 21; NATURALISTS, 24.

Significance   Positivists, such as Cornelius van Bynkershoek and
Richard Zouche, argued that the practice of nations defined international law, not abstractions found in laws of nature. Positivist thought
blended well with the rise of the modern territorial state system, with
the latter's emphasis upon sovereignty and, in the nineteenth century,
nationalism. By looking to the norms provided by treaties created by
states as well as customary practices to which states gave their consent, a
body of tangible norms could be identified by which the international
system could be regulated. One of the weaknesses of positivist thought
is the assumption that for a norm to be binding, it must be explicitly
consented to by the state. To extreme positivists, this totally discounts
the existence of natural law, thereby denying the existence of any
ethical standards beyond those which the state itself decides are acceptable. Moderate positivists do accord a sort of natural law a place in the
scheme of things, albeit a minor one.

Publicists: Bynkershoek, Cornelius van (1673–1743)   (27)

A leading proponent of the positivist school of international law. Bynkershoek, a Dutch judge, held that states were bound only by those
norms to which they had consented, thereby looking to treaties and
customs as the sources of international law. But like other classical
writers on the law of nations, Bynkershoek did not discount natural
law, maintaining that customary law derived from reason (the basis of
natural law). *See also JUS NATURALE*, 21; POSITIVISTS, 26; TERRITORIAL SEA,
249.

Significance   Bynkershoek, like his fellow Dutchman Hugo Grotius,
played an important role in the evolution of the law of nations in the
seventeenth through the nineteenth centuries via such major writings
as *Quaestionum Juris Publici Libri II* (Two Questions of Public Law) and
De Dominio Maris (Sovereignty of the Sea). Unlike Grotius, however, he
produced no general treatise on the law of nations. His major contributions were in the areas of maritime and commercial law. Bynkershoek is
best remembered for having suggested that the breadth of a state's
territorial sea (maritime belt) be a width equal to the range of coastal
guns that could defend such waters (the "cannon-shot rule"). In his day,
the assumed range of such guns was approximately three miles. The
acceptance by states of the "three-mile limit" became widespread
(though not universal) in the nineteenth century, but it has recently lost
ground in favor of twelve-mile limits.

Publicists: Gentili, Alberico (1552–1608) (28)

Professor of civil (Roman) law at Oxford University, England. Gentili or, in Latin, Gentilis, was of Italian birth, but fled his native land for religious reasons, settling in England as a political refugee. His major work was *De Jure Belli Libri Tres* (The Three Books on the Law of War), in which he dealt with such topics as causes and conduct of war, treaties, and acquisition of territory. The concept of the *rebus sic stantibus* clause is attributed to Gentili. *See also* ECLECTICS, 11; JUS GENTIUM, 20; JUS NATURALE, 21; POSITIVISTS, 26; PUBLICISTS: GROTIUS, HUGO, 29.

Significance Although recognizing natural law of divine origin, Gentili differed with his contemporaries in his emphasis upon looking to treaties and contemporaneous practice of states as evidence of international legal norms rather than natural law and universal principles. In so doing, Gentili has been called by some the father of the positivist school of international law. Others classify him as a member of the eclectic school, since he did not deny natural law as the main source of the law of nations. Regardless of where he is placed, Gentili was acknowledged by Hugo Grotius as influential in developing his thinking on the law of nations. Despite such a note of indebtedness, it has only been during the past century that the importance of Gentili has been recognized.

Publicists: Grotius, Hugo (1583–1645) (29)

A Dutch lawyer, mathematician, diplomat, theologian, and historian (to name but a few of the interests of the "miracle of Holland"), and a typical Renaissance scholar. The writings of Grotius ("De Groot" in Dutch) on international law, contained in his major work *De Jure Belli Ac Pacis* (On the Law of War and Peace), systematized the legal thinking prior to and of his time. He also laid stress upon such ideas as the freedom of the seas (an idea largely ignored since the time of the Romans, with the exception of Francisco de Vitoria and Alberico Gentili) in his work on *Mare Liberum* (The Free Sea). Like other classical writers on the law of nations, Grotius drew upon such diverse sources as biblical thought, Greek history, and Roman history and law; but, unlike Gentili, not current diplomatic practice. *See also* ECLECTICS, 11; FREEDOM OF THE HIGH SEAS, 231; JUS GENTIUM, 20; JUS NATURALE, 21.

Significance Grotius, known with some exaggeration as the "father of international law," emphasized the duality of the law of nations—*jus naturale* and *jus gentium*. Unlike some before him (such as Vitoria and Suárez), Grotius emphasized the rational nature of natural law (*jus naturale*) while recognizing its divine origin, thereby separating it from theology. *Jus gentium* was derived from customs and treaties; consequently it must also be considered as part of the law of nations. Therefore, the two were linked; and while states voluntarily established customary norms and treaties (man-made laws), having done so they were bound to observe those norms (*jus naturale.*) By systematically examining the field of the law of nations, Grotius was influential in the development of the modern territorial state system. Indeed, in terms of popularity and success his *De Jure Belli Ac Pacis* was exceeded only by the Bible. However, his doctrines—especially the distinction between just and unjust wars, borrowed from medieval theologians—were not accepted in the practice of states.

Publicists: Moser, Johann Jakob (1701–1785) (30)

A German professor and legal scholar who most clearly personified the tenets of positivism. To Moser, the law of nations consisted purely of treaties and practices to which states subscribed. Since it could not be observed and recorded, natural law had little to offer as instruction to the norms states were committed to obey. *See also* POSITIVISTS, 26; PUBLICISTS: ZOUCHE, RICHARD, 35.

Significance Moser was the most prolific legal writer of the classical period of the law of nations, contributing some five hundred volumes to the legal literature. While not noted for being a forger of new norms, he was a forceful exponent of positivism and was an influence in the predominant position positivism eventually gained in the battle with naturalists and Grotians over the nature and origin of international law.

Publicists: Pufendorf, Samuel von (1632–1694) (31)

German professor of law and holder of the first chair in the law of nations at the University of Heidelberg. Pufendorf was one of the leading exponents of the naturalist school, arguing that legal norms derived solely from God and reason (natural law), and that neither treaties nor customs bound nations (as that was voluntary law). His most important work was *De Jure Naturae et Gentium* (On the Law of Nature and of Nations). *See also* NATURALISTS, 24.

Significance Pufendorf's arguments were based upon the belief that eternal truths founded upon the laws of God and reason formed the foundation of international law. This implied that any norm not derived from or in conformity with natural law was not binding. Since such natural laws were, however, abstract or metaphysical, it was difficult to pinpoint exactly what those norms were. Even among naturalists the total rejection of treaties made Pufendorf somewhat the exception to the rule. While of some influence in his own time, Pufendorf did not leave a lasting legacy equal to that of the positivists and the eclectics.

Publicists: Suárez, Francisco (1548–1617) (32)

Spanish Jesuit professor of theology at the University of Coimbra in Portugal. Suárez's major works were *Tractatus de Legibus Ac Deo Legislatore* (A Treatise on Laws and God as Legislator), *Defensio Fideo* (Defense of Faith), and *De Triplici Virtute* (On Triple Virtue). In these works he developed such classical law of nations concepts and principles as the duality of the law of nations (consisting of both natural law and man-made law) the need for a state to consent to be bound by legal norms, good faith in observing agreements, and the interdependence of states. *See also* ECLECTICS, 11; *JUS GENTIUM*, 20; *JUS NATURALE*, 21; NATURALISTS, 24; POSITIVISTS, 26; PUBLICISTS: GROTIUS, HUGO, 29; PUBLICISTS: VITORIA, FRANCISCO, 34.

Significance Suárez made a philosophical attempt to broaden the origins of legal norms that bound states beyond the abstract metaphysics of natural law. He elaborated further Gentili's distinction between *jus naturale* (which was God-given) and *jus gentium* (which was created by states). *Jus naturale* must be observed by all, but *jus gentium* required the consent of all. While the norms of *jus naturale* were, therefore, immutable and universal, the norms of *jus gentium* were dynamic and subject to change over time. Suárez is included with Vitoria as one of the early legal theorists who had a major influence in laying the foundation of modern international law. He was acknowledged by Grotius to have had an effect upon his own thoughts about law.

Publicists: Vattel, Emerich de (1714–1769) (33)

The major figure of the Grotian school (eclectics) on the nature of international law. His thinking about international law did not quite correspond to that of Hugo Grotius, although there are those who would place him among the naturalists. Vattel's major work was *Le Droit des Gens* (The Law of Nations), which dealt with the principles of the law of nature as applied to the conduct and the affairs of nations and sovereigns. In that work, Vattel examined the relationship of the law of nature between man and the state. To him, the law of nature applied to man and, consequently, the state was also bound by it since the state consisted of a community of men. States in turn comprised a society of nations. In this community all states were equal and sovereign, regardless of their size or power, and should engage cooperatively in the betterment of each other (which he claimed was the "first general law"). *See also* ECLECTICS, 11; NATURALISTS, 24.

Significance   Vattel was second only to Grotius in his impact upon his contemporaries and subsequent generations. His major work (published in 1758) was relied upon by scholars and practitioners of international law throughout the nineteenth century and continued to be cited by judges into the twentieth century. His major contributions (built upon the work of the German philosopher Christian Wolff) were in bridging the law of nature as applied to man versus the state. While man was the subject of the law of nature, the state was the subject of the law of nations. There were situations in which the differences between right and wrong were clear, and thus principles of law were obvious (natural law). Vattel called these necessary laws of nations. In other situations the law of nature was much less clear, and there were thus voluntary laws of nations (conventional law), allowing states to selectively observe them. This conventional law of custom and treaties was appropriate so long as it conformed to the law of nature. But the independence of states basic to Vattel's thinking—sovereignty, equality, and voluntary observance of conventional law—made the concepts of state interdependence and a world community greater than the sum of its parts difficult to fit into Vattel's scheme of things.

Publicists: Vitoria, Francisco de (1480–1546)   (34)

Spanish Dominican professor of theology at the University of Salamanca in Spain. Vitoria was a humanist in an era of incipient colonialism marked by brutality. He emphasized the state's responsibility for the proper treatment of natives as wards of the state, as such obligations were founded within the principles of natural law. *See also* JUS NATURALE, 21; PUBLICISTS: GROTIUS, HUGO, 29; *See also* PUBLICISTS: SUÁREZ, FRANCISCO, 32.

Significance   Vitoria is considered to be one of the more important of the early pre-Grotian theorists who helped lay the foundation of modern international law. His ideas influenced the thought of Hugo Grotius, as had Francisco Suárez. While he never wrote a major legal treatise as such, his lectures were published posthumously as *De Indis ac de Jure Belli Relectiones* (Lectures on the Indians and the Law of War). This work reveals the range of Vitoria's interests, which included the interactions of states, just versus unjust wars, freedom of the seas, and the equality of states as well as the proper treatment of natives.

Publicists: Zouche, Richard (1590–1660) (35)

English professor of civil (Roman) law at Oxford and a judge of the English Admiralty Court. Zouche was Alberico Gentili's successor at Oxford and a forceful advocate of the positivist school of international law, arguing that customary behavior of states was based upon reason and that states voluntarily conformed to such norms because they were reasonable. His principal work was *Juris et Judicii Fecialis, Sive Juris Inter Gentes . . ., Explicatio* (Exposition of the Law and Judicial Process of the *Fetiales* [of War and Peace] or the Law among Nations), which is referred to by some as the first manual of international law. *See also* POSITIVISTS, 26; PUBLICISTS: GENTILI, ALBERICO, 28; PUBLICISTS: GROTIUS, HUGO, 29.

Significance Zouche based his observations and writings on his observations of state practice rather than upon abstractions. While he did not deny the existence of natural law, he argued that custom and treaties were the basis of international law as they were derived from the state system and states accepted them as binding. Since such norms were to be in conformity with reason, they were also in conformity with nature. On this basis, Zouche could be classified as an eclectic; but, along with Alberico Gentili, he is more often referred to as one of the principal founders of the positivist school. His writings and arguments were widely studied, and Zouche's impact was such that after Grotius, he is sometimes ranked as the "second father of international law."

Pure Theory of Law (36)

An approach in the debate over the nature of law, including also international law, which (in the case of international law) attempts to distill the essence of municipal and international law, asserting the common features rather than dissimilarities of the two. The pure theory of law was developed by the Austrian jurist from Vienna Hans Kelsen in his *General Theory of Law and State* and *Principles of International Law*. The essence of the pure theory of law is that all law— municipal or international—rests upon the ultimate obligation to obey the law. Because of the central role that Kelsen played in the development of this line of thought, those who follow his arguments are called the Vienna school. *See also* AUSTINIANISM, 2; AUTOLIMITATION, 3.

Significance   The pure theory of law school takes the position that the basic question posed by English jurist John Austin—whether or not international law is true law—is irrelevant. International law is valid law because it has customarily been followed and because it is believed to be obligatory, as is the case of municipal law and canon law. Customary law is the first stage in the international legal order from which come treaties that derive their authority from custom.

Resolutions of the United Nations General Assembly   (37)

Decisions and recommendations adopted by the United Nations General Assembly. The legal status of United Nations General Assembly resolutions and declarations is a controversial matter. In the traditional view, followed by the United States and other Western nations, they are not legally binding acts unless (1) they are decisions made by the General Assembly on certain "internal" matters which the Assembly is specifically authorized to make under the Charter (for example, budgetary questions; elections of members of other United Nations principal organs; etc.); or (2) they reflect an otherwise existing rule of customary international law. On the other hand, in the opinion of Third World countries, resolutions and declarations of the United Nations General Assembly in which they have the majority of voting power are legally binding international law. Many such resolutions and declarations have furthered economic and political interests of these countries; for example, the 1974 Declaration on the Establishment of a New International Economic Order; the Charter of Economic Rights and Duties of States of the same year; and numerous anticolonial resolutions. While it is true that resolutions and declarations of the United Nations General Assembly do not represent a source of binding law, since conventions voted upon by the Assembly still require separate acceptance and ratification by each member state, nevertheless such resolutions and declarations may be instrumental in the development of international law if supported with sufficient frequency and number of states. Even then, however, the legal effect of such acts would vary considerably, depending on the type of resolution and the conditions attached to its adoption and its provisions. *See also* SOURCES OF INTERNATIONAL LAW, 38.

Significance   Despite the hopes of world federalists and others for the creation of a supranational authority, the resolutions passed by the United Nations General Assembly are not automatically binding, because they have been passed by member states acting in their sovereign capacity and require being processed through a state's ratification or promulgation procedure before becoming binding upon the state. The conferees at San Francisco made it quite clear when drafting the United Nations Charter that they did not intend to endow the General Assembly with the power to make international law. Despite such observations, General Assembly resolutions can aid in the creation of international law by highlighting the concerns of its members and suggesting the direction norms might take. Some observers refer to such resolutions as "quasi law" or "pre-law."

Sources of International Law (38)

Those processes and materials to which the origin of the laws regulating the international community can be traced. The sources of international law include international conventions and treaties, international custom, and the general principles of law recognized by civilized nations. While judicial decisions and the writings of publicists are not sources of international law *per se,* Article 38 of the Statute of the International Court of Justice, in enumerating the sources which the Court is to apply in deciding disputes submitted to it, includes them as subsidiary means for the determination of rules of law. *See also* SOURCES OF INTERNATIONAL LAW: CUSTOM, 39; SOURCES OF INTERNATIONAL LAW: GENERAL PRINCIPLES OF LAW, 40; SOURCES OF INTERNATIONAL LAW: JUDICIAL DECISIONS, 41; SOURCES OF INTERNATIONAL LAW: PUBLICISTS, 42; SOURCES OF INTERNATIONAL LAW: TREATIES, 43.

Significance   The sources of international law do not provide so clear and evident rules as exist in domestic (municipal) law in which one can point to constitutions, statutes, legislative decrees, court judgments, and other sources for the laws with which we must comply. The international system does not have central agencies with universal authority, being instead a decentralized system of sovereign states. Article 38 of the Statute of the International Court of Justice does not explicitly rank the sources of international law according to their importance, but treaties have become the major source of international legal norms in the twentieth century. Should a conflict arise between or among these sources, there is some dispute as to which should prevail. As a general rule, a treaty would prevail over a customary practice; but whether the latter prevails over a general principle of law is more problematic, with the caveat that none of them can conflict with a peremptory rule of international law (*jus cogens*).

Sources of International Law: Custom (39)

Practices and usages which have been observed over a long period of time and are considered by states to be law. Two elements are necessary for the formation of customary international law—behavioral and psychological. The former requires consistent and recurring action (or lack of action) by states, meaning official government conduct, which is indicated by such activities as official statements, court decisions, legislative action, administrative decrees, and diplomatic behavior, as examples. The latter entails the conviction that in each case such behavior is required or permitted by international law (*opinio juris sive necessitatis*). Custom is included in Article 38 of the Statute of the International Court of Justice as one of the primary sources of international law. *See also* COMITY, 5.

Significance   Custom constituted the bulk of international law historically, with legal scholars tracing norms and usages back through the ages. If a usage was found to be habitually observed by a large number of states over a lengthy period of time and felt by them to be obligatory, it then became customary law and was deemed a norm of behavior binding upon the community of nations. A practice is not customary international law simply because a large number of states conform to it. It must also be considered to be legally obligatory for states to do so. How many states are necessary for a norm of customary international law to emerge is difficult to say. There is no need for all states to be included, but there should not be a significant number of states that have consistently objected to it. Clearly, a state that consistently objected to a practice would not be bound by it. The emergence in recent decades of many new states that played no part in the development of customary international law and that object to those norms they feel are essentially Western or place new states in an inferior position has weakened the universality of customary law. The Western view is that newly independent states are bound to conform to such customary laws as were operative at the time of those states becoming subjects of international law.

Sources of International Law: General Principles of Law   (40)

The principles of law common to all civilized nations. Article 38 of the Statute of the International Court of Justice includes the general principles of law recognized by civilized nations as a source of law to be applied by the Court. While the term "civilized nations" is inherently vague, it is presupposed that such a notion is founded upon a developed legal system and, therefore, includes all but the most primitive of societies. There is no agreement on the meaning of the general principles of international law. Some publicists interpret them as referring to certain basic principles of municipal law common to all national systems and applicable to international relations (e.g., the principle that no one can be judge in his own suit). In another view, represented by Soviet jurists, the general principles of law mean only general principles of international law as opposed to specific rules of this law. International tribunals have applied general principles in both meanings, and there is no reason why such principles should not be derived both from municipal law systems and from international law. *See also* JUS NATURALE, 21; NATURALISTS, 24.

Significance   General principles of law are considered to be at the foundation of any legal system, including international law. General principles are those which go beyond positive international law and, instead, trace their origins to their commonality among varieties of municipal legal systems. Concepts such as morality, justice, equity, and good faith predate the voluntary norms of positive international law. One of the general principles cited above, good faith, is considered by many theorists to be the very essence of international law itself from which all other legal norms derive. General principles of law are suggestive of natural law (reason) and refute the arguments of the extreme positivists in favor of the moderate positivists and the eclectics (Grotians). They also resemble the Roman *jus gentium* (law common to all nations). Indeed, some of these norms classified as general principles of law have their antecedents in the ancient Roman law from which legal theorists of the sixteenth and seventeenth centuries derived their observations. The determination of a general principle of law is often subjective (a matter of judgment) and makes a Court that employs it an active participant in the growth of international law.

Sources of International Law: Judicial Decisions   (41)

Decisions of international courts and tribunals as well as national courts. Judicial decisions are considered in Article 38 of the Statute of the International Court of Justice to be a "subsidiary means for the determination of rules of law."

Significance   Judicial decisions are, in the narrowest sense, not a true source of international law. Unlike national courts in countries such as the United States and others of the Anglo-American system of law, which are governed by the concept of *stare decisis* (that is, the duty to follow judicial precedents), international courts and tribunals are not obliged to follow precedents. Their decisions are binding only upon the parties involved and only for the particular case, as stated in Article 59 of the Statute of the International Court of Justice. Since states voluntarily go before judicial bodies and in the case of arbitral tribunals often tailor the case and circumstances by which the body will make a judgment, each case is in a sense unique. Nevertheless, such decisions are presupposed to be founded upon existing legal norms and, consequently, are a record of the existence and nature of such norms. Judges do take heed of the judgments of their peers, regardless of the theory in the matter. This is no less the case at the international level than at the national level. Nor is it less so in civil law countries than in common law countries. Finally, international courts may sometimes charter new paths in international law, as demonstrated by the advisory opinion on *Reparations for Injuries Suffered in the Service of the United Nations* case (International Court of Justice, 1949).

Sources of International Law: Publicists   (42)

International legal scholars whose writings serve as a subsidiary source for the determination of the rules of law. Article 38 of the Statute of the International Court of Justice specifies "the teaching of the most highly qualified publicists of the various nations, as subsidiary means for the determination of rules of law." Like judicial decisions, the writings of legal experts—while not usually definitive in the outcome of cases—can be influential where other sources are silent, by providing evidence of the existence of a particular legal norm. *See also* PUBLICISTS, 27–35.

Significance   Publicists such as Hugo Grotius and Emerich de Vattel were historically a major factor in the evolution of international law. They were the scholarly compilers of legal norms from antiquity to the modern state system as well as the originators of new norms. Much of what they had to say has since been either codified or rejected. While modern courts are less prone to draw upon this source for decisions, legal scholars have played an important role in court decisions, as demonstrated in the classic American case of *The Paquete Habana; the Lola,* 175 U.S. 677 (1900). Modern legal scholars still play an important though rather behind the scenes and anonymous role in the evolution of international law (particularly in such new areas as marine pollution, deep seabed mining, and outer space) by identifying areas that require further investigation, proposing changes in existing norms, and suggesting new norms. Learned writers in international law are also often quoted in diplomatic disputes and in materials provided by states before international tribunals.

Sources of International Law: Treaties   (43)

Written agreements between or among two or more states that generate rules of international law. Treaties are the most important source of international law. If a treaty is between two parties, it is a bilateral treaty binding only upon the signatories and is an example of *particular* international law. If the agreement is among a large number of states, it is a multilateral treaty—a "law-making treaty"—that might produce a *general* international legal norm. Article 38 of the Statute of the International Court of Justice recognizes as applicable "international conventions, whether general or particular, establishing rules expressly recognized by the contesting States." While there are many terms other than treaty for an international agreement such as pact, protocol, charter, convention, statute, and covenant, all are equally binding upon signatories. *See also* TREATIES, 279.

Significance Treaties have replaced custom as the major source of international law in the twentieth century. In a sense treaties represent international "statutes," as they often codify customary international law as well as create new international legal norms and international institutions. The bulk of treaties, however, are bilateral and have little impact upon the international legal order. The utility of treaties as a source of international law is in clarifying, codifying, and redefining customary law, as well as committing new norms to paper, thereby escaping the debate over norms founded upon custom and usage.

Transformation, Doctrine of (44)

The principle that for international law to become the "law of the land," it must become part of municipal law, i.e., there must be a legislative enactment to transform an international norm into a municipal (domestic) norm. *See also* DUALISTS, 10; INCORPORATION, DOCTRINE OF, 14; MONISTS, 23.

Significance The doctrine of transformation rests, in part, upon the belief in the sovereign character of the state. The state must consent to be bound by international legal norms, and this consent must take a more explicit form than the automaticity implied by the doctrine of incorporation. In the absence of a municipal statute, therefore, the courts of a state subscribing to the doctrine of transformation might not enforce that norm. The doctrine can also result from the constitutional peculiarities of a specific state. In Great Britain, for example, for a treaty to become part of domestic law, it is necessary to pass an Act of Parliament to give the treaty municipal effect. If the act is not passed, however, the treaty is still binding from the point of view of international law. Passing an Act is necessitated in the absence of the British Parliament in the treaty-making process of the government, which is the domain of the monarch. Consequently, the effect of a treaty upon

Great Britain is not the same in international law and municipal law. In contrast, the ratification process for a treaty in the United States automatically gives it effect in municipal law as provided for in Article VI of the Constitution. Treaty provisions can thus be enforced through the courts without legislative action by Congress or the state legislatures.

Transnational Law   (45)

That body of municipal and international norms governing public and private transactions that transcend national boundaries or national jurisdiction. Transnational law is an emerging body of law based upon universally accepted general principles of law supplemented by that portion of the municipal law of disputants applicable in an attempt to resolve conflict.

Significance   Proponents of transnational law, a term coined by Philip C. Jessup in the 1950s, suggest that there are major gaps in traditional international law and these needs can best be bridged at levels other than universal. Such gaps are particularly evident in such areas as contracts and concessions between governments and foreign nationals.

2. States as Subjects of International Law

Association   (46)

A concept developed by the United Nations General Assembly as part of its anticolonialist trend. An association is a formal arrangement between a non-self-governing territory (an associate) and an independent state (the principal) whereby the territory becomes an associated state with internal self-government, but the independent state is responsible for foreign affairs and defense. Apart from the final approval in the United Nations, two general conditions must be met for an association to be lawful under the guidelines of General Assembly Resolution 1541 (XV) of 14 December 1960: (1) the population must consent to the association; and (2) the association must promote the development and well-being of the dependent state. The first of these stipulations distinguishes an association from a protectorate, in that the latter could be formed at the will of the monarch or ruling elite. The second stipulation reflects the goals of the United Nations trusteeship system. *See also* NON-SELF-GOVERNING TERRITORY, 59; TRUSTEESHIP SYSTEM, 80.

Significance   Associated states resemble former protectorates or dependent states, but the use of the new term has less of a pejorative connotation. In practice, the United Nations General Assembly has shown a preference for complete independence rather than association status for non-self-governing territories. The associated status of former U.S.-administered Trust Territories of the Pacific Islands with the United States is an example of association. The termination of the trusteeship of the four entities to be associated with the United States must still be approved by the United Nations.

Community of Nations (47)

An idealistic, almost poetic, but often used concept which suggests that based upon their common features the collection of various states are members of an international "family" or "community" by virtue of being recognized as such by its existing members. In joining the community of nations (or international community) a state is recognized as a sovereign entity with all rights and privileges accorded the other members. In gaining these rights, the new state in effect agrees to accept the correlative duties and responsibilities of the community, including the international legal norms subscribed to by its member states.

Significance   Rooted in the ancient Stoic and medieval Christian tradition, the concept of a community of nations (or, more strictly, "sovereign states") results in part from the parallel evolution of international law and the European territorial state system. Although territorial states existed before 1648, the emergence of the territorial state system is conveniently linked to the Treaty of Westphalia (1648). New states were admitted to this community by an initial select group of great powers on the basis of candidates' acquiescence in the "public law" of that community. Russia was admitted in 1721; the United States in 1783; the newly independent states of the Western Hemisphere (formed from the colonies of Spain and Portugal) in the early decades of the nineteenth century; and the Ottoman Empire (Turkey), the first non-Christian state, by terms of the Treaty of Paris in 1856. It should be noted that the term "nation" should be thought of as "state," since the members of the community are sovereign legal entities, while a nation—a sociopolitical term not easy to define—is a grouping of people who have a psychological attachment to one another based upon ethnic, cultural, linguistic, or other common ties.

Condominium (48)

Jurisdiction over a territory shared by two or more states. A condominium arrangement is formally defined by the legal regime sharing authority over the territory. Jurisdiction may be shared either concurrently or sequentially. A condominium arrangement typically allows for equal exercise of sovereignty by the states concerned.

Significance   The motives behind establishing a condominium can derive from historic peculiarities or geopolitical considerations. Great Britain and Egypt had a condominium arrangement over the Sudan from 1898 to 1953 in order to protect the headwaters of the Nile. Great Britain and France exercised a condominium in the New Hebrides from 1887 until its independence in 1980. Australia and New Zealand have exercised joint administration over the mines of the Christmas Islands. Today condominiums are largely of historical interest except for Andorra, which is a condominium ruled jointly by the head of France and the Bishop of Urgel in Spain, and Ile des Faisans (Isle of Pheasants) which is a French-Spanish condominium.

Confederation (49)

A formal association of states loosely tied together by a treaty, often establishing a central governing mechanism with certain power over member states but not directly over the citizens of those states. In a confederation, the constituent states are sovereign and independent with the right of secession. A confederation must be distinguished from a federation (federal state), which forms one single subject of international law and exercises direct power over the citizens of the subordinate units. *See also* FEDERAL STATE, 53.

Significance   There have been few true confederations in the modern period. Although in their French, Italian, and Latin terminologies the Swiss still refer to their system established in 1848 as the Helvetic Confederation, Switzerland is a federal state. Prior to 1848, Switzerland was a confederation in the years 1291–1798 and 1815–1848. The United States was a confederation under the Articles of Confederation from 1781 to 1789. A confederation called the Republic of Central America (consisting of Honduras, Nicaragua, and San Salvador) existed from 1895 to 1898. A confederation was officially created in 1981 when Gambia and Senegal established a "Senegambia Confederation." The union of Libya with Morocco created by a treaty between the two countries in 1984 and denounced by Morocco in 1986 was, practically speaking, a kind of very loose confederation, much like six previous "unions" arranged by Libya with various other Arab states. All of the previous Libyan arrangements collapsed after a short period of time.

Continuity of States (50)

The principle that once a state is established as an international person, subsequent changes in government or constitution do not affect the existence of the state. The continuity of states refers to their continued existence as subjects and persons of international law. Continuity and identity of a state must be distinguished from state succession when one international personality takes the place of another. *See also* SUCCESSION, STATE, 79.

Significance   The continuity of states acquires importance in those instances where there have been alterations in names or changes in sovereignty through cession, annexation, or mergers. Continuity of a state's name or its change may or may not affect its international personality, and the concept of continuity is not consistently applied in international practice. The Austrian Republic, which emerged in the aftermath of World War I, was hardly synonymous with the Austro-Hungarian Empire from which it was derived. But the Austria that had been annexed into the German Third Reich and was reborn after World War II is, for most purposes, considered a continuation of the pre-*Anschluss* Austrian state. Serbia continued after World War I as the Kingdom of Serbs, Croats, and Slovenes, later known as Yugoslavia. The states of Egypt and Syria merged their separate existences in 1958, but subsequent dissolution of the relationship did not affect the separate existence of either entity in the eyes of the rest of the international community.

**Declaration on Principles of International Law   (51)
Concerning Friendly Relations and Cooperation
among States (1970)**
An annex to United Nations General Assembly Resolution 2625 (XXV)—a United Nations proclamation—adopted without vote by the General Assembly in 1970 to encourage the development and application of international law. The "Declaration on Principles of International Law Concerning Friendly Relations and Cooperation among States in Accordance with the Charter of the United Nations" highlights the areas of agreement by United Nations members on the purposes and meaning of the principles contained in the United Nations Charter, including refraining from the threat or use of force; peaceful settlement of disputes; nonintervention in the domestic affairs of other states; international cooperation according to the Charter; equal rights and self-determination; sovereign equality of states; and carrying out international obligations. *See also* FORCE, ILLEGAL THREAT OR USE OF, 308; SELF-DETERMINATION, RIGHT OF, 74.

Significance   The Declaration on Principles of International Law reaffirms those principles in the United Nations Charter which the Declaration declares are basic principles of international law. These principles are held to be interrelated, and each should be "construed in the context of the other principles." Although adopted without vote, the Declaration on Principles of International Law suggests that there exists consensual agreement upon basic international legal principles among the member states of the United Nations. The Declaration is also one of several contemporary statements by the United Nations General Assembly dealing with the issue of self-determination. Unlike some United Nations statements on the issue, which remain vague on the matter of who may exercise the right of self-determination, the Declaration is more explicit. It defines self-determination largely in terms of decolonization, as it specifically cautions that nothing within the section encouraging self-determination authorizes or encourages the dismemberment of the territorial integrity or political unity of sovereign states.

Dependent State (52)

A member of the community of nations with qualified or limited status. A dependent state has a relationship with another state such that the former's sovereignty or freedom of independent action is formally (as a rule by a treaty) curtailed to such a degree that there is a dependency upon the other state, which can range from collaboration in foreign affairs to establishing a colonial status. The status of dependency is not to be confused with the political realities of states being subjected to outside pressures and of global interdependence. Historically, dependent states have been alternately referred to as vassal states, semisovereign states, or protectorates. *See also* ASSOCIATION, 46; NON-SELF-GOVERNING TERRITORY, 59; PROTECTORATE, 61.

Significance Dependent states are largely a historical phenomenon. They were viewed as imperfect or partial subjects of international law. The extent to which the head of state of a dependency had personal immunity, was allowed to enter into commercial agreements, and had the authority to formulate treaties and conduct foreign policy in general was determined by the arrangements establishing the dependency. Treaties generally established the nature of the relationship between the suzerain and the protected state. Dependent states have occurred frequently over the past several centuries. They included, for example, Romania (Turkey); Serbia (Turkey); Egypt (Great Britain); the Transvaal (Great Britain); Tibet (China); Outer Mongolia (China; Soviet Union); and the various Malay states (Great Britain). Other territories of the British Empire also went through a period of "dependency" in the process of becoming independent.

Federal State (53)

A merger or union of previously autonomous or independent entities into a single state. The federal state obtains direct power over the citizens of such an entity and becomes a single, composite international legal person, the components of the state losing any individual international personality they may previously have possessed, although they retain their identity in municipal law. *See also* CONFEDERATION, 49.

Significance   The central government of a federal state typically represents its component units in foreign affairs, although the prescribed areas of state authority may allow the subdivisions a limited role in international affairs (e.g., Switzerland and the Federal Republic of Germany). The most extreme example of this is the membership of two components of the Union of Soviet Socialist Republics (USSR) in the United Nations—the Byelorussian and the Ukrainian Soviet Socialist Republics. Done for political reasons at the time of the creation of the United Nations, these two entities are generally held to have international standing only for purposes of membership in the organization. Although the constitution of the Soviet state ostensibly permits each of its republics to engage in foreign relations, this has remained a fiction.

Government-in-Exile   (54)
A government established outside of its territorial base. A government-in-exile or "absentee government," which has been in existence as the *de jure* government of the now-occupied state, remains the *de jure* government in the eyes of those so recognizing it as long as it views its exile as temporary. In such a case, there has been no break in the continuity of the government. In the case of a government created outside the territory of the state, there is no link to the former government and the new government-in-exile must be recognized by states before it has the proper authority to represent the state. In such a case, the government-in-exile is anticipating that it will eventually be the government in both fact and law for the state. *See also* BELLIGERENT OCCUPATION, 326; RECOGNITION, 63; RECOGNITION: *DE FACTO*, 67; RECOGNITION: *DE JURE*, 68.

Significance   There were many examples of governments-in-exile displaced or created abroad as a result of Nazi Germany's invasion before and during World War II—Czechoslovakia, Ethiopia, Greece, the Netherlands, Norway, Poland, and Yugoslavia to name but a few. Military occupation does not transfer sovereignty over the occupied territory, but rather gives the occupier the authority to exercise such administrative, political, and judicial authority as needed to maintain its own security and provide for as normal a state of affairs for the populace as can be expected under the circumstances. Continued recognition of the government-in-exile challenges the *de facto* authority of the occupier. While the authority of the government-in-exile is temporarily in abeyance within its own territory (although it may have an underground network of authority there), it is the legal representative of the state for those states that continue to recognize it. Should that recognition cease, so will the legal standing of the exiled government.

Holy See (55)

The juridical international person of the Roman Catholic church, with its physical location at the Vatican in Rome and its sovereign the pope. The Holy See (sometimes used interchangeably with the Vatican) is a subject of international law and as such exchanges diplomatic representatives with other states, enters into bilateral treaties (called concordats), and is a party to multilateral treaties.

Significance   The Holy See has been the subject of much debate as to the nature and extent of its international personality. It is not a state in the normal sense of the word, combining the features of the personality of the Holy See as a religious entity with its territorial base in Vatican City. Apart from some one thousand functionaries, it has no population and only about one hundred acres of its sovereign territory granted it by Italy in the Lateran Treaty of 1929. Nevertheless, the Holy See does send agents abroad to represent it (papal nuncios, who have the same standing as ambassadors), enters into bilateral agreements with other states (concordats), and is not subordinate to any other sovereign. While some have argued that maintaining diplomatic relations and honoring the sovereignty of the Holy See are merely acts of courtesy to honor a prior historic arrangement, the consensus among modern writers and the actions of states is that the Holy See is a unique international person. In 1984, the United States appointed its first ambassador to the Vatican.

International Legal Personality (56)

A legal (juridical) term signifying that an entity has standing as a member of the community of nations and possesses certain rights and obligations as a subject of international law. International persons are primarily states, although belligerent communities, international organizations (such as the United Nations), corporate bodies, and individuals also possess some degree of international legal personality for certain purposes. International personality reflects the capacity to stand in court, to sue or to be sued, and to be a subject of law. *See also* SOVEREIGNTY, 75; STATE, 76.

Significance   International legal personality indicates that the entity is a subject of international law and a member of the community of nations. In the case of states, changes in territory, population, or form of government do not, in most cases, affect the international personality of a state. The extinction of a state, however, can terminate its international legal personality, whether voluntarily (such as the annexation of the independent Republic of Texas into the United States in 1845) or through conquest and annexation (such as the Soviet absorption of the Baltic states of Lithuania, Latvia, and Estonia in 1940). Whether or not such forceful annexation results in loss of international personality is partly determined by the attitudes of the rest of the international community. The final, third partition of Poland in 1795 meant the loss of a state and its personality, as it was so perceived by the rest of the European community. The Italian conquest of Ethiopia in 1936 was also recognized by many states but condemned by others. The United States does not recognize the annexation of the Baltic states by the Soviet Union. The determination of loss of international personality is significant as it terminates all rights and duties of the extinct state, voids the bulk of its treaties, and absolves its contracts and financial obligations. Under the present international law based on the United Nations Charter, extinction of a state brought about by aggression or other means contrary to the Charter cannot be recognized as legal under international law.

Mandate System   (57)
An institution of the League of Nations whereby a territory was placed under the tutelage and guardianship of a victorious ally after World War I, on behalf of the League of Nations, until such time as the territory was ready to take its place as an independent member of the community of nations. Mandated territories, like the subsequent United Nations trust territories, were unique in that they fell under no state's sovereignty. The mandate system was established by Article 22 of the Covenant of the League of Nations to cover those colonies and territories formerly held by Germany and Turkey before their defeat in World War I. Each mandate was placed under the administration of a mandatory power responsible to the League of Nations for its proper administration. *See also* TRUSTEESHIP SYSTEM, 80.

Significance   The mandate system of the League of Nations established the principle that advanced nations were entrusted with the responsibility to see to the development and well-being of less advantaged, subject peoples. The mandate system consisted of three classes of territories—A, B, and C. Class A mandates (Arab territories formerly under Turkish sovereignty) were those that had reached a state of development requiring minimum supervision before they could become full members of the international community (Iraq, Lebanon, Palestine, Syria, and Transjordan). Class B mandates were judged to require a longer period of tutelage (the former German colonies of Cameroons, Ruanda Urundi, Tanganyika, and Togoland). Class C mandates were backward territories and scattered island groupings lost by Germany (South-West Africa, Samoa, Nauru, the Carolines, the Marianas, and the Marshall Islands). Mandatory powers were held accountable for the administration of their mandates, although ironically no such stipulation held for the colonies of the victors of the war. The general principles underlying the League of Nations mandate system were later embodied in the Charter of the United Nations by the creation of trust territories and the Trusteeship Council of the United Nations. Mandates that had not gained their independence by 1945 were placed under the new trusteeship system. South Africa refused to place its mandate, South-West Africa (now known as Namibia), under the trusteeship system and today worldwide pressures generated through the United Nations, several International Court of Justice decisions, and a guerrilla war for independence are moving South-West Africa toward full statehood.

Neutralized State (58)

A state subject to the condition of permanent neutrality both in peace and in war, recognized by other states. Unlike "neutrality," which applies only in the case of an ongoing war between third countries, the status of "permanent neutrality" or "neutralization" binds the state to neutral behavior at all times. A neutralized or "permanently neutral" state, in return for a pledge of impartiality, nonparticipation in any alliance, and defense of its neutrality, territorial integrity, and independence, may have its status guaranteed by other powers. It should be noted that states not parties to the neutralization agreement are not bound to come to the defense of the neutralized state in case it is attacked. It is not clear whether or not a signatory remains bound by the agreement in case of noncompliance by other signatories. However, one can argue that the permanent neutrality of Switzerland, and perhaps even Austria, has become part of general customary international law. From a neutralized or permanently neutral state, one must distinguish states such as Sweden and Finland, which are *de facto* permanently neutral without any legal obligation, and numerous states in the Third World that follow (or claim to follow) a strategy of "nonalignment." Unlike the legal status of neutralization (permanent neutrality), the status of nonalignment ("neutralism") is not based on any international legal obligation. *See also* NEUTRALITY, 351.

Significance   Neutralized states are not very common. Historically they are a product of the European balance of power system. Those that were included (or remain) in this category are Switzerland (the classical model of permanent neutrality), Belgium, Luxembourg, Laos, and Austria. Today, only Switzerland since 1815 and Austria since 1955 are examples of truly neutralized states. Belgium, Luxembourg, and Laos neutrality were violated by wars and are no longer classified as neutralized states. Both Belgium and Luxembourg are members of the North Atlantic Treaty Organization (NATO), while the now communist Laos is tied to the regional aspirations of the pro-Soviet Vietnam. Discouraged by its negative experience of membership in the League of Nations, Switzerland desires to ensure that its permanent neutrality status, internationally legalized by the Congress of Vienna (1815) and reaffirmed by the Treaty of Versailles (1919), is not jeopardized. This has led it to refuse membership in the United Nations on the legal grounds that the collective security feature of that organization would violate the intent of strict permanent neutrality. (A popular referendum in 1986 decidedly rejected the idea of joining the United Nations.) Switzerland is, however, a member of United Nations specialized agencies and a party to the International Court of Justice (ICJ). Austria is a United Nations member, however. The latest addition to the list of permanently neutral countries is Malta which, in 1980, declared a status of neutrality "based on nonalignment," explicitly recognized by Italy and several other states, including the USSR, China, and Libya. A new type of "unarmed" permanent neutrality was proclaimed by Costa Rica in 1983. However, this unilateral act has no automatic legal effect upon other states.

Non-self-governing Territory   (59)

The United Nations' term for a territory under the control of a colonial power, whatever its name—external territory; overseas territory; overseas *département;* dependency; self-governing territory; territory; or simply colony. Article 73 of the Charter of the United Nations charges all United Nations members responsible for administering non-self-governing territories to govern in such a manner as to promote the well-being of the inhabitants, including insuring the political, social, economic, and educational advancement of the territory in such a manner as to aid them in developing their own institutions. *See also*

DEPENDENT STATE, 52; PROTECTORATE, 61; SELF-DETERMINATION, RIGHT OF, 74.

Significance　Almost all non-self-governing territories have, since the end of World War II, become independent states. Indeed, Article 73 of the United Nations Charter was interpreted by some as a call for national independence and set the stage for the wholesale movement by colonies to seek independence. The attitude of the United Nations General Assembly suggested that this Article applied only to extra-European overseas colonies of the European states. The United Nations General Assembly Declaration of 1960 on the Granting of Independence to Colonial Countries and Peoples recognized that a non-self-governing territory could choose either independence or integration with a state or association. But in practice the Assembly and the territories in question have shown a preference for independence. In the mid-1980s, only a handful of non-self-governing territories remain in existence.

Personal Union (60)

An arrangement whereby several states accidentally share a single head of state (typically a monarch). A personal union does not create a single international person; rather, each state retains its separate legal personality.

Significance　Personal unions are of historical interest, although they were common in the past. Examples included Great Britain and Hanover (1714–1837), Brazil and Portugal (1808–1821), the Netherlands and Luxembourg (1815–1890), and Belgium and the Congo Free State (1885–1908). There are no personal unions today.

Protectorate (61)

A legal status largely of historical interest whereby a dependent state retains control over its internal affairs, while leaving its external protection in the hands of another state. Protectorates were sometimes referred to as autonomous states, semi-sovereign states, dependent states, or vassal states. The term protectorate is felt by some to convey a distinct relationship by formal agreement wherein the affected state relinquishes a portion of its sovereignty in return for protection by the guarantor state (or states). *See also* CONDOMINIUM, 48; DEPENDENT STATE, 52.

Significance   Protectorate as a term had replaced that of "vassal state" by the nineteenth century. The term vassal state was more accurate in a feudal or tributary system, and there were other distinct differences in the arrangements. Protectorates were viewed as a looser arrangement since the actions of the protecting state in such matters as signing a treaty or going to war did not necessarily involve the protected state, whereas they would have affected a vassal state. The extent of international personality held by a protectorate would depend upon the arrangement between the protector and the protected state (as well as the attitude of other states), but generally such arrangements would constitute that of partial personality at best. Examples of protectorates include the Ionian Islands, a British protectorate from 1815–1863; Morocco, under Great Power guardianship from 1906–1911 and then a French protectorate until 1956; and a portion of Morocco under Spanish control, 1912–1956. There are no more protectorates of colonial powers overseas after Brunei, the last protected state, became independent in 1984. Today, Europe houses the principality of Andorra—considered by some as a condominium and by others a joint protectorate of France and the Bishop of Urgel, the latter on behalf of Spain.

Real Union   **(62)**
A treaty arrangement whereby two or more states form a union, making them a single composite international legal person. A real union does not, however, create a single state; consequently, each state would regain its individual international personality should the real union be dissolved.

Significance   Real unions resemble federal states, but an important distinction is the loss of international personality and indissoluble nature of the latter case. Real unions have included Austria-Hungary, 1867–1918; Sweden and Norway, 1814–1905; and Denmark and Iceland, 1918–1944. Libya has been very active since the early 1970s in encouraging various kinds of unions with other Arab states, for example Egypt, the Sudan, Syria, and Tunisia. The latest state entering into a kind of union was Morocco in 1984. On the one hand, the various Libyan attempts are difficult to classify in traditional concepts; on the other hand politically they have proved a fiction.

Recognition   **(63)**
The discretionary function exercised unilaterally by the government of a state officially acknowledging the existence of another state or gov-

ernment or belligerent community. Recognition attaches certain legal consequences to an existing set of facts, as applied to either an entity claiming to be a state or a government claiming to be the legal representative of a state. Recognition carries with it entitlement to the rights and privileges held by states under international law. Recognition of a government should not be confused with recognition of a state. When a state is recognized, so also is its government; but subsequent governments may not be recognized, even though the state's recognition is permanent for the existence of that state. Recognition may be either explicit (express) or implicit (tacit). It may be recognition *de facto* or *de jure*. Recognition of a new state automatically involves recognition of its government, although the latter may be recognized only *de facto*. If a state's government is changed as a result of a regular constitutional change (normally elections), no problems of recognition arise, even if slight irregularities occurred but the new government is firmly in power and secures stability of the country. As a rule, problems of recognition of government arise in cases of a serious violation of normal constitutional practice (typically, a government is overthrown) and especially when a revolutionary change occurs in the political and usually economic and social system of a country. *See also* INTERNATIONAL LEGAL PERSONALITY, 56; RECOGNITION: BELLIGERENCY, 64; RECOGNITION: CONSTITUTIVE THEORY, 65; RECOGNITION: DECLARATORY, 66; RECOGNITION: *DE FACTO*, 67; RECOGNITION: *DE JURE*, 68; RECOGNITION: ESTRADA DOCTRINE, 69; RECOGNITION: IMPLICIT, 70.

Significance   Recognition of a state defines its membership in the world community, and consequently supports its claim as a separate juridical personality, i.e., an international person. It allows for the exercise of the rights and duties of states. For many well-established states with a long history of existence, recognition was never of consequence, at least for those involved in the development of international law. For most non-European states—especially the newly independent ones (as well as those seeking independence)—recognition could be important. By acknowledging the ability of a state to conform to the duties and obligations of the international community and subscribe to its legal norms, the European states formally admitted into the community of "civilized" nations such states as (1) Turkey, by the Treaty of Paris in 1856 (although relations had been maintained before); (2) Japan (later in the nineteenth century); (3) China in 1907 (by virtue of its acceptance as a participant at the Second Hague Conference). Recognition can also be important in instances where mergers or separations of international persons take place, such as the North German Confederation (1866) and the separation of Sweden and Norway (1905). Recognition has played an important role in the decolonization process in the post–World War II era, and in the question of the German Democratic Republic (not recognized by the Western powers until 1973), the two Koreas, and Vietnam. Recognition of the government of the People's Republic of China by the United States was a major political issue in relations between the two countries for more than two decades. Although *de facto* recognition took place in the early 1970s, formal recognition of the government in Beijing did not follow until 1979. Finally, the continued refusal of states to recognize an entity results in a situation of "collective nonrecognition," whereby the international community refuses to legitimize a situation they find objectionable. Such was the case with Manchukuo, which the Japanese created after their conquest of Chinese Manchuria, and is presently the case with the South African–created "independent" black homelands, called "bantustans." Recognition of a state or a government is in all cases a political act with legal and political consequences.

Recognition: Belligerency (64)

The formal acknowledgment by third parties of the existence of a state of war between a state's central government and a portion of that state. Belligerency exists when a portion of the state's territory is under the control of an insurgent community seeking to establish a separate state and the insurgents are in *de facto* control of a portion of the state's territory and population, have a political organization able to exert such control and maintain some degree of popular support, and conduct themselves according to the laws of war. Further evidence of a state of belligerency occurs when the state blockades the rebelling portion of its territory and invokes rights of visit and search upon vessels. Two conditions should exist before an outside state extends belligerent recognition: (1) the insurgency should have progressed to a state of general war; and (2) the effects of that war have spilled beyond the boundaries of the state and affected other states. Such recognition provides the rebelling unit with a degree of international personality, although much less than that possessed by the state itself. The lesser degree of personality results from it being both nonpermanent (the insurrection may fail) and particular (personality exists only for those states extending recognition). *See also* ARMED CONFLICT: INTERNATIONAL, 323; ARMED CONFLICT: NONINTERNATIONAL, 324; INSURGENCY, 71; NEUTRALITY, 351.

Significance Recognition of belligerency elevates an insurrectionary movement to the status of a quasi-international person, granting it the rights and imposing upon it the duties of the laws of war. This means that the belligerent community may legally establish a blockade; exercise visit and search of vessels on the high seas; confiscate contraband goods; enter ports of recognizing states (i.e., operate as a navy rather than as pirates); and be treated according to the laws of war rather than as common criminals. The timing of recognition of a status of belligerency is critical, for if done too hastily it constitutes an unfriendly act against the parent state and interference in that state's domestic affairs. The incentive to recognize a state of belligerency can be either to normalize relations with the warring parties by providing the recognizing state with the status of neutrality (as this becomes a duty upon recognizing such a status), or it can be a political incentive to help support the legitimacy of the rebellion. During the American Civil War, Great Britain recognized a state of belligerency with reference to the Confederate States of America in 1861, despite the protest of the U.S. government that the rebellion by the southern states did not result in a legal state of war. In fact, the Union naval blockade against the South seriously undermined the U.S. government's case and gave Great Britain valid incentive to protect its shipping and economic interests. Great Britain's supplying commerce raiders to the South, however, led to the postwar *Alabama Claims* (United States–Great Britain Arbitration, 1871) arbitral settlement. It should be noted that a rebellion may seek simply to change the government rather than seek existence as a separate state. This is then a civil war in the more limited sense and does not involve the issue of separate international personality.

Recognition: Constitutive Theory (65)

The theoretical proposition that the existence of a state begins with its recognition by other states. The constitutive theory of recognition propounds that the act of recognition constitutes or creates the new international person. *See also* RECOGNITION: DECLARATORY THEORY, 66.

Significance   The constitutive theory of recognition has few followers today and is not reflected in international practice. The major difficulty with this school of thought is in its assumption that recognition of a state is a legal process based upon objective criteria. In reality, the process is political and based upon both objective and subjective criteria, the criteria being objective, but their evaluation or verification being subjective. The constitutive approach can lead to confusing situations, with a state existing for those states that have recognized it while not existing for others. There are, however, instances where recognition can create a subject of international law for limited purposes, such as recognition of a state of belligerency during a civil conflict.

Recognition: Declaratory Theory (66)

A theory concerning the legal significance of recognition, according to which recognition is merely an acknowledgment of the facts; namely, of an already existing state or government. Under this theory, recognition does not create any state that did not already exist. Recognition of a new state implies recognition of its government as well, but thereafter a change in government could result in the refusal to recognize that government. *See also* RECOGNITION, 63; RECOGNITION: CONSTITUTIVE THEORY, 65; STATE, 76.

Significance The declaratory theory of recognition is one side in the theoretical dispute over the legal effect of recognizing a new state. The other side is the constitutive theory of recognition, which suggests that the act of recognition creates a new international person. Declaratory recognition acknowledges the *de facto* existence of the state. In cases of states that enter the community of nations as independent entities with prior existence and are able to meet the definitional conditions for being classified as a state, recognition would seem to be a declaratory statement of fact. On the other hand, recognition can have constitutive effects when a degree of international personality is granted even though an entity might fail to meet all the requirements for classification as a state as, for example, when a belligerent community exists within a state. Recognition is important because, *inter alia*, states have often refused to give unrecognized states access to their courts on the grounds of lack of standing.

Recognition: *De Facto* (67)

A provisional recognition by the government of one state that another regime in fact exercises authoritative control over its territory and people. A rather confusing distinction exists between *de facto* and *de jure* recognition (a distinction usually arising in the case of governments, although there have been some cases of recognizing states *de facto*). *De facto* recognition, or rather recognition of a *de facto* government, suggests that it is in actual control of the governmental machinery of the state and its authority is generally accepted by the populace. By extending *de facto* recognition, the recognizing state conveys a desire to enter into relations with the newly recognized government, but on a less than inclusive basis. This suggests that other conditions must be met or the circumstances of the government's coming to power clarified before full (*de jure*) recognition is extended. As such, it is implied that *de facto* recognition is provisional and temporary and could be withdrawn at some future date, although it is usually followed by full recognition. *See also* RECOGNITION, 63; RECOGNITION: BELLIG-

Significance   De facto recognition is usually not an issue when governments change according to the constitutional processes of the state. It is, however, very much an issue of political legitimacy in those cases where a new government has come to power through means outside the constitutional process, such as revolutions or coups. In such cases, the new government must meet the objective tests of effectively controlling the machinery of government and having popular support. It must be a government in fact (*de facto*). Sometimes additional, subjectively perceived conditions are attached to the two tests described above, such as the conveyance of a willingness to abide by international obligations. The type of government that has been formed or the manner in which it came to power may constitute subjective factors influencing the extension of recognition. The British government, for example, recognized the Soviet government as *de facto* in 1921 and later extended *de jure* recognition in 1924. In contrast, the United States simply extended *de jure* recognition in 1933. The addition of subjective considerations to recognition of governments leaves states open to charges of interference in the domestic affairs of the state in question. A major consequence of extending recognition to a new government is the access of that government to the recognizing state's domestic courts. Without such recognition, there is the real possibility of the unrecognized government being denied access to domestic courts of another state.

Recognition: *De Jure*   (68)

One of the two basic forms of recognizing a new government, the other being *de facto* recognition. *De jure* recognition, or rather recognition of a *de jure* government, acknowledges the legal status of the government as being the valid authority to speak and act for the state. It is, therefore, complete recognition of the government in question as not a government in fact, but rather the legal government. *De jure* recognition implies a permanence missing in *de facto* recognition, which can be withdrawn. States can normally be recognized only *de jure*. *See also* RECOGNITION, 63; RECOGNITION: *DE FACTO*, 67; RECOGNITION: ESTRADA DOCTRINE, 69; RECOGNITION: TOBAR DOCTRINE, 72.

Significance   De jure recognition conveys an uncontested legality to the target government, meaning permanent and full recognition. Unlike *de facto* recognition, it is held by many authorities to be irrevocable, but this may be too strong a statement. *De jure* recognition has a retroactive effect upon all actions of the recognized government; it allows for the exchange of diplomatic personnel and inaugurates full relations between the states concerned. As with *de facto* recognition, *de jure* recognition has the potential for abuse in a rapidly changing world of decolonization and internal revolutions, particularly when ideological considerations are injected. As a political instrument, granting or withholding *de jure* recognition is often viewed as intervention in the affairs of the state in question, as it suggests passing judgment on the internal political processes of that state.

Recognition: Estrada Doctrine   (69)

The doctrine asserting that a state should not apply subjective considerations to extending recognition of a new government, but rather accept the existence of that government. This is also known as the doctrine of effectiveness because it holds that the only test of recognition should be whether or not the government is in effective control of the machinery of state and the populace. *See also* RECOGNITION: *DE FACTO*, 67; RECOGNITION: *DE JURE*, 68; RECOGNITION: TOBAR DOCTRINE, 72.

Significance   The Estrada Doctrine was named for Secretary of Foreign Relations of Mexico Genaro Estrada, who espoused it in 1930. Its premise was a natural consequence of the tumultuous years of Mexican governmental changes in the aftermath of the Mexican Revolution and the strains this placed on the subjective recognition practices of such states as the United States. Chafing at the nonrecognition of the Huerta regime, Mexico deemed such discrimination insulting. The Estrada Doctrine reaffirms the objective test for recognition: Is the government in control of the machinery of government, and does it have popular support? and ignores the manner in which the government came to power. Indeed, strictly constructed, the Estrada Doctrine seeks to remove recognition from a state's political initiative, replacing it with automatic recognition of a new government and establishing diplomatic relations. This suggests that governmental changes do not interrupt the continuous relations of states. Many states are reluctant to yield recognition as a tool in interstate relations, but accept much of the argument for applying solely objective considerations for recognition decisions. This had been the practice of the United States before the Civil War and was called the Jefferson Doctrine, as it was during Thomas Jefferson's presidential term that the United States recognized the revolutionary government of France without concern for the manner in which it had come to power. During the latter decades of the nineteenth century, several American presidents attached conditions to recognition, culminating in President Woodrow Wilson's withholding of recognition of the revolutionary government in Mexico in the early twentieth century because of the manner in which it had come to power and the need for proof of popular support. This became known as the Wilson test for recognition.

Recognition: Implicit Recognition   (70)

Recognition of a state through actions other than official statements or actions intended to extend recognition. Implicit recognition is also known as implied or tacit recognition. *See also* RECOGNITION, 63.

Significance   Implicit recognition can result from a variety of actions undertaken by a state in reference to an unrecognized state. Some actions are widely held to imply recognition of the unrecognized state, while others are considered innocuous enough to escape such effect. Included in the former category are official congratulatory statements upon independence, the conclusion of a bilateral treaty, or the acknowledgment of the new entity's flag. Actions which do not imply recognition include being party to a multipartite treaty to which the unrecognized state is also a party or belonging to an international organization of which the unrecognized state is also a member or becomes a member.

Recognition: Insurgency   (71)

The acknowledgment of a status of insurgency by third states. A recognition of insurgency acknowledges a state of rebellion or revolt within a country which has not yet reached the proportion warranted for extension of recognition of a status of belligerency. Recognition of insurgency generally means that the rebellion has not yet gained control over a significant portion of the territory of the parent state. Nevertheless, the third state may wish to control the contact of its citizens with the rebellion and safeguard its neutral status, as well as see the rebels treated as something other than mere criminals. Such recognition does not convey international personality. *See also* ARMED CONFLICT: NONINTERNATIONAL, 324; RECOGNITION: BELLIGERENCY, 64.

Significance   Insurgent recognition is a Western Hemisphere creation of the nineteenth century, which does not have universal acceptance. The United States extended such recognition to the Cuban insurgents in their rebellion against Spain in the 1890s. The motive behind this new form of recognition was the enforcement of U.S. neutrality laws to preclude U.S. citizens from aiding insurgents during their rebellion. This recognition of insurgency or political revolt does not give insurgents the range of rights granted by recognition of belligerency, such as the right to establish blockades, the right to visit and search on the high seas, and the right to seize contraband.

Recognition: Tobar Doctrine   (72)

The doctrine that a state should not recognize a government that has come to power in another state through unconstitutional means, such as a coup d'état or a revolution. The Tobar Doctrine was enunciated in treaties in 1907 and 1923 among the states of Central America and remained the basis of recognition among them for more than two decades. This position is also known as the doctrine of legitimacy. *See also* RECOGNITION: *DE FACTO*, 67; RECOGNITION: *DE JURE*, 68; RECOGNITION: ESTRADA DOCTRINE, 69.

Significance   The Tobar Doctrine enshrined in treaty a classic statement for the subjective test of government recognition. Named for Carlos R. Tobar, the foreign minister of Equador, it failed to receive hemispheric support and is not today widely subscribed to. The United States supported the doctrine until the beginning of the 1930s. The most notorious instance of U.S. use of the Tobar Doctrine was President Wilson's refusal to recognize the government of Mexican General Victoriano Huerta when the latter seized power in 1911. It was not until Huerta's loss of power to the forces of General Venustiano Carranza in 1915 that the United States recognized the Mexican government. President Wilson stated that the United States would not recognize any change in government by those who had seized power for their own gain or ambition. This became known as the Wilsonian test for recognition or the Wilson policy. The emergence of ideologies politically unacceptable to some states is another motive for nonrecognition. The United States withheld recognition of the government of Soviet Russia and then the Union of Soviet Socialist Republics (USSR) for some sixteen years after the success of the Bolshevik Revolution in 1917. A similar reluctance to recognize a Marxist government occurred with the Chinese Communist takeover of the government of China in 1949. The U.S. unambiguous and formal acceptance of this change did not take place until 1979. Such examples illustrate the proposition that recognition of governments can be a political rather than legal decision.

Reparation (73)

A settlement (remedy) due to a state from another state for the injury sustained by a breach of international law by that state. Reparation is alternately called compensation, damages, indemnity, or recompense. Any breach of international law involves an obligation to make reparation. The breach of international law may produce either a material injury or a "moral" injury. Material injury may be an injury to an individual (or his or her property) or to a state's property, but in both cases it is considered an injury suffered by the state itself; hence, under international law a moral injury always accompanies a material injury. On the other hand, a moral injury to a state need not necessarily cause material damage but still results in the duty of reparation. Reparation must, if possible, relieve all the consequences of the illegal act and reestablish things to their previous state as if the act had never been committed. This is known as the principle of *restitutio ad integrum* and it may involve restitution in kind, but in most cases it is impossible because of changed circumstances; hence, reparation must be at least partially in the form of monetary compensation. For example, the International Court of Justice (ICJ) ordered Iran to pay reparation for the taking over of the U.S. embassy and the consulate and their personnel in Tehran in the *Case Concerning United States Diplomatic and Consular Staff in Tehran* (*United States v. Iran,* 1980). If the damage was suffered by a private person, this damage (which is never identical with that suffered by the state) can only provide a convenient scale for the calculation of the reparation due to the state. Indeed, in international practice reparation is measured not by the fault of the state that violated international law, but by the loss to the private person arising from the injury, although under the circumstances it may involve additional monetary damages for the moral injury to the state. *See also* STATE RESPONSIBILITY, 77.

Significance   A major problem with claim for reparation is the form and the magnitude of the claim. The judgment in the *Chorzów Factory* case (Permanent Court of International Justice, 1928) is instructive. In this case the Court declared that reparation must absolve the consequences of the act and restore things to their previous state as if the act had not been committed (*restitutio ad integrum*). The restitution should be in kind, or if not possible, payment of a sum reflecting the value of restitution in kind. A similar position was taken by the Court in the *Case Concerning Certain German Interests in Polish Upper Silesia* (Permanent Court of International Justice, 1926). Other than these basic principles, the nature of reparation will depend upon the circumstances of the case. Reparation or compensation is as much a matter of politics and economics as it is a judgment based upon legal considerations. This is particularly true in cases arising from the expropriation or nationalization of foreign property which is a major area of dispute over compensation or reparation. The U.S. position has been—at least on grounds of principle and for bargaining purposes—that, in case of expropriation, foreign investors are entitled to the fair market value of their interests ("adequate" compensation); whereas many Third World countries claim that the amount of reparation depends entirely upon their sovereign discretionary power.

Self-determination, Right of   (74)

The right of a people to choose their own legal and political institutions and status in the community of nations. It remains a matter of dispute as to whether national self-determination is a political concept, a theoretical principle, or a legal right. While many governments deny its legal status, the communist and Third World states strongly support it as both a legal principle and a political statement but apply it only to those peoples who are still under colonial rule in extra-European territories of European powers (and apply it inconsistently even in those territories.) *See also* DECLARATION ON FRIENDLY RELATIONS, 51; NON-SELF-GOVERNING TERRITORY, 59.

Significance   There remains considerable dispute as to whether the alleged right of self-determination deals only with colonies seeking their independence and creation of their own political institutions, or also includes any dissident group seeking to obtain its international identity (e.g., the Kurdish movement in Iran, Iraq and neighboring countries; the Sikhs in India; the Moluccans in Indonesia; Eritreans in Ethiopia; Tamils in Sri Lanka; and many others). In 1960 the United Nations General Assembly passed an important resolution entitled the Declaration on the Granting of Independence to Colonial Countries and Peoples by a vote of 89 to 0 with 9 abstentions (including the United States, Great Britain, and France). This Declaration asserts that alien subjugation, domination, and exploitation of peoples violates human rights and is contrary to the Charter of the United Nations; that all peoples have the right of self-determination; that failure to prepare a people for independence should not be a pretext for delaying independence; that all armed measures of repression against dependent peoples should cease; that in all territories not yet having achieved independence a transfer of power should take place; and that any attempt to disrupt the national unity and territorial integrity of a country is incompatible with the Charter of the United Nations. While the United Nations Covenant on Civil and Political Rights, the Covenant on Economic, Social, and Cultural Rights, and Article 1 of the United Nations Charter mention self-determination without qualification, the territorial integrity of United Nations members is also expressly guaranteed in the United Nations Charter (Article 2). Thus, a conflict can exist between the right of a state to maintain its territory intact and the right of a minority national group within that state to realize its destiny through the right of self-determination. The issue is unlikely to be resolved with the end of colonialism, given the vague concept of "people" and dissatisfied ethnic minorities present in countries on all continents.

Sovereignty (75)

A fundamental concept of international law denoting the supreme undivided authority possessed by a state to enact and enforce its law with respect to all persons, property, and events within its borders. Sovereignty is unfettered by the control of other states. By being sovereign "externally," a state enjoys certain immunities and privileges, such as sending and receiving diplomats, engaging in treaty making, and possessing immunity from the jurisdiction of other states. In reality, however, the exercise of sovereignty is not absolute. Through the corollary doctrine of state consent, each state may accept limitations on its sovereign powers by accepting the restrictions under international law and by virtue of decisions rendered by international organizations of which it is a member. States must abide by the legal norms established by the international community and are subjected to particular restraints embodied in treaties and set by international organizations. *See also* DEPENDENT STATE, 52; INTERNATIONAL LEGAL PERSONALITY, 56; STATE, 76.

Significance   Sovereignty is the benchmark of the international personality of an entity seeking a status legally equal to other members of the community of nations. The degree of sovereignty possessed by dependent states, protectorates, and associated states was once a matter of interest and debate but today is of historical interest only. Such appellations were used in situations where some degree of control or limitations upon a state's foreign and/or domestic policy was exercised by another state or states. At one time some states used to be admitted to the community of nations with stipulations attached to their acquiring international personality. For example, Bulgaria, Romania, Serbia, and Montenegro were obligated by the Treaty of Berlin (1878) to respect religious and ethnic minorities (suggesting conduct befitting "civilized" nations). Protection of minorities by Poland, Czechoslovakia, the Kingdom of the Serbs, Croats, and Slovenes (Yugoslavia), and some other countries was stipulated in the treaties concluded with these states by the principal allied and associated powers after World War I. The 1903 treaty between the United States and Cuba restricted Cuba's financial and treaty-making powers as well as providing the United States the right of military intervention. Where and at what point such a state of dependency undermines an entity's international personality is not clearly answered in international law, it being largely a political judgment. Such restrictions were generally held not to be contraventions of sovereignty to the extent that these less-than-sovereign states were unequals or second-class states.

State (76)

The primary legal (juridical) person and subject in international law. A state, by evidencing a separate legal and corporate personality, fulfills the basic requirements for entrance into the community of nations. This suggests that the entity is free from political control by another state and is free to contract and enter into relations with other states. A state has several characteristics it shares in common with other states as outlined, for example, in Article 1 of the Montevideo Convention on the Rights and Duties of States (1933): (1) territory; (2) population; (3) government (the political agent for the state); and (4) independence of action (sovereignty). States as international persons are formed through the creation of a new state, the merger of existing states, or the division of existing states. See also COMMUNITY OF NATIONS, 47; INTERNATIONAL LEGAL PERSONALITY, 56; PROTECTORATE, 61; SOVEREIGNTY, 75.

Significance Quite naturally, states are not similar in their attributes. The People's Republic of China contains almost one quarter of the human race, while the population of Nauru is some eight thousand. Canada's territorial size is twenty-nine thousand times that of Grenada. All have equal standing in international law, despite such statistical inequalities. This is called the legal equality of nations and is enshrined in the United Nations Charter as the most important principle of the organization; namely, "the principle of the sovereign equality of all its members" (Article 2[1]). It is commonplace among political scientists to use the terms "nation," "state," and "nation-state" interchangeably, but in international law "state" is the accepted term. To be a state, the entity must have the capacity to enter into international relations and act according to international law. For international law, the ethnic origin of the population is basically irrelevant except for the vague, ambiguous, and controversial principle of "self-determination of peoples."

State Responsibility (77)

The obligation of the state to make reparation arising from a failure to comply with an obligation under international law. State responsibility is predicated on an act or omission in violation of an international legal obligation resulting in injury to the claimant state. Although frequently associated with responsibility for injuries to aliens, state responsibility may be based upon many substantive grounds of international law, including violation of the prohibition of resort to force in international relations. State responsibility can result from actions directly attributable to the state through its agents (original responsibility) or from actions that only indirectly involve the state (vicarious responsibility). State actions that incur original responsibility include those performed by executive, legislative, or judicial organs of the government. Vicarious responsibility occurs as a consequence of unauthorized actions performed by subordinate or minor agents of the state or by private persons. *See also* IMPUTABILITY, 165; REPARATION, 73; STATE RESPONSIBILITY, DRAFT ARTICLES ON, 78.

Significance State responsibility remains an unsettled area of international law. There are those who argue that original responsibility of the state occurs only in the instances pertaining to the consequences of executive actions, as there are political systems in which the executive branch has only incomplete control over the actions of the legislative and judicial organs of the government. The area of indirect (vicarious) state responsibility is equally unsettled where issues of mob violence, actions by private individuals, and unauthorized actions by state officials confuse the picture. As a general proposition, there is vicarious state imputability in such circumstances as failure to exercise due diligence, failure to apprehend and punish those responsible for injurious acts, and unauthorized actions by state agents. The extent of the state's imputability insofar as reparations are concerned depends upon the severity of the offense, the persons involved, and the particular circumstance of the incident. Responsibility of states for other harmful acts, such as environmental damage caused by air and water pollution, nuclear contamination from accidents, and other activities that produce "created risk" has been an area receiving much attention in recent years. In general, the theory of state responsibility is not very well developed. Especially difficult is the issue of "objective responsibility"; that is, liability of a state for injurious consequences of acts not prohibited by international law. The liability of the USSR for radiation damage caused by the Chernobyl disaster in 1986 is one example.

State Responsibility, Draft Articles on   (78)

A draft convention in preparation by the International Law Commission designed to codify and develop the law of state responsibility. The Commission has divided the subject of state responsibility into three parts. Part 1, consisting of 35 draft articles, deals with the origin of international responsibility and includes such topics as general principles, the act of state doctrine, breach of international obligation, the implication of a state in the internationally wrongful act of another state, and circumstances precluding wrongfulness. Part 2 deals with the content, forms, and degrees of international responsibility, i.e., reparative and punitive consequences of wrongful acts. Part 3 concerns the implementation of international responsibility and settlement of disputes. The International Law Commission has distinguished primary rules of international law—those which impose particular obligations on states—from secondary rules—those which determine the consequences of violation of obligations—and decided to concentrate its efforts upon the latter.

Of major importance in the Draft Articles is the division of internationally wrongful acts into two categories: (1) international crimes; and (2) international delicts. The first category includes a serious breach of an international obligation of essential importance to (1) the maintenance of international peace, e.g., prohibition of aggression; (2) for safeguarding the right of self-determination of peoples, e.g., prohibition of colonial domination; (3) for safeguarding human beings, e.g., prohibition of slavery, genocide, and apartheid; and (4) for the safeguarding and preservation of the environment, e.g., prohibition against massive air or water pollution. Any wrongful act not covered in these four categories is considered an international delict. *See also* STATE RESPONSIBILITY, 77.

Significance   The Draft Articles on State Responsibility have been part of the codification efforts of the International Law Commission since 1955, and to date only Part 1 has been fully developed. Such slow progress attests to the central importance of the topic to the field of international law and the consequent difficulty of states coming to an agreement on the codification of its content. It was not until 1963 that any real progress was made as a result of distinguishing primary rules from secondary rules of state responsibility. This allowed for the successful drafting of Part 1 of the Draft Articles on State Responsibility.

Progress on Part 2 of the Draft Articles has been problematic since it is difficult to deal with the breach of an obligation without devoting attention to the content of the obligation and the distinction between primary and secondary rules challenging.

In 1982, however, six articles were proposed as a foundation for further work, dealing *inter alia* with quantitative proportionality and the peremptory subsystems of *jus cogens*, the United Nations system, and international crimes. The distinction between international crimes and international delicts is troublesome to some because it confuses the law concerning the responsibility of states with that concerning the responsibility of individuals and, by labeling specific serious breaches of international law as international crimes, politicizes a very sensitive area of state activity. The concept of international crime is controversial and opposed by the United States and other Western states who argue that only individuals can be subject to criminal responsibility and cite the Nuremberg Tribunal's pronouncement that crimes against international law are committed by men, not by abstract entities.

Succession, State (79)

The transfer of sovereignty over a territory from one subject of international law to another. Succession problems may result from total extinction of a state or from transfer of part of its territory to another state. Total extinction results in universal succession and may be brought about by (1) conquest and subjugation—a development legal in traditional international law but illegal under the present law; (2) division of a state into two or more states, e.g., Malaysia into Malaysia and Singapore in 1965 or Pakistan into Pakistan and Bangladesh in 1971; or (3) a merger of two or more states into one new state, e.g., Tanganyika and Zanzibar into Tanzania in 1964 or the absorption by a state of another state (such as the absorption of Texas by the United States in 1845). In practice, it may be difficult to decide whether the resulting entity is a new state or only an enlargement of one state. Partial succession results from cession or other methods of transferring sovereignty over territory, but transfer brought about by force is illegal. State succession raises complex legal problems concerning the extent to which rights and obligations of the predecessor state are transferred to the successor state. Until recently, state succession was based entirely upon customary international law; but the Vienna Convention on Succession of States in Respect of Treaties (1978) and the Convention on Succession of States in Respect of State Property, Archives, and Debts (1983) regulate large areas of the law of state succession. These two conventions were not yet in force in 1986. Succession of states involves problems of succession to treaties, membership in international organizations, public and private property rights, international claims, and contractual obligations, to name the most important areas. State succession must be distinguished from government succession, as the latter merely replaces the political agent of the state with another. *See also* CONTINUITY OF STATES, 50; INTERNATIONAL LEGAL PERSONALITY, 56.

Significance   Succession raises questions about the obligations and rights of the extinct state as they pertain to the new sovereign. In general, those rights and obligations that are linked to the international personality of the extinct state (*in personam*) are not automatically transferred to the successor state. Those rights and obligations that are linked to the physical territory of the state (*in rem*) generally do survive, such as dispositive treaties, which deal with rights over territory; boundary treaties; servitudes; and title to public property. Treaties of a political nature, military alliances, trade and commercial treaties, extradition treaties, etc. are examples of *in personam* obligations and would not be automatically transferred to the new state. The matter of contractual obligations, debts, or torts tied to the former state is largely left to the judgment of the successor state. Private property rights and obligations have historically been viewed as unaffected by state succession, but in this modern period witnessing the spread of state socialism, such a blanket statement is open to dispute. In general, as demonstrated by international practice of new states created by decolonization, these states follow the "clean state" approach to succession, preferring to decide according to their respective national interests the extent to which they will step into the rights and duties of the metropolitan power. Succession can also take place with regard to international organizations. The United Nations and the International Court of Justice are successors to the League of Nations and the Permanent Court of International Justice respectively. The International Court of Justice has held (in an advisory opinion) that the mandates of the League of Nations were transferred upon its demise to the Trusteeship Council of the United Nations as the successor to the League's mandate system.

Trusteeship System (80)

A United Nations-created institution whereby a trust territory would be administered by a state or the United Nations itself, under the supervision of the Trusteeship Council of the United Nations. Operating under the overall authority of the United Nations General Assembly, the trusteeship system was created by Chapters XII and XIII of the

United Nations Charter as a means of promoting the political, economic, and social betterment of the people in trust territories until such time as self-government and then independence could be granted. *See also* ASSOCIATION, 46; MANDATE SYSTEM, 57.

Significance The trusteeship system replaced the mandate system of the League of Nations, and the mandates of the older system were, with one exception, transferred by the Mandatory Powers to the Trusteeship Council. The exception was the South African mandate over Southwest Africa (now known as Namibia), which South Africa refused to relinquish. It was South Africa's contention that upon the demise of the League of Nations the mandate lapsed, and South Africa could incorporate the mandate into its own territory. This position was refuted in the *International Status of South-West Africa* advisory opinion by the International Court of Justice (1950). Potential or actual categories of territories that could or did come under the aegis of the Trusteeship Council were, in addition to the category mentioned (transfer of mandates), territories previously under control of the defeated powers of World War II and territories voluntarily transferred to the Trusteeship Council by colonial states. No examples of the third category occurred. A total of eleven territories under the control of seven states were placed under the trusteeship system. The United States trust over the Marianas, Carolines, and Marshall Islands produced an unusual relationship, as these were classified as strategic trust areas in view of their geopolitical importance. The strategic trust territories came under the supervisory authority of the Security Council rather than the Trusteeship Council and the General Assembly. An interesting feature of the trusteeship arrangement of the United Nations (which was not found in the League of Nations' mandate system) was that territories could be placed directly under the Trusteeship Council as trustee. Today the trusteeship system is virtually of historical interest only as the last of these territories, the United States Trust Territory of the Pacific Islands—the Commonwealth of the Northern Marianas Islands, the Federated States of Micronesia, the Republic of Palau, and the Marshall Islands—have signed compacts of association with the United States likely to be in force in the near future.

3. Individuals, Human Rights, and International Organizations

American Convention on Human Rights (1969) (81)

A treaty of the Organization of American States (OAS), adopted at its Costa Rica session of 1969, dealing with international legal protection of human rights in the Western Hemisphere. The American Convention on Human Rights is a comprehensive document closely modeled after the European Convention for the Protection of Human Rights and Fundamental Freedoms (1950). It guarantees some twenty-two basic political and civil rights, including rights to juridical personality; life; humane treatment; personal freedom; fair trial; privacy; compensation; reply; assembly; family; name; property; participation in government; equal protection; judicial protection; rights of children; freedom from slavery and ex post facto laws; and freedom of conscience and religion, thought and expression, association, movement, and residence. It also provided for the creation of an Inter-American Court of Human Rights and an Inter-American Commission on Human Rights (which is actually the OAS Commission). The Convention entered into force in 1978. *See also* INTER-AMERICAN COMMISSION ON HUMAN RIGHTS, 89; INTER-AMERICAN COURT OF HUMAN RIGHTS, 90; INTERNATIONAL COVENANT ON CIVIL AND POLITICAL RIGHTS (1969), 91; INTERNATIONAL COVENANT ON ECONOMIC, SOCIAL, AND CULTURAL RIGHTS (1966), 92; UNIVERSAL DECLARATION OF HUMAN RIGHTS (1948), 102.

Significance Despite the inclusion of most of the states in the Western Hemisphere (those not yet signatories include Brazil and the United States), the record on human rights remains poor in the region as a whole. The Inter-American Commission on Human Rights has issued a number of reports to the OAS on alleged human rights violations by member states, but little of substance has emerged from such investigations. One major success was the Commission's participation in resolving the diplomatic hostage crisis in Colombia in 1980. One difference between the American Convention and its European counterpart is the provision in the former enabling federal states to assume slightly different arrangements of obligations than those of unitary systems.

Crimes against Peace   (82)

The planning, preparation, initiation, or waging of a war of aggression; or a war in violation of international treaties, agreements, or assurances; or participating in a common plan or conspiracy for the accomplishment of any of these acts. Arguments on the existence of the crimes against peace point to the pertinent articles in the Covenant of the League of Nations, the Pact of Paris (Kellogg-Briand Pact), and of the Charter of the United Nations, which charges the United Nations Security Council to take such measures as necessary to restore and maintain international peace and security against any threat to or breach of international peace or any act of aggression. Crimes against peace were one of the three categories of crimes over which the Nuremberg and Tokyo International Military Tribunals sat in judgment after World War II. The Nuremberg Tribunal acted on the premise that the principles enunciated in its Charter were the expression of international law existing at the time of creation of the Tribunal. Those principles included the definition of crimes against peace offered above. In 1946, the United Nations General Assembly passed a resolution reaffirming the principles of international law recognized by the Charter of the Nuremberg Tribunal and the Judgment of Tribunal. *See also* AGGRESSION, 303; FORCE, ILLEGAL THREAT OR USE OF, 308; WAR, 320.

Significance   Crimes against peace are perhaps the most debated of the three categories of crimes enunciated in the Charter of the International Military Tribunal. The other two were crimes against humanity and war crimes. Before the Nuremberg Charter, the Covenant of the League of Nations and the Kellogg-Briand Pact did ban war other than in self-defense but did not specifically brand it as such. The Charter of the United Nations prohibits the use of force and makes it unlawful to resort to force, but does not explicitly label doing so a crime; yet, the principles of the Charter of the International Military Tribunal have been repeatedly reaffirmed by the United Nations General Assembly. Several major questions are central to the debate about crimes against peace. The first is whether or not the aggressive acts of the defeated powers in World War II could be considered a violation of customary or treaty law at the time of their commission. While one school argues that the treaties previously cited constituted a prohibition against aggression, another refutes existence of either custom or treaty prohibiting it, and furthermore, leading to the second major question, no definition of aggression had ever been agreed upon. While the first question may never be conclusively settled, the latter was finally addressed by the United National General Assembly in Resolution 3314 (XXIX) of 14 December 1974. Aggression is defined as "the use of armed force by a state against the sovereignty, territorial integrity or political independence of another state, or in a manner inconsistent with the Charter of the United Nations." Specific acts that would constitute acts of aggression are then detailed. The definition is not exhaustive and cannot be so; consequently, the ultimate source for the determination of an act of aggression is the United Nations Security Council under Article 39 of the United Nations Charter. However, with the existence of the veto power in the Council it is unlikely that a decision would be made under most circumstances. Therefore, the practical application of the concept of crimes against peace is not likely.

European Convention for the Protection of Human   (83)
Rights and Fundamental Freedoms (1950)

A treaty listing the rights and freedoms that the western European signatory states guarantee to their citizens. The rights and freedoms contained in the Convention include those of life and liberty; the prohibition of slavery and servitude; freedom from arbitrary arrest, imprisonment or exile; right to fair trial; and freedom of thought and speech, association (including unions), and religion. They do not include social security, full employment, or adequate standards of living—matters covered by a separate agreement, the European Social Charter (1960). The Convention provides for a European Commission of Human Rights to receive and investigate complaints pertaining to human rights disputes filed by signatory states or by individuals in individual petitions. (It also established a European Court of Human Rights.) The Commission's membership equals the number of signatories to the Convention. Its members are chosen for six-year terms by the Committee of Ministers of the Council of Europe on the basis of recommendations by the national delegations to the Consultative Assembly of the Council of Europe. The Convention is unusual in that many of the signatories allow private associations and individuals as well as states to file complaints. The Commission's jurisdiction to respond to individual petitions is optional; namely, a state must have ratified not only the Convention but also have declared the right of the Commission to hear cases brought against it by individuals. If the complaint is found admissible then the Commission will investigate the matter, but only after all local remedies available within the state in question have been exhausted. Should the Commission not succeed in facilitating a friendly settlement, its report and recommendations are sent to the Committee of Ministers of the Council of Europe for final disposition. The signatory states have the option of accepting the compulsory jurisdiction of the European Court of Human Rights in all matters concerning the interpretation and applications of the Convention. The European Convention on Human Rights was adopted by the foreign ministers of fifteen European states (the members of the Council of Europe) in 1950 and entered into force in 1953. Currently, twenty-one states are parties to the Convention. The Convention is supplemented by a number of protocols. *See also* EUROPEAN COURT OF HUMAN RIGHTS, 84.

Significance   The European Convention for the Protection of Human Rights and Fundamental Freedoms is the most ambitious operational experiment dealing with human rights. It has met with some, albeit limited, success in large part because of the similarity in political and legal traditions of its signatories. While only a relatively small number of complaints have been found to be admissible before the Commission and the Court, the threat of an adverse decision by the Committee of Ministers or the Court has in several instances stimulated the state in question to alter its policies rather than suffer the publicity of a hearing or review. A major weakness in both the Convention and its protocols is the lack of enforcement power by the Commission or the Court. These agencies must rely upon adverse publicity in instances of state noncompliance or, in an extreme case, expulsion from the Council of Europe. At present, the major importance of the Convention is the fact that it provides individuals access to and standing before international agencies.

European Court of Human Rights   (84)

The judicial organ of the European Convention on Human Rights empowered to hear cases pertaining to human rights complaints submitted by either signatory states or the European Commission of Human Rights. Created by a protocol to the European Convention on Human Rights, the Court consists of judges elected for nine-year terms by the Assembly of the Council of Europe from a list submitted by the Council. Its jurisdiction is optional; namely, a state signatory to the

European Convention does not automatically accept the Court's jurisdiction, but it must make a declaration to that effect by subscribing to a
protocol to the Convention. The Court is empowered not only to
determine violations of the Convention but also to award damages. Its
decisions are binding upon the parties.

Significance   The European Court of Human Rights is empowered
to hear cases only after the European Commission of Human Rights
has dealt with it and been unable to effect a friendly settlement. Cases
may be submitted by the Commission or any interested state party.
Ironically, while individuals and private groups may appear before the
Commission, making it a very unusual body, they are not technically
parties before the Court (although they have a right to be represented).
Since its creation, the European Court of Human Rights has established a commendable record of compliance in the cases for which it
has rendered decisions. The complex nature of human rights and the
difficulty of resolution is amply reflected in the *Belgian Linguistic* case
heard before the Court in 1968. This is the only case thus far in which
the judgment of the Court has been challenged in compliance.

Genocide   (85)

An act which has as its intent the destruction of a national, ethnic,
racial, or religious group, either in whole or in part. The term was
coined by Raphael Lemkin in 1944 as a result of the mass murders by
Nazi Germany of persons of Jewish origin and other ethnic groups in
both Germany and conquered territories before and during World
War II. Under the Genocide Convention, genocidal acts include those
that involve (1) killing, maiming, physical, or mental harm; (2) creation of deleterious living conditions; (3) imposing birth control; or
(4) forcibly removing the children from their families. *See also*
GENOCIDE, CONVENTION ON THE PREVENTION AND PUNISHMENT OF THE
CRIME OF (1948), 86.

Significance   Unfortunately, genocide occupies a prominent place in
the history of mankind, but historically has been viewed as a matter of
domestic concern and not subject to interference by other states. The
magnitude of the genocidal policies of Nazi Germany changed this
attitude, and noninterference was replaced by a universal belief that
such actions were crimes against international law. This change in
attitude led to the adoption of the Genocide Convention by the United
Nations in 1948, which confirmed that genocide was a crime under
international law. The Israeli Court in the (Adolf) *Eichmann* case

(Jerusalem District Court of Israel, 1961) held that the crime of genocide was a crime against humanity and, therefore, the Court had the right to hear the case even though Eichmann was a resident of Argentina and the crimes had been committed on German territory. The case is highly controversial in its invocation of the Genocide Convention, as Article 6 indicates that an individual charged with such an act is to be tried by the courts in the territory where the act took place or before an international tribunal empowered to have such jurisdiction. A flaw in the Convention is the failure to include destruction of a political or social group in those acts defined as genocidal. Does this then suggest that the suppression or elimination of political opponents or of social classes is not a crime within the context of the Genocide Convention?

Genocide, Convention on the Prevention and Punishment of the Crime of (1948) (86)

An international treaty, confirming that genocide is a crime under international law. Genocide is defined as any act committed with the intention of destroying either in whole or in part a national, ethnic, racial, or religious group. (Political or social groups are excluded.) Offenses that constitute crimes of genocide include (1) killing members of a group; (2) causing serious bodily or mental harm; (3) imposing conditions of life calculated to bring destruction to a group; (4) prohibiting propagation; and (5) removing children from a group. A product of the Economic and Social Council of the United Nations, the Convention on Genocide was approved by the United Nations General Assembly in 1948 and, having been signed by the required minimum of twenty states, came into force in 1951. More than ninety countries are parties to the Convention today, including the United States with its ratification of the Convention in 1986. *See also* GENOCIDE, 85; INTERNATIONAL CRIMINAL LAW, 93; WAR CRIMES, 367.

Significance   The Genocide Convention is a response to the brutality of the period just prior to and during World War II and a specific response to the extermination practices of the German Reich. It includes as punishable conspiracy, incitement, directing and planning, attempts, and complicity to commit genocide, as well as acts of genocide themselves. Nor is the plea of obedience to superior orders (*respondeat superior,* "let the superior be responsible") acceptable, since heads of state, public officials, and private individuals are equally punishable. Genocide is not considered a political crime for purposes of extradition, and signatories agree to honor extradition requests. Furthermore, genocide is considered a crime regardless of its taking place in time of peace or of war and regardless of whether or not the victims are nationals of the delinquent state. The Convention is particularly important for the extent to which individuals are held accountable for their acts, rather than being protected in the guise of state responsibility. The Convention is an example of the growing area of international criminal law which directly affects individuals rather than just states, but the Convention is weakened by the lack of international enforcement machinery, failure to create an international criminal court to hear such cases, and by the number of reservations states have attached to their acceptance of the Convention.

Human Rights (87)

The rights considered as fundamental or natural to any individual, as defined by civilized nations. Such rights are felt to be inalienable and essential if a state is to be counted among those that are included in the category of so-called civilized states. Human rights were historically concerned mostly with civil and political rights but have expanded in the contemporary period to include economic, social, and cultural rights. Traditional constitutional guarantees by states of rights of citizens are being supplemented in the modern period by international efforts through the United Nations and various regional organizations. The term encourages some confusion, as it connotes that individuals have rights under international law, whereas the more precise interpretation is that there are norms of international law created by treaties for the benefit of individuals. The "rights" are those that states signatory to such treaties commit themselves to provide through municipal statutes. *See also* AMERICAN CONVENTION ON HUMAN RIGHTS (1969), 81; EUROPEAN CONVENTION FOR THE PROTECTION OF HUMAN RIGHTS AND FUNDAMENTAL FREEDOMS (1950), 83; INTERNATIONAL COVENANT ON CIVIL AND POLITICAL RIGHTS (1966), 91; INTERNATIONAL COVENANT ON ECONOMIC, SOCIAL, AND CULTURAL RIGHTS (1966), 92; MINORITY CLAUSES, 95; UNIVERSAL DECLARATION OF HUMAN RIGHTS (1948), 102.

Significance   Human rights has been an area of major concern of both regional and international organizations since the end of World War II, but interest in this area is of long standing. National efforts include the United States Bill of Rights, the French Declaration of the Rights of Man, and the English Magna Carta and Bill of Rights. There were treaties in the nineteenth century that outlawed the slave trade and white slave traffic. The early twentieth century saw treaties prohibiting the employment of women at night, protecting minorities, and dealing with hazardous working conditions. The World War I peace treaties contained minority rights clauses, and the Covenant of the

League of Nations contained many references to various aspects of human rights, as does the Charter of the United Nations. In 1948 the United Nations General Assembly adopted a Universal Declaration of Human Rights.

Despite the energies expended in this area, the concrete results have been more modest than might be expected. There have been conventions adopted by international organizations that deal with protection of the rights of women; outlawing genocide and slavery; torture; reduction of statelessness; elimination of discrimination in education; and more than 100 conventions dealing with the protection of workers, to name but some of the major examples. While there are those writers who contend that the sum total of codification efforts in this area represents international legal obligations amounting to a new area of international law, it is as yet difficult to support such a conclusion. Most declarations and treaties that posit the ideals of a decent life and opportunity for peoples of all nations remain in the realm of the abstract, as there is no enforcement machinery attached to such conventions except for some modest steps in western Europe. The United Nations established a Commission on Human Rights and has been experimenting with such new investigatory machinery as the Special Committee on the Policies of Apartheid of the Government of the Republic of South Africa, established in 1962, and the Ad Hoc Working Group of Experts of the Human Rights Commission established in 1967; but they lack real power and must rely upon the publicity of findings. Stimulating the controversy in this area are the philosophical differences between those states (mostly Western) that hold to the more traditional interpretation of human rights (that is, civil and political rights) versus socialist-oriented and emerging states which view the issue in terms more focused upon economic and social rights. Despite the disappointing results of such efforts, it can be said that serious attention to the status of individuals as a component of international law is supplanting the state as only subject of that legal regime.

Individuals (As Subjects of International Law)   (88)

A subject of law is one to whom the law provides rights and assigns duties. The traditional requirements to be met for an entity to be considered a subject of international law are (1) the ability to have such rights and duties under the international legal regime; (2) have the capacity to enter into agreements with other subjects; and (3) have standing before international courts and tribunals. States are clearly subjects of international law since they fulfill all of these conditions, whereas the status of individuals is less clear. It is clear that individuals are objects of international law, in that they are bound to obey those norms, but whether or not they can be subjects of those norms remains controversial. On the one extreme is the proposition that individuals are invisible and have no rights or standing before any tribunals other than national ones; on the other is the argument that they are as logically subjects of the law as are states, since international law norms create obligations that are enforceable by national courts. Between these two extremes is the acknowledgment that individuals do have standing before their national courts in matters dealing with international legal norms and are gaining access to regional and international machinery as well. There is no doubt that individuals are subjects of international law insofar as certain duties are concerned, such as not to commit piracy, not to commit crimes against peace, not to commit crimes against humanity, and war crimes. *See also* HUMAN RIGHTS, 87; INTERNATIONAL CRIMINAL LAW, 93; WAR CRIMES, 367.

Significance   The issue of individuals as subjects of international law has had an erratic record. In the early period of the evolution of the modern state system, international law had its roots in natural law which did not make a great distinction between municipal and international law; consequently, there was not much concern about distinguishing between individuals and states. By the nineteenth century, positivism had become the foundation of international legal thinking, and states were held to be the only subjects of international law. The general rule at the current stage in the evolution of international law is that individuals have some degree of international personality, but what this implies is controversial. The position of Soviet publicists is that individuals have duties under international law, i.e., that they can be guilty of crimes such as war crimes, but have no rights under international law. To conclude that individuals are on the same level as states as subjects of international law is as yet a distinctly minority view. Yet there is much evidence to suggest that the trend is following a more liberal direction. As early as the post–World War I period, mixed arbitral tribunals provided for by the Treaty of Versailles (and the Central American Court of Justice) both gave individuals access to international legal machinery. In the German-Polish Convention on Upper Silesia (1922), individuals from ethnic minorities were allowed to petition an international organ concerning acts of their state that infringed upon their political or civil rights. Today the European Coal and Steel Community gives individuals and private corporations access to the European Court of Justice; the European Human Rights Convention grants individuals and private groups access to settlement machinery in the form of the European Commission of Human Rights;

and the Optional Protocol to the International Covenant on Civil and Political Rights provides similar access at the international level through access to United Nations machinery.

Inter-American Commission on Human Rights   (89)

An organ of the Organization of American States (OAS) established in 1960, whose function is to promote the human rights enunciated in the American Declaration of the Rights and Duties of Man (1948). The Commission makes recommendations on human rights issues to members of the OAS, performs studies it deems pertinent to its mission, investigates allegations of human rights violations, encourages members to provide it with information on their human rights activities, and is the advisory organ to the OAS on human rights issues. *See also* AMERICAN CONVENTION ON HUMAN RIGHTS (1969), 81; INTER-AMERICAN COURT OF HUMAN RIGHTS, 90.

Significance   The Inter-American Commission on Human Rights is a very cautious move in the human rights area in comparison to its more ambitious European counterpart. Prior to the amending of the Charter in 1970, the Commission was an autonomous entity of the OAS. While elevating the Commission to the level of an OAS organ enhanced its constitutional status, the Commission cannot directly hear individual claims, although it can receive and examine individual complaints. It has no power to force OAS members to respond to its requests or enforce decisions. The Commission's major leverage is that of adverse publicity resulting from its investigations and reports, and even this has been only minimally effective.

Inter-American Court of Human Rights   (90)

A regional court established by the American Convention on Human Rights of the Organization of American States (OAS) and headquartered in San José, Costa Rica, which has both contentious and advisory jurisdiction in the human rights area. The Court and its relationship to the Inter-American Commission on Human Rights is somewhat analogous to the European Court of Human Rights and the European Commission on Human Rights. As is the case with the latter Court, individuals have no standing before the Inter-American Court. Cases are brought before the Court by signatory states or the Inter-American Commission on Human Rights, with the consent of the parties involved. The Court's advisory jurisdiction provides for opinions interpreting the Convention as well as other treaties relating to hemispheric human rights. *See also* AMERICAN CONVENTION ON HUMAN RIGHTS (1969), 81; INTER-AMERICAN COMMISSION ON HUMAN RIGHTS, 89.

Significance   The Inter-American Court of Human Rights is of too recent origin to make an assessment of its performance. The Convention of 1969 creating it came into force in 1978, and the Court has heard only one case which dealt with procedural issues (*Viviana Gallardo et al.*, 1981). The record of the Inter-American Commission on Human Rights has not been such as to give cause for much optimism, however, suggesting that Latin American states are very reluctant to open the treatment of their nationals to outside scrutiny.

International Covenant on Civil and Political Rights   (91) (1966)

One of the two major international agreements transforming the rights listed in the Universal Declaration of Human Rights into legally binding rules. The Covenant contains a list of political and civil rights common to all peoples, which governments pledge to protect or to promote. These rights include life and security; freedom of movement, association, and assembly; freedom of thought, speech, and religion; and prohibition of slavery and torture. Initially drafted by the United Nations Commission on Human Rights and reported to the United Nations General Assembly in 1954, it was not adopted by the General Assembly until 1966. The Covenant came into force in 1976 upon ratification by thirty-five states. The United States has not ratified the Covenant because of concerns related to the constitutional distribution of federal-state powers. *See also* HUMAN RIGHTS, 87; INTERNATIONAL COVENANT ON ECONOMIC, SOCIAL, AND CULTURAL RIGHTS (1966), 92; UNIVERSAL DECLARATION OF HUMAN RIGHTS (1948), 102.

Significance   The Covenant on Civil and Political Rights is a major step in the advancement of universal human rights, as it transforms the civil and political rights listed in the Universal Declaration of Human Rights into legal obligations binding upon signatory states. These rights are guaranteed without regard to sex, race, religion, ethnic origin, or minority status. The Covenant further creates a Human Rights Committee of eighteen members to review reports of violations. While the Covenant is a legal instrument binding upon ratifying states, it is not self-executing, for those states that do not already guarantee such rights are charged with adopting appropriate measures in accordance with their constitutional processes. The lack of enforcement machinery or sanctions other than world public opinion, as well as the non-self-executing nature of the Covenant, limits its immediate impact. Furthermore, in time of public emergency a signatory state can unilaterally absolve itself of obligations contained in the Covenant.

International Covenant on Economic, Social, and   (92)
Cultural Rights (1966)

One of the two major international agreements transforming the rights listed in the Universal Declaration of Human Rights into legally binding rules. The Covenant lists the economic, social, and cultural rights aspired to by all peoples and charges governments to protect or promote such rights. The initial work was done by the United Nations Commission on Human Rights and reported to the United Nations General Assembly in 1954. It was not until 1966, however, that the Covenant was adopted by the General Assembly. It came into force in 1976 upon ratification by thirty-five states. The United States has not ratified the Covenant because of concerns related to the constitutional distribution of federal-state powers. *See also* HUMAN RIGHTS, 87; INTERNATIONAL COVENANT ON CIVIL AND POLITICAL RIGHTS (1966), 91; UNIVERSAL DECLARATION OF HUMAN RIGHTS (1948), 102.

Significance   The Covenant on Economic, Social, and Cultural Rights is a major step in transforming the ideals expressed in the Universal Declaration of Human Rights into obligations binding upon signatory states. Rights enumerated in the Covenant include *inter alia* those of decent working conditions and jobs; the ability to form and join unions; and rights to social security, education, health, and a decent standard of living. Unlike its sister Covenant on Civil and Political Rights, which has a Commission to review alleged violations, the Covenant on Economic, Social, and Cultural Rights depends upon the reporting process to the United Nations Economic and Social Council to enforce its norms. As in the case of its sister Covenant, the absence of effective enforcement machinery or sanctions other than world public opinion limits its impact. It also is a non-self-executing treaty, which requires those states that do not already have the Covenant's rights defined in municipal legislation to make efforts to do so. While there is only one Universal Declaration of Human Rights, there are two Covenants—one on civil and political rights and a second on economic, social, and cultural rights. This reflects the difference between a document expressing aspirations and one which binds signatories. Since there exist a number of states that ideologically oppose private ownership of property and means of production, it was necessary to separate civil and political rights from economic rights.

International Criminal Law   (93)

The area of international law dealing with piracy, war crimes, crimes against peace and against humanity (genocide), and such other specified crimes as counterfeiting, illicit traffic in dangerous drugs, and engaging in the slave trade. International criminal law is as yet a relatively uncharted area of international law, as there is no comprehensive code dealing with the field. Engaging in such acts can be directly attributed to individuals rather than their state. There is no consensus on whether apartheid is an international crime. It was proclaimed as such in the International Convention on the Suppression and Punishment of the Crime of Apartheid (1973), in force in 1976, but only Third World and communist states were parties to it in 1984. *See also* GENOCIDE CONVENTION (1948), 86; WAR CRIMES, 367; WAR CRIMES TRIALS, 103.

Significance   While international law governs relations among states and applies to states as subjects of that law, international criminal law suggests that there are specific legal prohibitions applying directly to individuals and for violation of which they are held directly responsible. This means that, in a limited sense, individuals are subjects of international law, as the individual cannot be protected behind the cloak of state responsibility for his or her actions in areas such as those listed. Attempts to formalize an international criminal code and create an international criminal court to handle such cases have not been successful. As early as the 1920s, the International Law Association (ILA) proposed the establishment of a separate chamber of the Permanent Court of International Justice to handle solely criminal cases, and the Interparliamentary Union drafted an international criminal code in the same decade. Following the creation of the United Nations, the subject of international criminal law has been periodically addressed, with such results as the Genocide Convention and the Draft Code of Offenses against the Peace and Security of Mankind. The International Law Commission has also recommended the creation of an international criminal court. Since such a court would by necessity be empowered to deal directly with individuals rather than through the intermediary of states, in the eyes of most states it represents too radical a departure from traditional legal concepts at this stage in the evolution of international law.

International Organizations (As Subjects of   (94)
International Law)

Associations of states, established by treaties between two or more states, whose functions transcend national boundaries and which are for certain purposes subjects of international law. The appearance of public international organizations from the early part of the nineteenth century raises the critical question of their standing in the international legal order. Public international organizations are generally considered to be subjects of international law (as are states) even though their legal personality is not comparable to that of states establishing them and their international legal personality is limited to possessing specific rights and duties. Their standing is determined by conventions among states and, therefore, some argue that the recognition of the international personality of an international organization is limited to signatory states of the convention creating such an organization.

Significance   Public international organizations (as distinguished from private or nongovernmental organizations) include global, all-purpose organizations; specialized agencies of the United Nations; other global functional organizations; and regional organizations. Such organizations of one type or another have existed since the early part of the nineteenth century, but it has been only in the more recent period that their international legal personality has become an issue. Generally, the treaty establishing an international organization will indicate the nature of its purpose and its powers. Its international personality is, therefore, relative—limited to the rights, duties and powers outlined in the treaty creating it (subject perhaps to the argument that the organization may have implied powers as well in order to carry out its expressed purpose and duties). The international legal personality of the United Nations and its specialized agencies, for example, is derived from the United Nations Charter, the Convention on the Privileges and Immunities of the United Nations (1946), the Conventions on the Privileges and Immunities of the Specialized Agencies (1947), and the Headquarters Agreement between the United Nations and the United States (1947). The legal capacity of the United Nations was a question in the advisory opinion in the *Reparation for Injuries Suffered in the Service of the United Nations* case (International Court of Justice, 1949). The Court held that the United Nations was an international person, although not a state, and therefore not having the same rights and duties as a state. The United Nations can enter into agreements (treaties) with member states and with other international organizations, enter into contracts, and borrow money. Such capacity to contract is a prerequisite of international legal personality. Historically, the position of Soviet writers has been more restrained, and they were reluctant to acknowledge the international personality of international organizations until the 1950s, holding instead to the traditional view that only states could possess international personality.

Minority Clauses   (95)

Clauses in treaties between states that provide for the protection of national minorities. Post–World War I treaties between the Allied and Associated Powers and certain East European and Balkan states, e.g., Hungary, Bulgaria, and Turkey, provided for the protection of racial, religious, or linguistic minorities in those states. Such minorities were to be equal before the law, and their life, language, and religious beliefs protected. The Greco-Bulgarian Convention of 1919 allowed for the free migration of minorities between the signatories. The League of Nations was to supervise these obligations, and any violation was subject to action by the League. A similar situation occurred at the end of World War II with minority clauses in Allied treaties with Finland, Italy, Bulgaria, Hungary, Romania and, some years later, Austria.

Significance   Although not very successful, minority clauses were early attempts in this century to provide for the protection of human rights. The post–World War I efforts fell victim to the decline of the League of Nations and the rise of dictatorships in the interwar period. Numerous complaints of minority rights violations found their way before the Permanent Court of International Justice, e.g., the Advisory Opinion relating to *German Settlers in Poland;* the Advisory Opinion on the *Treatment of Polish Nationals in Danzig;* and the Advisory Opinion on *Minority Schools in Albania.* One of the justifications for Nazi expansion in the 1930s was alleged ill-treatment of German minorities in central European states. Nor were complaints of violations by Bulgaria, Romania, and Hungary in the early post–World War II period any more successfully handled by the United Nations. It should be noted that stipulations in treaties dealing with minorities are not the same as treatment of resident aliens, since the latter are not classified as national minorities.

Nongovernmental Organization (NGO)   (96)

A private, international organization that serves as a mechanism for cooperation among private national groups in international affairs, particularly in economic, social, cultural, humanitarian, and technical fields. Under the United Nations Charter (Article 71), the Economic and Social Council is empowered to make suitable arrangements for consultation with NGOs on matters within its competence. NGOs are also known as transnational associations. NGOs are not subjects of international law, except for limited purposes under international humanitarian law, e.g., the International Committee of the Red Cross, from the viewpoint of international law the most important of the nongovernmental organizations.

Significance   Nongovernmental organizations have been active in international affairs for many years, some dating back over a century. Over two thousand are active in today's world, and more than three hundred have entered into arrangements as consultants for the Economic and Social Council (ECOSOC). Examples of NGOs include the International Committee of the Red Cross (ICRC); consumer and producer associations; religious groups; teacher organizations; professional, legal, and medical societies; and trade unions.

Offenses against the Peace and Security of Mankind,   (97) Draft Code of (1954)

A product of the International Law Commission that embodies the principles of international law espoused at the war crimes trials at Nuremberg and Tokyo after World War II. The Draft Code was not acted upon because it did not adequately deal with the question of what constituted aggression. After aggression had been defined by the United Nations General Assembly in 1974, attention was once again focused upon the Draft Code. To date, no final action upon the Code has transpired. *See also* AGGRESSION, 303.

Significance   The Draft Code of Offenses against the Peace and Security of Mankind is an undertaking initially propelled by the victorious allies of World War II to validate their claims of the existence of international legal norms against crimes against peace and against humanity (genocide), which formed the basis of judgments of the postwar military tribunals. It contains the basic principles and norms enunciated by the tribunals, such as individuals being held accountable for their actions and the rejection of the defense plea of complying with superior orders. It also lists numerous acts falling within the definition of crimes against peace and genocide. The Draft Code suffers from the absence of clear penalties for violations, and its recommendation of the creation of an International Criminal Court has not generated widespread support among United Nations member states. The obvious fact that the Code would sanction the injection of the United Nations into the domestic affairs of states does not augur well for its success in the near term.

Optional Protocol to the International Covenant on   (98) Civil and Political Rights (1966)

A treaty attached to the Covenant on Civil and Political Rights giving individuals access to international machinery by providing them with the right of petition before a special eighteen-member Human Rights

Committee in matters pertaining to violation of human rights under the Covenant. The Optional Protocol came into force in 1976.

Significance   The opportunity for individuals or groups to petition an international authority is a relatively new development in international law. Only the now defunct Central American Court of Justice, several post–World War I arrangements, and the European Convention for the Protection of Human Rights and Fundamental Freedoms have allowed individuals or private groups standing before international machinery prior to the Optional Protocol. The Protocol is also unusual in that it allows the individuals to protest actions of their own government before such machinery. As yet, only a minority of the world's states have become signatories to the Optional Protocol that otherwise contains a renunciation clause allowing signatories to withdraw from the agreement.

Racial Discrimination, International Convention on   (99)
the Elimination of All Forms of (1965)

A Convention prepared by the Commission on Human Rights of the United Nations Economic and Social Council that lists prohibited discriminatory practices based upon race; specifically, any preferential or discriminatory act based on race, color, ancestry, nationality, or ethnic origin. The Convention guarantees that no racial discrimination will take place in the general areas of rights subsequently enumerated in 1966 in both the Covenant on Civil and Political Rights and the Covenant on Economic, Social, and Cultural Rights. It further condemns racial segregation, apartheid policies, and groups espousing theories of racial superiority. A Committee on the Elimination of Racial Discrimination was created by the Convention, consisting of eighteen experts of high moral standing and acknowledged impartiality elected by signatory states and empowered to handle complaints and disputes by states. The Convention was adopted by the United Nations General Assembly in 1965 and entered into force in 1966. At present, over one hundred states are signatories, although not the United States. *See also* OPTIONAL PROTOCOL TO THE INTERNATIONAL COVENANT ON CIVIL AND POLITICAL RIGHTS (1966), 98.

Significance   The International Convention on the Elimination of Racial Discrimination is illustrative of the postwar efforts by the United Nations to implement the humanitarian goals expressed in the Universal Declaration of Human Rights, taking its place alongside other agreements to protect civil, political, economic, social, and cultural rights and the status of women, children, and stateless persons. It should be noted that the Convention does not apply to discrimination against noncitizens of signatory states. An Optional Protocol to the Convention provides the opportunity for individuals to petition a special Racial Discrimination Committee on matters violating the Convention, although there are as yet few signatories to this optional protocol.

Transnational Corporation   (100)

An enterprise, comprising entities in two or more countries, which operates under a system of decision making, permitting a common policy in which these entities are so linked by ownership or otherwise, that they are able to exercise significant influence over the activities of others and share knowledge, resources, and responsibilities. Transnational corporations are difficult to define, as their external activities may be limited to investments in enterprises abroad or, at the other extreme, consist of managerial, financial, labor, and physical plant links among various countries that are interchangeable or autonomous. They may consist of a central headquarters with foreign branches (or subsidiaries) or of large units each incorporated under their state's laws and loosely tied together through some contractual arrangement.

Significance   Transnational corporations have been a feature of the international system for some time, but it has only been within the past several decades that they have become the center of major attention of the international community. It is a controversial matter whether and to what extent transnational corporations (or any business enterprise for that matter) can be a subject of international law. A state may conclude a contract with a private corporation and agree that it be governed by international law or general principles of law. To that extent, a transnational corporation may acquire rights and be otherwise bound by international law. It is estimated that between two-thirds and three-fourths of the industrial output of the nonsocialist world is in the hands of from three hundred to four hundred such entities. They are difficult to regulate because of their pervasiveness in the international market and their domestic influence and difficult to monitor when their activities extend to various countries, making it difficult to determine nationality, source of income, and proper state of taxation. In the case of many developing states, the assets of such companies operating in those states exceed the budgets of the governments themselves. Efforts were begun at the United Nations Conference on Trade and Development (UNCTAD) in 1968 to deal with the issue of transnationals with the creation of a United Nations Commission on Transnational Corporations. A primary activity of the Commission has been the drafting of a Transnational Code of Conduct for corporations, which would deal with (1) corporate influence in other countries; (2) corporate responsibility for observing the sovereignty and laws of the nation in which they are active; and (3) abstaining from intervening in the domestic affairs of the host country and from bribery and influence peddling of its public officials.

United Nations Commission on Human Rights   (101)

A subsidiary organ of the Economic and Social Council established in 1946 pursuant to Article 68 of the United Nations Charter and charged with the responsibility of developing proposals to implement the human rights ideals advanced in Articles 55 and 56 of the Charter. The first major product of the Commission was the Universal Declaration on Human Rights (1948) followed by years of work on two covenants to operationalize and transform into law the ideals embodied in the Declaration—the Covenant on Civil and Political Rights (1966) and the Covenant on Economic, Social, and Cultural Rights (1966).

Significance   At its inception, many member states of the United Nations assumed that the Commission on Human Rights would be the sounding board for human rights violations. Such did not prove to be the case, as the Commission invariably forwarded such complaints to other United Nations organs. Since the early 1970s, however, the Commission has cautiously expanded its activity to include the examination of violations and making recommendations. However, the absence of sanction or enforcement powers limits the effectiveness of the Commission in this area.

Universal Declaration of Human Rights (1948)   (102)

A United Nations General Assembly resolution intended to establish a "common standard of achievement for all peoples and all nations" in the observance of civil, political, economic, social, and cultural rights. Prepared by the Commission on Human Rights and the Economic and Social Council (ECOSOC), the Declaration was adopted by the United Nations General Assembly in 1948. In its thirty articles, the Universal Declaration of Human Rights proclaims two broad categories of rights and freedoms that people should share equally—political and civil rights and economic, social, and cultural rights. Rights universally shared include *inter alia* life, liberty, and security; freedom from slavery; freedom from arbitrary arrest and imprisonment, torture, or inhuman punishment; freedom of movement and domicile, association, religion, thought and expression, and marriage; the right to work and organize; and rights to education, a decent standard of living, and participation in the state's political process. As a resolution of the General Assembly, the Declaration is not a legally binding agreement, but rather was designed to serve as a model for more specific future codification efforts. Indeed, in 1954 the General Assembly began work on two draft covenants—one containing civil and political, the other economic, social, and cultural rights—to implement the concepts contained in the Declaration. These were adopted by the United Nations General Assembly in 1966, and both came into force in 1976. *See also* HUMAN RIGHTS, 87; INTERNATIONAL COVENANT ON CIVIL AND POLITICAL RIGHTS (1966), 91; INTERNATIONAL COVENANT ON ECONOMIC, SOCIAL, AND CULTURAL RIGHTS (1966), 92; OPTIONAL PROTOCOL TO THE INTERNATIONAL COVENANT ON CIVIL AND POLITICAL RIGHTS (1966), 98.

Significance   Although most of the rights set forth in the Universal Declaration have not yet been adopted as universal international law through treaties, the document has not been without impact. Its aspirations are reflected in the constitutions of many newly independent states, it has been noted in national court decisions, and it is often cited in resolutions and reports of various organs of the United Nations. In several cases before the International Court of Justice (ICJ), the Declaration has served as a basis for condemning discriminatory practices of Southern Rhodesia and South Africa. The absence of any mention in the Declaration of enforcement machinery or a judicial body suggests that the primary purpose of the Declaration is that of goal setting (rather than implementation or regulation) by clarifying and expanding the very basic human rights outlined in the United Nations Charter. A resolution passed by the 1968 United Nations Conference on Human Rights proclaiming the Universal Declaration of Human Rights to be binding upon its members must be viewed with considerable circumspection, although suggestions that some of its provisions are general principles of law or humanity rest upon a more solid foundation.

War Crimes Trials   (103)

Trials of individuals to determine their individual guilt and punishment for crimes against peace, crimes against humanity, or war crimes. After World War I the Treaty of Versailles set a precedent by providing for the trial and punishment of the German Emperor Wilhelm II and members of the armed forces of Germany (Article 227), although the Allies never carried out the trials. The London Agreement of 1945 created an International Military Tribunal, representing Britain, France, the Soviet Union, and the United States. German war criminals were tried at Nuremberg by this Tribunal. Charged with crimes against peace, war crimes, and crimes against humanity, twelve defendants were sentenced to death, three acquitted, and the rest imprisoned. Similar proceedings took place in Tokyo where Japanese war criminals were tried before the International Military Tribunal for the Far East, consisting of the eleven states at war with Japan. All twenty-five defendants were found guilty, and seven of them were sentenced to death. *See also* CRIMES AGAINST PEACE, 82; INDIVIDUALS, 88; WAR CRIMES, 367.

Significance   The war crimes trials at the termination of World War II added a new dimension to efforts geared toward enforcing the laws of war. Historically, individuals were held liable for violations of the laws of war. As early as the American Revolution, with the trials of Nathan Hale and John André for espionage, states have established military tribunals to handle attempted assassinations, mistreatment of prisoners, and violations of laws of land and naval warfare. However, the paucity of codified laws of war and a reluctance by states to try their own nationals for actions against their enemies meant that few allegations of war crimes were ever brought to trial; those that were dealt with nationals before their own national tribunals. Lastly, there was the practice of granting general amnesty at the time of a peace settlement for violations which had occurred during the course of the war. At the end of World War I, twelve cases (out of some nine hundred Allied allegations of war crimes incidents) were heard before Germany's national supreme court, but most of the outcomes were disappointing to the Allies. Consequently, during the course of World War II, the Allies determined that those guilty of major war crimes would be tried by an international military tribunal rather than in the national courts of the defeated nations. Scholarly evaluation of the legality of the Nuremberg and Tokyo trials has been mixed, with general agreement that decisions based upon long-standing customary and treaty law regarding war crimes were well-founded, but that judgments based upon crimes against the peace and crimes against humanity were open to interpretation as *ex post facto* judgments. In the years following the conclusion of the war crimes trials, the United Nations attempted to formulate what constituted crimes against peace by drafting a Code of Offenses against the Peace and Security of Mankind, which would stipulate crimes against peace and spell out crimes constituting genocide, as well as more clearly define the meaning of aggression. While there is no rule in international law against *ex post facto* legislation, United Nations efforts in the areas just cited go far in clearing the confusion previously existing in the areas of crimes against peace and against humanity. However, as long as victorious powers rely upon quasi-international tribunals to judge guilt or innocence in war crimes charges against defeated states and their nationals rather than entrust jurisdiction to truly international tribunals, charges of revenge against the vanquished are difficult to refute.

Women, Status of (104)

The international legal status of women has much improved over their historic relegation to a secondary position in terms of their rights and equal place before the law. This has been achieved through both national laws and the efforts of international bodies. A major achievement has been the Convention on the Political Rights of Women, adopted by the United Nations General Assembly in 1952. The Convention guarantees equal voting rights to women and the right to seek and hold public office. In addition, the United Nations Economic and Social Council has established a Commission on the Status of Women, which works to improve their status in regard to educational opportunities, job opportunities and equal pay, and their position before the law. A major international instrument regarding the position of women is the 1979 Convention on the Elimination of All Forms of Discrimination against Women, in force in 1981.

Significance The status of women varies from state to state, as well as by issue, nationality, etc. In numerous countries, women have been subjected to humiliating treatment; denied access to political offices and the right to vote; and have risked losing nationality upon marriage, to mention but a few of many traditional discriminatory practices. In the area of nationality law, for example, the traditional practice was for the nationality of the woman to follow that of her husband, which resulted in the woman's loss of her original nationality if different from that of her husband at the time of marriage. Should she subsequently divorce, statelessness could ensue. The practice of the United States was clarified by the Cable Act (1922), which provides that a woman does not automatically lose her U.S. citizenship upon marriage to an alien nor does an alien woman automatically become a U.S. citizen upon marriage to a U.S. national. This modern view of the independence of a woman's nationality from that of a male is reflected in such agreements as the Montevideo Convention on the Nationality of Women (1933) and the Convention on the Nationality of Married Women (1957) which provide that marriage does not automatically affect a woman's nationality, but rather requires subsequent action on her own volition to alter her status. Since the establishment of the Commission on the Status of Women in 1946—a subsidiary organ of the United Nations Economic and Social Council—the United Nations has been actively involved in encouraging the expansion of women's rights in the educational, economic, political, and social fields by adopting resolutions, drafting conventions, and organizing conferences devoted to the status of women.

4. Jurisdiction and Jurisdictional Immunities

Agrément **(105)**
The formal notification by a state that the diplomatic agent selected to be sent to it by another state would be acceptable (*persona grata*) and can be accredited to it. The *agrément* is the response to a query by the sending state which precedes the formal nomination and public announcement of the diplomatic accreditation under consideration. The procedure followed by the two states is called *agréation*. *See also* PERSONA NON GRATA, 141.

Significance   *Agrément* is a necessary procedure to ensure that a diplomatic agent will be allowed to carry out normal diplomatic functions in the host state, particularly in the area of being the normal communications link between the sending and receiving states. A state can refuse *agrément* without giving reasons for refusal, and the appointing state has no legal grounds for protest or appeal. Its only recourse is to select a replacement and determine whether that person is *personal grata* by going through the *agrément* and accreditation process once again.

Asylum: Diplomatic **(106)**
The use of a state's diplomatic or consular residence or a state's warship as a place of refuge for fugitives from the authorities of the host state in which the residence is located. Diplomatic asylum is distinguished from territorial (or political) asylum, as the former is done on the basis of the fiction of the extraterritorial nature of the state's presence outside its territory. Diplomatic asylum is not recognized by general international law nor in the Vienna Convention on Diplomatic Relations, and it is not supported in practice by many states, including the United States, except in those instances where a person's life is threatened by mob

87

violence. It is, however, still practiced in Latin American states. *See also*
ASYLUM: POLITICAL (TERRITORIAL), 107; POLITICAL OFFENSE, 142.

Significance   Diplomatic asylum was historically viewed as an acceptable practice. It was often the case that individuals seeking escape from
the local authorities would find refuge in the section of the city in which
foreign missions were located. Such enclaves provided asylum known
as *franchise du quartier*. The modern view is that diplomatic and consular
premises are not to be used as places of asylum; however, asylum
occasionally is granted in regions where political unrest is prevalent.
The Inter-American Convention Fixing the Rules to Be Observed for
the Granting of Asylum (1928), for example, allows for political asylum
on the premises of diplomatic missions, but not for criminal actions.
Diplomatic asylum is, therefore, considered an acceptable practice in
Western Hemispheric regional international law for those states signatory to the Convention. Indeed, even among those states that do not
view diplomatic asylum as an acceptable practice, there are circumstances in which even they have condoned its use, such as an unusually
notorious incident or in a region where it is common practice. Reasons
such as these have led the United States to grant asylum in its embassies
on some fifty occasions, while continuing to object to the practice. One
of the most celebrated cases was diplomatic asylum granted to Hungarian Cardinal Mindszenty by the United States in its legation in
Budapest during the Hungarian uprising in 1956, where he remained
until 1971.

Asylum: Political (Territorial)   (107)
Sanctuary offered to fugitives accused of political offenses or who are
victims of persecution in other states. As long as the individual remains
in the territory of the state granting asylum, the police power of the
political fugitive's state is ineffectual unless summarily handed over to
that state (*refoulement*). Should that individual move on to another state,
however, the risk of being formally or informally extradited reappears,
as would be the case should the individual be expelled at some later
date from the state of asylum for wrong conduct occurring after the
granting of asylum. A right of territorial asylum is provided for in the
Universal Declaration of Human Rights (1948), the Geneva Convention on the Status of Refugees (1951), and many state constitutions. *See
also* ASYLUM: DIPLOMATIC, 106; POLITICAL OFFENSE, 142.

Significance   Political asylum is founded upon other than purely
legal considerations. Defining a political offense, for example, is subjective and imprecise, particularly when an action is criminal but has

political motives behind it (particularly in an age of ideological conflict). Broadly speaking, a political crime is one that is politically motivated and has a political purpose. The intent or motive, rather than the nature of the act, becomes the guide for determining the outcome. In many cases there will have been no crime committed at all, simply an attempt to escape persecution in one's country. An attempt to clarify the matter was made by the United Nations General Assembly's Declaration on Territorial Asylum (1967), which offers guidelines for granting asylum but is not legally binding upon states nor very specific in its content, although it does exclude those suspected of war crimes, crimes against peace, or crimes against humanity. The Universal Declaration of Human Rights (1948) proclaims the right of an individual to seek and enjoy asylum from persecution, but any right of asylum is more accurately the right of the state to grant asylum to individuals rather than the state's duty to honor an individual's request for asylum. An Inter-American Convention on Political Asylum (1933) establishes political asylum as a right but is only operative among signatories and is, therefore, a regional norm at best.

Attentat Clause (108)

A clause in many extradition treaties, stipulating that attempts against the life of a head of state or members of his or her family are not classified as political offenses for purposes of extradition; they are criminal acts and extraditable offenses. *See also* ASYLUM: POLITICAL (TERRITORIAL), 107; EXTRADITION, 120; POLITICAL OFFENSE, 142.

Significance The term *Attentat* is derived from German, meaning attempt at someone's life. Historically, acts of violence against rulers were a classical symbol of political protest, particularly when Europe was undergoing the political and ideological transformations of the nineteenth century. The assassination attempt against Napoleon III of France, in which the perpetrators fled to Belgium and escaped extradition on the grounds of political asylum, initiated efforts to make such acts extraditable. The *Attentat* clause became a clause in bilateral extradition treaties until its regional utility was recognized in the Montevideo Convention on Extradition in 1933. Not all states support the concept, on the grounds that actions against a head of state are by their nature political and are, therefore, excluded from extradition.

Consul (109)

A state agent sent abroad to represent the political and economic interests of the state and to serve its citizens. Establishment of consular relations is normally based on bilateral treaties (consular, or treaties of commerce, friendship, or navigation). The law developed by such treaties was codified and developed by the 1963 Vienna Convention on Consular Relations. Consular duties include services related to (1) shipping, commerce, navigation, and trade; (2) citizens, passports, visas, and immigration; and (3) notary and other quasi-legal matters between the sending and receiving state. In more recent decades, the practice of some states is to accord consular officials roles more traditionally assigned to diplomatic agents, so that the distinction between the two is in some cases nebulous. Consular ranks in descending order of importance are consul general, consul, vice-consul, and consular agent. Should a state appoint a nonnational (normally a citizen of the host state) to look after its interests, that individual often carries the title of honorary consul. Consuls have a more limited range of privileges and immunities than do diplomatic envoys unless otherwise provided for by law or treaty or unless they are members of a diplomatic mission (normally its consular section). *See also* EXEQUATUR, 118; VIENNA CONVENTION ON CONSULAR RELATIONS (1963), 147.

Significance   Consular agents have been a feature of the international system since antiquity, as international trade, commerce, and shipping began to develop. Consular codes and maritime regulations, often based upon Greek and Roman practices, were developed in the Middle Ages, particularly as the Crusades moved Europe into the Levant. Protecting traders and smoothing commercial relations were major responsibilities of these consuls. Today, diplomatic and consular activities are closely coordinated by the state. No state is obligated to permit foreign consuls to operate within its jurisdiction. The extent of their authority and the nature of their duties is determined by their commission (or patent) and rank. Unlike diplomatic missions, which are located only in the capital of the host state, there may be several foreign consular offices located in the host state.

Consular Privileges and Immunities   (110)

The rights and exemptions from the host state's jurisdiction that, by customary law and treaty, are accorded to consular officials. Consular privileges and immunities are much less extensive than those accorded diplomatic officials, but do provide for the consular official's protection; the inviolability of the consular building, archives, and official correspondence; immunity in certain civil and criminal matters (if related to the consul's official duties); and exemption from local taxation. Consular privileges and immunities are detailed in the 1963

Vienna Convention on Consular Relations. *See also* CONSUL, 109; VI-
ENNA CONVENTION ON CONSULAR RELATIONS (1963), 147.

Significance   Consular privileges and immunities are less extensive
than those accorded diplomats, because a consular official works for
two states. Consular functions concern economic and trade relations
between the two states, as well as working with the nationals of both
states in matters pertaining to visas, tourism, and protection. Both
states must, therefore, have some control over the consular official's
actions. The official's private affairs or actions are not, for example,
exempt from the jurisdiction of the host state. More extensive immunities can be extended to consular officials through bilateral treaty
arrangements; such is the case, for example, with the U.S.-Soviet Consular Convention of 1964.

Convention on the Reduction of Statelessness (1961)   (111)

A United Nations effort to eliminate the condition of statelessness
(being without nationality) by asserting that every individual has a right
to a nationality. The Convention on the Reduction of Statelessness
enumerates those conditions (such as marriage, divorce, adoption,
naturalization, or expatriation) under which an individual will not lose
his or her nationality upon the risk of becoming stateless should a new
nationality not be provided. Conditions under which an individual
could lose his or her nationality include the swearing of allegiance to
another state, renunciation of nationality, serving in a public capacity in
another state, or acts of treason or other actions endangering the
security of the state. The Convention further prohibits states from
depriving their nationals of their identity as punishment or as a discriminatory instrument for political, racial, religious, or ethnic reasons.
Reported to the United Nations General Assembly by the International
Law Commission in 1954 and signed in 1961, the Convention came
into force in 1975. *See also* EXPATRIATION, 119; NANSEN PASSPORT, 134;
NATIONALITY OF INDIVIDUALS, 137; STATELESSNESS, 145.

Significance   Historically, the loss of nationality was a common occurrence and an accepted power of the state over its nationals. Should
an individual serve in the armed forces of another state, vote in its
elections, or occupy one of its public offices, he or she often lost
citizenship (as is still the case today). Marriage and divorce were equally
risky, since a woman often lost her nationality upon marriage—
acquiring that of her husband—only to lose the new nationality if there
was a subsequent divorce. Wars were often major causes of mass

statelessness, with conquest and transfer of territory producing changes in and loss of nationality. The Convention on the Reduction of Statelessness proclaims the status of statelessness to be an affront to the dignity of individuals and the possession of nationality a basic right held by all under international law. Of particular interest is the providing of nationality by signatories for individuals who have resided within the state for a certain period of time.

Diplomatic Agent   (112)
One of a special class of state officials responsible for representing a state and its interests in the territory of another state or in international organizations. Diplomatic agents are broadly classified into two groups: (1) heads of a mission; and (2) members of the staff of the mission having diplomatic rank. Diplomatic agents may be permanent or sent on a special temporary mission, a situation governed by the 1969 Convention on Special Missions. Diplomats who are part of the state's permanent diplomatic mission have the functions of (1) representing the sending state in the receiving state; (2) negotiating with the host state; (3) reporting on events within the receiving state; (4) protecting the interests of the sending state and its nationals; and (5) promoting friendly relations between the sending and receiving state. *See also* VIENNA CONVENTION ON DIPLOMATIC RELATIONS (1961), 148.

Significance   While diplomacy is as old as recorded history (scholars note temporary envoys being sent by states of antiquity—Egypt, China, Indian states, Greek city-states, and Rome), permanent diplomatic missions first appeared in the fifteenth century in relations between Italian states, and then in the period of the emergence of the territorial state system in Europe during the sixteenth and early seventeenth centuries, which created the need for a permanent class of persons skilled in the arts of diplomacy. Since their skills were employed in the courts of monarchs and, therefore, required that they speak the language of the courts and be familiar with the requisite social graces and court practices, the diplomats typically were drawn from nobility. This practice produced a general perception that diplomatic careers were elitist, a perception that persists even today. While initially considered a skill employable for a head of state other than one's own, the practice eventually settled upon employing only nationals to represent the state abroad. In the period of primitive transportation and communication, diplomatic agents were the principal means by which states interacted. They negotiated and made commitments in the name of their state and were the major means of keeping their state alert to developments in the host state. With the transportation and communications revolution, the emergence of the central authority of foreign ministries and executive advisors, and the penchant for summit diplomacy by heads of state and government, the central political role of diplomatic agents has declined and social and informational roles emphasized instead. The permanence of diplomatic missions and the members of the diplomatic staffs led to the need for ranks and diplomatic precedence so as not to offend state sensibilities of equality. The Congresses of Vienna (1815) and of Aix-la-Chapelle (1818) established the diplomatic classification system of heads of missions confirmed in general by the Vienna Convention on Diplomatic Relations (1961): (1) ambassador, nuncio, and other heads of missions of equivalent rank, e.g., in relations between the British Commonwealth members, high commissioner; (2) ministers, envoys, and internuncios; and (3) *chargé d'affaires*. Heads of missions take precedence within their respective classes in the order of the date and time of taking up their functions in the host state, although some states have traditionally given precedence to the representative of the Holy See. The former third class of minister resident has now been eliminated with the Vienna Convention on Diplomatic Relations (1961). The first two classes are accredited to heads of state, the third one to the foreign affairs ministry.

Diplomatic Agent: Ambassador (113)

The highest rank of diplomatic agent and head of mission accredited to a head of state by the head of the sending state. Ambassador is the highest rank, as established by the Congress of Vienna (1815) and reiterated by the Vienna Convention on Diplomatic Relations (1961). An individual holding this rank is responsible for overseeing all the activities of the state's embassy in the state to which he or she is accredited. Equal in status to ambassador is the rank of papal nuncio, a designation for ambassadors of the Holy See. In relations between members of the British Commonwealth of Nations, ambassadors are called high commissioners. *See also* DIPLOMATIC AGENT, 112; VIENNA CONVENTION ON DIPLOMATIC RELATIONS (1961), 148.

Significance   Ambassadors were historically a rank of royal or other princely agents or representatives, sent or received by one monarch to another. The United States did not employ the rank until the end of the nineteenth century. In the twentieth century, particularly after World War II, it became more common to provide such rank to diplomatic envoys of lesser powers, although the Soviet Union refused to employ the rank until the outbreak of World War II. Today it is unusual for any head of a mission not to be of ambassadorial rank, regardless of the size or importance of the state. This is primarily due to the sensitivity of new states to the principle of equality in international law.

Diplomatic Agent: *Chargé d'affaires*   (114)

The lowest class of head of diplomatic mission. A *chargé d'affaires* is sometimes also referred to as *chargé d'affaires en titre* to distinguish the individual from a *chargé d'affaires ad interim*. The latter title indicates that the individual is acting provisionally as head of the mission if the post of head of the mission is vacant or the head of the mission is temporarily unable to perform his or her duties. A *chargé d'affaires* has fewer honors than those of higher ranks but retains normal diplomatic privileges and immunities.

Significance   *Chargés d'affaires*, along with the now rarely used class of ministers resident (a term used historically for envoys of European powers in overseas countries), were usually sent to relatively less important states. Today, they are normally assistants of ambassadors and envoys. If the regular head of the mission is recalled, the *chargé d'affaires* heads the mission—sometimes for several years—a situation reflecting deterioration in the relations between the states concerned. An important distinction between this rank and that of ambassador, envoy, or minister is that a *chargé d'affaires* is accredited from one foreign ministry to another instead of from one head of state to another.

Diplomatic Agent: Envoy   (115)

A diplomatic head of mission of the second class (below that of ambassador), to which also belong the ranks of minister and papal internuncio. An envoy is not accorded the privilege of requesting direct audiences with the head of state of the host state, as diplomatic agents in this second rank are not considered to be the personal representatives of their head of state. Today, such distinctions between the first two diplomatic ranks are often muted.

Significance   An envoy (or minister) is a title often given to someone on a special mission of limited duration. Although not accorded the full panoply of honors granted to ambassadors, envoys and ministers are given the full range of diplomatic privileges and immunities enjoyed by other diplomatic envoys.

Diplomatic Mission   (116)

A diplomatic presence of one state (the sending state) in the territory of another (the receiving state) for which special treatment is accorded by the latter state. The diplomatic mission is the official representation of the sending state to the receiving state and is permanently housed in the capital of that state, for which it receives the protection of that state and full diplomatic privileges and immunities. The traditional so-called "right of legation" is the authority of a state to send (active right) and to receive (passive right) diplomatic representatives. While the state is not required to exercise such a right, to do so has been used as evidence of it being an international person. *See also* DIPLOMATIC AGENT: AMBASSADOR, 113.

Significance   The institution of diplomatic missions was an important means for organized communities to interact and communicate during the long historical period of primitive means of transportation and communication. While the practice of sending them is an ancient one, permanent diplomatic missions became a common feature of international relations only in the early period of the territorial state system. The first permanent diplomatic missions were established among the Italian city-states during the fifteenth century, and the practice became common throughout Europe in the sixteenth and seventeenth centuries. The emergence of the territorial state system as the central feature of Europe by the mid-seventeenth century saw diplomatic missions become a permanent feature of that system. The tangible evidence of the exercise of the "right of legation" is the building of the diplomatic mission of the sending state. Headed by a chief of mission (an ambassador, envoy, or *chargé d'affaires*), it normally consists of a deputy chief of mission; the embassy diplomatic staff organized into substantive sections, e.g., consular, economic, political, public affairs; attachés, e.g., cultural or military; administrative and technical staff, such as secretaries and communications personnel plus attachés assigned to the embassy; and the service staff, maids, gardeners, chauffeurs, etc.

Diplomatic Privileges and Immunities   (117)

The special status and inviolability of diplomatic agents (and to a lesser extent of members of the administrative and technical staff and service staff of the mission) and family members from the authority of the receiving state as a consequence of the position of the member of the mission as an agent representing the sending state. The customary law of diplomatic privileges and immunities was codified and developed in the Vienna Convention on Diplomatic Relations (1961). The person of the diplomatic agent is inviolate, and he or she is immune from the criminal jurisdiction of the receiving state, as well as the civil proceedings of the receiving state's courts. Exceptions to this rule include lawsuits relating to private immovable property, to succession of property in which the diplomat is involved as a private person, and to any commercial or professional activity conducted by the diplomat outside of official duties. The diplomat is immune from customs duties and taxation other than indirect taxes and taxes pertaining to private commercial and unofficial activities. The diplomatic mission, its premises, archives, all property, and transportation are immune from the receiving state's authority, as are the official correspondence and communications of the mission, including the diplomatic bag or pouch. The increase in terrorist acts against diplomats during the 1960s and 1970s led to the United Nations Convention on the Prevention and Punishment of Crimes against Internationally Protected Persons, Including Diplomatic Agents (1973), which covers (1) threats; (2) attempts or commission of murder or kidnapping of a head of state, head of government, foreign minister, or other representative of a state in the territory of a state or on board ships or aircraft; and (3) attacks against the official premises, private accommodations, or transportation of such protected persons. Those accused of such crimes are to be extradited or punished where located. *See also* VIENNA CONVENTION ON DIPLOMATIC RELATIONS (1961), 148.

Significance Diplomatic privileges and immunities are among the oldest and most sacrosanct rules of international law. Diplomatic privileges and immunities result from the need to not impair the ability of diplomatic agents to fulfill their functions effectively, as well as acknowledge that the diplomat is the official representative of the sovereign state in the host country. Diplomatic immunity does not mean that the individual is not accountable for his or her actions. It means that, unless immunity is waived by the sending state, diplomatic agents cannot be prosecuted in the host state's courts; instead, the matter will be handled in the courts of the sending state. Privileges and immunities extend to members of the diplomat's family. The administrative and technical staff enjoy a lesser degree of privileges and immunities. They are not immune from civil proceedings for actions not relating to official duties and are exempt from customs duties only for goods imported at the time of their taking up their posts. Members of the service staff are not immune from criminal jurisdiction and are immune from civil jurisdiction only for acts performed as part of their official duties. They are exempt from income taxes, however. Being a party to the Vienna Convention of 1961 does not bar a state from providing more inclusive privileges and immunities, as is the case with the U.S. Diplomatic Immunities Act of 1978. The names of persons attached to the diplomatic mission (including the accompanying family members) for whom the head of the mission claims diplomatic status or immunity are submitted to the appropriate state agency that conducts foreign affairs. They become part of an official diplomatic list to which reference can be made in any cases in which the matter of immunity arises. Privileges and immunities cease upon the expiration of the diplomat's mission and do not normally apply in third states except in cases where the diplomat is in transit to or from his or her assigned post. Violations of diplomatic privileges and immunities are relatively rare, but the Iranian hostage crisis illustrates most strikingly how vulnerable diplomatic agents are in a receiving state. After the 4 November 1979 Iranian seizure of the American embassy in Teheran and its diplomatic personnel being made hostages, the United States filed application before the International Court of Justice (ICJ) in the *Case Concerning United States Diplomatic and Consular Staff in Teheran (U.S. v. Iran)*. In its 1980 judgment, the Court ruled that Iran had violated the rules of international law pertaining to the immunity of embassies and its diplomatic personnel.

Exequatur   (118)

The certificate by which the issuing state admits and recognizes the official status of a consular officer. The sending state issues the consular official a commission or a patent, which authorizes the individual to represent the state's interests in the host state, and the receiving state provides the consular officer with an *exequatur,* which authorizes the individual to carry out consular functions in that country. This process occurs at the government level of foreign ministries rather than between heads of state. *See also* CONSUL, 109.

Significance   States are not required by international law to receive foreign consuls, but if they do so they should not be discriminatory, although this stipulation does not affect the right of the issuing state to rule on the acceptability or nonacceptability of the consular official seeking an *exequatur*. In essence, the *exequatur* is a consul's work permit that authorizes the consul to function in the host state. Since its issuance is a formal action, the granting and acceptance of an *exequatur* implies tacit recognition in the case of a previously unrecognized government or state. The revocation of the *exequatur* by the issuing state terminates the consular mission for the individual to whom it was directed.

Expatriation   **(119)**

Any act whereby an individual loses or renounces his or her former
citizenship, breaking the tie to the country of origin or last nationality.
Expatriation can be premeditated or accidental. Actions that constitute
grounds for expatriation in most countries include taking an oath of
allegiance to another state, serving in foreign military forces without
permission, voting in foreign elections, and publicly renouncing one's
citizenship. The key to expatriation lies in a voluntary action undertaken by the individual rather than by a government. Some states view
this as an individual right, while other states require that their nationals
seek permission to expatriate themselves. The latter category of states
follow what is known as the "doctrine of indelible allegiance," which
holds that an individual cannot lose nationality without the prior approval of the state of which he or she is at that time a national. Should
the state deprive the individual of nationality, the process is known as
denationalization. *See also* NATIONALITY: INDIVIDUALS, 137.

Significance   Individuals who expatriate themselves are often un-
aware that they are doing so and may not understand the consequences
of their actions. Unless assured of naturalization elsewhere, they may
become stateless persons unable to obtain a residence permit, a
passport, or visas to travel to other countries. In short, they could claim
no protection as a matter of right from any state. To preclude such a
situation, some states provide for the reinstitution of the individual's
former citizenship in instances of denationalization—a procedure
known as redintegration. The Universal Declaration of Human Rights
(1948) proclaims that no individual should be arbitrarily denied the
right to a nationality, and the Convention on the Status of Refugees
(1951), the Convention on the Status of Stateless Persons (1954), and
the Convention on the Reduction of Statelessness (1961) suggest that
everyone has a right to a nationality.

Extradition   **(120)**

A judicial or—in some states—administrative procedure whereby a
fugitive from justice (whether accused or convicted) found in one state
is surrendered to the state from which the fugitive fled. Extradition is a
formal procedure between states governed largely by bilateral extradition treaties, as there is no general body of international law dealing
with the subject; although there are some multilateral extradition
treaties, such as the 1957 European Convention on Extradition and the
Inter-American Convention on Extradition (1981). In the absence of a
bilateral treaty between states, unofficial extradition (rendition) depends upon the relations of the states involved and the general attitude

toward extradition held by the state hosting the fugitive. Extradition agreements establish specific conditions and offenses for which extradition requests will be honored. The offense must be one listed in the agreement and the fugitive must be tried for the extradited offense and no other (the principle of speciality). Furthermore, the offense must be a crime in both states (the principle of double criminality). Generally, a political crime is not an extraditable offense. *See also* ASYLUM: POLITICAL (TERRITORIAL), 107.

Significance   Extradition has historically been an important tool to penetrate the protective cloak state sovereignty offers an individual against the police power of the fugitive's own state, as the latter's authority does not extend into the jurisdiction of another state. To attempt to inject that authority into another state is interference in its domestic affairs and a violation of that state's sovereignty. By cloaking oneself in the protection of another state's authority, a fugitive can escape the punishment for violation of law in the country from which he or she fled. Not all states have extradition agreements with all other states and there are, therefore, states considered havens or sanctuaries for fugitives from certain states. Furthermore, some states do not like to surrender their own nationals for trial in another state and will instead try them in their own courts for the crime committed in the other state. Should the crime not be considered a crime in that national's own state, the fugitive will have successfully escaped punishment. Efforts to codify or standardize this area have only been partially successful, such as the 1907 Central American Republics Convention; the Convention on Extradition (1933) drafted by the Conference of American States; the European Convention on Extradition (1957); and the Inter-American Convention on Extradition (1981). In the absence of a universal agreement, it cannot be said that there is a right of extradition, an obligation to extradite being self-imposed through treaties or else a matter of comity between states. Indeed, we are witnessing a decline in the importance of extradition in this century. States have moved instead in the direction of deportation of aliens, as it frees them of the constraints contained in extradition treaties, such as the principles of speciality and double criminality.

Extradition: Double Criminality, Principle of   (121)

The rule in extradition procedure whereby, in order for the request to be honored, the crime for which extradition is requested must be a crime in both the requesting state and the state to which the fugitive has fled.

Significance   Double criminality does not require that the crime be precisely defined as equivalent in both states nor that the punishment be comparable, only that it be a crime in both states. In the *Eisler* case (1948), a British court concluded that while an act in question was similar to perjury in Great Britain, it was actually not perjury and, therefore, the party in question could not be extradited to the United States. Should the offense listed in the extradition request not be a crime in the state where the accused has taken refuge, then the state is under no obligation to honor the request. In such situations, it is possible for an individual to commit a crime and escape punishment. The caveat is that the individual not move to a state in which the act is a crime since a subsequent extradition request would likely be honored.

Extradition: Speciality, Principle of   (122)
The principle that a state requesting the extradition of a fugitive from another state must specify the crime for which the accused is to be extradited and try the individual only for the crime specified in the extradition request.

Significance   The principle of speciality is designed to preclude blanket extradition requests. Furthermore, should a state seek the extradition of an individual on one charge and then try that individual on a different charge, the practice of higher courts in some states is to deny the decision of lower courts.

Extraterritoriality   (123)
A legal fiction whereby heads of state, diplomatic agents and other individuals enjoying diplomatic immunity, the premises of diplomatic missions and residences of its diplomatic agents, diplomatic documents and communications, etc., are immune from the jurisdiction of the host state as if they were not located in its territory. *See also* DIPLOMATIC PRIVILEGES AND IMMUNITIES, 117; VIENNA CONVENTION ON DIPLOMATIC RELATIONS (1961), 148.

Significance   Extraterritoriality is a useful legal fiction adopted for an effective carrying out of diplomatic functions. Since these functions entail communications with the mission's government, representing the sending state's interests and nationals in the host country, and dealing with the official agents of the host government, to restrict these activities would undermine the purpose of sending and receiving diplomatic missions. Therefore, diplomatic agents must be accorded certain privileges and immunities not enjoyed by other individuals. Extraterritoriality ceases at the termination of the diplomatic agent's official status or when he or she leaves the state to which he/she is accredited; although adequate time to leave the country is provided. At one time, extraterritoriality meant that embassies and their personnel were beyond the territorial jurisdiction of the host state; but the modern interpretation is more restrictive, considering extraterritoriality as a useful legal fiction. The older interpretation had its antecedents in the representational theory of diplomatic functions during the Middle Ages and earlier centuries of the modern state system when diplomatic agents were viewed as the personal representative of their sovereign. The modern view is that diplomatic privileges and immunities serve a functional role, although obviously the representational role of diplomats continues and is listed among the functions of diplomatic agents in the Vienna Convention on Diplomatic Relations (1961).

General Convention on the Privileges and Immunities of the United Nations (1946)   (124)

Adopted by the United Nations General Assembly at its first session, the General Convention on the Privileges and Immunities of the United Nations (1946) deals with the legal capacity of the United Nations and the diplomatic privileges and immunities of United Nations personnel that are alluded to in general terms in the United Nations Charter (Articles 104 and 105). It provides the United Nations with juridical personality and immunity from legal process and grants its high ranking officials and representatives of member states diplomatic privileges and immunities comparable to those enjoyed by diplomatic agents accredited to individual states. The organization, its property, and assets are immune from legal process; its premises and archives are inviolable; and it is exempt from customs duties and most direct taxation. Diplomatic privileges and immunities are extended to the representatives of member states who are assigned to the principal and subsidiary organs of the United Nations and include delegates, deputy delegates, advisers, technical experts, and secretaries of delegations. Major United Nations officials are covered in the Convention, including judges of the International Court of Justice (ICJ), but most employees of the United Nations Secretariat are not granted diplomatic immunity and are exempt from legal process in the country where they perform their functions only in those instances where they are acting in their official capacity as United Nations officials. Lower ranked officials enjoy only specified immunities. *See also* HEAD-QUARTERS OF THE UNITED NATIONS AGREEMENT (1947), 125; VIENNA

CONVENTION ON THE REPRESENTATION OF STATES IN THEIR RELATIONS
WITH INTERNATIONAL ORGANIZATIONS OF A UNIVERSAL CHARACTER
(1975), 149.

Significance   Since the United Nations is a subject of international
law, it must have the freedom to function independently as well as have
its property and archives protected. Under traditional international
law, however, there was no special recognition given to the immunities
of international organizations and their agents. The General Convention on the Privileges and Immunities of the United Nations is critical,
therefore, for the effective functioning of the organization. It under-
scores the capacity of the United Nations to contract, to acquire and
dispose of immovable and movable property, and to institute legal
proceedings. The specialized agencies of the United Nations are covered in a separate Convention on the Privileges and Immunities of the
Specialized Agencies (1947).

Headquarters of the United Nations Agreement   (125)
(1947)

An agreement between the United Nations and the United States
entered into in 1947. The Headquarters Agreement establishes the
headquarters district of the United Nations and guarantees its independent existence, detailing the status and conditions under which it
operates in the United States. The Agreement guarantees rights of
transit to delegates to the United Nations; diplomatic privileges and
immunities to delegations; the providing of public services to the
district; the right to operate communications equipment; and prohibits
the district from being a place of asylum.

Significance   Since the United Nations is a person in international
law, special measures are required in order for it to carry out its
functions and responsibilities. Not being a state with the traditional
feature of territory, it needs a physical base from which to operate. Real
estate in New York City was provided for the Organization and is
referred to as the Headquarters district for the United Nations. This
district is inviolable and is under the control and authority of the
United Nations.

Jurisdiction   (126)

The capacity of a state under international law to prescribe and enforce
a rule of law. Jurisdiction is the authority or power of a state over
persons, property, or events within its purview and is of three types:

(1) jurisdiction to prescribe norms; (2) jurisdiction to enforce the norms prescribed; and (3) jurisdiction to adjudicate. Since jurisdiction is spatial, personal, and material (pertaining to the subject matter), there exist a number of principles or grounds for jurisdiction. These include (1) the nationality principle; (2) the territorial principle; (3) the protective principle; (4) the universality principle; and (5) the passive personality principle. The first is based upon the link of nationality, the second upon the power of the state over its territory, the third upon the state's right to protect itself, the fourth upon select acts of universal proscription, and the fifth upon the nationality of the object of the action. Of these five principles, the first three are widely accepted, the fourth only insofar as it pertains to crimes which are universally defined, and the fifth less so. *See also* JURISDICTION: NATIONALITY PRINCIPLE, 127; JURISDICTION: PASSIVE PERSONALITY PRINCIPLE, 128; JURISDICTION: PROTECTIVE PRINCIPLE, 129; JURISDICTION: TERRITORIALITY PRINCIPLE, 130; JURISDICTION: UNIVERSALITY PRINCIPLE, 131.

Significance   Jurisdiction is derived primarily from the sovereignty of the state over its spatial domain. A state's jurisdiction extends over all persons and things within its land boundaries, its national air space, and its internal and territorial waters. But its jurisdiction is also personal and extends to persons and things beyond its boundaries for which there is a national link. Finally, certain acts proscribed under international law allow for any state's jurisdiction to enforce and punish. Since states jealously guard their sovereignty, there is frequent opportunity for jurisdictional conflicts, as the five basic jurisdictional principles suggest. Such conflicts afford the opportunity for concurrent jurisdiction. For example, an accused may be tried and punished in more than one country. While some countries have constitutional or statutory guarantees against double jeopardy (being tried more than once for the same crime), such is not the case with all countries, and international law makes no provision for such circumstances.

Jurisdiction: Nationality Principle   (127)
The position held by many states that a state's jurisdiction extends to its nationals and actions they take beyond the territorial jurisdiction of the state. The nationality principle is based upon the notion that the link between the state and the individual is a personal one independent of location. In Anglo-American practice, criminal jurisdiction based on the nationality principle is claimed only with respect to such major crimes as treason or murder. Other states make a more extensive use of the nationality principle, for example, continental Europe.

Significance   The nationality principle assumes that a state has primary jurisdiction over its nationals and, consequently, clashes with the territorial principle, which assumes primary jurisdiction based upon location of the action rather than the nationality of the person involved. States that hold to the nationality principle do not look positively upon their nationals being tried in courts other than their own and are loath to honor extradition requests that involve jurisdictional disputes of this variety. For example, should a French national be accused of a crime committed within the territory of the United States, France would claim jurisdiction based upon the nationality principle and the United States upon the territoriality principle. Should the accused return to France, the French government would likely not honor a United States extradition request and choose instead to try the accused in a French court. A similar emphasis upon nationality can occur in cases where jurisdiction is based on the nationality of the plaintiff or injured party, in which case it is referred to as the principle of passive personality. This principle is viewed as much weaker than either the territorial or nationality principle as a basis for jurisdiction.

Jurisdiction: Passive Personality Principle   (128)

The notion held by many states that acts committed by an alien against their nationals abroad accord them jurisdiction in the matter. The passive personality principle is viewed as a secondary basis for determining state jurisdiction and is a matter of considerable dispute among authorities.

Significance   The principle of passive personality as the basis for state jurisdiction evokes much controversy because it suggests that individuals carry the cloak of the law of the state with them to protect them when beyond the territorial jurisdiction of their own state. Such being the case, the sovereign jurisdiction of a state over its own territory is challenged, and the passive personality principle therefore undermines the fundamental principle of territorial sovereignty. One area in which the principle of passive personality could conceivably take on major importance would be those instances in which an offense took place where no territorial authority was obvious, e.g., outer space.

Jurisdiction: Protective Principle   (129)

The notion that the jurisdiction of the state can be applied in those cases in which the action of a person takes place outside the territorial jurisdiction of the state but is viewed as prejudicial to its security interests. The protective principle is usually viewed as a secondary basis for determining state jurisdiction over individual actions rather than sharing primary authority with the principles of territoriality and nationality.

Significance   The protective principle is a means by which the state protects its interests and security from actions abroad, particularly in those instances where the action undertaken is of little consequence to the state from which it emanates. The protective principle is used in a narrower sense than either the territoriality or nationality principles. It would apply in those instances where an individual's action that took place outside the state injured or was a crime against the sovereignty of the state. Examples are subversive activities, treason, economic and securities activities, and counterfeiting. A leading American case, *United States v. Pizzarusso*, 338 F.2d 8 (1968), highlights the protective principle. In that case, an individual made false statements on an application for an immigrant visa to the United States before a U.S. consul in Canada. While none of the elements of the offense occurred in the United States (a requirement of the objective territorial principle), the Circuit Court held that the false statements could have an adverse effect upon the United States and, therefore, it had jurisdiction.

Jurisdiction: Territoriality Principle (130)

The absolute and exclusive jurisdiction of the state over all persons and things within its territory. This is known as the principle of territoriality and means that the state has primary jurisdiction with regard to all events taking place in its territory and over crimes committed there, regardless of the nationality of the person responsible. It is the dominant type of jurisdiction in international law. All other states must respect the supremacy of the state over its territory and neither interfere with nor intervene in its internal affairs or territorial jurisdiciton. The latter encompasses not only the land mass of the state but also its national airspace, internal waters, and territorial sea. Should the crime affect more than one territory, then a case of concurrent jurisdiction occurs—subjective jurisdiction (the state in whose territory the crime was committed) and objective jurisdiction (the state in whose territory the effect of the crime was felt).

Significance   The territoriality principle is derived from the concept of state sovereignty; namely, that within its sphere of authority no power exceeds that of the state. Sovereignty and territoriality are tied to the emergence of the territorial state system in the sixteenth and seventeenth centuries. As the monarchies of Europe challenged the worldly political authority of the pope in Rome, they replaced his authority with the concept of monarchical sovereignty over their domain in matters other than spiritual. Sovereign authority was bound to the monarch's territoriality. While a state retains a link with its nationals beyond the confines of its territory, such a link cannot extend into another state without acceptance by that state as the authority of the state within its territory is dominant. The territoriality principle does not, however, exempt states from conforming to the tenets of international law since they affect the affairs of a state in its own territory; for example, as the right of innocent passage and proper treatment of aliens.

Jurisdiction: Universality Principle   (131)

The authority of a state to assume criminal jurisdiction over an individual regardless of nationality or where the crime was committed. The universality principle is normally contrary to international law except for crimes against international law (*delicta juris gentium*). An individual guilty of such crimes is considered to be *hostis humani generis* and can be arrested and tried by any state without concern for the person's nationality. This principle is, as is the case with the protective principle and the passive personality principle, one of secondary importance in international law. JURISDICTION: NATIONALITY PRINCIPLE, 127; JURISDICTION: PROTECTIVE PRINCIPLE, 129; JURISDICTION: TERRITORIALITY PRINCIPLE, 130.

Significance   The universality principle suggests that there are certain crimes that adversely affect the orderly relations of nations or constitute conduct repugnant to civilized nations. These crimes, therefore, are crimes against all nations regardless of whom the action was directed against. Crimes in this category include piracy, the slave trade, white slavery, aerial hijacking, counterfeiting, war crimes, and crimes against humanity (genocide). The universality principle is not universally accepted by states in the absence of commonly recognized definitions of international crimes and the obvious threat that it represents to the jurisdiction of states over their nationals.

Letter of Credence   (132)

A formal document by which the head of the "accrediting" state introduces its newly appointed diplomatic agent to the head of the host state. The letter of credence (*lettre de créance*) states the diplomat's rank, mission, and powers, and asks that full faith and credit be given to acts undertaken on behalf of his or her government. The letter of credence is presented to the head of state in a formal audience, except in the case of a diplomatic official with the rank of *chargé d'affaires,* in which case the procedure takes place at the level of foreign ministry.

Significance   The letter of credence is necessary to ensure normal diplomatic relations between states. It provides the receiving state with information on the diplomat's status and mission needed to determine what the state's relationship with the diplomat will be and how much weight and latitude the agent has in dealing and negotiating with the host state. Conversely, the acceptance of the letter of credence by the receiving state indicates that the state will deal with the diplomat and recognizes his or her official or formal status. The diplomat's status is not official and he or she cannot begin formal duties until the completion of the procedure of accreditation and reception.

Letter Rogatory   (133)

A sworn statement made before proper judicial authorities that is admissible as testimony before the court of another state. The letter rogatory procedure enables the court in question to call upon their counterpart in the state in which the individual is located and ask for a deposition pertaining to the matter at hand. To honor such a request is a matter of bilateral arrangements or international comity but is not a norm of general international law.

Significance   The procedure of letters rogatory serves to alleviate the expense and inconvenience of individuals traveling from one country to another to appear as witnesses in a case or to provide other testimony. The extent to which it is employed is partly a matter of the municipal juridical and constitutional processes of the state. In the United States, for example, the constitutional right of accused to be confronted by witnesses against them would seem to preclude the use of letters rogatory in U.S. federal courts. On the other hand, there is no reason why courts in the United States could not provide the courts of another state with such a sworn deposition.

Nansen Passport   (134)

A document similar to a passport and actually called so, provided to stateless persons in the aftermath of World War I. The Nansen passport was named after its creator, Dr. Fridtjof Nansen, the Norwegian High Commissioner for Refugees of the League of Nations. *See also* STATELESSNESS, 145.

Significance   The Nansen passport was instrumental in alleviating the human suffering attended by the flood of refugees from communist Russia and transfer of territories after World War I. Statelessness meant that displaced persons could not gain the protection of any government, be granted visas or passports to travel, or have their condition represented by any state. An analogous problem occurred as a result of World War II, but a similar response was not forthcoming. A few states did adopt an international passport agreement after that war, but it did not gain the institutionalization in the United Nations enjoyed by the Nansen passport in the League of Nations.

Nationality: Dual   (135)

A situation in which an individual holds citizenship in more than one country. Dual nationality can occur at birth when an individual acquires the parents' citizenship through *jus sanguinis* but is born in a country that practices *jus soli*. It can also result when a person is naturalized whose country of origin does not allow nationals to expatriate themselves. It can also occur in instances of marriage and adoption. In such instances, the individual may be subject to nationality jurisdiction of more than one state. Some states allow for the selection between nationalities at the age of majority. It is also possible for an individual to have more than two nationalities. *See also* EXPATRIATION, 119; NATIONALITY: INDIVIDUALS, 137; NATIONALITY: *JUS SANGUINIS*, 138; NATIONALITY: *JUS SOLI*, 139; NATURALIZATION, 140.

Significance   Dual nationality occurs because states have the right to determine the conditions under which an individual becomes one of its nationals. At first glance dual nationality might seem attractive, as it allows individuals to select among several countries for purposes of gaining visas and passports, being provided preferential treatment, or taking advantage of differences in national laws. The reality can be quite different, however, since citizenship imposes duties and obligations as well as conveying rights or privileges. A dual national, for example, might be liable for compulsory military service in both states, might be subject to double taxation, or might lose the diplomatic protection of the other state. Since both states have jurisdiction over their nationals, there is little that can legally be done to interpose on behalf of such an individual. To alleviate such dilemmas, some states have agreements covering such issues. In the absence of specific agreements, claims are frequently resolved in favor of the state possessing *de facto* jurisdiction over the individual; namely, the state in which the individual habitually resides and over whom the state exerts primary jurisdiction. A person with dual or multiple nationality is well advised to investigate his or her status thoroughly before moving between different jurisdictions claiming their allegiance.

Nationality: Genuine Link   (136)

The notion that there must exist a real tie between an individual or entity and the state of which nationality is claimed. A genuine link (also referred to as an "effective bond of attachment" or "effective nationality") is one in which the tie of nationality is real and effective, rather than one of convenience. *See also* FLAG OF CONVENIENCE, 229; NATIONALITY: INDIVIDUALS, 137; NATIONALITY OF CLAIM, 168; NATIONALITY OF SHIPS, 245.

Significance   In any action in which an individual seeks the support or protection of his or her government, it must be established that the individual or entity is indeed a national of that state. For most individuals, nationality is acquired through their parents or location at birth and would normally provide basis for proof of a genuine link between the individual and the state. However, is is not uncommon for individuals to purchase nationality and passports or become naturalized for self-serving reasons, which often amount to nominal or doubtful claims to nationality. In the controversial *Nottebohm* case (*Liechtenstein v. Guatemala*, 1955), the International Court of Justice (ICJ) held that "nationality is a legal bond having as its basis a social fact of attachment, a genuine connection of existence, interests and sentiments, together with the existence of reciprocal rights and duties." In the 1958 Geneva Convention on the High Seas and in the United Nations Convention on the Law of the Sea (1982), the genuine link concept is applied to merchant vessels as a challenge to the practice of flags of convenience. With the degree of personal and corporate mobility that exists in the contemporary world, however, what constitutes a genuine link is more difficult to determine than the statement provided in the *Nottebohm* case. "Genuine link" approach could also be applied to the nationality of legal entities, such as business corporations. Their nationality follows, however, the state of incorporation, but the state where business is effectively carried out or other circumstances can, in some situations, be the determining factor.

Nationality: Individuals   (137)

The legal link between an individual and a state. Nationality provides an individual with the protection of the state and accords the individual certain rights and duties. Some states distinguish between the terms national and citizen—the former connoting an individual's obligations toward a state and the latter an individual's political rights as well as obligations. Any such distinctions between citizen, national, and subject are a matter of municipal rather than international law, although in international law terminology the term "national" is used for all. An individual's nationality is determined either by birth or by legal process. Most individuals acquire nationality through birth, but the increase in human migration in the nineteenth and especially the twentieth centuries saw the legal process of naturalization attain greater popularity. Nationality may also be acquired through marriage, adoption or legitimation, and transfer of territory. Nationality may be lost by renunciation, by acquiring new nationality (except in countries following the principle of "indelible allegiance"), by deprivation, or by transfer of territory. *See also* EXPATRIATION, 119; NATIONALITY: DUAL, 135; NATIONALITY: GENUINE LINK, 136; NATIONALITY: *JUS SANGUINIS*, 138; NATIONALITY: *JUS SOLI*, 139; NATURALIZATION, 140.

Significance   Nationality is the central bond linking an individual to the state. Since the individual does not have unquestioned standing in international law, the state is the means of providing that standing. The protection the state can give an individual (such as interposing on his or her behalf in instances of dispute with another state, providing benefits through the medium of treaties, and sanctuary from the incursion of other states into the individual's daily life) is a function of the link of nationality. If an individual is not a national of a state, the state can provide none of these services. To be without nationality (stateless) is, therefore, a serious problem for an individual, particularly when traveling abroad.

Nationality: *Jus Sanguinis*   (138)

The principle that at birth an individual acquires the nationality of the parents. In some states, either parent being a national will suffice to convey nationality upon the child. In others, preference is given to the father being the national, while in other states (such as the Soviet Union) both parents must be nationals. Nationality is acquired either through birth or by legal process—naturalization, legislative statute, executive decree, etc. *Jus sanguinis* (literally, the "law of blood") is one of two principles used by states in determining nationality by birth. The other principle is *jus soli* (the "law of soil"). Rules governing the acquisition of nationality are largely a matter of domestic law, as each state is free to determine who may be its nationals. *See also* NATIONALITY: *JUS SOLI*, 139.

Significance   *Jus sanguinis* is the principal method employed by the majority of the world's states, establishing nationality through that of the parents (particularly the father) rather than that of the place of birth. Even in such cases, however, provision is usually made for the acquisition of nationality through place of birth. Most continental European and Asiatic countries embrace the principle of *jus sanguinis*, although many grant secondary status to *jus soli*.

Nationality: *Jus Soli* (139)

The principle that a person's nationality is determined by place of birth. Nationality is acquired either by birth or by legal process (naturalization, legislative enactment, executive decree, etc.). *Jus soli* (literally the "law of soil") is one of the two principles governing nationality by birth; the other is *jus sanguinis* (meaning the "law of blood"). Rules governing the acquisition of nationality are largely a matter of domestic law, as each state is free to determine who may be its nationals. *See also* NATIONALITY: *JUS SANGUINIS*, 138.

Significance   *Jus soli* is rooted in European feudal practice and remains the principal means of determining nationality in most English-speaking and Latin American countries. Children born in countries following this principle are citizens even if their parents are aliens or ineligible for citizenship. Exceptions to this rule are children born to foreign diplomats, visiting heads of state, and other aliens enjoying diplomatic status. No state that bases its nationality practices upon *jus soli* does so exclusively, however. To do so would be to deny citizenship to children of its nationals who are born beyond the territory of the state. Such states provide for a secondary means of acquiring nationality by birth through *jus sanguinis*.

Naturalization (140)

The legal process whereby an individual acquires a new nationality. The naturalization process varies from state to state but usually includes a formal renunciation of allegiance to one sovereign (expatriation) and an oath of allegiance to the new state. Naturalization is not a right of aliens and each state is free to determine the conditions for naturalization.

Significance   Naturalization is the means by which a person who cannot claim citizenship in a state by right of birth can acquire citizenship in that state. Naturalization is usually an individual process (direct naturalization, through the normal naturalization process) but (depending upon the laws of the state in question) can also be done (1) collectively, an entire category of individuals being granted nationality through treaty, legislation, or executive decree; (2) by adoption or legitimation in the case of children whose nationality is unknown; or (3) by derivation, e.g., marriage, a child or spouse gaining nationality as a consequence of the naturalization of the parent or spouse. A state can restrict naturalization to particular categories of persons as well as exclude specific individuals. Furthermore, many states have procedures whereby a naturalized citizen can lose his or her citizenship under certain conditions, e.g., subversive activities, or fraud in applying for naturalization, a process known as denaturalization. Should this occur, it is possible for the individual to become stateless. To preclude such a situation, some states provide for the reacquisition of the individual's previous citizenship, a process known as redintegration.

Persona Non Grata   (141)

A Latin term indicating that a diplomatic agent of a state is unacceptable to the receiving state. This can take place either before the individual is accredited, indicating that the proposed appointee is unacceptable to the host state and will not be received, or after the accreditation process in response to some real or alleged impropriety by the diplomatic agent. Proclaiming a diplomat *persona non grata* usually results from an unfriendly attitude toward the (prospective) receiving state, violation of its laws or of international law, or improper diplomatic behavior or indiscretions, although the host state may proclaim a diplomat *persona non grata* for any or no reason. The sending state must then recall its agent or, should not recall occur, the host state may ignore the presence of the diplomatic agent or expel the diplomat from its territory.

Significance   Since the function of diplomatic agents is to represent the sending state's interests in the host country and to communicate the host state's concerns and interests to the diplomat's state, a situation in which the diplomat is unable to effectively carry out these responsibilities does neither state any good. To be *persona non grata* is to be without standing in the host state. The only course of action for the sending state is to replace the diplomat or, if a candidate for a diplomatic post is involved, to nominate another individual. When one state's diplomatic agent is proclaimed *persona non grata*, it is common for that state to reciprocate in kind by singling out one of the other state's agents for similar treatment. Since it is an attribute of sovereignty for a state to be free to determine who is or is not acceptable to it, no reason need be given for proclaiming a diplomatic agent *persona non grata.*

Political Offense   (142)

An act committed for a political purpose or from a political motive. The action may be a mix of a politically motivated but criminally implemented act, or it may be more narrowly political, or indeed be simply an attempt to escape the political system or discriminatory persecution. *See also* ASYLUM: POLITICAL (TERRITORIAL), 107; EXTRADITION, 120.

Significance   Defining a political offense is difficult because of the subjective nature of the offense, the political climate between parties concerned, and the general values held by the international community at a point in time. Without objective criteria upon which to base a judgment, each case must be viewed independently. An early case that attempted to distinguish political offense from a mere criminal act and remains instructive is that of *In re Castioni* (Great Britain, Queen's Bench Division, 1890), in which the Court denied a Swiss extradition request for a Swiss national involved in a local uprising on the grounds that the act was political, since there had been an open struggle for power, the fugitive was a member of the rebelling party engaged in the political activity, and the rebellion was part of a political movement between two contending groups. The subject of "relative" political crimes (*délits complexes*) clouds the picture, with incidents where the actions are criminal, e.g., arson, murder, robbery, but the motives could be interpreted as political. In the case of *In re Kavic, Bjelanovic and Arsenijevic* (Swiss Federal Tribunal, 1952), the Court held that air hijacking and jeopardy of passengers and crew, while criminal acts, were done for the purpose of escaping to freedom from a communist state and was, therefore, sufficient reason to determine the crime to be relatively political. More liberal than this is the case of *In re Ktir v. The Federal Public Prosecutor* (Swiss Supreme Federal Court, 1961) in which the Court ruled that murder is a political crime if it is "designed to further a higher interest and to attain a political aim." Broadly speaking, therefore, a political crime is one that is politically motivated and has a political purpose. The intent or motive, rather than the nature of the act, becomes the guide for determining the outcome, as does the nature of the state involved. In many cases, there will have been no crime committed at all, simply an attempt to escape persecution in one's country.

Sovereign (State) Immunity   **(143)**

The principle that a state, its agents, and its property are immune from the judicial process of another state. Until the twentieth century, states leaned in the direction of absolute immunity from state action, but as more commercial and other activities classified as private were undertaken by the state in the twentieth century, the need to separate state actions from actions that a private person could perform became apparent. Some states, especially socialist systems, still hold to the classical absolute theory of sovereign immunity. But the modern position separates state actions connected with official, public activities (known as *jure imperii*) from those state actions which are commercial, economic, or private activities (*jure gestionis*). *See also* DIPLOMATIC PRIVILEGES AND IMMUNITIES, 117; VIENNA CONVENTION ON DIPLOMATIC RELATIONS (1961), 148.

Significance   Since all states are legally equal and are independent in dealing with one another, no state may impose its authority or extend its jurisdiction upon another without the approval of the state itself through its waiver of immunity. With the expansion of contacts among states through the commercial and transportation revolution of the nineteenth century and the emergence of socialized economies, the interpretation of the nature and extent of state sovereignty has become an issue. In the practice of several European civil law states, the distinction between public and private acts by governments became common and restrictive immunity more popular. The choice by states as to absolute or restrictive immunity can result from their socioeconomic system or their legal tradition. Communist states uniformly subscribe to the absolute theory of state sovereignty, given that their commercial enterprises are state owned and all economic activity is centrally controlled by the state. Absolute immunity also has a long tradition in Anglo-American law. With the appearance of the "Tate letter" in 1952 (a statement of the acting legal advisor of the U.S. Department of State outlining the U.S. position on sovereign immunity), the United States announced its decision to follow those European states that had adopted the restrictive theory and later incorporated this position in the Sovereign Immunities Act of 1976. Among this latter group of states, there is some difficulty in distinguishing between acts *jure imperii* and *jure gestionis*. Some look to the nature of the acts while others look to their final purpose. Distinguishing between public and private acts and public and commercial acts is not always clear and practice varies among states, particularly in contrasting common law and civil law countries. In the influential American court case of *Victory Transport, Inc. v. Comisaria General de Abastecimientos y Transportes*, 336 F.2d 354 (1964), the Court of Appeals, Second Circuit listed those acts that are held to be clearly within a state's public domain: (1) internal administrative acts; (2) legislative acts; (3) acts concerning the armed forces; (4) acts concerning diplomatic activity; and (5) public loans. In 1976, the United States Congress passed the Foreign Sovereign Immunities Act, which became effective in 1977. The act transferred immunity decisions from the Department of State to the courts, reaffirmed the restrictive immunity outlined in the Tate letter (*viz.*, only public official acts would be included in the theory of sovereign immunity, not commercial or private acts), outlined processing procedures for lawsuits against foreign sovereigns, and gave U.S. citizens means of judgment against another state.

Sovereign Immunity: Waiver of Immunity   (144)

The requirement that, in order for a state to submit to the jurisdiction of a foreign court, that state must waive its immunity from the jurisdiction of the other state. Such waiver of immunity applies to such state agents as the head of state, diplomatic agents, and those persons and organizations engaged in actions labeled *jure imperii* (official state actions, as opposed to commercial or other private actions).

Significance   Waiver of immunity is required as a consequence of state sovereignty and the consequent freedom of the state from control or accountability by or to other states. The Vienna Convention on Diplomatic Relations (1961) is quite clear on the procedural matters of waiver of immunity for diplomatic personnel. Such waiver must be expressed; that is, the government must indicate that immunity has been waived for its agent. The mere appearance of the agent in a court can no longer imply that immunity has been waived. Once immunity is waived, the agent is open to counterclaims arising from the same action and cannot reinvoke immunity in such cases. Nor is the agent immune from the appeals process in the case at issue. It should be noted that waiver of immunity from jurisdiction does not imply waiver of immunity from the court's decision. In Anglo-American practice, for example, consent to waiver of state immunity does not imply consent to have state property attached or seized in executing judgment. This is a separate action required before judgment can be carried out.

Statelessness   (145)

A situation in which an individual is not recognized by any state as one of its nationals. Statelessness may result (1) from dislocations caused by war, revolution, or other political reasons (statelessness *de facto*); or (2) from a conflict of nationality laws, by some act of denationalization undertaken by a government against some of its citizens, or by an individual act of expatriation which is not followed by the acquisition of a new allegiance (statelessness *de jure*). *See also* CONVENTION ON THE REDUCTION OF STATELESSNESS (1961), 111; NANSEN PASSPORT, 134; NATIONALITY: INDIVIDUALS, 137.

Significance   Statelessness means that a person has no legal claim to protection from any country. The international and human problems of statelessness and of refugees have been of particular concern to the United Nations General Assembly, the Economic and Social Council, the International Law Commission, and the Office of the High Commissioner for Refugees. In 1961, the United Nations General Assembly opened for signature a Convention on the Reduction of Statelessness that establishes circumstances under which a country could be required to grant nationality to stateless individuals.

Status of Forces Agreement   (146)

A treaty defining the host state's jurisdiction over foreign military forces present upon its soil which belong to the other contracting state. Status of forces agreements normally provide for exclusive jurisdiction by the contracting state over its own military personnel in instances where its military law has been violated (e.g., disobeying orders or desertion) and the offense is not a crime against the laws of the host country, and for the exclusive jurisdiction by the host state for violations of its laws that are not an offense in the other state. In cases where the offense violates the laws of both states, the agreements provide for some form of concurrent jurisdiction. In these cases, determination of primary jurisdiction becomes important. If the act is an offense against persons and property of the sending state or occurred in the line of duty, then the sending state has primary jurisdiction. While at one time U.S. status of forces agreements included civilians and military dependents, today such individuals are subject to the jurisdiction of the host state. At present, the United States has more than twenty such agreements in force. *See also* JURISDICTION: NATIONALITY PRINCIPLE, 127; JURISDICTION: TERRITORIALITY PRINCIPLE, 130.

Significance   Bilateral and multilateral status of forces agreements are a response to the problem of the permanent presence of military forces in another country during peacetime. Historically, military forces were present in other states during war, or foreign ships would call upon a port for friendly visits and revictualing. Traditionally, military forces were subject to the law of their state, and violations of law were prosecuted by that state, although there were those who argued for local jurisdiction or the need to waive local jurisdiction. Any concept of extraterritoriality was clearly unacceptable to those states that would be hosting large contingents of foreign troops on their soil for extended periods during peacetime. Status of forces agreements became the means of linking the jurisdiction of the host state and the state whose forces are on its soil. The rather large realm of concurrent jurisdiction results in jurisdictional disputes, and their settlement is often based upon political considerations involving local sensitivities rather than technical merit or legal issues.

Vienna Convention on Consular Relations (1963)   (147)

The product of a United Nations conference attended by ninety-two states in 1963 at Vienna, called to codify the norms pertaining to consular functions, privileges, and immunities, and based upon a draft prepared by the International Law Commission (ILC). The Vienna Convention outlines the immunities to be accorded consular officials, including freedom from arrest until trial (except for grave offenses) and from imprisonment until final judgment by the court; freedom of travel and communication; free access to the consul's nationals held in the jails of the host country; and immunity from jurisdiction in cases arising from the consul's performance of official duties. In addition, the consular premises are inviolable as are its archives and documents. The Convention entered into force in 1967. *See also* CONSULAR PRIVILEGES AND IMMUNITIES, 110.

Significance   The Vienna Convention on Consular Relations is the first global multinational agreement to establish norms governing the status, privileges, and immunities of consular officials. Prior to the Convention, such norms were the product of municipal legislation, bilateral treaties, and such regional agreements as the Havana Convention on Consular Agents (1928). The only universal norms were customary practices guaranteeing the inviolability of consular archives and official correspondence and the exemption of the official from local jurisdiction in certain types of cases.

Vienna Convention on Diplomatic Relations (1961)   (148)

The product of a United Nations conference of 81 states at Vienna in 1961 called to codify the norms pertaining to diplomatic relations; namely, diplomatic functions, accreditation, *agrément,* classes of heads of missions, precedence, breaking off of diplomatic relations, and similar matters. The Convention is based upon a draft prepared by the International Law Commission (ILC). The codification efforts of the conference were successful because the final product in general reflected the customary norms and established practices of states, although in certain areas the Convention establishes new, more restrictive rules pertaining to diplomatic immunities. While diplomats and their families retain the traditional immunity from criminal and civil jurisdiction of the receiving state, they do not retain such immunity from actions arising from professional or commercial activity outside of their official duties. Administrative and technical staff no longer have similar full immunities but are immune from criminal jurisdiction of the receiving state and from civil jurisdiction only for official actions. The service staff's immunity has been even further constrained to grant the receiving state both criminal and civil jurisdiction for acts of an unofficial nature. Further matters covered include inviolability of the premises of the mission (including furnishing, property, vehicles, and documents); exemption from various forms of taxation; conditions of movement and travel; communications and correspondence; customs duties; household goods; and diplomatic transit through third states, among others. The Convention entered into force in 1964. Over 130 states are signatory to the Convention. *See also* DIPLOMATIC PRIVILEGES AND IMMUNITIES, 117.

Significance   Prior to the Vienna Convention, diplomatic law and especially diplomatic privileges and immunities were based upon custom as well as contained in bilateral treaties and municipal statutes. Nor were the customary rules uniform in state practice. Diplomatic ranks and precedence were established by the Congress of Vienna (1815) and the Conference of Aix-la-Chappelle (1818). In addition, the Sixth International Conference of American States in 1928 drafted a convention on diplomatic privileges and immunities that had the effect of regional international law. The Vienna Convention compiles and delineates these norms, making them clearer and less subject to state interpretation. In particular, the Convention attempts to bridge the gap between those states that hold to inclusive diplomatic immunity versus those that define immunities in relation to official versus unofficial acts. It also elevates the exemption from customs duties from the realm of comity (friendly gestures) to that of law. It should be noted that those portions of the Convention that codify customary practices are also binding upon nonsignatory states, since custom is a source of international law. At the same time, the Convention clearly states that customary international norms remain applicable in instances not covered by the Convention; but, in general, the Convention reflects current international norms on the subject.

Vienna Convention on the Representation of States   (149)
in Their Relations with International Organizations
of a Universal Character (1975)

Patterned after the Vienna Convention on Diplomatic Relations (1961) and the work of the International Law Commission (ILC), the Convention covers the missions that states send to international organizations and delegations to special conferences called by such organizations. Such missions and delegations are granted the same immunities as diplomatic personnel under the 1961 Convention; indeed, the immunities provided are more inclusive as they provide more liberal immunities to service and private staff than those provided under the 1961 Convention.

Significance   Prior to the Vienna Convention on the Representation of States in Their Relations with International Organizations of a Universal Character, conventions dealt with the status of international organizations themselves, but the privileges and immunities of diplomatic missions were the result of treaties and arrangements with the host state as opposed to being based on customary law. The 1975 Convention fills this gap, although it has received criticism from some quarters for being too inclusive by slighting the special problems of the host state which result from the exceedingly liberal immunities provided by the Convention.

5. Treatment of Aliens

Alien (150)

An individual who is not a citizen or a national (in international law and diplomacy terminology) of the state in which he or she is located. Aliens are usually classified as either resident aliens (domiciled in the host country) or transient aliens (temporarily in the host country on business, travel, study, etc.). States are under no obligation to admit aliens nor, should they elect to do so, must they be nondiscriminatory in their admission policy. States may require entry visas from aliens, but many states waive them for transient aliens, usually on a basis of state reciprocity. Subject to the minimum international standard of justice, aliens are to be extended legal protection comparable to citizens of the host state, subject to any limitations concerning ownership of property or contractual rights. They will usually not be extended political rights (voting, holding public office, access to government jobs, etc.). In return for such protection and rights, aliens must obey local laws, pay taxes, and in some states are liable to military service. (In the last case, their international legal position is not entirely clear.) The activities of aliens can be regulated by such means as requiring periodic notification of domicile to proper government authorities or having restrictions placed upon their economic activities, travel in the host country, or exercise of their profession. Aliens may be expelled or deported from the host state as the state sees fit, based upon its municipal law. *See also* MINIMUM INTERNATIONAL STANDARD OF JUSTICE, 167; NATIONAL TREATMENT, 169.

Significance Aliens have always been a subject of great concern in international law and increasingly so in this century as a result of the revolution in travel and demographic migration, the dislocation of peoples as a consequence of war and revolution, and the increasing economic interdependence, foreign investment, and presence of multinational companies in other states. Discriminatory immigration practices, job restrictions, regulations governing ownership of property, expropriation and nationalization, and ill-treatment of aliens by citizens are common irritants to peaceful relations between states. As a rule, however, aliens are extended traditional rights and protections so that the state's nationals abroad are properly treated. Efforts to codify international norms have not been very successful, with the exception of the American Republics' Havana Convention on the Status of Aliens (1928) of which fifteen American states, including the United States, are parties.

Calvo Clause   (151)

A clause in public contracts with aliens requiring that disputes arising from a contract be settled solely by local remedies. By agreeing to a contract containing the Calvo Clause, aliens waive their right of appeal to their government for espousal of their claim and agree to be treated as a national of the host country. What distinguishes the Calvo Clause from the rule of the exhaustion of local remedies is exclusion of diplomatic protection by the alien's state after the local remedies have been exhausted. Named after the renowned Argentine jurist, historian, and diplomat of the nineteenth century, Carlos Calvo, it has received mixed reviews before courts and tribunals. In recent decades, it has been less frequently the central issue in cases concerning contract disputes with governments. The Calvo Clause must not be confused with the Calvo Doctrine, which deals with state responsibility for acts against aliens by nationals of that state. *See also* NATIONAL TREATMENT, 169.

Significance   The Calvo Clause illustrates the conflict between a state's ties to its nationals abroad (the nationality principle) and a state's sovereignty over its territory (the territorial principle). The clause has been widely supported by Latin American and Third World states as testimony to the sovereign equality of states. To them, foreign interjection in their domestic processes is a form of neocolonialism. Critics of the Calvo Clause point out that, while aliens can agree to such a stipulation, they cannot waive their government's right to interpose on behalf of citizens since the right to protect its nationals is a governmental rather than a private right. Such was the opinion of the Commission in the *Mexican Union Railway (Ltd.)* case (Great Britain–Mexico Claims Commission, 1929–1930) when it affirmed that "no person can, by such a clause, deprive the Government of his country of its undoubted right to apply international remedies to violations of international law committed to his hurt." Calvo Clauses have virtually disappeared from contracts between Latin American states and foreign nationals.

Calvo Doctrine (152)

The proposition that a state cannot be responsible for acts of insurrectionists against aliens or, more broadly, for any damages resulting from domestic uprisings, mob violence or revolutions, irrespective of whether or not the state took all reasonable measures to protect the aliens. The Calvo Doctrine was espoused by Carlos Calvo of Argentina on the grounds that the disruption caused by revolutions or other domestic upheavals affects nationals as well as aliens, and the latter are not entitled to greater protection than a state's nationals. *See also* DUE DILIGENCE, 159; NATIONAL TREATMENT, 169.

Significance   The Calvo Doctrine illustrates the position of those states that hold mob violence or insurrections as a matter of *force majeure*—actions for which the state cannot be held responsible. Whether a state can be held responsible for actions of mob violence or insurrections is a matter of much controversy, but the Calvo Doctrine cannot be regarded as a principle of universal international law. At best, it is a reflection of Latin American regional international law. The general principle held by the United States is that the responsibility of governments for acts of insurgents or mobs depends upon the failure of the government to exercise due diligence when it knows of the likelihood of the event or is in a position to affect the outcome. Conversely, should an insurgency prove successful, then the new government can be held responsible for its past actions.

Capitulations (153)

The once practiced granting of certain privileges to nonnationals, used in reference to Christians in states under Muslim rule and in countries of the Orient. Capitulations were a form of extraterritoriality that exempted or limited local jurisdiction over aliens. The term is derived from the agreements formulated between European states and the Levantine rulers of Egypt, Turkey, and Persia (Iran), which were arranged by chapters (*capituli*).

Significance   Capitulations are now of historical interest only. They were necessitated by the commercial revolution in Europe where European powers confronted cultures and politico-legal-religious systems dissimilar to theirs. The practice had its origins in medieval

Europe when it was common for foreign traders to be domiciled in a particular portion of the town and be subject to their own laws. While the practice died out with the emergence of the concept of territorial sovereignty in Europe, it was retained in other regions. In Moslem countries, restrictions upon host state jurisdiction over Europeans resulted from the nonapplicability of Islamic law to those of other faiths and, therefore, the need to employ European law in regulating alien activities in the European trading centers in the Levant. While today this seems surprising, in that period it was commonly held that individuals' laws went with them beyond the limits of their state. While non-European capitulations originated in Asia Minor, the practice became more universal in the period of imperialism in the form of extraterritoriality, which was imposed upon Japan, China, and several other oriental countries. While originally a means of providing for justice in those cases where law was religiously based and inapplicable to nonbelievers, it became an instrument of dominance and abuse in its extraterritorial form. The practice was not completely abolished until the post–World War I period when extraterritorial arrangements with such states as Persia (Iran), Turkey, and China were terminated.

Charter of Economic Rights and Duties of States   (154) (1974)

A resolution adopted by the United Nations General Assembly in 1974 (with the opposition of a half a dozen of the developed states, including the United States), which sets forth the Third World's perceived proper international economic relationships. The Charter of Economic Rights and Duties of States was prepared by the United Nations Conference on Trade and Development (UNCTAD). Subjects covered within the Charter include *inter alia* (1) the regulation of transnational corporations operating within the state; (2) nondiscrimination in international trade; (3) the right to create producers organizations; (4) the obligation of developed states to take into consideration the interests of developing states in economic cooperation and development (including technology transfer); (5) treatment of alien property and foreign investments; and (6) a reiteration of the principle that every state has full sovereignty over its wealth, natural resources, and economic activity. As a resolution of the United Nations General Assembly, the Charter has no legally binding force.

Significance   The Charter of Economic Rights and Duties of States was in effect a proclamation by the developing states in their campaign to create a New International Economic Order (NIEO). Particularly important is Article 2 of the Charter, which proclaims the right of every state to nationalize or expropriate private property, provided that appropriate compensation is paid. No detailed definition of appropriate is made and, indeed, the provision is further confused by the caveat that the state take into account its laws, regulations, and all circumstances that it considers pertinent. Furthermore, in any question of compensation, the matter will be settled under the domestic law of the nationalizing state unless other means are agreed upon by the states involved. While the Charter does not explicitly refute the traditional assumptions about expropriation, neither does it clarify this very unsettled area of international law.

Claims Commission (155)

A type of arbitral tribunal formed to hear a claim or series of claims of similar nature between states and nationals of other states. A claims commission can operate on a case-by-case basis and make individual awards or can make a lump sum award for a category of claims. Claims commissions became popular by the middle of the nineteenth century and, in the course of the next hundred years or so, over sixty such arrangements have been formulated through agreements by affected states.

Significance   Claims commissions are often established to consider an accumulation of incidents affecting the normal relations between two states and dispatch them quickly rather than each seeking its remedy through a variety of forums and tribunals. Such a technique was frequently used in U.S.-Mexican relations, with claims commissions established in 1839, 1848, 1868, and 1923. A claims commission handled Venezuelan claims involving some ten states in 1903, and the United States and Great Britain handled disagreements by claims commissions in 1853, 1871, and 1908. Today, the United States has a permanent Foreign Claims Settlement Commission, which is a national commission. Established in 1955 through the amending of the 1949 International Claims Settlement Act, this Commission decides on the merits of cases before presenting them to foreign governments. Lump sum settlements with a foreign state are then distributed to each claimant. While the Commission has the potential for greater efficiency, foreign governments have cause for concern that it is biased toward claimants rather than giving equal weight to the position of the foreign state. Great Britain has a comparable commission, the Foreign Compensation Commission.

Convention on the Settlement of Investment   (156)
Disputes between States and Nationals of Other
States (1965)
An international agreement concluded in 1965 and in force in 1966
that created, at the suggestion and approval of the World Bank (International Bank for Reconstruction and Development [IBRD]), an International Center for the Settlement of Investment Disputes. The
Center is located in the World Bank and handles disputes relating to
investments between states and nationals of other states, upon the
consent of the parties involved. Panels of individuals qualified to serve
as arbitrators or conciliators are maintained by the Center, and disputants can select from such individuals, providing they are signatories to
the Convention. *See also* EXPROPRIATION, 162; EXPROPRIATION OF CON-
TRACTUAL RIGHTS, 163.

Significance   The Convention on the Settlement of Investment Disputes between States and Nationals of Other States was a response to
the increasing incidence of expropriation of alien property by newly
independent and other developing states, and investment disputes
taking place in the postwar decolonization process. The arbitral process of the Center for the Settlement of Investment Disputes is similar
to that of other tribunals in that once the parties agree to take their
dispute before it, they are bound by that agreement and by the decision
of the Center's arbitration panel. The parties agree upon the rules of
law that are to apply in the proceedings and, in the absence of such an
agreement, the panel applies the law of the contracting state and
pertinent international norms. Thus far few disputes have found their
way before the Center for resolution, but more than eighty states were
parties to the Convention as of 1984, including the communist states of
Romania and Yugoslavia.

Denial of Justice   (157)
An action by a state that denies or obstructs an alien's access to local
courts, constitutes deficiencies of the administrative or remedial process, or represents discriminatory or unjust judgment by a local court.
Denial of justice entails international responsibility of the state. Technical error by a court, however, would not constitute a denial of justice
unless it produced a gross injustice to the alien. Aliens are subject to the
laws of the state in which they are present and must utilize that state's
judicial machinery if injured. An alien must exhaust all local remedies
in seeking rectification for injury or wrong and the state is obligated to
give the alien access to local remedies. *See also* EXHAUSTION OF LOCAL
REMEDIES, 161.

Significance   Denial of justice, as defined, should be viewed as illustrative rather than definitive, as there is no agreed upon international standard. The term is used alternately to mean any action that violates international law, failure to provide a remedy for a wrong, failure to apprehend the party or parties guilty of the wrong, or treatment of an alien that deviates from normal substantive or procedural law of the state. Latin American and generally Third World states interpret denial of justice very restrictively, limiting it to questions of access to local courts. This is known as the procedural view of denial of justice. To go any further, they argue, is to allow other states to judge the validity of their municipal law and the quality and effectiveness of their administrative and judicial processes. In a broader sense, such states contend that an alien casts his or her lot with the state's nationals and accepts local laws and procedures. The traditional European outlook is more inclusive and liberal, as it is based upon concepts of minimal international standards and illegality of discriminatory treatment, including violation of international legal standards by corruption of the court, intimidation of alien or witnesses, or manifestly unjust judgment. This inclusive view is reflected in the *El Triunfo Company* case (United States–El Salvador Special Arbitration Tribunal, 1902) where the issue concerned the enactment of executive decrees that cancelled contracts. The Tribunal ruled that denial of justice was not limited solely to courts, but rather included actions by other government organs as well.

Drago Doctrine (158)

The proposition that states cannot use force in the recovery of debts incurred by other states. The Drago Doctrine holds that a state's defaulting on its public debt owed to aliens or another state does not give that state the right to intervene militarily to collect that debt. The Doctrine is named after Luis María Drago, an Argentine foreign minister, diplomat, lawyer, and international arbiter, who formulated the proposition in 1902 as a consequence of the British-German-Italian naval blockade of Venezuela defaulted on its debt.

Significance   The Drago Doctrine received immediate support from various quarters, including the United States (as a corollary to the Monroe Doctrine) and the rest of the Latin American states. The Second Hague Conference in 1907 dealt with the issue and the result was Hague Convention II Respecting the Limitation of the Employment of Force for the Recovery of Contracts Debts, the so-called Porter Convention, which affirmed the principles embodied in the Drago Doctrine with the important stipulation that nonintervention need not apply in those instances in which the state refuses to negotiate or abide by an arbitral decision. Ironically, the absence of state intervention for the recovery of debts in the present era of massive indebtedness of many—especially Third World—states has less to do with the Drago Doctrine than it does with superpower competition and the nuclear age, the cost of military intervention, the proliferation of sophisticated military equipment through arms sales to debtor states, disrepute of imperialism, and the legal prohibitions against intervention and aggression. States rely instead upon diplomatic suasion and such economic measures as resort to the International Monetary Fund (IMF), refinancing of debts, and trade arrangements to resolve debt burdens and the threat of repudiation of debts.

Due Diligence (159)

The obligation of a state to exercise reasonable effort to protect aliens and their property, once the state has decided to allow them to enter the country or carry on commercial activities. A concept borrowed from civil law, due diligence takes both a positive form (such as insuring that aliens are not wronged by government agencies) and a negative form (protection of aliens against wrongful acts by private citizens). A wrong requires the state to apprehend and punish the guilty party. If there is a failure or lack of due diligence, the state is held responsible and liable for making compensation for injury to the alien or to the alien's estate. *See also* CALVO DOCTRINE, 152; STATE RESPONSIBILITY, 77; STATE RESPONSIBILITY, DRAFT ARTICLES ON, 78.

Significance   Due diligence is not synonymous with absolute protection. Just as a state cannot guarantee absolute protection to its nationals, it is not expected to guarantee it to aliens. However, due diligence does mean that a state should exercise prudence and make a reasonable effort to safeguard the lives and property of aliens, just as it would in regard to its own nationals. In the *Home Missionary Society* case (United States–Great Britain Claims Arbitration, 1920) for example, the Tribunal held that while the imposition of a hut tax upon the natives of Sierra Leone sparked a revolt in which several missionaries were killed and much property of the American religious group was destroyed, the British authorities had no advance indication that such an action would produce such a result and, once the revolt had begun, made every immediate effort to put down the revolt. Consequently, the Tribunal concluded that there was no lack of due diligence on the part of the British authorities in Sierra Leone.

Espousal of Claim   (160)

The injection of a state into the quest by one of its citizens for redress of grievances allegedly committed by another state in whose territory the injury occurred. The alien must exhaust all local remedies available in that state and there must still be a denial of justice before the alien can petition his or her government to represent ("espouse") their claim before the other state. Espousal of a national's claim can take several forms, including normal diplomatic channels possibly followed by the creation of an arbitral tribunal or, in the case of numerous grievances between the two states, the creation of a mixed claims commission to handle all the claims. *See also* DENIAL OF JUSTICE, 157; EXHAUSTION OF LOCAL REMEDIES, 161.

Significance   Espousal of claim is a sensitive area, as it involves a state in the domestic affairs of another state and, consequently, is a form of intervention. It derives from the basic principle that a state has a right to protect its subjects and, when they are injured by actions of other states that are contrary to international law, the state is only seeking to ensure that legal norms are respected by taking up the cause of its nationals.

Exhaustion of Local Remedies   (161)

A well-established rule of customary international law that when an alien (individual or company) has been wronged, all local court remedies available to the injured party in the host country must be exhausted before the alien can appeal to his or her government to intervene and "espouse" their claim in instances where there is evidence of such a denial of justice. Local remedies generally entail the use of local courts and, should access to them be denied to the injured alien, a case of denial of justice can be made. Local remedies need not be exhausted if it is obviously futile to have to resort to them or if it is clear that the local courts will not provide redress. The rule of local remedies therefore serves two functions: (1) it is the means of achieving redress for grievances; and (2) should such be denied, is the basis for state responsibility. There is no need to exhaust local remedies when the injury was inflicted directly upon a state organ or its property. *See also* DENIAL OF JUSTICE, 157; ESPOUSAL OF CLAIM, 160.

Significance   Exhaustion of local remedies is a reasonable requirement. It is founded upon the principle of state sovereignty and the state's exclusive territorial jurisdiction, whereby aliens are subject to the laws of the state in which they are located. Were it otherwise, the alien would have a privileged status in that country. The emphasis upon local remedies allows the state to settle the problem and abide by its international legal obligations. Most claims by aliens are handled without difficulty by due process in the courts of the host state; the problems are usually minor issues of little or no interest to the alien's government. Furthermore, states dislike intervening in another state's domestic affairs as it encourages reciprocal intervention. While refusing an alien access to the local courts would constitute denial of justice (as would discriminatory expropriation legislation or other legislation which could not be refuted in the local courts), an adverse ruling in a local court would be much more difficult to prove as a denial of justice.

Expropriation   (162)

The seizure of foreign-held property and transfer of ownership to the expropriating state or third parties. Expropriation is not prohibited *per se* in international law, but the conditions under which it is acceptable are disputed. The traditional view holds that to be acceptable, expropriation must be neither discriminatory nor retaliatory, and just compensation must be made, meaning prompt, adequate, and effective compensation. Furthermore, expropriation must be for a public purpose (not contravene a treaty) and take place according to due process of law. If such conditions are not met, then the action of expropriation is often called "confiscation." Expropriation should not be confused with nationalization. Nationalization differs from expropriation in that the compulsory transfer affects both nationals and aliens and encompasses classes of property rather than specific properties, i.e., the nationalization of a state's rail system rather than the expropriation of a specific railroad. It is similar to expropriation in that the nationalization must be for a public purpose and compensation provided. *See also* CONVENTION ON THE SETTLEMENT OF INVESTMENT DISPUTES BETWEEN STATES AND NATIONALS OF OTHER STATES (1965), 156; INVESTMENT PROTECTION, 166; MINIMUM INTERNATIONAL STANDARD OF JUSTICE, 167; NATIONAL TREATMENT, 169; REPARATION, 73.

Significance   In this century, expropriation has become not only a major legal concern but an economic and political concern as well. Many developing states and socialist-based revolutions have used it as a tool to counter neocolonialism in the form of foreign investment. There is a wide range of opinion as to the validity of expropriation and the criteria contained in the traditional view as outlined. Nor are the definitions of just, adequate, and effective compensation agreed upon or what constitutes the public good. What is agreed upon is the realization that expropriation has an adverse effect upon the flow of investment capital to the Third World. Most states do agree that some form of compensation is obligatory, but many argue that the obligation extends only to the level of compensation the state provides to its own nationals. Even communist states have in some cases paid at least token compensation. Beyond that, little is firmly established and the practice is not consistent. Many developing states simply cannot meet the hope of full and prompt compensation, and any attempt to do so could adversely affect domestic social programs and national security concerns. As a consequence of such dilemmas, today more consideration is being given to a state's capacity to pay rather than the technical value of the property in question. Furthermore, it is widely held that there are situations in which there is no obligation to provide compensation. These would include cases provided for by treaty; in response to criminal acts, tax arrears, or debts; or reprisals in kind. Expropriation can take forms other than the confiscation of property, such as requiring special permits of foreign companies, imposing discriminatory taxes, placing ceilings upon profits which a foreign company can generate, imposing currency restrictions, or devaluing the local currency. Such subtle actions are examples of what is often referred to as "creeping" or "disguised" expropriation. In order to avoid the disruption of peaceful interstate relations that expropriation causes, many states sign bilateral treaties for the protection of foreign investment that prohibit discriminatory or improper measures against the other state's nationals.

Expropriation of Contractual Rights (163)

The confiscation or negation by the state of acquired rights other than property such as concessions, contracts, licenses, or investments, granted to an alien by the state. Should a breach of contract or denial of justice involve an abuse of a state's governmental power, it gives substance to the alien's request for the diplomatic protection of his or her state. Contractual rights often involve the extraction of minerals or other natural resources, the operation of transportation systems or public utilities, or the state obligation attached to public bonds. *See also* CONVENTION ON THE SETTLEMENT OF INVESTMENT DISPUTES BETWEEN STATES AND NATIONALS OF OTHER STATES (1965), 156; EXPROPRIATION, 162; INVESTMENT PROTECTION, 166.

Significance Expropriation of contractual rights is a more complex and difficult problem than the expropriation of alien property, because the state is a party to the contract and can alter the terms of the arrangement through its legislative powers, which makes the arrangement an imbalanced one. Expropriation of contractual rights has given rise to two schools of thought—the noninterventionist and the interventionist. The noninterventionist school holds that aliens who make contracts with foreign governments know beforehand of the risks involved in hazardous investments and accept those risks in anticipation of the profits to be made. Furthermore, a sovereign state cannot be sued without its consent. The interventionist school holds that if all local remedies have been exhausted and there still exists a denial of justice, then the alien's state can interpose on behalf of its nationals. Advocates of this school argue that a contractual agreement between a state and an alien is no less binding than a treaty and, consequently, the principle of *pacta sunt servanda* (treaties shall be observed) applies to contracts just as it does to treaties. A violation of an agreement requires restitution or compensation.

To avoid the disruptive effects of contractual expropriation, many states have entered into bilateral treaties for the protection of foreign investment in each other's country, which pledges nondiscriminatory treatment of the investment or acquired rights of the other's nationals in its territory. Some states have created national investment guarantee programs to cover nationals against the risk of foreign expropriation and encourage them to undertake activities in regions where there is a risk of expropriation. Finally, there have been attempts at multipartite agreements, such as the Draft Convention on the Protection of Foreign Property (1967) of the Organization for Economic Cooperation and Development (OECD). A major problem in cases concerning contractual disputes is the determination of which body of law is to apply to settlement efforts—the municipal law of the injured alien; the municipal law of the contracting state; international law; general principles of law; some other body of law; or a combination of legal systems? The particular system of law to apply is often stipulated in the contract in order to avoid such a problem. Usually only the municipal law of the contracting state governs the contracts; but, in recent decades, a body of opinion has emerged that advocates the creation of legal rules that would bridge national and international law in order to handle just such problems and issues. Called "transnational law" (a term coined by Philip C. Jessup), it would consist of those general principles of law common to disparate legal systems (rather like the Roman *jus gentium*) that could be applied to state contracts.

Expulsion (164)

Removal of aliens considered undesirable or a threat to the state. Just as a state is free to admit or refuse admittance to aliens, it also has the right to expel them. While each state determines conditions for expulsion, generally they involve matters of security, illegal entry, public order, or health. In time of war, on the other hand, a state can expel all enemy aliens found within its territory apart from the right to intern them. Deportation is a procedure under municipal law that is distinct from expulsion in that it refers to aliens who have entered a state in violation of its immigration law, whereas expulsion affects all and primarily legally settled aliens.

Significance   Expulsion can easily be abused. There are few international legal norms prescribing just and unjust causes of expulsion, although most authorities hold that a state should not be arbitrary in its exercise of the power of expulsion and that cause must be offered for the action. Failure in these stipulations suggests the right of the alien's state to protest. In most states, expulsion is an executive rather than a judicial action, and whether or not the alien has the right to appeal an expulsion order to a judicial authority depends upon the state's municipal process. This is derived from the nature of expulsion, which is usually viewed as an administrative action rather than a punishment. The major deterrent to extensive abuse of the power of expulsion is that of reciprocity against the state's own nationals.

Imputability   (165)

The principle whereby internationally illegal acts or omissions of an individual or group of persons, usually state organs, are attributable to the state and, thereby, involve that state's responsibility. Imputability (or "attribution") pertains to any state organ (legislative, administrative, or judicial), other state agencies, and (under certain conditions) subordinate political organs. Actions of private individuals and groups can also lead to state responsibility under certain circumstances. *See also* DENIAL OF JUSTICE, 157; STATE RESPONSIBILITY, 77; STATE RESPONSIBILITY, DRAFT ARTICLES ON, 78.

Significance   The concept of imputability is a necessity in international law since the state, which is the international person to which such law applies, is in a real sense invisible. Its agents act on its behalf and their actions are called acts of state. Conduct that is attributable or imputable to the state and that causes injury to aliens is wrongful under international law if it deviates from general international legal norms or is in violation of an international agreement. Imputability can be a problem in those instances where there is a distinction between the actions of state officials that take place in their official capacity—called "direct" or "original" responsibility—and those actions of officials that are in excess of their authority (*ultra vires*) or actions performed by private citizens, called "indirect" or "vicarious" responsibility. The

Youman's Claim (United States–Mexico General Claims Commission, 1926) is an example of imputability. Mexican troops were dispatched to protect U.S. nationals from mob violence, but rather than protect them fired upon them. Mexico was held liable as the troops were under an officer, acting as a unit, and in clear disregard of superior orders.

Investment Protection (166)

Legislative action taken by states to protect foreign investment in developing states or to encourage new or increased investment. Such stipulations protect foreign investment against expropriation or, in the case of expropriation, guarantee or insure compensation.

Significance   Investment protection legislation offered by developing states has a major drawback in that it is subject to the whims of politicians and can be amended, repealed, or selectively suspended. Therefore, a number of developing countries have supplemented their legislation with agreements with developed countries. On the other hand, developed states can employ the technique to encourage overseas investment by their nationals. Investment protection in the United States, for example, is governed by the Investment Guaranty Program administered by the Agency for International Development (AID). The Program offers three types of coverage: (1) specific risk insurance against inconvertibility of foreign currencies into U.S. dollars, expropriation or confiscation, and the effects of civil wars or revolutions; (2) extended risk insurance to cover development projects; and (3) protection against extended risk in specified regions. Other developed states, such as Japan, the Federal Republic of Germany, and Switzerland have comparable programs.

Minimum International Standard of Justice (167)

The principle that a state must accord an alien at least a minimal standard of treatment befitting a civilized nation, even if this treatment exceeds that accorded nationals of the state. While no clear definition of conduct befitting a civilized nation is universally accepted, that provided by the Tribunal in the *Neer Claim* (United States–Mexico General Claims Commission, 1926) is instructive. Conduct falling below a minimum acceptable standard is that which would amount to an "outrage, to bad faith, to willful neglect of duty, or to an insufficiency of governmental action so far short of international standards that every reasonable and impartial man would readily recognize its insufficiency." *See also* EXPROPRIATION, 162; NATIONAL TREATMENT, 169; STATE RESPONSIBILITY, DRAFT ARTICLES ON, 78.

Significance   There is considerable variance among states as to what constitutes a minimum international standard of justice. Among both communist and Third World states, the view commonly shared is that aliens are to be accorded the same treatment as nationals—no more, no less. This is known as the equality of treatment doctrine or the rule of national treatment, first upheld by the Latin American countries in the nineteenth century. In contrast, Western governments contend that aliens must be accorded a minimum international standard, regardless of how a state treats its nationals. In this view, there may occur instances in which an alien must receive better treatment than a state's own nationals. At the 1930 Hague Conference for the Codification of International Law, the international standard position was narrowly upheld. With the large increase in Third World states, it is highly unlikely that a similar outcome would occur today. Third World states charge that the minimum international standard serves as a cloak for special status for aliens, protection of foreign investments, and justification for foreign intervention in their domestic affairs. In such a view, it is neocolonialism disguised as a legal norm. The other side of the coin is that the torture and killing of aliens is not excusable simply because the state does that to its own nationals, just as one does not expect that a state should grant aliens the right to vote or hold public office simply because nationals do these things. About all that can be said with reasonable confidence is that excessive severity in punishing violations of law and order by a state—such as maiming, harsh punishment for a trivial offense, punishment without trial, excessive delay in the administration of justice, and the like—would generally be recognized as forming part of the principle of the minimum international standard. However, in many other areas, such as compensation for expropriation of aliens' property or expulsion, the content of this standard is very controversial.

Nationality of Claim (168)

The rule that before a claim based on denial of justice, lack of due diligence, or improper expropriation of property of aliens will result in the interposition of the alien's state on his or her behalf (espousal of claim), the nationality of the claimant must be determined. This is necessary because, in general, a state will represent only its own nationals. (Exceptions include aliens serving in the armed forces of the state or serving on the state's merchant vessels.) For most individuals this is a simple matter since they possess a single nationality. But some individuals possess dual nationality through birth or marriage. Others have been expatriated or naturalized in another country. Should individuals be stateless, then no state can claim on their behalf. The existence of the bond of nationality between the person injured and the state must, for purposes of presenting the claim before an international tribunal, continue from the time of injury until the date of the tribunal's judgment (award). *See also* NATIONALITY: INDIVIDUALS, 137.

Significance   Nationality of claims can present problems in determining exactly what nationality is possessed by the claimant. There is no single rule governing nationality in cases of conflict, and one must generally look to treaties and municipal law for guidance in instances where nationality is in dispute. The fundamental test is to establish a linkage between the claimant and the state. In the case of individuals, the *Nottebohm* case (International Court of Justice, 1955), although certainly not binding as a precedent and much criticized, is instructive. Nottebohm was a German national who owned land in Guatemala. Fearing that his German nationality might result in his holdings being seized should Guatemala enter World War II against Nazi Germany, he acquired Liechtenstein nationality while on a short visit with his brother in that state in 1939, thereby losing his German nationality under the then applicable German law. Subsequently, Guatemala declared war on Germany, Nottebohm's property was seized, and he was interned on the grounds of being a German national. Liechtenstein interposed on his behalf, claiming that he was a national of Liechtenstein. The Court held that there must be a "genuine link" between the individual and the state and that Nottebohm's acquisition of Liechtenstein nationality was for convenience, as he had no intention of taking up residence in that state. Therefore, Nottebohm's naturalization was not sufficient to establish Liechtenstein's right to bring a claim on his behalf.

Should the individual have dual nationality, the issue is more complex. Generally, the state having primary control over the individual will have primary authority. In the case of corporations, it is even more complex. The basic test is where the entity was incorporated and had its registered office, but there are other tests that "pierce the corporate veil." These tests include determining the nationality of the majority of the shareholders; determining the nationality of the board of directors; the state in which the corporation is physically located; and the state in which the corporation conducts most of its business. In the *Barcelona Traction* case (International Court of Justice, 1970), the Belgian government attempted to bring claim against Spain for losses incurred by the Barcelona Traction, Light, and Power Company on the grounds that while the company was incorporated in Canada, the bulk of its shareholders (88 percent) were Belgian and, therefore, the company was really Belgian. The Court rejected the Belgian contention, noting that the company had maintained its offices, shares, accounts, board meetings, and tax receipts in Canada for more than fifty years and had disclosed from the onset of its incorporation that its activities were geared for business outside of Canada.

National Treatment (169)

The view that aliens cast their lot with the nationals of the country in which the alien is located. National treatment means that the alien will receive the same treatment as the state's nationals, rather than be extended special treatment or status. The national treatment view is derived from concepts of state equality and territorial sovereignty and, for these reasons, is alternately referred to as the equality of treatment doctrine. The position is widely supported by Latin American and Third World states, as well as by communist states. *See also* ALIEN, 150; CAPITULATIONS, 153; EXPROPRIATION, 162; MINIMUM INTERNATIONAL STANDARD OF JUSTICE, 167.

Significance   The advocacy of national treatment is founded as much in the realm of politics and economics as it is in legal theory. Historically, nationals of European powers were often accorded privileged treatment in foreign territory amounting to being cloaked in their own country's laws and protection. Privileged status through major economic interests in developing states was also common. In some extreme cases, this privileged status was called "extraterritoriality," since foreigners were exempted from local laws and jurisdiction. In the aftermath of the decolonization process in the post–World War II period and the rejection of Western imperialism, the national treatment view has gained wide popularity as the favored position rather than the concept of a minimum international standard. The latter retains support among Western states that look with favor upon such cases as the *Roberts* case (United States–Mexican General Claims Commission, 1927), which held that equality of treatment of aliens and nationals is an important—but not the ultimate—test of the acts of authorities; rather, the ultimate test is whether aliens are treated according to ordinary civilized standards. Treatment of aliens is often governed by bilateral treaties, particularly with regard to investments, inheritance, and ownership of property.

Permanent Sovereignty over Natural Resources (170)
(1962), Resolution on

A United Nations General Assembly Resolution of 1962 proclaiming the right of "peoples and nations" to permanent sovereignty over their national wealth and resources and establishing general principles governing nationalization, expropriation, or requisitioning of both domestic and foreign interests. The Resolution was the product of the efforts of the Commission on Permanent Sovereignty over Natural Resources established in 1958 (as well as the United Nations Economic and Social Council) in response to aspirations for economic self-determination and rights of "peoples" freely to dispose of their own national wealth expressed in the United Nations Draft Human Rights Covenant and in a General Assembly Resolution of 1952. The Resolution on Permanent Sovereignty over Natural Resources declares that a nation's resources must be used for the national development and well-being of its people. Foreign investment agreements between states will be observed in good faith. At the same time, nationalization, expropriation, or requisitioning will be based on grounds of public utility, security, or national interest, overriding foreign and domestic private interests. Owners will be paid "appropriate compensation," and pacific settlement techniques will be utilized in cases of dispute after exhaustion of local remedies. *See also* CHARTER OF ECONOMIC RIGHTS AND DUTIES OF STATES (1974), 154; EXPROPRIATION, 162; EXPROPRIATION OF CONTRACTUAL RIGHTS, 163; MINIMUM INTERNATIONAL STANDARD OF JUSTICE, 167; REPARATION, 73.

Significance   The Permanent Sovereignty over Natural Resources Resolution is a useful benchmark in suggesting the direction an eventual legal regime on expropriation might take, as international legal norms relative to expropriation of foreign assets are far from a settled area of international law. Based upon the sovereign equality of states and the need for respect of their economic independence, the Resolution notes that, in cases where foreign economic activity is allowed, the profits of that activity will be governed by agreement, municipal law, and international law, but consideration must be given the state's sovereignty over its natural wealth and resources. The thoughts contained in the Resolution have been reiterated in amended form by a General Assembly Resolution of 1973, which makes no mention of international legal guidelines pertaining to compensation for expropriation, and by the Charter of Economic Rights and Duties of States Resolution adopted by the United Nations General Assembly in 1974 over the protests of many developed states. The Charter does mention the principle of good faith in contractual undertakings by states and recognizes the right to compensation but does not mention international law in this context, which means that the law of the expropriating state will be decisive. Such provisions are not international law as yet, but reflect the challenge to traditional views by the developing world and the North-South debate over the Third World's proposal for a "New International Economic Order."

6. Territory: Land

Accretion (171)

The very slow, almost imperceptible, process of creating land through the natural action of water, such as river currents and ocean tides. Land added through the process of accretion is an example of original title to territory. Accretion is not to be confused with avulsion, or rapid change, which does not affect title to territory. *See also* AVULSION, 176; ORIGINAL TITLE, 186.

Significance Accretion is a natural phenomenon of the world's rivers, streams, bays, gulfs, straits, lakes, and oceans. The banks and coastlines of such bodies of water are subject to continual erosion and buildup from the movement of water. The material deposited through accretion is called alluvium, and the course of the shoreline, riverbed, or coastline can be altered as a consequence of the redistribution of such deposits. Since original title results from the process of accretion, it means that changes in the course of boundary rivers will change the boundaries of the affected states, and alluvial deposits on shorelines or river deltas and islands will alter the baseline from which a state delineates its territorial waters. Although an ongoing natural process, accretion is of negligible interest in international law.

Administered Province (172)

A territory under the technical jurisdiction of one state while under the real control of another. An administered province arrangement is presumed to be only temporary in nature, but in reality can last for many years. The institution of administered provinces is of historical interest only.

Significance   Administered provinces such as have existed in the past were simply an administrative unit of a state. History provides several examples, including Cyprus (under administrative control of Great Britain under an agreement with Turkey, 1878–1914), and Bosnia-Herzegovina (administered by Austria-Hungary from 1878–1908, although technically under Turkish sovereignty). The more recent period provides the example of Germany, under some form of Allied administrative control in the early post–World War II years, and of Austria, under Allied administrative control until 1955.

Annexation   (173)

The extension of sovereignty over a territory by its inclusion into the state. Annexation normally (but not always) accompanies conquest and, if all of the territory of the defeated state is annexed, then it is called subjugation. If only a portion of the state is annexed, then forcible cession of territory has taken place. *See also* CONQUEST, 180; STIMSON DOCTRINE, 192.

Significance   Annexation has been a common feature of international relations over the centuries and was traditionally an acceptable and legal means of acquiring territory. Historically, annexation (whether in whole or in part) was judged to be appropriate only after successful conquest and could not, therefore, take place while a conflict was still in progress. A modern example of annexation was Germany's annexation (in conjunction with a plebiscite) of Austria in 1938 (known in German as the *Anschluss*), in violation of the post–World War I settlements. Annexation after conquest is no longer viewed as acceptable in international law. But, in the absence of successful opposition by other states, it has the practical effect of transfer of territory just the same.

Antarctic Treaty System   (174)

An international legal system based on the Antarctic Treaty of 1959, which holds in abeyance the territorial claims by states to portions of the Antarctic continent and consigns the continent to use only for peaceful purposes. Seven countries—Argentina, Australia, Chile, France, New Zealand, Norway, and the United Kingdom—are claimant states. A small sector of Antarctica is not claimed by any state. Although there are more than thirty-five signatories of the Antarctic Treaty, only the original twelve—Argentina, Australia, Belgium, Chile, France, Japan, New Zealand, Norway, South Africa, Great Britain, the Soviet Union, and the United States, plus Poland, the Federal Republic of Germany, Brazil, China, India, and Uruguay (as countries undertaking "substantial scientific research activity" in Antarctica)—have so-called "consultative party" status and represent an elite with executive decision-making power. The other signatories of the Treaty have no such powers. The Convention for the Conservation of Antarctic Marine Living Resources (1980) and the Convention for the Conservation of Antarctic Seals (1972) as well as "recommendations" of the Consultative Powers complement the Antarctic legal regime. The Treaty went into force in June 1961 and may be reviewed in thirty years. *See also* SECTOR THEORY, 189.

Significance   The Antarctic Treaty freezes territorial claims to the continent, although the seven claimant states do not renounce their claims by virtue of adhering to the Treaty. Signatories pledge to use the continent only for such peaceful purposes as scientific research and exploration on a basis of international cooperation. The Treaty demilitarizes and prohibits disposal of radioactive waste in Antarctica and prohibits the introduction and/or testing of nuclear weapons or any other type of military weapon. Signatories have a right to on-site inspection of installations of one another so as to insure compliance with the Treaty. The passage of time provided some new issues which could not be dealt with by the original signatories, such as the exploration and exploitation of the seabed off Antarctica. Exploitation of living resources in the seas surrounding the continent is regulated by the Living Resources (1980) and the Seals Conventions (1972). The potential mineral resources of the Antarctic, especially of the continental shelf, became a subject of negotiations by the Consultative Powers. The nature of issues such as these suggests that economics might undermine the Treaty. Still, the Antarctic Treaty System is instructive for its successful confrontation with contentious political issues; indeed, it was the prototype for the Outer Space Treaty. Currently, however, the club of the Antarctic Consultative Powers has been subjected to criticism for its exclusiveness and secrecy, and the whole matter of Antarctica is likely to be subjected to pressures by the developing countries in the name of the principle of the "common heritage of mankind." A resolution to prepare a comprehensive study of Antarctica was adopted by the United Nations General Assembly at the initiative of the less developed countries in 1983. The study was prepared in 1984 and discussed at the 1984 and 1985 sessions of the Assembly, but no action was taken.

Arctic Region   (175)
The north polar region contiguous to the United States, the Soviet Union, Canada, Norway, Denmark (Greenland), and Iceland. Claims

to portions of the Arctic are based upon discovery, the sector theory, and such concepts as continuity of the continental tableland and contiguity (proximity of the aforementioned states to portions of the frozen wastes). *See also* CONTINENTAL SHELF, 225; EXCLUSIVE ECONOMIC ZONE, 227; SECTOR THEORY, 189.

Significance   The Arctic region—mostly frozen sea—comprises some 5 million square miles of land, ice, and water. It is an important region for scientific, economic, and military reasons. The extension of coastal states' jurisdiction to large offshore areas of the ocean has resulted in a number of disputes between Arctic states concerning the delimitation of the boundaries of the exclusive economic zones and the continental shelves of those states. The continued exploration and growing exploitation of oil and gas (primarily by the United States and Canada) and building of bases and research sites suggest that a permanent presence by the contiguous states and conflicts between them can be anticipated.

Avulsion   (176)

A rapid change in the course of a river or the banks of bodies of water caused by some natural force or disaster such as floods, tidal waves, or hurricanes. The alteration of territory as a consequence of avulsion does not affect title to territory. *See also* ACCRETION, 171.

Significance   Avulsion can create serious territorial problems for affected states. While a slow change (accretion) in the course of a boundary river, for example, will alter the boundary between the affected states, the boundary will remain unaffected by avulsion. Consequently, the new course of the river would flow completely through one of the states while the old river bed would remain the boundary. In addition, it is sometimes difficult to judge whether or not the changes that occur result from accretion or avulsion, particularly if changes over time occur from both actions. Such problems formed the basis of the *Chamizal* arbitration (U.S.-Mexico International Boundary Commission, 1911). The case was a boundary dispute over a six-hundred-acre tract of land called the El Chamizal tract along the Rio Grande River between El Paso, Texas and Ciudad Juárez, Mexico. At issue was whether the change in the course of the Rio Grande River that created the tract was the consequence of accretion or avulsion. A ruling by the tribunal adverse to the position of the United States resulted in its refusal to abide by the decision, which subsequently affected U.S.-Mexican relations. The dispute was finally resolved by the Chamizal Treaty of 1963, which provided for the rerouting of the riverbed of the

Rio Grande and its being permanently set in concrete. The bulk of the Chamizal tract reverted to Mexican sovereignty. Although always a natural threat, avulsion is of negligible interest in international law.

Barcelona Convention on the Regime of Navigable   (177)
Waterways of International Concern (1921)

Negotiated under the auspices of the League of Nations, the Barcelona Convention and Statute on the Regime of Navigable Waterways of International Concern, in force since 1922, established the general principle of free navigation by signatory states on navigable waterways of international importance flowing through each other's territory. According to the Statute, all natural navigable waterways of the signatories were open to navigation by other signatories without distinction as to riparian or nonriparian states. Artificial waterways were also open for inclusion.

Significance   The Barcelona Convention and Statute dealt with two important issues: (1) the principles and guidelines of usage of navigable waterways of international importance; and (2) the transit of goods and people over such waterways. Efforts to extend the same principles to purely national rivers failed. However, an additional protocol provided that signatories might concede, on a reciprocal basis, navigation access to all rivers in their jurisdiction whether of international significance or not. While an admirable expression of the concept of the right to access and navigation of international rivers by all nations and of considerable theoretical influence, the Protocol's guidelines were, in the final analysis, not fully accepted even by the signatories, and it has had little practical effect. There have been efforts in recent decades by the International Law Commission (ILC) and other bodies to reassess the norms reflected in the Barcelona Convention.

Boundary   (178)

An imaginary line that delineates the territorial limit of a state. Boundaries, often referred to as political boundaries, are three-dimensional in that they include the airspace and subsoil of the state as well as the horizontal plane of the state's land and the maritime domain of its internal waters and territorial sea. Boundaries are either (1) natural-topographical, having physically distinguishable features, or (2) imaginary and artificial, such as lines of latitude and longitude, surveyor lines, concrete posts, etc. Both have equal legal standing and are usually based upon treaties or historic title. *See also* SOVEREIGNTY, TERRITORIAL, 191; THALWEG, 194.

Significance   Boundaries determine the reach of a state's sovereignty; consequently, clearly delineated, agreed upon, and demarcated (surveyed) boundaries minimize confusion and overlapping claims. Natural boundaries such as mountains, rivers, lakes, and sea-coasts are, therefore, to be preferred over artificial boundaries. Treaties typically determine the precise location of boundaries but, in the absence of a boundary treaty, customary norms exist to apply to natural boundaries. In the case of a mountain range, the watershed (the divide or ridge system separating the flow of water) is the boundary. For rivers, it is the *Thalweg;* that is, the middle of the main navigable channel and, in the case of unnavigable rivers, it is generally the middle of the river. Treaties can provide, however, for a boundary mountain or river to be wholly within one state. A major problem for many of the new states that have emerged from colonial status is the artificiality of their boundaries. They are often little more than lines arbitrarily drawn in the colonial period to separate the territorial or administrative limits of colonial powers. The disruptive legacy of such colonial boundaries, often drawn in complete disregard for ethnic groups or tribal lands, can be seen in the political map of Africa and Latin America. In the case of the former Spanish colonies in Central and South America, the boundaries of the newly independent states of the nineteenth century corresponded to the former Spanish administrative boundaries.

Cession   (179)

A derivative mode of acquisition of territory by a state. Cession is usually based upon a treaty. Consequently, it is a formal procedure for changing sovereignty over territory, in contrast to forcible annexation without formalization by treaty. Cession can be effected by purchase, exchange, a gift or dowry, voluntary merger, or other voluntary manner, or it can be a result of use of force against the state ceding the territory. The latter is unlawful in international law. *See also* ANNEXATION, 173; CONQUEST, 180; DERIVATIVE TITLE, 181; PLEBISCITE, 187; STIMSON DOCTRINE, 192; SUCCESSION, STATE, 79.

Significance   Cession can prove disruptive to both individuals and property, as well as to state obligations. While in theory private property and private rights are unaffected by cession, the reality is often different. At the very least, an individual's nationality can be affected and, in the case of radically different political systems, perhaps the individual's property as well. Cession may affect a state's treaties and other obligations tied to the ceded territory. History provides innumerable examples of cession, including cession by sale by Denmark of the Danish West Indies (Virgin Islands) to the United States in 1916 as well as such purchases by the United States as the Louisiana territory from France (1803), the Floridas from Spain (1819), the Gadsden purchase from Mexico (1853), and Alaska from Russia (1867). Examples of cession by exchange include the exchange of a portion of Bessarabia by Romania to Russia (1878) in exchange for Dobrudja and the exchange of Heligoland in 1890 by Great Britain to Germany in return for Zanzibar. Historical examples of gifts include Austria's cession of Lombardy to France (1859) and France's gift of Venice to Italy (1866). Cessions through voluntary merger include the Republic of Texas' merger into the United States and Duchy of Courland's merger into Russia in 1795.

Conquest   (180)

The acquisition of territory through force. While an accepted means of acquiring title to territory under traditional international law, conquest is no longer legal. After World War I, the growing movement to restrict the right of states to go to war was exemplified by the Covenant of the League of Nations and the Kellogg-Briand Pact (1928). This movement culminated in the Charter of the United Nations (1945), which banned the use of force, thereby making the acquisition of territory by conquest illegal. Other international acts include the United Nations General Assembly Declaration on Principles of International Law Concerning Friendly Relations and Cooperation among States in Accordance with the Charter of the United Nations (1970), and such regional pronouncements as the Lima Declaration of Nonrecognition of the Acquisition of Territory by Force (1938). Like forcible cession, conquest results in transfer of territory under duress, but unlike cession, it involves no treaty. *See also* ANNEXATION, 173; CESSION, 179; COERCION OF A STATE, 264; FORCE, ILLEGAL THREAT OR USE OF, 308; STIMSON DOCTRINE, 192.

Significance   Under traditional international law, conquest did not lead immediately to claim of title but was merely military occupation. If followed by formal annexation of the conquered territory, then it was called subjugation and could be considered a valid derivative title to territory. The traditional view of conquest as a mode of acquiring territory was subsequently tempered by the League Covenant, the Pact of Paris, and regional declarations, and completely reversed by the Charter of the United Nations, since its signatories pledge to respect each other's territorial integrity.

Today, conquest is no longer a legal means of acquiring title to territory. Even a victim of aggression cannot, according to the United

Nations Declaration on Principles of International Law, acquire territory by conquest. However, since no effective international community mechanisms exist to enforce the rule against acquisition of territory by conquest, there is a discrepancy between the law and the reality of international relations. The issue may be even more perplexing if other states *de jure* recognize an aggressor state's acquisition of territory by conquest. Also, as demonstrated by India's conquest of Portuguese Goa in 1960, legality of acquiring territory by force can be rationalized in the name of anticolonialism. Over the recent two decades or so, the issue of conquest has acquired special significance in the context of the Arab-Israeli conflict and Israel's annexation of some Arab territories occupied as a result of the 1967 round of war.

Derivative Title   (181)

A claim of sovereignty over territory having a previous sovereign. The concept of derivative title is, like that of original title, borrowed from the Roman law. Derivative title occurs through cession or—now illegal—conquest of territory. With the land surface of the globe claimed by states, most new title acquisitions in the modern period are based upon cession—either peacefully or by force. *See also* ANNEXATION, 173; CESSION, 179; CONQUEST, 180; PRESCRIPTION, 188.

Significance   Derivative title to territory involves the transfer (cession) of title from one sovereign to another. Peaceful cession can take several forms, including purchase, exchange, a gift, or voluntary merger. Transfer of title can also take place under duress through forcible cession, conquest and/or annexation. While under the present international law force is no longer recognized as a valid mode of acquiring title to territory, a change in sovereignty through illegal use of force may, if unopposed or unresolved over time, eventually have the practical effect of transfer of title.

Discovery   (182)

A means of gaining title to territory by claiming land previously unclaimed (*terra nullius*). Discovery was an important means of territorial acquisition during the fifteenth and sixteenth centuries—the age of discovery in European history. It provides only an inchoate (imperfect or temporary) title and must be followed by effective occupation and control within a reasonable period of time for the title to take full effect.

See also ACCRETION, 171; OCCUPATION, 185; ORIGINAL TITLE, 186; PRE-SCRIPTION, 188.

Significance   Discovery is a concept closely tied to the evolution of the territorial state system and European history. The Western Hemispheric land mass, for example, was "discovered" thousands of years ago during the Paleolithic Age when the predecessors of the natives who confronted Columbus (and later visitors to the continents of North and South America) crossed the now-submerged land bridge across the Bering Strait from Asia to North America. From a European perspective, however, such tribes were not states in the European sense but merely inhabitants of the territory, and uncivilized at that. A similar outlook prevailed in Africa, the South Pacific, and other regions. In many instances, however, the European discoverers and colonizers negotiated agreements with local tribal chiefs and rulers, which had the practical effect of derivative title to territory through cession. Of course not all territory that was discovered was inhabited; the polar regions and numerous atolls and small islands dotting the world's oceans are examples.

While discovery is no longer an important means of acquiring title to territory, the historical circumstances surrounding discovery and subsequent actions by claimants can have bearing upon the outcome of contemporary territorial disputes. An excellent case in point is the *Western Sahara* case (Advisory Opinion of the International Court of Justice, 1975). The case centered upon the nature of the Spanish claim to Western Sahara (Rio de Oro and Sakiet El Hamra) and the legal ties of that territory to Morocco and Mauritania. The event precipitating the dispute was a United Nations move to allow a referendum on self-determination in Western Sahara as a non-self-governing territory of Spain. Both Morocco and Mauritania claimed parts of the Western Sahara on historical grounds and, consequently, the issue was whether the Spanish claim to the territory was based upon occupation of territory considered to be *terra nullius,* meaning territory belonging to no one. The Court concluded that the Spanish establishment of a protectorate over the region had been based upon agreements with the chiefs of local tribes, and Spain did not look upon it as *terra nullius.* The claims by both Morocco and Mauritania to historic ties of territorial sovereignty were not sufficiently founded in the Court's advisory opinion and, consequently, nothing existed to hinder decolonization and self-determination for Western Sahara. Morocco invaded Western Sahara in November, 1975, precipitating a guerrilla war in the region, which Morroco continues alone today against the Polisario guerrillas following the withdrawal of Mauritania from the territory.

Environment, Protection of   **(183)**
States are governed by the general principle of not using their territory
for acts that adversely affect the rights of other states, in keeping with
the Roman law maxim *sic utere tuo ut alienum non laedas* (use your
property in such a manner as to not injure another). The protection of
the environment has become a major issue in international law, as
witnessed by the United Nations Stockholm Conference on the Human
Environment (1972). In the aftermath of the Stockholm Conference, a
new United Nations specialized agency, the United Nations Environment Programme, was created, headquartered in Nairobi, with the
charge of developing more specific international environmental law.
See also LONG-RANGE TRANSBOUNDARY AIR POLLUTION, 208; MARINE POL-
LUTION, INTERNATIONAL LAW OF, 243; PROHIBITED WEAPONS, 357.

Significance   While protection of the environment is not without
legal foundation, states are sovereign within their own territory, and
environment is, as yet, not subject to any authority empowered to
regulate all its aspects. Rather, most legal obligations beyond general
abstract concepts are the result of national legislation and bilateral and
multilateral treaties. These cover specific areas such as marine pollution (oil discharges from ships), air pollution, changing climatic conditions, research, and so forth. Examples of these include regulation of
marine pollution by many global and regional agreements, the United
States–Canadian agreement on pollution of boundary waters (1909),
and prohibition of hostile use of environmental modification techniques under the Environmental Modification Convention (1977).
There have been arbitral awards as well, such as the *Trail Smelter*
arbitration (United States–Canada Arbitral Tribunal, 1941), in which
Canada was held liable for polluting air entering the United States; and
the *Lake Lanoux* case (France-Spain Arbitration, 1957), concerning
alleged diversion of waters flowing from France to Spain. An inclusive
environmental legal regime is hampered not only by state adherence to
national sovereignty, but to economic and ideological arguments as
well. The developing nations of the world are convinced that most of
the world's environmental problems are caused by the developed,
industrialized nations, and to impose environmental regulations upon
developing states would make them economically noncompetitive—a
form of neocolonialism. Nuclear waste disposal; nuclear weapons tests;
nuclear plant disasters such as the one that occurred in the Soviet
Union (the Chernobyl reactor) in 1986; fossil fuel burning and
greenhouse effects; destruction of the ozone layer in the atmosphere;
acid rain; damage to marine life from fertilizer runoff; and the destruction of bird and insect life from pesticides are but some illustrations of

the complexity of the environmental problem and suggest the enormity of the political and economic issues involved. The international community will be severely tested in confronting and resolving such environmental problems in progressively developing international environmental law.

Lease (184)

A contractual arrangement between states whereby a portion of one state's territory is provided to another state for the latter's use. Of mostly historical interest today, leases usually had time limits attached to them and did not imply transfer of sovereignty to the leasing state, only the temporary transfer of administrative control and use of the territory for a specified (or unspecified) period. Nor could such rights be transferred by the lessee to another party.

Significance Leases in international relations seem, at first glance, to be comparable to those in municipal law but are more often than not the result of unequal relationships, frequently amounting to a *de facto* cession of territory. In the last decade of the nineteenth century, for example, China leased several of its ports to Great Britain, France, and Russia—none of them willingly. Some Chinese leases were even transferred to third parties without the prior approval of China. The Russian leases of Port Arthur and Dalny, for example, were transferred to Japan as part of the settlement of the Russo-Japanese War (1904–1905); and Japan acquired the German lease of Kiao-Chao after World War I. The U.S. lease of the Panama Canal Zone was unusual in that, through the Convention of 18 November 1903, Panama granted to the United States the use of the Zone in perpetuity as if the United States were sovereign (recently replaced by the Panama Canal Treaty of 1977). Examples of leases of current interest in international politics are the lease of the bulk of Hong Kong set to expire in 1997 and the U.S. Guantánamo facility in Cuba.

Occupation (185)

An original mode of acquisition by a state of title to territory belonging to no state (*terra nullius*), through its real, permanent and effective presence and control upon a territory to which it lays claim, in order to make final the inchoate (temporary) title which it acquired through discovery. Occupation does not necessarily mean that an entire territory must be occupied, but by the same token the occupation of a coastal area does not automatically create title to the hinterland. *See also* ANTARCTIC TREATY SYSTEM, 174; DISCOVERY, 182; ORIGINAL TITLE, 186.

Significance   Occupation establishes the permanent presence of the claimant state, but the legal meaning of such terms as "real," "permanent," or "effective" control is less than precise. In the early period of European discovery (the fifteenth and sixteenth centuries), failure to immediately colonize or even the temporary abandonment of a colony did not necessarily affect a claim to the territory. Inclusion of territory in administrative decrees and in statutes was evidence of a claimed title. However, by the eighteenth century effective control came to be interpreted more strictly to mean the creation of a governing presence in the territory and a permanent population.

The more inhospitable portions of the globe, such as guano islands and polar regions, are another matter. Even today one part of the Antarctic continent remains unclaimed by any power. Cases such as the *Clipperton Island* arbitration (France-Mexico Arbitration, 1931) and the *Legal Status of Eastern Greenland* case (Permanent Court of International Justice, 1933) suggest that claims can be supported with minimal physical presence under certain geographical conditions. The thinking of the Court in the *Eastern Greenland* case is most illuminating. The dispute concerned the clash of Norwegian and Danish claims to sovereignty over Eastern Greenland. Norway announced claim to the region in 1931 and Denmark immediately protested, claiming sovereignty over the whole of Greenland. During the course of its deliberations, the Court noted that Denmark's claim to the whole of Greenland could be traced as far back as 1721 and, subsequent to that time, that state had enacted numerous legislative and administrative actions that applied not only to Denmark but to the whole of Greenland as well. Combined with the lack of challenge to Danish sovereignty until 1931, this led the Court to decide that minimal exercise of sovereignty required in such an arctic and inhospitable environment were all that was necessary to substantiate Danish title to the whole of Greenland, especially since Norway could not prove superiority of its claim to sovereignty.

Original Title   (186)

A claim to sovereignty over territory that has not previously been claimed by any state. Original title includes occupation, accretion, and—a debatable theoretical issue—prescription. Most hold prescription to be original, since lapse of title or abandonment has taken place, while others hold to prescription being derivative, since formally there is a previous holder of title to the territory. *See also* ACCRETION, 171; DISCOVERY, 182; OCCUPATION, 185; PRESCRIPTION, 188.

Significance   Original title to territory through discovery is initially only an inchoate (temporary) title, which must then be followed by effective control. The concept of unclaimed land (*terra nullius*) was a product of European colonialist powers' perception since many of the lands discovered during Europe's age of discovery (the fifteenth to seventeenth centuries) were already occupied. However, since the natives that were present were perceived to be merely uncivilized individuals rather than organized entities displaying similar political and religious traditions as their discoverers, the lands were subject to claims of possession by the discoverers. In many cases, treaties were negotiated with the natives of the discovered territory and, subject to the position taken by the European power in dealing with natives, could be viewed as derivative title to territory (in those cases where the territory was not viewed as *terra nullius*). In the contemporary period, original title is relegated to the very slow process of land being formed through accretion, although the sudden appearance of a volcanic island in international waters could provide an opportunity for original title through discovery.

Plebiscite   (187)
A public referendum or vote by the population of a territory to determine their choice of a sovereign. A plebiscite is often applied in a cession of territory from one state to another.

Significance   Plebiscites gained some popularity in the nineteenth and twentieth centuries as a means for implementing the principle of "national self-determination." The hardship upon the population that transfer of title to territory imposes was also cited as justification for the calling of a plebiscite. The population in the ceded territory become nationals of the new sovereign and can lose their former citizenship. Because of this, many treaties of cession contain a proviso giving individuals the option of retaining their old citizenship or emigrating. Historic examples of plebiscites include those conducted by Napoleon Bonaparte in the early nineteenth century; the cession of Nice and Savoy to France (1860); cession of Venice (1866); the plebiscites in the German-Polish and German-Danish border areas after World War I; and in the Saar (1935). The United Nations has conducted several plebiscites or "quasi-plebiscites" to settle disputes that emerged out of the process of change from colonial status to independent statehood.

Prescription   **(188)**

The acquisition of title to territory through uncontested exercise of sovereignty over an extended period of time. An institution derived from Roman (civil) law, prescription presupposes a prior sovereign whose control over the territory in question has lapsed through failure to occupy, abandonment or neglect, wrongful claim, or failure to contest a new claim. See also OCCUPATION, 185; ORIGINAL TITLE, 186.

Significance   Prescription must be judged on a case by case basis, as there is no time limit in international law that bars a state from challenging prescriptive title. Indeed, the concept itself has not been universally accepted by legal scholars because of this lack of specific time limits. Its application in court decisions, however, attests to its international acceptability. A classic case illustrating the concept of prescription is *The Island of Palmas* case (Permanent Court of Arbitration, 1928). The immediate event precipitating the case between the United States and the Netherlands was the transfer of title to the territory of the Philippines from Spain to the United States in the settlement of the Spanish-American War of 1898. Upon taking occupation of the various islands comprising the Philippine archipelago, the United States discovered a Dutch presence on the Island of Palmas (situated midway between the Philippines and the Dutch East Indies), which had been included in the Spanish transfer of title. The Dutch contended that they had exercised sovereignty over the island since the latter part of the seventeenth century without Spanish protest and that the Spanish claim was nullified by abandonment, since discovery was not followed by continued and effective display of state authority, namely occupation. The sole arbitrator—Swiss publicist Max Huber—agreed with the Dutch claim by reason of prescription. Prescription has also been acknowledged in such cases as the *Fisheries* case (*United Kingdom v. Norway*, International Court of Justice, 1951) and the case concerning *Sovereignty over Certain Frontier Lands* (Belgium/Netherlands, International Court of Justice, 1959).

Sector Theory   **(189)**

A proposed basis for national claims to sovereignty over the polar regions. The sector theory draws meridian lines from the pole to the farthest extremity of the contiguous state's land mass. All the land area within that sector is purported to be under the sovereignty of the claiming state. The theory is not an internationally recognized basis for claiming territory. See also ANTARCTIC TREATY SYSTEM, 174; ARCTIC REGION, 175.

Significance   The sector theory is a means of skirting the traditional rule of international law that discovery of territory must be followed by effective occupation. It also places greater emphasis upon such concepts as continuity (of continental landmasses) and contiguity (proximity) to the territory in question. In the Arctic, the states contiguous to that polar region are the United States, Canada, Norway, Denmark, Iceland, and the Soviet Union. Canada and the Soviet Union are the two proponents of the sector theory for the Arctic, with Soviet writers claiming that regardless of the nationality of those who discover and claim territory in the Arctic, lands falling within a state's sector belong to that state. Both Denmark and the United States are more reluctant to endorse the sector theory. The situation in the Antarctic polar region is even more complex, as claims to portions of that continent are based upon the sector theory, principles of continuity and contiguity, and landings and exploration. Such diverse bases for claims to territory produce overlapping titles such as those of Argentina, Chile, and Great Britain to Antarctic territory. It should be noted that territorial claims based solely upon such concepts as continuity or contiguity are not well founded in international law, although they may be of supplemental use in specific cases. To forestall conflicts over such claims in the Antarctic, all states concerned negotiated the Antarctic Treaty in 1959, which, *inter alia*, holds in abeyance all territorial claims to the continent, at least until 1991 when the treaty may come up for review.

Servitude   (190)

A restriction upon the exercise of a state's sovereignty over its territory. An institution derived from Roman law and similar to the common law institution of easement, servitude can be either positive or active (authorizing something) or negative or passive (prohibiting something) and today is usually defined by treaty. It can also be terminated by agreement among the parties concerned. Some scholars include universal restrictions or obligations in the category of servitudes and classify them as "natural" servitudes (*servitutes juris gentium naturales*). An example of such is the universal right of innocent passage.

Significance   Servitude is a controversial concept in international law. Servitudes are contrary to the legal premise of the equality of nations, as they impose restrictions amounting to interference with the sovereign authority of a state over its territory. Nevertheless, situations resembling a servitude occur more frequently than one might assume, particularly since servitudes are usually designed to preserve a status quo beneficial to those encouraging the servitude. Most servitudes can be classified as either military or economic in nature and cover such activities as the fortification of territory, transit rights across a state's territory or use of its rivers, and transit through certain straits or canals. A historic servitude that has captured international attention on more than one occasion was the nonfortification of the Aaland Islands, which are strategically situated in the Baltic Sea at the mouth of the Gulf of Bothnia between Sweden and Finland. In 1856, Russia agreed by treaty not to fortify the Islands. When the Islands were transferred to Finland in 1917, a Committee of Jurists appointed by the Council of the League of Nations reiterated the stipulation that they not be fortified, concluding that the demilitarization provisions of the Convention of 1856 applied to them. By the terms of the Soviet-Finnish Agreement of 1940 (later reaffirmed by the Soviet-Finnish Peace Treaty of 1947) the Islands were once again demilitarized. Other illustrations of servitudes include the dismantling of Italian fortifications along the Italian-Yugoslav border by the terms of the 1947 Peace Treaty, and the Swiss commercial free zone in Genoa, Italy. The concept of universal (natural) servitudes is not widely supported, as it is argued that servitudes are usually based upon a written agreement (*servitutes juris gentium voluntariae*).

Sovereignty, Territorial   (191)

The geographic framework within which the state exercises its control under international law. Territorial sovereignty extends over all land and subterranean areas, internal waters and the territorial sea, and the airspace over the land areas. Since the state's jurisdiction is three-dimensional, some prefer to speak of spatial sovereignty rather than territorial sovereignty. Extending the concept of territorial sovereignty to include such state activities beyond its borders as diplomatic missions, ships on the high seas, and aircraft in flight is a legal fiction since such activities represent an extension of state jurisdiction rather than territory. *See also* BOUNDARY, 178; DERIVATIVE TITLE, 181; ORIGINAL TITLE, 186.

Significance   Territorial sovereignty is a concept subject to confusion. For example, is the state's control over its territory comparable to an individual's control over property? Prior to the French Revolution, the territory of a state was considered to be the property of the ruler. This was known as the patrimonial theory and was replaced by the theory of state ownership after the French Revolution. But the modern view of territorial sovereignty contrasts the state's ownership of property (*dominium*) with the state's power of government, administration, and disposition (*imperium*), the latter being more correctly territorial jurisdiction. The final answer must rest to some extent in the realm of municipal law, as there are state-owned properties and, in common law systems, there is the state's right of eminent domain. Territorial sovereignty is unaffected by the nature of the configuration of a state's territory. Most states consist of a single piece of the earth's surface, but there are some whose parts are separated from their continental component. Quite a few are archipelagoes, for example, Indonesia and the Philippines; or are enclaves totally or partially enclosed by another state, such as Lesotho, which is totally surrounded by South Africa, and the Spanish enclave of Llivia in France. While there are practical problems of transportation and communication with enclaves and fragmented states, there is no effect upon the nature of their territorial sovereignty.

Stimson Doctrine (192)

The principle, named after U.S. Secretary of State Henry Stimson, proclaiming, *inter alia*, that any situation or treaty that would bring about change in territorial status by means contrary to the Pact of Paris (Kellogg-Briand Pact) would not be recognized. *See also* CONQUEST, 180; GENERAL TREATY FOR THE RENUNCIATION OF WAR (1928), 309.

Significance   The Stimson Doctrine was precipitated by the Japanese takeover of Manchuria in 1931–1932. The Doctrine was endorsed by the League of Nations and invoked in the cases of conquest and annexation of Albania, Austria, and Ethiopia but was largely ineffectual. Condemnation of conquest as a legal means of acquiring territory has been repeatedly supported by Latin American states at inter-American conferences, so that many assert that the Stimson Doctrine is a valid part of regional (Western Hemispheric) law. In any case, acquisition of territory by conquest is illegal under general international law.

Territory, Acquisition of (193)

The extension of the sovereign authority of a state over additional land and/or water. Territory is the space within which the state exercises sovereign authority. Title to territory is acquired either through (1) the claim of land not previously owned (*terra nullius*) or (2) the transfer of title from one state to another. Title acquired in the first category is called original title; that in the second derivative title. Modes of original acquisition of territory, adopted from Roman law, include discovery and occupation, prescription and accretion. Derivative modes include cession (voluntary or forcible) and conquest. *See also* ACCRETION, 171; ANNEXATION, 173; CESSION, 179; CONQUEST, 180; DERIVATIVE TITLE, 181; DISCOVERY, 182; OCCUPATION, 185; ORIGINAL TITLE, 186; PRE- SCRIPTION, 188; STIMSON DOCTRINE, 192.

Significance   While some modes of acquiring territory (such as dis- covery) are of only historical interest today, the particulars surround- ing a title to territory are important in instances where title is in dispute. Historically, for example, discovery of territory was of itself enough to establish title; but by the eighteenth century the accepted practice was that it had to be followed by effective occupation. If a claim was abandoned, then another state could lay claim to the territory. A contemporary dispute that illustrates these modes of acquiring title or claims is the British-Argentine dispute over the Falkland (Malvinas) Islands, which briefly erupted into open and costly war between the two in 1982. Spain and Great Britain both claimed the Islands through discovery, neither making a significant attempt at permanent occupa- tion until the end of the eighteenth century, when Spain and later the government of Buenos Aires did so. Later, they were forced out by the British who reasserted control over the Islands in 1833 and remained in control of the Islands since then. The Argentine claim is based upon the alleged British abandonment of the Islands between 1774 and 1810, while the British claim is based upon the failure of Spain to protest the British claim announced in 1765, even though French rights were transferred through purchase to Spain in 1767. Another contemporary issue involving legality of acquisition of territory is Is- rael's annexation of Arab territories after the 1967 Arab-Israeli round of war.

Thalweg   (194)
The path taken by boats in their navigation in a river or other body of water; in essence, the main navigable channel of a body of water. The *Thalweg* rule is used to delineate territorial jurisdiction over boundary rivers, bays, estuaries, etc., the boundary (in the absence of a treaty to the contrary) being the middle of the main navigable channel. *See also* ACCRETION, 171; BOUNDARY, 178.

Significance   A German term, the *Thalweg* rule is founded upon the principles of equality and justice. By placing the boundary of states in the middle of the main navigable channel (or its principal channel if the river has more than one), both states have equal use of the river for commerce and travel. Should the river simply be divided down the middle (as was advocated by such early writers as Hugo Grotius), the use of the river or other body of water might be denied one of the parties if the navigable channel fell completely within the jurisdiction of the other state. As the main channel shifts through the process of accretion, so also does the boundary.

7. Air, Outer Space, and Telecommunications

Air Defense Identification Zone (ADIZ)   (195)

A zone, extending in some cases up to 300 miles beyond the territorial sea, established for security reasons by some states off their coasts. All aircraft entering an ADIZ are required to identify themselves, file flight plans, and report their position to ground identification stations of the coastal state. *See also* AIRSPACE, 197; FREEDOM OF THE HIGH SEAS, 231.

Significance   The practice of maintaining ADIZs is of questionable validity. It has not become part of customary international law, and treaty practice tends to reject exercise of jurisdiction over foreign aircraft beyond the territorial sea. Nevertheless, ADIZs are maintained by the United States, which also established a Distant Early Warning Identification Zone, Canada, and a dozen or so other countries. During the Algerian War France maintained an ADIZ, known as the "zone of special responsiblity," extending eighty miles off the coast of Algeria.

Air Hijacking   (196)

Unlawful seizure of aircraft in flight carried out by private individuals for personal reasons or out of political motives. The first attempt to deal with aircraft offenses was the Tokyo Convention of 1963 on Offenses and Certain Other Acts Committed On Board Aircraft (1963). It deals with air hijackers only incidentally, treating them as any other offenders. It was not until 1970 that the Hague Air Hijacking Convention made unlawful seizure of aircraft a separate crime. A year later the Montreal Convention against Aircraft Sabotage covered aircraft offenses other than hijacking, such as placing explosives in aircraft and similar acts of sabotage, destruction of aircraft in service, damage to air

159

navigation facilities, acts of violence against persons on board, and extortion hoaxes aboard an aircraft. *See also* HAGUE AIR HIJACKING CONVENTION (1970), 201; MONTREAL CONVENTION AGAINST AIRCRAFT SABOTAGE (1971), 209; TOKYO CONVENTION ON OFFENSES AND CERTAIN OTHER ACTS COMMITTED ON BOARD AIRCRAFT (1963), 218.

Significance   Air hijacking became a serious problem in the 1960s when a series of aircraft seizures, initiated with a 1961 hijacking of a U.S.-registered airliner to Cuba, made the international public and governments cognizant of the need to take appropriate measures. Governments also increasingly recognized that dangers posed by hijacking and similar offenses should not be overridden by real or alleged political considerations motivating the offenders. This point of view was endorsed not only by Western countries but also by the Soviet Union and other communist states after they realized that their own aircraft were not immune to the menace of hijacking. Yet it soon became evident that international agreements alone could not be an effective weapon in combating the menace of hijacking in the absence of full cooperation of all states, particularly if certain governments afforded shelter to hijackers or were otherwise in breach of international obligations. Proposals designed to strengthen the enforcement of antihijacking regulations, discussed within the framework of the International Civil Aviation Organization (ICAO) and other global international agencies, have not so far resulted in more stringent and comprehensive enforcement rules to deal with aircraft offenses. On the other hand, this failure has prompted national, bilateral, and regional action aimed at combating air hijacking. On the national level, stringent antihijacking legislation and security measures contributed to a marked decline of air hijacking incidents by the late 1970s. There have also been cases of unilateral self-help action against hijackers, such as the Entebbe raid in 1976 by Israeli commandos who rescued passengers of an Air France airliner in Uganda against that country's protests, and the Mogadishu raid in 1977 in which a hijacked Lufthansa plane was recaptured by West German troops with the Somali government's approval. On the bilateral level states have signed agreements providing for the return of hijackers to the state of registration or trial in the country of shelter. The U.S.-Cuban Memorandum of Understanding of 1973, subsequently denounced by Cuba in retaliation for an alleged U.S.-organized sabotage of a Cuban airliner, is an example of such an agreement. On the regional level the major Western industrialized countries agreed in 1978 to act in concert in suspending air traffic to and from states that failed to surrender hijackers and hijacked aircraft promptly to the state of the aircraft's registration. Beyond all these explicit agreements customary international law does not seem to have developed a rule obligating states to take action against hijackers. Return of the hijacked plane and passengers appears to be enjoined by customary international law, however.

Airspace (197)

The pillar of air above the subjacent territory. National airspace, including airspace above the internal waters and the territorial sea, is under complete and exclusive sovereignty of the subjacent state, without any right of innocent passage by foreign aircraft. Consequently, except for aircraft in distress, any use of national airspace by foreign aircraft is allowed only with the consent of the territorial sovereign, granted either unilaterally or more commonly—especially in case of commercial flights—through a bilateral treaty, usually on conditions of reciprocity. Specific permission is normally required for foreign military or other governmental aircraft to enter the national airspace of a country. Moreover, foreign aircraft are normally required to fly only within designated corridors and—under some national laws—only after notification to the relevant air defense authorities of the subjacent state. Airspace above the sea beyond the territorial sea—that is, the high seas—as well as the exclusive economic or similar zones, is free for use by all states' aircraft without any control by the coastal state. Therefore, air defense identification zones (ADIZs) and similar zones are of questionable validity under international law. The principle of national sovereignty over the superjacent air space is a firmly established rule of general international law, but there is no agreement on the boundary between national airspace and outer space. *See also* AIR DEFENSE IDENTIFICATION ZONE (ADIZ), 195; CHICAGO CONVENTION ON INTERNATIONAL CIVIL AVIATION (1944), 198; INTERNATIONAL AIR SERVICES TRANSIT AGREEMENT (1944), 203; INTERNATIONAL CIVIL AVIATION ORGANIZATION (ICAO), 205; OUTER SPACE, INTERNATIONAL LAW OF, 211.

Significance   The rule that states have exclusive sovereignty over their airspace developed rapidly following the invention of the airplane. It was included in the Paris Convention of 1919 for the Regulation of Aerial Navigation and in numerous other international agreements, in particular the Chicago Convention on International Civil Aviation (1944). Sovereignty over national airspace is unquestionably one of the most fundamental and sacrosanct principles of contemporary international law. Violation of national airspace by foreign aircraft is considered a serious breach of international law and has led to many international incidents and disputes. Among them the shooting down over the Soviet Union of a U.S. high-flying U-2 reconnaissance aircraft in 1960 and the affair of the South Korean civil airliner brought down, with the loss of all 269 crew and passengers, by Soviet interceptor fighter aircraft over the far eastern territory of the USSR in 1983 are perhaps the two most publicized cases. What measures the territorial sovereign may take under international law in case of illegal aerial intrusion is not entirely clear. In any case the foreign aircraft may be ordered to leave the national airspace, change its course, or land at some designated area. Use of weapons against foreign military aircraft disobeying such orders seems to be allowed under customary international law on grounds of threat to national security. On the other hand, military action against an intruding civilian aircraft, for example, the downing of an Israeli airliner over Bulgaria by Bulgarian military aircraft in 1950; the shooting down of a Libyan airliner over Israeli-occupied Egyptian territory by Israel's air force in 1973; and the destruction by the Soviet interceptor aircraft of the South Korean plane in 1983, is generally considered illegal. Some states (and part of the doctrine) argue, however, that absolute prohibition of attacks on intruding civilian aircraft is not a rule of general international law and the violation of the law occurs only if the subjacent state's reaction to the intrusion is unreasonably disproportionate under the circumstances. Following the South Korean airliner incident of 1983, the Chicago Convention on International Civil Aviation (1944) was unanimously amended by the ICAO Assembly in 1984 to the effect that every state must refrain from resorting to the use of weapons against civil aircraft in flight and that in case of interception the lives of persons on board and the safety of aircraft must not be endangered. However, even under this amendment, rights and obligations of states under the United Nations Charter are not in any way modified, which means that the right of self-defense might still be invoked in cases of intrusion by foreign civil aircraft that can be reasonably suspected of being deliberately used by a foreign state against the security of the subjacent territorial sovereign.

Chicago Convention on International Civil Aviation   (198) (1944)

An international multilateral agreement, concluded at the Chicago Conference of 1944, which set out the fundamental principles of international air law and established the International Civil Aviation Organization (ICAO), eventually one of the specialized agencies of the United Nations. The Chicago Convention reaffirms the basic principle of customary international air law that every state has complete and exclusive sovereignty over its air space. It lays down the principle that aircraft have the nationality of the state in which they are registered. The basic distinction of the Convention between scheduled and unscheduled air services has continued until today in international air law. No foreign aircraft scheduled international services may be operated over or into the territory of the subjacent state except with the consent of that state. Aircraft not engaged in scheduled international air services have the right to make flights into or in transit nonstop across the territory of another state and to make stops for nontraffic purposes without obtaining prior permission of that state, subject to the right of the subjacent state to order immediate landing and impose various restrictions, such as routes and off-limits areas. Foreign government-owned aircraft, including military planes, need special prior authorization of the subjacent state for flying over or landing in the territory of that state. Equality of treatment and nondiscrimination in regard to aircraft of other states must be observed in all cases of flights by such aircraft. More than 150 states are parties to this Convention. *See also* AIRSPACE, 197; INTERNATIONAL AIR SERVICES TRANSIT AGREEMENT (1944), 203; INTERNATIONAL AIR TRANSPORT AGREEMENT (1944), 204; INTERNATIONAL CIVIL AVIATION ORGANIZATION (ICAO), 205.

Significance   The Chicago Convention did not bring any major changes in the international law of the air, previously codified in the Paris Convention of 1919. It did lay down more detailed and refined rules, reflecting agreement on standards of air navigational practices and certificates of airworthiness. It did not, however, provide the legal framework for international air traffic, which had to be left to regulation by bilateral agreements. As a result of the absence of a multilateral agreement allocating traffic among competing scheduled international services and the very limited application of the "Five Freedoms" agreement of 1944, states have entered into a vast and complex network of usually reciprocal bilateral agreements covering routes, traffic volume, and other matters of concern to the prodigiously expanded airline industry. Thus today international scheduled flights take place largely on the basis of such agreements.

Direct Television Broadcasting   (199)

Transmission of television pictures by satellite directly to individual dish antennae linked to receivers. International law rules governing direct television broadcasting are still uncertain and the whole subject is bedeviled by thorny technological, legal, and especially political issues. There is, however, a Convention of 1974 Relating to the Distribution of

Programme-Carrying Signals Transmitted by Satellites, which is designed to prevent unauthorized rebroadcasting of signals received from satellites and thereby to protect the copyrights of legitimate broadcasters. As far as the issue of direct television broadcasting is concerned, the United Nations General Assembly, at its 37th session (1982–1983), adopted a Resolution on the Principles Governing the Use by States of Artificial Earth Satellites for International Television Broadcasting, accepted by a vote of 107 in favor to 13 against (mostly Western nations) and 13 abstentions. There seems to be consensus that direct satellite broadcasting should be conducted in accordance with international law, including the Charter of the United Nations, the Outer Space Treaty, and the relevant provisions of the International Telecommunications Union (ITU) and its radio regulations, and that access to the technology of communications satellites should be freely available to all states without discrimination and without any country's having a monopoly in launching and operation of such satellites. *See also* INTELSAT, 202; INTERNATIONAL COVENANT ON CIVIL AND POLITICAL RIGHTS (1966), 91; INTERNATIONAL TELECOMMUNICATIONS UNION, 206; OUTER SPACE TREATY (1967), 212; RADIO COMMUNICATION, INTERNATIONAL LAW OF, 214.

Significance   Matters raised by the use of artificial earth satellites for international direct television broadcasting have been on the agenda of the Legal Subcommittee of the United Nations Committee for the Peaceful Uses of Outer Space for more than a dozen years, and the desirability to adopt an international agreement to govern this issue has been reiterated in several resolutions of the United Nations General Assembly since 1972. However, because of the fundamental divergence of view between the Western states, favoring freedom of information and the communist and Third World countries opposing it, no such convention has so far been concluded. Most Western nations, while accepting the necessary ITU restrictions concerning allocation of frequencies, refuse to accept a general legal principle imposing restrictions on broadcasts across national borders. They are particularly concerned that such a principle would apply to technologically unavoidable overspill, that is, unintentional flow of transmission over to contiguous countries. Most developed nations opposed the United Nations General Assembly Resolution because it provides for prior consultation and agreement between a state intending to establish an international direct television broadcasting satellite station and receiving states. In the Western view, the principle of prior consent constitutes censorship and would give states the right to control even what they themselves transmit to their own populations.

Geostationary Orbit   (200)

That orbit above the equator at which a satellite circles the earth at a rate of speed synchronized with that of the earth's rotation and thus appears to be stationary. The utilization of the geostationary orbit is essential for telecommunication services and other application of artificial satellites since it enables continued relay of a signal from a station on earth to a satellite in the orbit and back to a wider area on earth. *See also* DIRECT TELEVISION BROADCASTING, 199; OUTER SPACE, INTERNATIONAL LAW OF, 211; OUTER SPACE TREATY (1967), 212.

Significance   As long as the issue of the airspace-outer space delimitation is unresolved, international law concerning the geostationary orbit remains uncertain. At this time the prevailing view opposes a state's permanent right to any orbit around the earth. Taking advantage of the fact that international law does not have any rule concerning the boundary between the airspace and outer space, in 1976 eight equatorial states, asserting that the geostationary orbit was part of their natural resources, claimed sovereign rights over that segment of the orbit which lies above their respective territories to a height of 36,000 km above sea level. Although these states subsequently lessened their emphasis on sovereignty, they continue to be concerned about access to the orbit and, like other developing nations, demand an equitable management and use of the orbit and consequently also of space telecommunications technology.

Hague Air Hijacking Convention (1970)   (201)

An International Civil Aviation Organization (ICAO)-drafted multilateral convention for the suppression of unlawful seizure of civilian aircraft, of which some 130 countries are signatories. The Hague Hijacking Convention is the main international agreement providing a legal framework to deal specifically with seizure of aircraft in flight. Without using the term "hijacking," the Convention defines this offense and obliges each signatory state to make it punishable by "severe penalties." Consequently each party to the Convention must make hijacking a part of its domestic criminal law in order to establish its jurisdiction over this offense. Jurisdiction is exercised on one or more of the following grounds: (1) commission of the offense on board an aircraft registered in the contracting state; (2) landing of the hijacked aircraft in a contracting state with the alleged offender still on board, including a universality jurisdiction provision allowing for the apprehension of a hijacker who escapes from or is allowed to leave a state with jurisdiction under item one; and (3) commission of the offense on board an aircraft leased by the contracting state without crew to a lessee who has his principal place of business or permanent residence in that state. Any contracting state in the territory of which the hijackers are present is obliged to take them into custody and must either extradite or prosecute them under its law irrespective of whether or not the hijacking was committed in its territory and, in principle, without regard to motivation. Under the Convention, hijacking is made an extraditable offense in any existing or future extradition treaties or reciprocal practice of surrendering offenders between the contracting states. *See also* AIR HIJACKING, 196; EXTRADITION, 120; JURISDICTION: UNIVERSALITY PRINCIPLE, 131; MONTREAL CONVENTION AGAINST AIR- CRAFT SABOTAGE (1971), 209.

Significance   The Hague Hijacking Convention is the first global international agreement to deal with hijacking as a distinctly separate offense. A major weakness of the Convention is that it contains no legal obligation to extradite a hijacker except under the terms of an extradi- tion treaty or reciprocal practice of surrendering offenders. This means that even if hijacking is included in an extradition treaty as an extraditable offense, extradition may still be refused on the basis of any provisions in the extradition treaty exempting political offenses from extradition or denying extradition of nationals.

INTELSAT
(202)

An intergovernmental organization in the area of satellite telecom- munications whose main objective is to provide, on a commercial base, the "space segment" for international public telecommunications ser- vices, including satellites and other equipment and services required to support the operation of the satellites. Membership in the Interna- tional Telecommunications Satellite Organization (INTELSAT) is open to states members of the International Telecommunications Union (ITU), which participate in it by way of investment shares determined by the percentage of utilization of INTELSAT's space segment by all parties. The structure of INTELSAT includes an Assembly of the states' parties which considers the aspects of INTESAT of import to the members as sovereign states; a Meeting of Signatories dealing with the "nonsovereign" operational and financial matters; a Board of Gover- nors; and an executive organ headed by a Secretary-General. The decision-making system is based on weighted voting adjusted to the amount of the investment share each governor on the board of INTELSAT represents, but no governor may cast more than forty percent of the total votes. Decisions on substantive matters require the support of at least four governors representing at least two-thirds of the shares or all but three governors irrespective of the total investment share represented by the majority. *See also* DIRECT TELEVISION BROADCASTING, 199; INTERNATIONAL TELECOMMUNICATIONS UNION (ITU), 206; RADIO COMMUNICATION, INTERNATIONAL LAW OF, 214; REMOTE SENSING, 216.

Significance   The origins of INTELSAT date back to 1964 when an International Telecommunication Satellite Consortium without legal personality was established in which all members of the ITU could invest as a commercial venture providing services to any customer country. This early INTELSAT was dominated by a private U.S. corporation known as COMSAT (Communications Satellite Corporation), which was, however, established by the U.S. Congress and subject to federal control. Other parties to the original INTELSAT were represented either by governments or publicly controlled telecommunications organizations. With rise in INTELSAT membership, pressures increased to reorganize it and limit the U.S. influence in the consortium. The result was transformation of a loose international consortium into an international organization with its own legal personality. Two international agreements provided the legal basis for this reorganization: one concluded by the participating states and the other (the "Operating Agreement") by the states or public or private "telecommunications entities" designated by member states. For example, COMSAT has been so designated by the United States. Although COMSAT has lost its position as the operating agency of INTELSAT, it has continued to play the leading role in the activities of the Organization. There is a similar organization in the Eastern bloc, namely the INTERSPUTNIK, created in 1971 by nine communist countries under the aegis of the USSR but, in principle, open for membership by all nations. For purposes of maritime communications, the Convention on the International Maritime Satellite Organization (1979) established a new intergovernmental organization, INMARSAT.

International Air Services Transit Agreement (1944)   (203)

An international multilateral agreement, concluded at the 1944 Chicago Conference on International Civil Aviation, which provides for the so-called "two freedoms" for scheduled air services, namely the privileges to (1) fly across foreign territory without landing and (2) land on foreign territory for nontraffic purposes such as refueling.

The Agreement, otherwise known as the Two Freedoms Agreement, is in effect for some one hundred states, including the United States, but not the USSR. *See also* AIRSPACE, 197; CHICAGO CONVENTION ON INTERNATIONAL CIVIL AVIATION (1944), 198; INTERNATIONAL AIR TRANSPORT AGREEMENT (1944), 204.

Significance   Unlike the International Air Transport Agreement, the International Air Services Transit Agreement grants only limited rights for foreign scheduled flights. That is why it obtained approval of most states participating in the Chicago Conference of 1944. One can conclude therefore that the two freedoms of scheduled flights (flying without landing and landing for nontraffic purposes) command much more general acceptance in international practice than the other three freedoms specified in the International Air Transport Agreement.

International Air Transport Agreement (1944)   (204)

An international multilateral agreement, concluded at the 1944 Chicago Conference on International Civil Aviation, which provides for the so-called "five freedoms" for scheduled air services; namely, the privileges to (1) fly across foreign territory without landing; (2) land there for nontraffic purposes such as refueling; (3) disembark in a foreign country passengers and/or cargo originating in the territory of the state whose nationality the aircraft possesses; (4) embark traffic destined for that state; and (5) embark traffic destined for, or disembark traffic coming from, a third contracting state. Additionally the Agreement includes a provision on international air traffic (air *cabotage*), which may be reserved entirely to domestic airlines. *See also* AIRSPACE, 197; CHICAGO CONVENTION ON INTERNATIONAL CIVIL AVIATION (1944), 198; INTERNATIONAL AIR SERVICES TRANSIT AGREEMENT (1944), 203.

Significance   Unlike the International Air Services Transit Agreement, the International Air Transport Agreement did not obtain the support of a majority of states represented at the Chicago Conference of 1944, at which the extent of the freedoms of the air was the most debated issue. As a leading air services nation, the United States favored the widest scope of the freedom of the air, but only the first two freedoms were acceptable to a majority of states that favored some kind of centrally controlled and equitable allocation of the world's rapidly growing air traffic. So few states became parties to the Five Freedoms Agreement that the United States (which had joined in 1945) withdrew as a party in 1947. Since that time the Agreement has not been of great significance as a legal source for regulating international civil air traffic.

International Civil Aviation Organization (ICAO)   (205)

An intergovernmental organization, created by the Chicago Convention on International Civil Aviation (1944), whose objectives are to develop the principles and techniques of international air navigation and to foster the planning and development of international air transport. ICAO, headquartered in Montreal, became a specialized agency of the United Nations in 1947. Its principal organs include an Assembly composed of all members (that is, the parties to the Chicago Convention), each with one vote, which meets every three years, and an Executive Council composed of delegates elected for a three-year term by, and answerable to, the Assembly. Membership of the Council must include delegates both from states with a major role in air transport and other states. The Council adopts international standards of navigation and recommends practices, which are subsequently incorporated into the Chicago Convention in the form of annexes. Through various subsidiary bodies the Council studies all aspects of civil aviation. It arbitrates disputes between member states with regard to implementation of the Convention and investigates any situation that poses an obstacle to international air transport. ICAO works in close cooperation with regional civil aviation commissions composed of states of a particular geographical region. *See also* AIRSPACE, 197; CHICAGO CONVENTION ON INTERNATIONAL CIVIL AVIATION (1944), 198; INTERNATIONAL AIR SERVICES TRANSIT AGREEMENT (1944), 203; INTERNATIONAL AIR TRANSPORT AGREEMENT (1944), 204.

Significance   In view of the rapid expansion of civil aviation, ICAO has been a very active specialized agency of the United Nations with considerable achievements to its credit both in technical and legal fields. It is under the auspices of the ICAO that a number of international agreements in the field of air transport have come into being or have been amended. Examples are the Geneva Convention of 1948 on international recognition of property and other rights in aircraft on flights crossing different territories; the Rome Convention of 1952 dealing with damage caused by foreign aircraft to third persons on the ground; and amendment protocols to the Warsaw Convention of 1929 regulating the liability of the air carrier to passengers and consignors. The action undertaken by the ICAO with regard to the downing in 1983 of the Korean airliner by the Soviet air force was an outstanding example of the ICAO's investigative functions in the area of the safety of international air transport.

International Telecommunications Union (ITU)   (206)

A specialized agency of the United Nations headquartered in Geneva and possessing virtually universal membership, whose primary purposes are to (1) maintain and extend international cooperation for the improvement and rational use of telecommunications; (2) promote the development and efficient operation of technical facilities; and (3) harmonize the actions of nations in the attainment of these ends. The ITU was created as early as 1932 by the Madrid Telecommunications Convention, which replaced the earlier telegraph and radiotelegraph conventions, the ITU itself being the successor to the Bureau of the International Telegraphy Union established in 1865. Following World War II, the ITU was reorganized by successive Conventions: at Atlantic City in 1947; at Buenos Aires in 1952; at Geneva in 1959; at Montreux in 1965; and finally at Málaga-Torremolinos in 1973. Among the ITU organs are a Plenipotentiary Conference, meeting every five years as the supreme organ of the Union and determining the general policy of the organization; two Administrative Conferences which adopt and revise regulations for each form of telecommunications; an Administrative Council which supervises the Union's administrative functions between the sessions of the Plenipotentiary Conference, reviews and approves the budget, and coordinates the ITU's activities with those of other organizations; and a General Secretariat headed by a Secretary-General. Radio frequencies are allocated by the International Frequency Registration Board. Other technical organs include an International Radio Consultative Committee and an International Telegraph and Telephone Consultative Committee. *See also* DIRECT TELEVISION BROADCASTING, 199; INTELSAT, 202; PIRATE BROADCASTING, 213; RADIO COMMUNICATIONS, INTERNATIONAL LAW OF, 214.

Significance   The ITU is the nerve center of global radio and other telecommunications. Rational use and efficient operation of telecommunications in international relations would be impossible without the coordinating and regulatory activities of this specialized agency of the United Nations, which include the allocation of radio frequencies in order to avoid harmful interference; the fostering of international collaboration in order to lower rates for telecommunications and improve telecommunications equipment and networks; the promotion of the adoption of measures for ensuring the safety of life through tele-communications services; and the undertaking of studies, preparation of recommendations, and dissemination of information.

Liability for Damage Caused by Space Objects   (207)
Convention (1972)

A multilateral convention spelling out the rules on the liability of states for damage caused by objects launched into space. The Convention develops in more detail the principles of international liability in this area established by Article 7 of the Outer Space Treaty. Under its rule a launching state is to be absolutely liable ("no fault" liability) to pay compensation for damage caused by its space objects to persons or property on the surface of the earth or to aircraft in flight, but only fault liability applies to damage caused to other space objects in flight and to persons in them. The Convention establishes joint and several liability in case of joint launching. Claims can be brought without the need to exhaust local remedies. Claims in respect of damage to individuals are brought by the state of their nationality, but the state where the damage has occurred or of which the individual is resident may also act. A claim that cannot be settled by diplomatic negotiations is to be resolved by a mixed claims commission established at the request of either party. The compensation due is to be determined "in accordance with international law and the principles of justice and equity" so as to restore the victim to the condition that would have existed if the damage had not occurred, but no ceiling on the amount of compensation is set by the Convention. More than sixty states are parties to this Convention. *See also* OUTER SPACE TREATY (1967), 212; STATE RESPONSI-BILITY, 77; STATE RESPONSIBILITY, DRAFT ARTICLES ON, 78.

Significance   With hundreds of satellites and other objects in orbit, there have been a number of instances recorded of debris of space objects falling to earth. So far there has been only one claim brought under the Convention. It resulted from the breakup of the Soviet nuclear-powered Cosmos 954 satellite that disintegrated over Cana-dian territory in 1978, depositing debris throughout a large area of remote parts of Canada. Canada presented a claim against the Soviet Union pursuant to the Liability Convention, requesting more than $6 million (Canadian dollars) compensation for damage to property by the deposit of hazardous radioactive debris, which rendered the af-fected part of Canada unfit for use. The claim was settled in 1981 by an agreement whereby the USSR paid Canada $3 million (Canadian dol-lars) in full and final settlement of all matters related to the incident.

Long-Range Transboundary Air Pollution   **(208)**

Air pollution whose physical origin is situated wholly or partially in one state but which has adverse effects in the territory of another state at such a distance that it is not generally possible to distinguish the contribution of individual emission sources to the resulting pollution of air space. Long-range transboundary air pollution is associated primarily with pollution by emissions of sulphur from industrial sources causing damage to natural resources, such as waters and forests, by acidification (hence the popular term "acid rain"). Although polluting the air of a neighboring country results in international responsibility of the country of origin, the international legal regulation of long-range transboundary air pollution is still based upon treaties, and general international law on this subject is only beginning to emerge. *See also* ENVIRONMENT, PROTECTION OF, 183; MARINE POLLUTION, INTERNATIONAL LAW OF, 243.

Significance   Responsibility for transboundary air pollution under international law is generally traced to the *Trail Smelter* arbitration (United States–Canada Arbitration, 1941), involving liability of a Canadian company for polluting U.S. air space by sulphur dioxide from its smelting operations in the Canadian territory. The Tribunal observed that under international law no state has the right to use or to permit to use its territory in such a manner as to cause injury by fumes in the territory of another state. More recently, as part of a general rise in environmental concerns, the Declaration of the United Nations Stockholm Conference on the Human Environment (1972) stressed the responsiblity of states to ensure that activities within their jurisdiction do not cause damage to the environment of other states and even of areas beyond the limits of national jurisdiction, such as the high seas. Also the Final Act of the Helsinki Conference on Security and Cooperation in Europe (1975) called for cooperation to control air pollution (including long-range transboundary pollution) and the development of a program for monitoring and evaluating this kind of pollution, starting with sulphur dioxide. As far as the conventional regulation of the problem is concerned, the most significant attempt so far to develop international law rules dealing with atmospheric pollution is the 1979 Convention on Long-Range Transboundary Air Pollution of virtually all European nations, sponsored by the United Nations Economic Commission for Europe. Under this Convention the contracting states are bound to gradually decrease air pollution from sulphur and nitrogen dioxide emissions. A number of these states have instituted measures for reducing sulphur emissions at least thirty percent by 1993, using the 1980 emissions as the base, the rule that was also adopted in 1984 in a declaration on acid rain of some Western European nations and Canada. The issue of acid rain has been a major irritant in the relations between Canada and the United States, both countries (but especially Canada) being concerned about the deleterious effects of acid rain originating in the other country. Cooperation to combat acid rain has been agreed upon by these two countries in a number of memoranda and agreements in the early 1980s, such as the Memorandum of Intent of 1980 and the Agreement on Acid Rain Research of 1983, and even an Agreement between the state of New York and the province of Quebec on coordinating efforts in research on acid precipitation. On the southern border of the United States a U.S.-Mexico Agreement of 1983 on cooperation in the solution of environmental problems in the border area also provides for coordinating the two countries' efforts in dealing with the problems of air, land, and water pollution. Although pollution from atmosphere is a form of land-based pollution, it is considered a separate source of marine pollution under the Montego Bay United Nations Convention on the Law of the Sea of 1982 (not yet in force), which calls upon states to enact and enforce national legislation to prevent pollution of the sea from the atmosphere and to establish global and regional rules to prevent atmospheric pollution, a concept that includes pollution resulting in acid rain. Contamination of air by radioactive substances resulting from nuclear weapons tests is prohibited by the Treaty of 1963 Banning Nuclear Weapons Tests in the Atmosphere, in Outer Space, and under Water (the "Partial Test Ban Treaty") to which more than 110 states were parties in 1986.

Montreal Convention against Aircraft Sabotage   (209)
(1971)

An International Civil Aviation Organization (ICAO)-drafted multilateral convention for the suppression of unlawful acts against the safety of civil aviation. The Montreal Convention (the "Sabotage Convention") supplements the Hague Air Hijacking Convention of 1970 in that it covers offenses against civilian aircraft other than hijacking an aircraft in flight, and in particular (1) violence against a person on board an aircraft in flight, likely to endanger the safety of the aircraft; (2) destroying or causing damage to an aircraft in service; (3) placing explosive devices on an aircraft in service; (4) destroying or damaging air navigation facilities or interfering with their operations; and (5) bomb hoax extortion and similar acts. The Montreal Convention applies only if an international element is involved, namely if the place of take-off or landing is located outside of the territory of the state of registry or the offense is committed in the territory of a state other than the state of the aircraft's registry. The Convention also applies if the offender is found in the territory of a nonregistry state. As far as destruction or damaging air navigation facilities is concerned, the Convention applies only if international facilities are the target of the offense. Each signatory country undertakes to establish its jurisdiction over the offenses covered by the Convention. Such jurisdiction is exercised when the offense is committed in a country's territory or against or on board an aircraft registered in that country or when the aircraft on which the offense is committed lands in its territory with the offender still on board; and if the offense is committed against or on board an aircraft leased by a contracting state without crew to a lessee who has his principal place of business or permanent residence in that state. *See also* AIR HIJACKING, 196; HAGUE AIR HIJACKING CONVENTION (1970), 201; TOKYO CONVENTION ON OFFENSES AND CERTAIN OTHER ACTS COMMITTED ON BOARD AN AIRCRAFT (1963), 218.

Significance   Generally speaking, the provisions of the Montreal Convention regarding the taking into custody of alleged offenders and their extradition and prosecution follow the rules of the Hague Air Hijacking Convention of 1970, suffering from the same weaknesses of enforcement provisions as that Convention. Attempts to institute tougher and more far-reaching international legal obligations in the matter of aircraft offenses, covered by the Montreal Convention, have so far proved unsuccessful.

Moon Treaty (1979)   (210)

A multilateral agreement spelling out the principles and rules of international law governing the moon and other celestial bodies. The Agreement Governing the Activities of States on the Moon and Other Celestial Bodies, briefly known as the Moon Treaty, was approved by the United Nations General Assembly in 1979 after seven years of drafting work carried out by the United Nations Committee on the Peaceful uses of Outer Space. The Moon Treaty applies, in relation to the moon and other celestial bodies, the provisions of the Outer Space Treaty and other relevant global agreements dealing with outer space. Under the Treaty, all activities on the moon are to be carried out in accordance with international law in the interest of peace and with due regard to interests of all states parties. The moon is demilitarized, and nuclear weapons or other weapons of mass destruction cannot be placed in lunar orbit. The exploitation and use of the moon is the province of all mankind, carried out for the benefit of all countries. Other provisions of the Moon Treaty stipulate freedom of scientific investigation without discrimination, protection of the moon's environmental balance, safeguarding the life and health of persons on the moon, and the mutual right of inspection. The Treaty reiterates the prohibition of national appropriation (already stated in the Outer Space Treaty) and declares the moon to be the "common heritage of mankind." Looking ahead to the time when technological advances will make it feasible to exploit the moon's natural resources, the Treaty calls for the establishment of an international regime whose main purposes would be an orderly and safe development and rational management of the lunar resources and expansion of opportunities in the use of these resources. *See also* THE "AREA," 220; LIABILITY FOR DAMAGE CAUSED BY SPACE OBJECTS CONVENTION (1972), 207; OUTER SPACE TREATY (1967), 212; REGISTRATION OF OBJECTS LAUNCHED INTO SPACE CONVENTION (1974), 215; RESCUE OF ASTRONAUTS AGREEMENT (1968), 217.

Significance   Although the draft of the Moon Treaty was approved by the United Nations General Assembly (without vote), the Treaty has so far been signed and ratified by a limited number of countries with little or no experience in outer space exploration. It entered into effect in 1984. Negotiations on the Treaty, whose first draft was originally proposed by the USSR in 1971, continued for years. The most controversial issue involved the vague concept of the "common heritage of mankind." This idea was adopted at the Third United Nations Conference on the Law of the Sea (UNCLOS III) for purposes of defining the world community's role in the exploration and exploitation of the deep seabed resources beyond national jurisdiction, and it was eventually incorporated in the Montego Bay United Nations Convention on the Law of the Sea (1982). The Moon Treaty calls for establishing a moon regime of the common heritage of mankind whose one major purpose would be an equitable sharing by all states parties in the benefits derived from lunar resources, whereby the interests and needs of the developing nations as well as the countries that have contributed either directly or indirectly to the exploration of the moon should be given special consideration. Concerned that the concept of the common heritage of mankind might hamper the U.S. ability to explore the moon and inhibit its commercial exploitation by U.S. companies, the United States has not signed the Treaty. The USSR has also been unwilling to subscribe to an agreement that proclaims the application of the common heritage principle to the moon. The exploitation of the moon's resources is still a matter of rather remote future, but in theory a state nonparty would appear to have the right to such exploitation since the otherwise undefined concept of the common heritage of mankind has not, at least as yet, become part of international law. Whether the Moon Agreement established a moratorium on lunar exploitation by states parties prior to the establishment of the projected international regime also remains an academic question at this time.

Outer Space, International Law of   **(211)**

The law governing space beyond the airspace surrounding the earth. The boundary between the airspace and outer space remains undetermined and uncertain. Neither the Chicago Convention of 1944 nor the Outer Space Treaty (1967) contains any provisions on the precise point where the airspace ends and outer space begins. However, state practice—including in particular that of the United States and the USSR—provides ample evidence for the existence of the rule of international law that, although for security reasons national sovereignty must extend over the airspace up to a certain limit, such sovereignty obviously ends at some altitude above the earth. No state has insisted on its sovereignty to an unlimited height (*usque ad coelum*) and all have acquiesced in innumerable overflights of foreign-registered artificial satellites and space vehicles over their territories. Thus, the conduct of states in the first decades of the space age has given rise to a new permissive rule of international law to the effect that states have the right to place their satellites and space vehicles in orbit over the territory of other states. On the other hand, although the question has been on the agenda of the United Nations Committee on the Peaceful Uses of Outer Space, so far states have not evidenced much urgency to establish a demarcation line between the airspace and outer space. The two major space powers—the United States and the Soviet Union—tend to reserve the right to counter hostile acts at whatever altitude they may occur. Proposals for the upper limit of national airspace, suggested by the doctrine, are based on a variety of scientific and technological criteria such as the aerodynamic lift. This idea involves the theoretical limits of air flight ("the Karman line") or the lowest altitude (perigee) at which an artifical satellite can remain in orbit, which would place the boundary of the airspace at around 80 to 90 km. Wherever outer space may begin, it is governed by international law, including the Charter of the United Nations. Among the fundamental principles of the international law of outer space are (1) prohibition of national appropriation; (2) ban on weapons of mass destruction; (3) freedom of exploration; (4) the duty to give due notice to the United Nations of the launching of satellites; (5) avoid injury to other states and not contaminate the environment; (6) availability of communication satellites to all nations without discrimination; and (7) the duty to provide assistance to space vehicles and astronauts in distress. *See also* AIRSPACE, 197; DIRECT TELEVISION BROADCASTING, 199; GEOSTATIONARY ORBIT, 200; LIABILITY FOR DAMAGE CAUSED BY SPACE OBJECTS CONVENTION (1972), 207; MOON TREATY (1979), 210; OUTER SPACE TREATY (1967), 212; REGISTRATION OF OBJECTS IN SPACE CONVENTION (1974), 215; RESCUE OF ASTRONAUTS AGREEMENT (1968), 217; REMOTE SENSING, 216.

Significance   Ever since space exploration began in 1957 with the launching of the first artificial satellite by the USSR, international law has had to keep pace with the rapid progress in space technology and exploration. Although no agreement exists on the boundary between the airspace and outer space, consensus has been reached on some fundamental principles governing the legal status of outer space, as reflected in six United Nations General Assembly Resolutions adopted in the years 1959–1963 and incorporated in the Outer Space Treaty of 1967. The latter act has been further implemented by the Rescue of Astronauts Agreement of 1968, the Liability for Damage Caused by Space Objects Convention of 1972, the Registration of Objects in Space Convention of 1974, and the 1979 Agreement Governing the Activities of States on the Moon and Other Celestial Bodies, to which only a limited number of states are parties. The global outer space law has been increasingly complemented by regional arrangements such as, for example, the Convention of 1975 for the Establishment of a European Space Agency of some Western European countries and the Agreement of 1976 on Cooperation in the Exploration and Use of Outer Space for Peaceful Purposes, adopted by nine communist states including the members of the Warsaw Pact, Cuba, and Mongolia. There are also numerous bilateral agreements on outer space cooperation, research, and communications. Despite the growing body of the rules of the international law of outer space, much remains to be done in the areas of the military uses of outer space (increasingly imperative as the United States and the Soviet Union expand their research on space defense weapons), space navigation, telecommunications, remote sensing, and the unresolved issue of the boundary between the airspace and outer space.

Outer Space Treaty (1967)   (212)

The international multilateral agreement setting forth the fundamental principles governing the international law of outer space. Drafted by the United Nations Committee on the Peaceful Uses of Outer Space, this Treaty on Principles Governing the Activities of States in the Exploration and Use of Outer Space, Including the Moon and Other Celestial Bodies builds upon and incorporates the principles enunciated in a number of unanimously adopted United Nations General Assembly resolutions, namely Resolution 1721 of 1961, Resolution 1884 of 1963, and in particular Resolution 1962 of 1963. The Treaty provides that outer space, including the moon and other celestial bodies, is free for exploration and use by all states and cannot be appropriated by any nation. Any exploration and use must be carried out for the benefit of all countries on a basis of equality and in accordance with international law, with due regard to interests of other states and without any harmful contamination of the environment of the celestial bodies and the earth itself. States conducting activities in outer space must, to the greatest extent feasible and practicable, disclose information about such activities and open their stations and equipment to inspection by other states. Activities of nongovernmental entities require authorization and supervision of the government bearing international responsibility for such activities. Responsibility for activities of an intergovernmental organization is borne both by the organization and by its members. A state that launches or authorizes the launching of an object into outer space is liable for damage caused by the object, a provision subsequently elaborated by the Convention of 1972 on Liability for Damage Caused by Space Objects. Ownership of objects launched into outer space is not affected by their presence there or by their return to earth; if found they must be returned to their state of origin. States must assist astronauts, "envoys of mankind in outer space," in distress and an astronaut landing in emergency in another state must be promptly returned to the state of the space vehicle's registry. The Agreement on the Rescue of Astronauts of 1968 further elaborates this rule. Finally the Outer Space Treaty demilitarizes the moon and other celestial bodies in a way analogous to the demilitarization of Antarctica under the Antarctic Treaty of 1959. However, as regards objects orbiting around the earth, the Treaty merely provides that nuclear weapons or any other kind of weapons of mass destruction must not be placed in orbit, which means that the earth's orbit may be used for other military purposes, in particular for launching reconnaissance satellites, such as those verifying compliance with arms control agreements. More than eighty states, including the United States and the USSR, are parties to the Outer Space Treaty. *See also* INTELSAT, 202; LIABILITY FOR DAMAGE CAUSED BY SPACE OBJECTS CONVENTION (1972), 207; MOON TREATY (1979), 210; OUTER SPACE, INTERNATIONAL LAW OF, 211; REGISTRATION OF OBJECTS IN SPACE CONVENTION (1974), 215; RESCUE OF ASTRONAUTS AGREEMENT (1968), 217.

Significance   Apart from its provisions concerning the military uses of outer space and mutual inspection of facilities on the moon and other celestial bodies, the Outer Space Treaty does not add much to the principles set forth in the United Nations General Assembly resolutions on outer space. Still the Treaty laid down mandatory general principles upon which the legal regime of outer space is now predicated and which can already be considered part of general (customary) international law.

Pirate Broadcasting   **(213)**
Unauthorized transmission of sound radio or television broadcasts by
private stations from a vessel or installation on the high seas, intended
for reception by the general public contrary to international regulations, but excluding the transmission of distress calls. Under the International Telecommunications Union Convention the establishment
and use of broadcasting stations outside national territory is prohibited, and the enforcement of this rule rests with the country of the
broadcasting vessel's registry. *See also* INTERNATIONAL TELECOMMUNICA-
TIONS UNION (ITU), 206; FLAG-STATE JURISDICTION, 230; RADIO
COMMUNICATIONS, INTERNATIONAL LAW OF, 214; UNITED NATIONS
CONVENTION ON THE LAW OF THE SEA (1982), 251.

Significance   The phenomenon of broadcasting for profit without a
license from the state where broadcasts were received made its appearance in northwest Europe in the late 1950s and acquired much publicity in the 1960s when a number of unauthorized radio stations carried
out their broadcasts off the coasts of Great Britain; the Netherlands
(including a "pirate" TV station in 1964); Denmark; and, in the early
1970s, the United States. Governments took enforcement action in
some cases, but it was not until several West European states concluded
the Agreement of 1965 for the Prevention of Broadcasting Transmitted from Stations outside National Territory that most pirate stations
were forced to close down. Under this Agreement the states agreed to
punish both their nationals and nonnationals engaged in unauthorized
broadcasting from vessels or installations registered in any of the
contracting states. Going further, the Montego Bay United Nations
Convention on the Law of the Sea (1982) calls upon all states to
cooperate in the suppression of unauthorized broadcasting from the
high seas. It allocates concurrent jurisdiction to prosecute offenders to
the flag state, to the state of registry of the installation, to the state of the
broadcaster's nationality, to any state where the transmission can be
received, and to any state where authorized radio communication is
suffering interference. When the Convention enters into effect, its
provisions will contribute to the enforcement of the prohibition of
pirate broadcasting.

Radio Communications, International Law of   **(214)**
The system of legal norms and regulations governing the use and
operation of radio communications in international relations. Unlike
the international law of the air, in radio communciations technical
reasons make it impossible to safeguard each country's absolute

sovereignty over its airspace against penetration by electromagnetic waves broadcast from another state. Hence the legal status of radio communications is based, at least in principle, on the freedom of broadcasting across national borders. However, in view of the shrinking spectrum of available radio frequencies and in order to avoid chaos in international broadcasting, this freedom is limited by each state's duty to see to it that radio stations operating in its territory avoid harmful interference with the communication services of other countries. Furthermore, as a corollary of the basic principles of international law concerning respect for the sovereignty of other states, each state is obliged to prevent its territory from being used for broadcasting injurious to other states and conversely each state has the right to prevent penetration of its airspace by harmful broadcasts originating abroad. However, these general principles are difficult to apply as demonstrated by the controversy over the jamming of Western broadcasts by the Soviet bloc countries. *See also* DIRECT TELEVISION — BROADCASTING, 199; INTELSAT, 202; INTERNATIONAL TELECOMMUNICATIONS UNION (ITU), 206; PIRATE BROADCASTING, 213.

Significance   International legal regulation of radio communications became necessary with the invention of wireless telegraphy at the beginning of this century and subsequent rapid development of worldwide telecommunications. The development of the rules of international law governing radio communications took place through global and regional agreements, beginning with the Berlin and London International Wireless Conventions of 1906 and 1912 respectively. Today the International Telecommunications Union (ITU) is the center for the development of the rules governing radio and other telecommunications in international relations. The two major regulatory acts of the ITU in the area of radio communciations have been the repeatedly revised Regulations of 1959 and the Regulations of 1979 which replaced them (in force since 1982). Regional telecommunications conventions have also contributed to developing new rules, as illustrated by the Inter-American Radio Conventions of Havana, Rio de Janeiro, and Washington of 1937, 1945, and 1949 respectively; the European Convention of Copenhagen of 1948; and the Asian Broadcasting Union Convention of 1964. There is also an international Agreement (1949) concerning telecommunications between the British Commonwealth and the United States. All these acts are designed to allocate radio frequencies and avoid harmful interference between stations of different countries. The Soviet bloc countries, claiming that Western broadcasts in the languages of their populations are unlawful hostile propaganda, have set up an extensive system of radio stations deliberately designed to interfere with ("jam") such broadcasts. Since jamming constitutes interference with radio communications of other states it is, in the opinion of most Western publicists, a violation of international law as set out in ITU conventions and regulations. However, from the viewpoint of international law it is not easy to draw a line between internationally disallowed hostile propaganda interfering in the domestic affairs of a country and legitimate dissemination of information in accordance with the freedom of information guaranteed by the United Nations Covenant on Civil and Political Rights of 1966 of which the Soviet Union and its allies are parties.

Registration of Objects Launched into Outer Space   (215) Convention (1974)

A multilateral agreement establishing a mandatory system of registering objects launched into outer space. The 1974 Convention introduces the duty of the launching state to register its satellites and other space objects in a national register and furnish to the United Nations Secretary-General, as soon as practicable, detailed information concerning the space object such as its registration number; date and territory or location of launch; basic orbital parameters, including nodal period, apogee, and perigee; and the general functions of the space object. This information is recorded in the central register of the United Nations to which full and open access is available. The Convention, to which some thirty countries are parties, implements a general provision of the Outer Space Treaty on registration of space objects. *See also* INTELSAT, 202; OUTER SPACE TREATY (1967), 212.

Significance   The Registration Convention makes it possible to keep an open record of all satellites and other space objects launched and authorized to be launched by signatory states. All the major launching nations are parties. The mandatory system of registration under the Convention is an improvement as compared to the original system under a United Nations General Assembly resolution that called only for the voluntary furnishing of such information.

Remote Sensing   (216)

A form of gathering information from a distance by surveying the earth from artificial satellites in the earth's orbit. Remote sensing is not governed by any specific international law rules, but general principles of the law of outer space as reflected in the Outer Space Treaty and other international agreements implementing it apply to remote sensing. For example, the duty of the launching state to inform the "sensed" state of the function of the sensing satellite can be implied from the provisions of the Registration of Objects Launched into Space Convention of 1974. Debate continues on the permissibility under international law of remote sensing and such questions as who, in addition to the "sensing" state, should be allowed access to data obtained from sensing, in what form the data should be available, and who is to decide in these matters. All these questions have been studied since 1971 by the United Nations Committee on the Peaceful Uses of Outer Space and its Legal Subcommittee, but no agreement has been reached on a mutually acceptable legal regime of remote sensing. The question of permissibility of sensing and the right to disseminate information received from it are the most controversial issues. *See also* LIABLITY FOR DAMAGE CAUSED BY SPACE OBJECTS CONVENTION, (1972), 207; OUTER SPACE, INTERNATIONAL LAW OF, 211; OUTER SPACE TREATY (1967), 212; REGISTRATION OF OBJECTS LAUNCHED INTO OUTER SPACE CONVENTION (1974), 215.

Significance   Remote sensing by satellites has enormous potential benefits for mankind in such fields as agriculture and forestry, geography and hydrology, geology, meteorology, and oceanography. On the other hand, it raises a host of controversial and interrelated technical, legal, organizational, and primarily political issues. Negotiations on a universally acceptable legal regime of remote sensing have been hampered by the conflict between the Western nations and the less developed countries of the Third World, with the USSR assuming a less committed attitude on the matter. The Western nations uphold the principle of permissibility of remote sensing from outer space, an area free from any nation's sovereignty, and of open dissemination of information obtained. On the other hand, focusing on the target of sensing (their territories and ocean areas over which they exercise jurisdiction) the less developed countries contend that remote sensing cannot be conducted without their consent. They invoke the principle of the states' permanent sovereignty over their natural resources which, they claim, might be compromised by remote sensing. National security considerations also contribute to the reluctance of many states to accept the freedom of remote sensing by satellites from other countries.

Rescue of Astronauts Agreement (1968)   (217)

A multilateral agreement designed to secure international cooperation in rescuing and returning home astronauts and objects launched into space. The Rescue Agreement develops the general principle on this subject, already stated in the Outer Space Treaty (1967), spelling out in greater detail the duties and rights of states with regard to the rescue of astronauts who land in the territory of a foreign country and return of any space objects to the country of launch. There are also general provisions concerning the rescue of astronauts in outer space. Some eighty countries are parties to the Rescue of Astronauts Agreement. *See also* OUTER SPACE TREATY (1967), 212.

Significance   The Rescue of Astronauts Agreement is an example of international law anticipating a future contingency. So far the contingency of astronauts landing in distress in a foreign territory has not occurred, but in view of the increasing frequency of space flights, the Agreement may be invoked in the future. Concerning the return of objects launched into outer space, in 1962 the United States returned a part of a Soviet satellite that had fallen on U.S. territory. The part was given to representatives of the USSR at a meeting of the United Nations Committee on the Peaceful Uses of Outer Space.

Tokyo Convention on Offenses and Certain Other   (218)
Acts Committed On Board Aircraft (1963)

An International Civil Aviation Organization (ICAO)-drafted multilateral convention dealing with the punishment of persons committing crimes aboard aircraft in flight. The Tokyo Convention does not deal specifically with hijacking. It is designed to insure, in general, that individuals committing criminal offenses aboard civilian aircraft in flight or in an area outside the territory of any country will not go unpunished. It provides that the state of the aircraft's registration has the competence to exercise jurisdiction over such offenses. For purposes of extradition, the offenses are to be treated as if committed also in its own territory. In addition, the Tokyo convention gives special authority to the aircraft commander, other crew members, and even passengers. For example, outside the airspace of the state of registration the commander has the authority to disembark an offender and deliver him to the competent authorities of a contracting party. More than one hundred countries are parties to the Tokyo Convention. *See also* AIR HIJACKING, 196; HAGUE AIR HIJACKING CONVENTION (1970), 201; MONTREAL CONVENTION AGAINST AIRCRAFT SABOTAGE (1971), 209.

Significance   The Tokyo Convention was the first modest step in combating crimes on board aircraft. With regard to hijacking, it did not tackle this offense specifically, but dealt with it only incidentally and in a limited manner. Hijackers are treated just like any other offenders— they may be taken into custody or subjected to restraint in the same way as other offenders, and the hijacked aircraft is, under the Convention, to be restored to the lawful commander. Hijacking and other terrorist offenses against the safety of aircraft had to be specifically dealt with by special conventions, in particular the Hague Convention of 1970 and the Montreal Convention of 1971.

8. The Law of the Sea

Archipelago

A group of islands—including parts of islands, interconnecting waters, and other natural features—so closely interrelated that they form or have been historically regarded as an intrinsic geographical, economic, and political entity. A special regime for the waters of an "archipelagic state," that is, a state constituted wholly by one or more archipelagos and possibly other islands, was created by the 1982 Convention on the Law of the Sea under the pressure of Indonesia, Philippines, Fiji, Mauritius, and some thirty other archipelagic states in the Caribbean Sea and the Pacific and Indian Oceans. Under the Convention, straight baselines can be drawn around states that consist exclusively of archipelagos and islands, the baselines surrounding either individual archipelagos or all of the state's archipelagos and islands. The Convention provides that an archipelagic state may draw straight baselines around the outermost perimeter of its islands, which serve as baselines from which its territorial sea and other zones—the contiguous zone, the exclusive economic zone, and the continental shelf—are measured. The waters within the baselines are "archipelagic waters." The archipelagic state has sovereignty over these waters, the superjacent airspace, and the subjacent sea bed and subsoil with their resources. Within its archipelagic waters the archipelagic state may draw closing lines across river mouths, bays, and ports of its individual islands according to the general rules on baselines. Foreign states have certain rights in an archipelagic state's waters: rights under existing agreements and traditional fishing rights and other legitimate activities of immediately adjacent neighboring states; rights to existing submarine cables; and navigational rights, namely the right of innocent passage of ships under the general rules of the law of the sea and the right of ships and aircraft of "archipelagic sea lanes passage" in designated lanes, or if none are designated, through the routes normally used for international navigation. This right is essentially the same as the "transit passage through straits used for international navigation," which means that the rights of foreign ships and aircraft in archipelagic waters are more extensive than those in an archipelagic state's territorial sea, which lies seaward of such waters. The Convention lays down precise mathematical rules designed to prevent archipelagic states from drawing baselines around remote islands in the archipelago (the ratio of land to water within the archipelagic baselines must not be less than 1:9) and not to allow drawing such baselines to states that consist of one large island and several smaller ones (the ratio of land to water must not be more than 1:1). The length of baselines must not exceed 100 nautical miles except that up to three percent of the total number of baselines may exceed that length up to a maximum of 125 miles. Other conditions relating to archipelagic baselines essentially follow the general rule governing the drawing of straight baselines of what geographers call "coastal" archipelagos; that is, the baselines along islands fringing a coast such as that of Norway. *See also* BASELINE, 221; INNOCENT PASSAGE, 236; STRAIT, 248; TERRITORIAL SEA, 249.

Significance   The provisions on archipelagic waters, introduced by the 1982 Convention, are an innovation in the law of the sea. The 1958 Geneva Conference on the Law of the Sea evaded the issue of archipelagos. Subsequently, more and more archipelagic states adopted the practice of enclosing their perimeters by baselines. This innovation was originally opposed by maritime states concerned about threats to the freedom of the seas and especially navigational rights. Yet the United Nations Convention on the Law of the Sea of 1982 codified and developed this practice by creating such new legal concepts as "archipelagic state," "archipelagic baselines," "archipelagic waters," and "archipelagic sea lanes passage." These concepts meet the perceived interests of some thirty archipelagic states, some of which, Fiji and Papua New Guinea, for example, drew straight baselines joining the outermost points of the outermost islands which enclosed "archipelagic" waters, even before the entry of the 1982 Convention into effect. However, some other states, in particular Indonesia and the Philippines (the first exponents of a special status for archipelagos), treat the enclosed waters as "internal." The validity of the latter claim is controversial. Still other states, such as Japan, New Zealand, and the United Kingdom, did not draw any archipelagic lines although in principle they would be entitled to do so. In the period of uncertainty, and especially before the entry of the 1982 Convention into force, claims to archipelagic waters were of questionable validity as against states persistently objecting to this new legal concept. On the other hand, in view of the concurrent emergence and universal acceptance of the institution of the exclusive economic zone (EEZ), the chances are that the concept of archipelagic waters will eventually be recognized by maritime nations if it fully accommodates their legitimate navigational interests. Such indeed was the position of these states at the Third United Nations Conference on the Law of the Sea (UNCLOS III).

The "Area" (220)

The seabed, ocean floor, and subsoil thereof beyond the limits of national jurisidction. The "Area" is a term of art used in the United Nations Convention on the Law of the Sea (1982) to denote the deep seabed with its subsoil, situated beyond the continental shelf in the legal sense as defined in the Convention. The legal status of the superjacent waters and air space remains unaffected, however. Under the projected deep seabed regime, spelled out in the lengthy Part XI and two annexes of the 1982 Convention, the Area and its resources (especially the polymetallic manganese nodules rich in manganese, cobalt, copper, and nickel) are the "common heritage of mankind" to be managed on behalf of mankind as a whole by a United Nations agency to be known as the International Sea-Bed Authority. No state shall claim or exercise sovereignty or sovereign rights over any part of the Area. Any rights with respect to the minerals recovered from it can be acquired or exercised exclusively through the Authority. Financial and other economic benefits from the exploitation of the Area (and the revenue generated from the national exploitation of the continental shelf beyond the 200-mile limit) will be equitably shared by all mankind on a nondiscriminatory basis, taking into particular consideration the interests and needs of developing states and non-self-governing peoples.

Under the 1982 Convention, the seabed policy of the Authority has two objectives: (1) the development of the resources of the Area; and (2) the promotion of just and stable prices for minerals on the world market. To minimize harm to land-based producers of the minerals, the Convention provides for production limitations according to a special formula. All seabed activities must be carried out either by the Authority through its "Enterprise" or by private and state entities by permission of, and in association with, the Authority. An annex to the Convention sets out in detail the qualifications required of applicants for seabed contracts to be granted by the Authority. They would have to be a state party to the Convention or an entity sponsored by such a state. Applicants would have to meet financial and technical standards, to be defined in advance by the Council of the Authority, and would have to accept the Authority's control over their activities and comply with the technology transfer requirements spelled out in great detail in the Convention and an annex to it. As envisaged by the Convention, deep seabed mining would be based on what has become known as the "parallel" system of exploitation. Under this system, a state (or a private or public firm under its jurisdiction) would submit to the Authority a site on the seabed with commercial possibilities. The Authority would allot half of it to the would-be miner under contract with the Authority, and the remaining part would be reserved for use by the Enterprise or by developing countries. Before starting operations the miner would need a plan of work in the form of a contract with the Authority, to be approved by the Council, and a production authorization, specifying the tonnage each contractor could mine, to be issued by the Council's Legal and Technical Commission. If the Enterprise could not obtain the necessary technology on the open market, contractors would be obliged to make it available to it "on commercial terms." Technology would also be transferred to a developing country the Authority had authorized to exploit a reserved site of the seabed. Under the Convention, the parallel system could be reviewed by a Review Conference fifteen years after the start of commercial production. If, within five years following the start of the review, no agreement was reached by the Conference, it could approve (by consensus or, if no consensus could be reached, by a two-thirds majority) amendments which would take effect for all state parties after ratification by three-fourths of them. Disputes with respect to activities in the Area would be handled by a special Seabed Disputes Chamber of the International Tribunal for the Law of the Sea or a special *ad hoc* chamber of this Tribunal.

In adopting the Final Act, UNCLOS III resolved to establish a special regime to protect the preparatory investment made by state and private investors, the so-called "pioneer investors" who were already capable of carrying out deep seabed mining. Under this regime, the pioneer investors, registered with the Preparatory Commission for the Seabed Authority, would be entitled to explore—but not commercially exploit—a selected site in the Area until the 1982 Convention came into effect. Special fees and other financial obligations would be due from such pioneer investors who would otherwise be guaranteed priority over other investors, except the Enterprise, once the commercial exploitation of the Area was permitted by the Authority. One group of pioneer investors—France, India, Japan, and the Soviet Union, including their state enterprises—was registered in 1985. Another group of potential pioneer investors consisted of entities made up of firms having the nationality of, or controlled by, Belgium, Canada, the Federal Republic of Germany, Italy, the Netherlands, the United Kingdom, and the United States. *See also* CONTINENTAL SHELF, 225; FREEDOM

OF THE HIGH SEAS, 231; INTERNATIONAL SEABED AUTHORITY, 238; THIRD
UNITED NATIONS CONFERENCE ON THE LAW OF THE SEA (1982), 250.

Significance   The legal status of the deep seabed was the most controversial issue before UNCLOS III, and because of the way the legal
regime of the Area was set up by the Conference, the United States, the
United Kingdom, and the Federal Republic of Germany refused to
sign the 1982 Convention. The developing countries, hoping to benefit
from the exploitation of the manganese nodules of the seabed, had
been pressing for a legal regime that would declare the deep seabed a
"common heritage of mankind" in the meaning of *res communis* (things
owned in common), that is, an undivided asset to be shared by all
nations irrespective of their technological capabilities and to be managed by the United Nations. In general, the legal regime of the Area, as
set out in the 1982 Convention, reflected this position, but it must not
be overlooked that a vital part of the common heritage, with already
exploitable oil and gas resources, was severed from this heritage as it
was conceived by Arvid Pardo and placed under national jurisdiction
by virtue of a generous definition of the continental shelf. The United
States and some other Western countries represented the view that
under the principle of the freedom of the high seas the resources of the
deep seabed were *res nullius*; that is, things belonging to no one and
available for appropriation by any nation capable of recovering them,
and that the principle of the common heritage of mankind would be
interpreted in that way. In this view, the Third World's interpretation
distorted the meaning of the concept and was contrary to international
law.

For the United States and some other Western states, the regime of
the Area was unacceptable for economic and political reasons. Particularly offensive to the United States were the provisions of the 1982
Convention that (1) enabled the Review Conference to adopt key
changes, in the otherwise unacceptable regime, over the objections of
member states; (2) deterred rather than promoted economic development of the Area; (3) discriminated against private operations;
(4) restricted U.S. access to strategically important minerals; (5) hampered production by imposing limits upon it; (6) created a cumbersome bureaucracy requiring unconscionable financial burdens for the
United States; and (7) effectively enjoined the mandatory transfer of
sensitive private technology to possibly unfriendly countries. Even
before the 1982 Convention was signed, the United States, the United
Kingdom, the Federal Republic of Germany, and France had signed
the Agreement Concerning Interim Arrangements Relating to
Polymetallic Nodules of the Deep Sea Bed (1982). The Agreement was

designed to make appropriate provisions for avoiding overlaps and conflicting mining claims between the parties to this reciprocating state regime and to coordinate national legislation that had already been adopted by the parties and some other countries. The Soviet Union, which also adopted legislation similar to that of the Western states, did not join the reciprocating states agreement.

In 1984, Belgium, France, the Federal Republic of Germany, Italy, Japan, the Netherlands, the United Kingdom, and the United States signed a second agreement, the Provisional Understanding Regarding Deep Seabed Matters, aimed at avoiding conflict over mine sites and providing for regular consultation with respect to deep seabed mining. The parties agreed that no exploitation shall occur prior to January 1988 and assured the Preparatory Commission that the Agreement was fully compatible with the Final Act of UNCLOS III and the 1982 Convention. However, the Group of 77 and the Group of Eastern European States reiterated their opposition to any reciprocating agreements and asserted that any deep seabed activities outside the Convention regime were illegal. Thus, although commercial exploitation of the manganese nodules still remains in the rather distant future, the legal status of the deep seabed Area in the mid-1980s continues to be the most controversial issue in the law of the sea.

Baseline   (221)

The line from which the breadth of the territorial sea and other coastal state zones (contiguous zone, exclusive economic zone, exclusive fishing zone) is measured. The baseline forms the boundary between the internal waters on its landward side and the territorial sea on its seaward side. The baseline is either normal or straight. The normal baseline, used for relatively unindented coastline, is the low-water line along the coast as marked on large-scale charts officially recognized by the coastal state. Permanent outermost harbor works (but not offshore installations and structures or artificial islands) are regarded as forming part of the coast and thereby the baseline itself. In the case of islands situated on atolls or of islands having fringing reefs, the baseline is the seaward low-water line of the reef, but it is not clear how close to the coast the reef must be to serve as a baseline. Low-tide elevations (naturally formed areas of land surrounded by and above water at low tide but submerged at high tide, such as sand banks, drying rock and the like) generate baselines if they are situated wholly or partly at a distance not exceeding the breadth of the territorial sea from the mainland or an island. Straight baselines are applied in localities where the coastline is deeply indented and cut into, or if there is a fringe of islands along the coast in its immediate vicinity. In such geographical circumstances, it is virtually impossible to follow closely all the irregularities of the coast and the fringing islands, and the coastal state may draw straight baselines across the sea joining appropriate points on headlands and islands and measure the breadth of the territorial sea and other zones from these baselines.

The drawing of straight baselines is subject to the following conditions. First, such baselines must not depart to any appreciable extent from the general direction of the coast and the sea areas lying within the lines must be sufficiently closely linked to the land domain to be subject to the regime of internal waters. Second, to prevent baselines from being drawn too far seaward, they must not run to and from low-tide elevations unless lighthouses or similar installations that are permanently above sea level have been built on them or where the straight baseline method has received general international recognition. Third, straight baselines may not cut off the territorial sea of another state from the high seas or an exclusive economic (fishing) zone, a provision applying to such exceptional situations as in the Aegean Sea where Turkey could, by a system of such lines, cut off the territorial sea of the Greek islands near its coast. In determining particular baselines, account may be taken of economic interests peculiar to the region concerned (in practice, mostly fishing), the reality and the importance of which are clearly evidenced by long usage. As well as being applied in cases of irregular coastline, straight baselines may be drawn across the mouths of rivers flowing directly into the sea and, according to special rules, across estuaries and bays. *See also* AR-CHIPELAGO, 219; BAY, 222; INTERNAL WATERS, 237; TERRITORIAL SEA, 249.

Significance   The straight baseline method has been applied since the nineteenth century by Norway to its coastline, which is cut into by fiords and other inlets and fringed by innumerable islands, islets, rocks, and reefs, known as *sjaergaard*. In its judgment of 1951 in the *Anglo-Norwegian Fisheries* case (*United Kingdom v. Norway*), the International Court of Justice held, against the U.K. contention, that the method of straight baselines was in conformity with international law if it met certain conditions. Both the 1958 Geneva Convention on the Territorial Sea and Contiguous Zone and the 1982 United Nations Convention on the Law of the Sea incorporated this principle which is also part of the customary law of the sea. In view of the fact that neither customary nor conventional rules governing the use of straight baselines are precise and, in particular because there are no rules limiting the length of individual lines, the system of straight baselines, which in principle is designed to take care of exceptional situations, frequently lends itself to abuse. In fact, numerous states have applied it in a way that conflicts with the criteria and the spirit of this method. In such cases, other states are at liberty not to recognize the validity of the baseline under international law. As an extreme example, one of Burma's straight baselines is 222 nautical miles long and at one point 75 miles from the nearest land. In such (and similar) cases, the straight baseline method has contributed to pushing the coastal state's sovereignty farther seaward by enclosing considerable marine spaces on the landward side of the lines as internal waters at the ultimate expense of the freedom of the seas.

Bay   (222)

A well-marked indentation in the coast which constitutes more than a mere curvature of the coast and deserves the status of internal waters. Customary international law does not offer any clear criteria indicating when an indentation may be recognized as a legal bay or what the maximum length of its closing line should be. Although the term "gulf" usually refers to a larger ocean inlet than a bay, in state practice the two terms are sometimes used interchangeably. The concept of bays was made more precise in the 1958 Geneva Convention on the Territorial Sea and Contiguous Zone whose provisions in this respect were repeated in the United Nations Convention on the Law of the Sea (1982). Both Conventions use the term "bay" only and apply it solely to one of the three categories of bay; namely, bays the coasts of which belong to a single state. Bays whose coasts belong to more than one state and so-called "historic bays" are not covered by these Conventions. In virtually the same language as the 1958 Geneva Convention, the 1982 Convention fixes twenty-four miles as the maximum distance between the low-water marks of the natural entrance points of the bay. If the entrance exceeds twenty-four miles, a closing twenty-four-mile straight line may be drawn within the bay in such a manner as to enclose the maximum area of water that is possible with a line of that length. To be regarded as a bay, a coastal indentation must be at least as large as the area of the semicircle whose diameter is a line drawn across the mouth of that indentation. If, because of the presence of islands, an indentation has more than one mouth, the diameter of the semicircle is a line as long as the sum total of the lengths of the lines across the different mouths. Islands within an indentation are treated as if they were part of its water area. The legal status of bays bordered by more than one state—Passamaquoddy Bay bordered by Canada and the United States, for example—is controversial. It appears that in such a bay the normal baseline—that is, the low-water mark around its shores—constitutes its legal baseline and, therefore, its area does not have the character of internal waters unless the coastal states can prove that the bay is a historic bay. As interpreted by a United Nations Secretariat study of 1962, a state or states may validly claim title to a bay on historic grounds if, with the acquiescence of other states, it has or they have claimed it as internal waters and effectively exercised authority in it for a considerable period of time. There exist no limits concerning the maximum permissible length of the line closing a historic bay. *See also* BASELINE, 221; INTERNAL WATERS, 237; TERRITORIAL SEA, 249.

Significance   Lacking widespread acceptance of conventional regulation, bays must be governed by customary rules of international law which, however, fail to provide clear criteria concerning the validity of a state's claim that an indentation in the ocean is a legal bay. However, even the conventional rules on bays are not entirely free of uncertainty. Particularly in the case of estuaries, it is sometimes difficult to establish where the natural entrance points of an indentation are located. Furthermore, the approximately forty bays whose coasts belong to more than one state are not regulated by the 1958 Convention on the Territorial Sea and Contiguous Zone or by the United Nations Convention on the Law of the Sea (1982). Also, the validity of a number of claims to historic bays is contested by third states. For example, the United States denies the character of historic bay to Hudson Bay, claimed by Canada, and to Peter the Great Bay, claimed by the USSR. Uncertainty of the law may produce extravagant claims with a serious potential of international conflict as evidenced by the 1981 and 1986 U.S.-Libya incidents over the Gulf of Sidra, unjustifiably claimed by Libya as a historical bay under international law, with consequent extension of Libya's internal waters, its baselines, and its territorial sea far north into the Mediterranean Sea.

Constantinople Convention (1888)   (223)

The multilateral convention governing the legal status of the Suez Canal. The Constantinople Convention, adopted at the time when the Ottoman Empire had sovereignty over Egypt, stipulates that the Canal must be open to ships of all nations both in peace and in wartime and can never be blockaded. In time of war, no act of hostility is allowed in the Canal or within three miles of its ports, even if the country within whose territory it is located should be a belligerent. The Convention places restrictions upon the right of stay in the Canal of warships of belligerents and bars permanent fortifications there and stationing belligerents' warships in the harbors of Port Said and Suez. *See also* KIEL CANAL, 240; PANAMA CANAL TREATIES (1977), 246; STRAIT, 248.

Significance   The Suez Canal, built by the Franco-British Suez Canal Company under a concession agreement with the Sultan of Turkey, was opened in 1869. Turkey agreed that the company should operate the Canal for ninety-nine years from the time of the opening, at the termination of which Egypt was to enter into full possession of the Canal. After the defeat of Turkey in World War I, Great Britain took over Turkey's rights and titles with respect to Egypt and, in 1922, when agreeing to Egypt's independence, reserved for itself the right of negotiating with Egypt the defense of the Canal. In 1936 Egypt agreed to the stationing of British troops in its territory to defend the Canal jointly with Egypt, a promise that was put to test in World War II. In 1956, Egypt nationalized the Suez Canal Company, assuming control and management of the Canal, an action which provoked the 1956 Suez War. In 1957, Egypt unilaterally assured all interested states in a declaration deposited with the Secretariat of the United Nations that it was Egypt's unaltered policy to respect and implement the Constantinople Convention and, subsequently, accepted the compulsory jurisdiction of the International Court of Justice (ICJ) under the optional clause of the Court's Statute with respect to any differences arising between the parties of the Convention regarding the application of its provisions. As a result of hostilities during the Six-Day War of 1967 the Suez Canal was made impassable until it was reopened in 1975, when the first Israel-bound cargo ship passed through the Canal.

Contiguous Zone   (224)

A maritime zone adjacent to the territorial sea where the coastal state may exercise the control necessary to prevent infringement of its customs, fiscal, immigration, or sanitary laws and regulations within its territory or territorial sea, and to punish infringement of the above laws and regulations committed within its territory or territorial sea. Under the 1982 United Nations Convention on the Law of the Sea, the contiguous zone may not extend beyond twenty-four miles from the baselines of the territorial sea. *See also* HOT PURSUIT, 235; TERRITORIAL SEA, 249.

Significance   The origins of contiguous zone can be traced back to the British "Hovering Acts," enacted in the eighteenth century against smuggling ships hovering within twenty-four miles from the shore (eventually repealed in 1876 after the firm establishment of the three-mile territorial sea). Although Great Britain and some other states refused to recognize any special zones beyond the territorial sea, an increasing number of states introduced zones to protect their customs, immigration, and similar interests. The United States Tariff Act of 1922, which subjected foreign vessels within twelve miles of the coast to prohibition laws, was the most notorious case raising much international opposition, especially on the part of Great Britain concerned about the possibility of infringing upon the freedom of the high seas by means of this "creeping jurisdiction." Eventually, opposition to the contiguous zone faded away, and such a zone was expressly allowed (up to twelve miles) in the 1958 Convention on the Territorial Sea and Contiguous Zone. The 1982 United Nations Convention also recognized this institution, raising the maximum breadth of the zone to twenty-four miles in view of the extension of the territorial sea up to twelve miles. In the mid-1980s, the status and breadth of the contiguous zone remained uncertain because of divergence in state practice which in some cases appears to go beyond the rules of the 1982 Convention, some states establishing zones for purposes other than those specified by the Convention. Security zones and zones for purposes of maritime control and vigilance are typical examples of such zones. North Korea, for instance, instituted a fifty-mile security zone in 1977 and Chile a one-hundred-mile customs and security zone in 1948.

Continental Shelf (225)

The seabed and subsoil of the submarine areas that extend beyond a coastal state's territorial sea throughout the natural prolongation of its land territory to the outer edge of the geographical continental margin, or to a distance of 200 nautical miles from the baselines where the outer edge of the continental margin does not extend up to that distance. Under the 1982 United Nations Convention on the Law of the Sea, the continental shelf cannot, in principle, extend more than 350 nautical miles from the baselines, or its outer limits cannot exceed 100 nautical miles from the 2,500 meter isobath (a line connecting the depth of 2,500 meters). A distinction must be made between continental shelf in the geographical sense of the term and continental shelf in the legal meaning. The former is only one section of the continental margin (that is, the submerged prolongation of the land mass of the coastal state) adjacent to the coast and averaging approximately 130 meters in depth at its outer limit. Beyond this first section lie the continental slope, extending to a depth of 1,200 to 3,500 meters, and the continental rise, a gently sloping area descending approximately 3,500 to 5,500 meters into the deep seabed. As it emerged by the 1980s, the legal meaning of the continental shelf differs from the geographical understanding of the term in that, on the one hand, it includes not just the shelf itself but the whole margin and, on the other, it may include a seabed that geologically is not a natural prolongation of the land mass at all. In the latter case the 200-mile limit, copied from the rule governing the exclusive economic zone, applies as the outer limit of the continental shelf in the legal sense of the term. The 1982 United Nations Convention on the Law of the Sea adopted the above definition, adding complex geophysical guidelines for establishing the outer edge of the continental margin wherever it extends beyond 200 miles from the baselines. Adoption of the 100 miles–2,500 meters isobath (depth) limit may in some cases result in the continental shelf exceeding the 350-mile limit, especially since under the Convention submarine elevations that are natural components of the continental margin (plateaux, rises, caps, banks, and spurs) count as the margin itself. However, on submarine ridges the outer limit of the continental shelf must not exceed 350 miles from the baselines. Under the Convention, the coastal state is obliged to delimit the boundaries of its continental shelf beyond the 200-mile limit by using straight lines, not exceeding 60 miles in length, connecting fixed points defined by coordinates of latitude and longitude. The coastal state must notify the boundaries to a special Commission on the Limits of the Continental Shelf and to the Secretary-General of the United Nations. Delimitation of the continental shelf between opposite and adjacent states is an issue that has generated numerous international disputes, some fifty of which have been resolved by agreement, others by arbitration or adjudication, and still others remain to be settled. In the case of the fifty-four parties to the 1958 Convention on the Continental Shelf, the boundaries are to be determined by agreement and in the absence of agreement by application of the principle of equidistance (median line) unless another boundary line is justified by special circumstances. Customary law appears to follow the same principles except that state practice has emphasized that the equidistance–special circumstances rule must have, as its ultimate objective, as equitable a division of the continental shelf as possible in such a way as to leave each state areas that constitute the natural prolongation of its coastline (see the *North Sea Continental Shelf* cases before the International Court of Justice [ICJ], involving the Federal Republic of Germany/Denmark and the Federal Republic of Germany/Netherlands in 1969), and with a reasonable degree of proportionality between the area of continental shelf allocated to a state and the length of its coastline (see the *Continental Shelf* case before the same Court involving Tunisia/Libya in 1982). The 1982 Convention simply provides that delimitation "shall be effected by agreement on the basis of international law . . . in order to achieve an equitable solution," a provision analogous to the one governing the delimitation of exclusive economic zones. On the continental shelf within the 200-mile zone, the coastal state has exclusive sovereign right to natural resources; that is, mineral and other nonliving resources of the seabed and subsoil, together with sedentary species—organisms which, at the harvestable stage, either are immobile on or under the seabed, or unable to move except in constant physical contact with the seabed or the subsoil (oysters and clams, for example). Wrecks are excluded since they are not natural resources. The coastal state must not unjustifiably interfere with navigation and other rights of third states (overflight and laying submarine cables and pipelines), but it may construct installations and establish safety zones up to 500 meters. The rights of the coastal state over the continental shelf beyond the 200-mile zone are somewhat different, since the superjacent waters are not an exclusive economic zone but rather the high seas. Since fishing on the high seas is open to all states, disputes might arise over whether a given seabed species is sedentary and thereby under exclusive sovereign rights of the coastal state. As a compensation for removing a sizable portion of the seabed from the "common heritage of mankind," the 1982 Convention imposes upon the coastal states the duty to pay to the International Sea-Bed Authority annual payments or contributions in kind in respect of the exploitation of the nonliving resources of the continental shelf beyond 200 miles. The payments would start after five years of exploitation of a site and would be in proportion to the value or volume of production, rising from one percent in the sixth year to seven percent in the twelfth and following years. A developing state net importer of the minerals exploited would be exempt from this obligation. The Authority would distribute the revenue to developing countries, especially to the least developed and landlocked ones. *See also* THE "AREA," 220; EXCLUSIVE ECONOMIC ZONE (EEZ), 227; INTERNATIONAL SEA-BED AUTHORITY, 238.

Significance   The law of the continental shelf offers an example of the formation of customary international law in recent times. Although prior to 1945 there had been some isolated cases of exclusive rights to harvesting specific living resources of the seabed beyond the territorial sea (for example, sponge fisheries off the Tunisian coast, claimed by France, and pearl fisheries off Ceylon, claimed by Great Britain), the general rule was that no state had exclusive right to any part of the seabed and subsoil beneath the high seas. The discovery of offshore oil and gas and the development of technology to exploit these resources brought about a fundamental change in this rule. President Truman's proclamation of 1945 was the first major assertion of a coastal state's exclusive rights to the living and nonliving resources of the continental shelf, in the case of the United States down to the depth of 100 fathoms (600 feet). Without any protests, the U.S. example was followed by certain other states. Moreover, a number of Latin American countries, especially those on the Pacific coast where there is hardly any geological continental shelf, extended their respective claims to the resources of the superjacent waters to a distance of 200 miles. By the time the Geneva Conference on the Law of the Sea (UNCLOS I) convened in 1958, a customary rule of international law had developed confirming the U.S. claim of 1945. The Conference adopted a special Convention on the Continental Shelf in which the outer limits of the shelf were fixed at the ocean depth of 200 meters (roughly corresponding to the U.S. claim) or, beyond that limit, to "where the depth of the superjacent waters admits of exploitation." The criterion of exploitability might suggest that, as technology progressed, ever deeper areas, extending to the deep mid-ocean and eventually covering the whole seabed, could be considered the "legal" continental shelf, a development that would have benefited only the industrialized nations possessing the required technology. Concern about such extreme consequences of the exploitability criterion (otherwise legally unfounded since the 1958 Convention in principle conceives the continental shelf as a prolongation of land territory and defines it as an area adjacent to the coast) led to calls for declaring the seabed a "common heritage of mankind" and to the convening of UNCLOS III, which adopted the aforementioned provisions on the continental shelf. By the mid-1980s, with the acceptance of the concept of the exclusive economic zone (EEZ), the coastal states could claim exclusive rights to the natural resources of the continental shelf not only on the basis of the customary law of the continental shelf but also, insofar as the shelf within the 200-mile limit is concerned, by virtue of the concept of the EEZ. In view of the fact that the continental shelf contains (in addition to other minerals and sedentary species), rich oil and gas deposits accounting for a quarter of the total oil and fifteen percent of gas production, competition for these resources is likely to increase with advances in technology and rising demand. Disputes over delimitation of the shelf have already proliferated. The general concept of "equitable solution" offers guidelines for settlement, developed in international adjudication and adopted by the 1982 Convention, but diversity of geographical and other elements involved in individual cases suggests that clarification of this concept will have to take a long time.

Enclosed or Semienclosed Sea (226)

A gulf, basin, or sea surrounded by two or more states and connected to another sea or the ocean by a narrow outlet or consisting entirely or primarily of the territorial seas and exclusive economic zones of two or more coastal states. Under the 1982 United Nations Convention on the Law of the Sea, states bordering enclosed or semienclosed seas should cooperate with each other in the exercise of their rights and in the performance of their duties under the Convention and "shall endeavor" to coordinate (1) the management, exploration, and exploitation of the marine living resources; (2) the implementation of their rights and duties with respect to the protection and preservation of the marine environment; and (3) scientific research. They also have the duty to invite cooperation of other interested states or international organizations. *See also* FISHERIES, INTERNATIONAL LAW OF, 228; MARINE POLLUTION, INTERNATIONAL LAW OF, 243.

Significance   There are more than twenty marine areas which, under the criteria specified in the 1982 Convention, can be regarded as enclosed or semienclosed seas. Among them are the Baltic, Bering, Black, Caribbean, East China, Mediterranean, Red, Solomon, and South China seas; the Gulf of Mexico; the Gulf of Oman; and the Persian (Arabian) Gulf. In actual international practice, cooperation among the littoral states of enclosed or semienclosed seas has taken place for some time in such matters as conservation of the living resources and marine pollution prevention and control. The Gdańsk Convention of 1973 on Fishing and Conservation of the Living Resources in the Baltic Sea and the Belts is an example of cooperation in the former area. However, it is the regional arrangements on the protection and preservation of the marine environment, that is, in the area of combating marine pollution, that have emerged in the 1970s and the 1980s as the major instance of cooperation of states bordering an enclosed or semienclosed sea. The Helsinki Convention of 1974 on the Protection of the Marine Environment of the Baltic Sea Area provides a pioneering case of a comprehensive approach of the littoral states to the problem of marine pollution in an extremely vulnerable marine area. The various arrangements set up under the auspices of the Regional Seas Programme of the United Nations Environment Programme (UNEP)—namely for the Mediterranean Sea (1976); the Persian Gulf and the Gulf of Oman (1978); the Gulf of Guinea (1981); the Red Sea and the Gulf of Aden (1982); and the Caribbean Sea and the Gulf of Mexico (1981)—are further examples of cooperation envisaged by the 1982 Convention. It must be stressed that the Convention does not impose any mandatory mechanisms upon the states bordering enclosed or semienclosed seas since such states are expected only to "endeavor" to coordinate their cooperation. Using this language, the Convention avoided imposing a regional regime upon coastal states which for various reason would not be willing to join it. It must also be emphasized that the concept of the enclosed or semienclosed sea under the 1982 Convention has nothing in common with the politically and strategically motivated doctrine, sometimes known under the same name, selectively promoted by the Soviet Union but categorically rejected by the Western nations.

Exclusive Economic Zone (EEZ)   **(227)**

The marine area (including the subjacent seabed and subsoil) beyond and adjacent to the territorial sea, extending up to 200 nautical miles from the baselines of the territorial sea, in which the coastal state has sovereign rights in relation to natural resources and with regard to other activities for the economic exploitation and exploration of the zone, but in which third states enjoy the freedoms of navigation and overflight and of laying submarine cables and pipelines. The EEZ is a new marine zone that emerged in customary law of the sea in the 1970s and early 1980s and was codified at UNCLOS III in the 1982 United Nations Convention on the Law of the Sea as a separate functional zone of the ocean between the territorial sea and the high seas. Where states, because of geographical circumstances, cannot claim a full 200-mile zone, delimitation of the EEZ between opposite or adjacent states must be effected by agreement in order to achieve an equitable solution. In practice, such delimitation usually follows the equidistance (median line) principle, frequently modified by taking into account special circumstances as illustrated by the *Delimitation of the Maritime Boundary in the Gulf of Maine Area* case before the International Court of Justice (Canada/United States of America, 1984). In its EEZ, the coastal state has, in addition to the already mentioned sovereign economic rights, jurisdiction with regard to establishment and use of artificial islands, installations and structures, marine scientific research, and the protection and preservation of the marine environment, and other rights and duties allowed under international law such as, for example, those resulting from the contiguous zone (which overlaps with the first twelve miles of the EEZ) and the right of hot pursuit. The freedoms enjoyed by third states in the EEZ and, in particular, the freedom of navigation, may be limited by the coastal state's rules on pollution control and the presence of artificial islands and similar structures. Attribution of other rights of third states in the EEZ (for example, the rights to salvage wrecks, conduct military exercises, or emplace antisubmarine listening devices) must be decided on the merits of each case. One corollary of the coastal state's sovereign rights to the living resources of its EEZ is its right and—under the 1982 Convention—duty to determine the total allowable catch, prevent overexploitation, and promote the objective of optimum utilization of its resources. However, in case of underfishing, other states—especially landlocked and geographically disadvantaged states of the same subregion or region—have access to the surplus through special arrangements with the EEZ country. The provisions of the 1982 Convention to this effect are ambiguous, and their precise content will ultimately have to be defined by actual practice both among parties to the Convention (when it is in effect) and other states. *See also* BASELINE, 221; CONTIGUOUS ZONE, 224; CONTINENTAL SHELF, 225;

Significance   Like the continental shelf, the EEZ provides an example of the creation of customary international law in recent times. Historically the concept of the EEZ can be traced to claims of some Latin American countries to a 200-mile exclusive fishery zone in the decade following 1945. Such claims were at that time considered extravagant and illegal by most developed countries. On the other hand, they gained support of an increasing number of less developed countries and even some Western nations (Canada, Iceland, Norway, Australia, and New Zealand, for example), all of them desiring to gain control of their offshore fishing resources, in some cases exploited by foreign fishing fleets. The idea of an EEZ was first proposed by Kenya at the Asian-African Legal Consultative Committee in 1971 and was similar to the concept of the "patrimonial sea" promoted by Latin American countries. By the opening of UNCLOS III the two concepts had merged into one concept of the EEZ, which soon received universal approval and reluctant acceptance even by those countries which, like the United States and the USSR, had originally opposed it as curtailing the traditional freedom of the seas. By the mid-1980s most coastal states, without waiting for the 1982 Convention to enter into force, had unilaterally proclaimed either an Exclusive Fishery Zone (EFZ) or an EEZ. Many of these acts follow the rules of the Convention, but some of them conflict with it and even claim a 200-mile territorial sea. The United States, which had introduced a 200-mile EEZ in 1976, proclaimed an EEZ in 1983, followed by the USSR in 1984. However, the United States did not claim jurisdiction to control foreign scientific research in its zone.

The almost universal establishment of the EEZ/EFZ has had a profound impact upon the law of the sea. It subtracted from the high seas area more than one third of ocean space containing some ninety percent of the world's fish stocks and—since the EEZ also includes the seabed and subsoil irrespective of their geological nature—almost the same proportion of seabed oil deposits and approximately ten percent of the ocean's manganese nodules. The extension of coastal jurisdiction has radically changed the system of management of the living resources of the sea, shifting the responsibility of management from fishery commissions to coastal states. One irony of the emergence of the EFZ is that, contrary to expectations of many developing nations which promoted it in the name of a "New International Economic Order," the introduction of the EEZ/EFZ has not resulted in any fundamental redistribution of the ocean resources in favor of the less developed nations. Although some of them (for example, India, Indonesia, Brazil, and Mexico) have gained large areas of the EEZ and others have benefited by gaining revenues from licensing fees on foreign fishing vessels, seven developed countries, the United States and France being the biggest winners, are among the ten major beneficiaries of the EEZ. Furthermore, the introduction of this zone has not significantly reduced the catches of the distant-water fishing nations, most of which were able to negotiate access to the exclusive economic (fishery) zones of other countries.

Fisheries, International Law of (228)

That part of the law of the sea which regulates marine fisheries and, in general, the exploitation, management, and conservation of the living resources of the sea. Because of universal extension of coastal jurisdiction by the introduction of the Exclusive Economic Zone (EEZ) or Exclusive Fishery Zone (EFZ), the international law of fisheries has undergone some fundamental changes since the mid-1970s. Under traditional international law, the coastal state's fishery jurisdiction was limited to its internal waters and the territorial sea, and the management and conservation of fisheries beyond the territorial sea was largely the function of numerous international commissions—the North East Atlantic Fishery Commission, for example—or was regulated on regional or bilateral bases. The introduction of the EEZ/EFZ has extended the coastal jurisdiction to 200 miles, with only the high seas remaining free for fishing by nationals of all states. The result is a reduction of the role of international fishery commissions in the management of the living resources of the oceans.

The law of fisheries was in a state of flux in the early 1980s, but its basic principles and rules were codified and developed in the 1982 United Nations Convention on the Law of the Sea which, in general, can be considered reflective of the customary international law of fisheries. Under the 1982 Convention, the coastal state must determine the total allowable catch of the living resources of its EEZ/EFZ and take proper conservation and management measures to ensure that they are not endangered by overexploitation. It must maintain harvested species at levels that can produce maximum sustainable yield; that is, the level at which the loss from fishing and natural causes is compensated by the increase from reproduction. If the coastal state does not have the capacity to harvest the entire allowable catch, on the basis of agreement, it must allow other states access to the surplus, taking into account such factors as the significance of the living resources to its economy, the needs of developing states of the same subregion or region, the rights of landlocked and geographically disadvantaged states, and the need to minimize economic dislocation in states whose nationals have habitually fished in the zone or that have made substantial efforts in research and identification of stocks. States must cooperate in conservation of stocks that migrate from one EEZ to another or to the high seas. Special rules apply to anadromous, catadromous, sedentary, and highly migratory species, and marine mammals. States in whose rivers anadromous species originate—species such as salmon, which spawn in fresh waters but subsequently live in the ocean— have the primary responsibility for managing such stocks and are not obliged to grant other states access to the surplus. Fishing for anadromous species beyond 200 miles is normally forbidden, and regional agreements such as the 1982 Convention for the Conservation of Salmon in the North Atlantic confirm this rule. Catadromous species—such as eels that spawn in the ocean but spend the greater part of their life cycle in fresh waters—are governed by the general rules on fishing in the EEZ. However, fishing for this species in the high seas is prohibited. Management of catadromous species migrating through exclusive economic zones is to be regulated by agreement. Sedentary species are subject only to the rules governing the continental shelf. The management by coastal states of highly migratory species such as tuna, marlins, and sharks is to be complemented by international cooperation through regional commissions such as the one set up under the 1966 International Convention for the Conservation of Atlantic Tunas. Coastal states must cooperate through appropriate international organizations for the conservation, management, and study of marine mammals—whales, porpoises, and seals, for example. A number of countries, including Australia, the United States, and the United Kingdom, have prohibited whaling in their respective zones. Whaling is regulated by the International Whaling Commission, established under the International Convention for the Regulation of Whaling (1946) in an attempt to save these cetaceans from extinction by large-scale whaling, conducted especially by the Soviet Union and Japan. The Commission sets quotas for commercial catches, which are gradually being reduced, with the final objective of a total ban on all commercial whaling. In 1985, the Commission voted to impose a total moratorium on commercial whaling beginning in 1986.

High seas fisheries are open to all states which must cooperate in their conservation through subregional or regional organizations. In actual practice, states had adjusted the work of existing fishery commissions to the conditions of the new legal regime of fisheries or established new commissions to manage the living resources beyond the 200-mile limits. The North West Atlantic Fisheries Organization (1978) and the North East Atlantic Fisheries Commission (1980) are examples of international cooperation envisaged by the 1982 Convention. *See also* CONTINENTAL SHELF, 225; EXCLUSIVE ECONOMIC ZONE (EEZ), 227; LANDLOCKED AND GEOGRAPHICALLY DISADVANTAGED STATES, 241; TERRITORIAL SEA, 249.

Significance   Apart from claims by some Pacific coast Latin American nations to 200-mile exclusive fishery zones in the late 1940s and early 1950s, a general trend toward extension of fishery jurisdiction beyond the territorial sea started, following the unsuccessful attempts of the First and Second Geneva Conferences on the Law of the Sea (1958, 1960) to agree on the breadth of the territorial sea and the failure to adequately implement the 1958 Geneva Convention on Fishing and Conservation of the Living Resources of the High Seas. That the trend to extend the coastal states' fisheries jurisdiction was irreversible was demonstrated by the fact that the United Kingdom had to give up its attempts, in three "cod wars" in the period between 1958 and 1976, to prevent Iceland from enforcing its laws extending such jurisdiction first to 12, then 50 and 200 miles. Eventually, even before the 1982 Convention went into effect, a 200-mile fishery jurisdiction of the coastal states, either in the form of an EEZ or an EFZ, became the rule, with 90 percent of the oceans' fish stock placed under national jurisdiction. The reasons behind this development include resentment of many coastal states over activities of foreign distant-water fishing fleets in their offshore waters, dissatisfaction with the work of international fishery commissions, and general concern over depletion of the living resources of the oceans. The success of the 200-mile fishery regime will depend on the rationality and effectiveness of the domestic management and enforcement measures, international cooperation, progress in scientific research, and the extent to which the developing countries are provided with know-how and appropriate technology in building up their fishery resources.

Flag of Convenience   (229)

The flag of a state whose law allows registration, in return for pecuniary consideration, and thereby the grant of nationality and the right to fly its flag to virtually any ship without laying down any requirements, such as those relating to the nationality of the shipowner or the crew or the country of construction. Panama and Honduras (and at one time Costa Rica) were the first countries to start the practice of "open registry" before World War II. Following the war, however, it was Liberia that rapidly grew to become the leading flag-of-convenience country (followed by Panama) to such an extent that since 1967 it has been by far the world's largest ship-owning nation in terms of registered tonnage. More recently Cyprus, Singapore, Somalia, Sri Lanka, and the Philippines have joined the practice of open registry. None of these states is party to the 1958 Geneva Convention on the High Seas, which requires the otherwise unclear "genuine link" to exist between the ship and the state of registry which must exercise effective jurisdiction in administrative, technical, and social matters over the ships flying its flag. In its advisory opinion on the *Constitution of the Maritime Safety Committee of IMCO* ([Intergovernmental Maritime Consultative Organization; now International Maritime Organization] 1960), the International Court of Justice (ICJ), indirectly upholding Liberia's and Panama's right to open registry, ruled that the concept of genuine link was irrelevant for determining the meaning of the phrase "the largest ship-owning nations" for purposes of membership in IMCO's Maritime Safety Committee, as formulated in the Convention establishing this agency. The Court held that the phrase simply meant that nation with the largest registered tonnage, irrespective of any link between ships and the state of the nationality, which meant that ownership was also an irrelevant factor. From an international point of view, the existence of flags of convenience raises a host of vexing questions, such as whether the state of ownership of a flag-of-convenience ship has the right to protect it or to requisition it in time of national emergency, possibly under the doctrine of "effective control," or whether the labor laws of the state of ownership can be extended to flag-of-convenience vessels. It is generally recognized, however, that the practice of flags of convenience is not contrary to international law. *See also* NATIONALITY: GENUINE LINK, 136; NATIONALITY OF SHIPS, 245.

Significance   The issue of flags of convenience aroused considerable controversy in the law of the sea and international shipping. These flags are used primarily by shipping companies from the United States, Greece, Hong Kong, and Japan, which by registering ships under them can avoid payment of taxes and greatly reduce their operating costs. In their view, flags of convenience are "flags of necessity" since, they contend, without them they would not be able to compete in the international shipping market. Open-registry countries claim that they allow foreign-owned vessels registration under their flags in the exercise of their sovereign powers and in accordance with international law. On the other hand, shipowners from traditional European maritime nations and their governments are in the forefront of the opposition against the flags of convenience, claiming that open registry gives American and other flag-of-convenience shipowners competitive advantage over shipping registered under traditional maritime nations' flags. International labor, and especially seafarers' unions, have also battled the flags of convenience since refuge under these flags allows shipowners to avoid the jurisdiction of labor and other social legislation of maritime nations and deprives seamen of these nations of job opportunities. Open-registry countries have also been criticized for laxity in crew standards, failure to comply with antipollution regulations, and jeopardizing safety of navigation. While it is true that numerous tanker accidents have involved open-registry shipping, it is a fact that the Liberian fleet has a relatively larger number of modern vessels than other fleets and that Liberia has made efforts to improve effective control over ships registered under its flag. At the international level, various attempts have been made to meet the challenge posed by the flags of convenience. The "genuine link" requirement of the 1958 Geneva Convention on the High Seas was one such attempt which, however, had little influence upon the growing practice of open registry. There is no reason to believe that the genuine link clause of the 1982 Convention on the Law of the Sea will have any more impact upon this practice. The issue of flags of convenience was also on the agenda of the International Maritime Organization (IMO) and the International Labor Organization (ILO). It was also discussed and studied by the United Nations Conference on Trade and Development (UNCTAD) where, although the open-registry flags belong to developing countries, the practice of flags of convenience was condemned by a great majority of these countries that demanded its gradual elimination as a phenomenon detrimental to the economy of the Third World. In 1986, as part of the anti-open-registry action, UNCTAD adopted a convention on the conditions for registration of ships under national flags.

Flag-State Jurisdiction   (230)

A fundamental principle of jurisdiction whereby, save in exceptional cases, a ship on the high seas is subject only to the jurisdiction of the flag state; that is, the state granting it the right to sail under its flag. Flag-state jurisdiction is a corollary of the rule that no state may validly purport to subject any part of the high seas to its sovereignty or jurisdiction and of the need to avoid a state of unregulated lawlessness and anarchy on the high seas. In the event of a collision or any other incident of navigation on the high seas, penal or disciplinary proceedings may be initiated against a crew member only before the judicial or administrative authority either of the flag state or the state of which the individual concerned is a national. This rule was confirmed in 1952 by the Brussels Convention for the Unification of Certain Rules Relating to Penal Jurisdiction in Matters of Collision or Other Incidents of Navigation and reiterated in the 1958 Geneva Convention on the High Seas and the 1982 United Nations Convention on the Law of the Sea.

The rule reversed the highly criticized judgment of the Permanent Court of International Justice in the *Lotus* case (*France v. Turkey*, 1927) which, however, otherwise reaffirmed the basic principle of customary international law that "vessels on the high seas are subject to no authority except that of the State whose flag they fly." Since the flag state is responsible for the safe operation of its ships, its jurisdiction is likely to have priority over the concurrent jurisdiction of the state of crew members' nationality. *See also* FREEDOM OF THE HIGH SEAS, 231; HIGH SEAS, 234; NATIONALITY OF SHIPS, 245; CUBAN QUARANTINE, 1982, 306.

Significance   A major consequence of the rule of flag-state jurisdiction is that on the high seas (and, subject to the coastal state's rights, also in the Exclusive Economic Zone [EEZ]) a merchant vessel can be stopped, boarded, or otherwise interfered with only by a public ship of its flag state. However, whereas warships and ships owned or operated by a state and used only on government noncommercial service enjoy complete immunity, there are a number of exceptional situations where a warship or another duly authorized public ship or aircraft may interfere with a nonpublic vessel or a vessel owned or operated by a state and used on commercial service of another state. Apart from the rule that the coastal state is allowed to exercise its jurisdiction over foreign vessels in its EEZ and contiguous zone, if they violate the coastal state's right in the respective zone, boarding a foreign ship on the high seas is justified if there are reasonable grounds for suspecting that it is engaged in piracy, slave trade, or unauthorized ("pirate") broadcasting, or that the ship is without any nationality or, though flying a foreign flag or refusing to show its flag, it is in reality of the same nationality as the warship. In such cases the warship may proceed to exercise the so-called "right of visit" or "visit and search" or "right of approach" in order to verify the ship's right to fly its flag. A boat may be sent to a suspected ship and, if suspicion remains after the documents have been checked, the ship may be boarded for a more thorough examination. Other exceptions to the flag state's jurisdiction include hot pursuit; arrest of a foreign vessel on the basis of a reciprocal treaty power to arrest one another's vessels (a practice common in the nineteenth century for suppression of slavery and today often followed under treaties for the conservation of marine living resources and protection of submarine cables); intervention in case of the threat of pollution from a foreign shipping casualty (the right recognized by the International Convention relating to Intervention on the High Seas in Cases of Oil Pollution Casualties, 1969, but today probably part of customary law); and finally if action against a foreign vessel has been authorized by the United Nations Security Council, as was the case during the Rhodesian crisis when, in 1966, such authorization was given to the United

Kingdom in order to stop ships on their way to the blockaded port of Beira in the then Portuguese Mozambique. Interference with foreign shipping on the high seas on grounds of self-defense, such as that asserted by France during the Algerian War, is highly controversial as was also the Cuban "quarantine" action of 1962 when, on the basis of an Organization of American States (OAS) Resolution, warships of the United States, Argentina, Venezuela, and the Dominican Republic interfered with foreign shipping to interdict transportation of offensive military equipment bound for Cuba.

Freedom of the High Seas   (231)

A fundamental principle of international law whereby all states, whether coastal or landlocked, have the right to exercise certain freedoms on the high seas with due regard for the interests of other states. Because of technological progress, the freedoms of the high seas cannot be exhaustively listed. Hence, both the 1958 Geneva Convention on the High Seas and the 1982 United Nations Convention on the Law of the Sea name only examples of such freedoms. The latter Convention lists the following freedoms: navigation and overflight; laying submarine cables and pipelines (sometimes known as "freedoms of immersion"); constructing artificial islands and other installations; fishing; and scientific research. *See also* EXCLUSIVE ECONOMIC ZONE (EEZ), 227; FLAG-STATE JURISDICTION, 230; HIGH SEAS, 234; HOT PURSUIT, 235; NATIONALITY OF SHIPS, 245; PIRACY, 247.

Significance   As an institution of international law, freedom of the high seas asserted itself universally by the first half of the nineteenth century. Its origins are commonly associated with the name of Hugo Grotius (De Groot) whose pamphlet *Mare Liberum* (The Free Sea) of 1609 (as discovered in the nineteenth century, one chapter of his treatise *De Jure Praedae*—On the Law of Prize and Booty) defended the principle of the freedom of the seas against Portuguese encroachments. This principle had been advocated by others before him, for example Alberico Gentili. Grotius' work eventually prompted the appearance of pamphlets defending the legality of claims to sovereignty over the high seas, of which English jurist and antiquarian John Selden's *Mare Clausum* (The Closed Sea) of 1635, representing England's claims, is the best known. In the second half of the twentieth century the emergence of new maritime zones, and especially the Exclusive Economic Zone (EEZ), reduced the area of the high seas and brought about certain limitations upon the exercise of some freedoms. For example, despite continued validity of the freedom of laying submarine cables and pipelines, constructing installations, and doing scientific research, the building of an artificial island or similar structure on another country's continental shelf or conducting research there requires that country's consent; and the exercise of the right to lay submarine cables and pipelines or to implant other installations on the seabed there is subject to the coastal state's regulatory power. There are certain activities related to the exercise of the freedom of the high seas that are controversial in international law. First, a fundamental disagreement arose in the 1970s over the question of whether or not the exploitation of the deep seabed is part of the freedom of the high seas. Whereas some Western nations (for example, the United States, the United Kingdom, and the Federal Republic of Germany) claim such freedom on the ground that the manganese nodules and other nonliving resources of the seabed and subsoil beyond the legal continental shelf are one kind of *res nullius* (a thing belonging to no one) free for appropriation by any nation able to recover them, most states, and especially the developing ones, deny this freedom to individual countries, regarding the minerals as *res communis* (a thing owned in common), subject to international management under the auspices of the United Nations. Second, since freedoms of the high seas must be exercised with due regard for the interests of other states, it is controversial whether nuclear weapons may be tested on the high seas (by a country which is not a party to the 1963 Partial Test Ban Treaty). Thus Australia, New Zealand, and other countries objected to France's atmospheric testing in the Pacific Ocean on the grounds that such activity interfered with ships and aircraft of other nations and that radioactive fallout constituted infringement and abuse of the freedom of the high seas. The International Court of Justice (ICJ) did not rule on the legality of this testing after France had announced its intention of conducting no further testing on the oceans (*Nuclear Tests* cases, *Australia v. France, New Zealand v. France*, 1974). Navigation of nuclear-powered ships and ships carrying nuclear materials does not appear to be contrary to international law. Naval maneuvers and conventional weapons testing are allowed on prior notification of all third states. The freedom to observe and monitor such activities is also part of the freedom of the high seas.

Geneva Conference on the Law of the Sea, 1958   (232) (UNCLOS I)

An international conference under the auspices of the United Nations convened to codify and develop the law of the sea on the basis of drafts prepared by the International Law Commission (ILC). This First

United Nations Conference on the Law of the Sea (sometimes referred to as UNCLOS I) brought together eighty-six states which adopted four conventions on (1) the Territorial Sea and Contiguous Zone; (2) the High Seas; (3) the Continental Shelf; and (4) Fishing and Conservation of the Living Resources of the High Seas. An Optional Protocol on the Compulsory Settlement of Disputes was also signed. *See also* GENEVA CONFERENCE ON THE LAW OF THE SEA, 1960 (UNCLOS II), 233; LAW OF THE SEA, 242; THIRD UNITED NATIONS CONFERENCE ON THE LAW OF THE SEA, 1973–1982 (UNCLOS III), 250.

Significance   The Geneva Conference of 1958 produced the first major codification of the law of the sea. In its preamble the Convention on the High Seas claims to be "generally declaratory of established principles of international law," but no such claims are made for the other three conventions adopted at the Conference, which represented a mixture of "codification" and "progressive development" as understood by the ILC. To a large extent, however, the Convention on the Continental Shelf was a codification of the existing customary law. All four conventions are still in force, but only for a rather limited number of states. As of January 1984, the Convention on the Territorial Sea and Contiguous Zone was in force for forty-five states; the Convention on the High Seas for fifty-seven; that on the Continental Shelf for fifty-four; and the Convention on fishing only for thirty-five states.

The Geneva Conference produced a considerable codificatory work; but it failed to reach agreement on some issues, in particular on the breadth of the territorial sea and the related question of the fishing rights of coastal states in the areas of the high seas adjacent to their territorial seas. What is more important, however, is the fact that the work of the Conference was soon overtaken by technological, economic, and political developments. The technology of seabed exploration and exploitation made it necessary to revise the rules of the Convention on the Continental Shelf and even to devise a completely new regime for deep seabed mining. Concern about depletion of fishing resources and marine pollution resulted in the expansion of the coastal states' jurisdiction at the expense of the high seas. Many, especially new, states claimed wide territorial seas and extensive fishing zones so that the Convention on fishing became virtually meaningless. Archipelagic states pressed for recognition of their claims and, in general, many states were dissatisfied with various provisions of the Geneva 1958 conventions in the drafting of which they had not played any part. These pressures eventually led to the convening of another conference to deal comprehensively with the law of the sea, taking account of recent developments.

Geneva Conference on the Law of the Sea, 1960   (233)
(UNCLOS II)

An unsuccessful international conference convened by the United Nations to deal specifically with the issues of the breadth of the territorial sea and the fishing rights of states in areas of the high seas adjacent to their territorial seas. *See also* GENEVA CONFERENCE ON THE LAW OF THE SEA, 1958 (UNCLOS I), 232; LAW OF THE SEA, 242; THIRD UNITED NATIONS CONFERENCE ON THE LAW OF THE SEA, 1973–1982 (UNCLOS III), 250.

Significance   The 1960 Geneva Conference (sometimes referred to as UNCLOS II) gathered eighty-seven states but failed to achieve its objectives. A joint U.S.-Canadian compromise formula for a six-mile territorial sea plus a six-mile fishery jurisdiction zone failed by one vote needed for the necessary two-thirds majority. In retrospect, it is clear that even if the compromise had been adopted, it would have been short-lived because of a trend among many countries (especially in the Third World) to claim territorial seas wider than six miles and fishery zones extending far beyond the limits proposed at the 1960 Conference.

High Seas   (234)

All parts of the sea that are not included in the Exclusive Economic Zone (EEZ), or Exclusive Fishery Zone (EFZ), the territorial sea, the internal waters of a state, or in the archipelagic waters of an archipelagic state. This definition of the high seas takes into account recent developments in the law of the sea, and in particular the emergence of the EEZ/EFZ and archipelagic waters, as codified and developed in the 1982 United Nations Convention on the Law of the Sea. However, in the view of some traditional maritime states, the high seas are all parts of the sea not included in the territorial sea or in the internal waters of a state (as codified in 1958 in the Geneva Convention on the High Seas). In this view, the EEZ is merely part of the high seas subject to special jurisdictional rights of the coastal states. The concept of the high seas also extends to the superjacent airspace, but whether or not it includes the subjacent seabed and subsoil is the most controversial issue in contemporary law of the sea. The high seas are open to all states whether coastal or landlocked. They may exercise freedoms of the high seas there, but no state may validly purport to subject any part of the high seas to its sovereignty and any such claims of sovereignty are invalid. The rather vague and general provision of the 1982 Convention to the effect that the high seas "shall be reserved for peaceful purposes" must reasonably be interpreted as implying only that aggression on the high seas is prohibited. A show of strength off the coast of another state could also be considered illegal as implying threat of force. *See also* THE "AREA," 220; EXCLUSIVE ECONOMIC ZONE (EEZ), 227; FREEDOM ON THE HIGH SEAS, 231; FLAG-STATE JURISDICTION, 230; HOT PURSUIT, 235; NATIONALITY OF SHIPS, 245; PIRACY, 247.

Significance   The concept of the high seas is of fundamental importance in international law and is closely related to the principle of freedom of the high seas. However, the principle that in peacetime no state may exercise sovereignty on the high seas in relation to other states did not assert itself until the nineteenth century. Earlier, in the fifteenth and seventeenth centuries, some states had laid claims to large portions of the ocean; for example, Venice to the Adriatic and England to the seas around its coasts. As overseas exploration and trade increased, even those states which, like England, had advocated the idea of a "closed sea" in opposition to the principle of the "free sea," gradually abandoned their claims realizing the advantages of the regime of the high seas. The traditional regime of the high seas endured until about the middle of the twentieth century, when the distinction between the territorial sea and the high seas underwent a fundamental revision by the emergence of the EFZ and then EEZ, which removed approximately one-third of the ocean space from this regime. Although the freedoms of navigation, overflight, and the laying of submarine cables and pipelines are guaranteed in these zones under the 1982 Convention, some traditional maritime nations concerned about the possibility of the EEZ being eventually converted into the territorial sea ("creeping jurisdiction"), would prefer to treat the EEZ as part of the high seas rather than a separate zone. However, their eventual acquiescence in the new order of the oceans, as laid down in the 1982 Convention, is likely to secure a universal acceptance of the shrinking of the high seas in the legal sense of the term.

Hot Pursuit   (235)
The right of a state's warships or military aircraft, or other public ships or aircraft, to pursue and arrest a foreign private vessel on the high seas that has violated that state's laws and regulations while within that state's internal waters or territorial sea. Hot pursuit must be commenced when the foreign ship or one of its boats is within the internal waters, the territorial sea (under the 1982 United Nations Convention on the Law of the Sea also the archipelagic waters), or—if customs, fiscal, immigration, or sanitary laws have been violated—the contiguous zone of the state effecting the pursuit. The pursuit may only be continued outside the territorial sea (or the contiguous zone) if it has

not been interrupted. With the emergence of the concepts of the continental shelf and the Exclusive Economic Zone (EEZ), hot putsuit may also be undertaken in case of violation of the coastal state's laws and regulations governing such zones. Hot pursuit may only be commenced after a visual or auditory signal to stop has been given, but the ship giving the order need not be within the territorial sea or the contiguous zone. A radio signal is not sufficient, however. Pursuit must be continuous and the right to pursue ceases as soon as the ship pursued enters the territorial sea of its own state or of a third state. Under the 1982 Convention, pursuit begun by an aircraft may be taken over by another aircraft or ship. It appears that a ship may also take over hot pursuit from another ship. Stopping or arresting a foreign ship outside the territorial sea in circumstances that do not justify the exercise of the right of hot pursuit results in the duty to compensate that ship for any loss or damage sustained. *See also* CONTIGUOUS ZONE, 224; EXCLUSIVE ECONOMIC ZONE (EEZ), 227; FLAG-STATE JURISDICTION, 230; TERRITORIAL SEA, 249.

Significance The right of hot pursuit (alluded to in the eighteenth century in the writings of Cornelius van Bynkershoek) is a well-established rule of customary international law, codified in the 1958 Convention on the High Seas and the 1982 United Nations Convention on the Law of the Sea. One of the most celebrated cases of the exercise of this right was the case of the *I'm Alone* (Canadian–United States Arbitration, 1935), involving a Canadian registry schooner pursued by a U.S. coastguard ship on suspicion of smuggling liquor at the time of prohibition in the United States. The right of hot pursuit is general in the sense that it is immaterial what law was infringed upon by the foreign vessel in the coastal state's waters. It is not clear under the 1982 Convention whether a foreign warship may be pursued (in particular for violating the coastal state's security interests) and whether hot pursuit of a ship may be undertaken if the violation of the coastal state's law occurred on a previous voyage of the foreign ship. Whereas hot pursuit was originally permitted to commence within the coastal state's internal waters or territorial sea, over the years a broadening of the zone from which such pursuit may begin has taken place. With the introduction of the EEZ and numerous incidents involving violation of the coastal state's fishing and other rights in this zone, the institution of hot pursuit is likely to be applied to pursuits commenced in the EEZ.

Innocent Passage (236)

Continuous and expeditious navigation of a foreign ship through the territorial sea of a state, without prejudice to the peace, good order, or security of the coastal state. Innocent passage involves the traversing of the territorial sea of another state without entering that state's internal waters, calling at a roadstead or port facility outside the internal waters, or proceeding to or from internal waters or a call at such roadstead or port facility. Under the 1958 Convention on the Territorial Sea and Contiguous Zone and the 1982 United Nations Convention on the Law of the Sea, foreign ships have the right of innocent passage through internal waters in cases where the establishment of a straight baseline for measuring the breadth of the territorial sea has the effect of enclosing as internal waters areas not previously considered as such. Under the latter Convention, the right of innocent passage also pertains to archipelagic waters. *See also* ARCHIPELAGO, 219; INTERNAL WATERS, 237; ISLAND, 239; STRAIT, 248; TERRITORIAL SEA, 249; WARSHIP, 252.

Significance The right of innocent passage developed along with the principle of the coastal state's sovereignty over the territorial sea and is a firmly established principle of the law of the sea. It includes not only navigation but also stopping and anchoring insofar as they are incidental to ordinary navigation or rendered necessary by *force majeure* (or distress). Submarines and other underwater vehicles are required to navigate on the surface and show their flag, an obligation which is not always observed as evidenced in the case of the Soviet submarine caught in Swedish internal waters and numerous other incidents involving unidentified foreign submarines in Swedish and Norwegian territorial sea and internal waters. The criterion of the "innocence" of passage was for a long time a controversial issue. In accordance with the prevailing practice, the 1958 Convention adopted the simple criterion of a passage that is "not prejudicial to the peace, good order or security of the coastal State." The 1982 Convention reiterates this definition of innocence, adding a long list of prejudicial activities which would render a foreign ship's passage automatically noninnocent if it engaged in any one of them. The list includes threat or use of force; weapons practice; spying and propaganda; launching, landing, or taking on board aircraft or any military device; customs, fiscal, immigration, or sanitary offenses; pollution; fishing, research, or survey; interference with the coastal state's communication or other facilities; and "any other activity not having a direct bearing on passage." It is possible that the inclusion of the last-mentioned general category may result in the eventual narrowing of the scope of the traditional right of innocent passage. Although the coastal state must not hamper innocent passage, it may prevent noninnocent passage (hovering ships, for example, are presumed to be noninnocent) and even temporarily suspend, for security reasons, innocent passage in specified areas of its territorial sea. It may not, however, suspend innocent passage through straits used for international navigation. The institution of the right of "transit passage" in such straits, introduced by the 1982 Convention, is different from the traditional right of innocent passage.

The right of warships to innocent passage is a most controversial issue. Whereas the Western states hold that such right exists under international law, the Soviet Union and other communist states (as well as many Third World countries) contend that foreign warships may exercise this right in their waters only with the coastal state's authorization or prior notification. The 1958 Convention's rules on innocent passage apply to ships in general (apart from a specific reference to submarines which, as a rule, are warships), but the USSR and some of its allies made reservations to the Convention, claiming that innocent passage of warships required authorization. The 1982 Convention simply evaded any express reference to warships and granted the right of innocent passage to ships of all states. No reservations are allowed to this Convention. The right of innocent passage of nuclear-powered ships and ships carrying nuclear or other dangerous substances is guaranteed in this United Nations Convention, subject to certain precautionary regulations.

Internal Waters   (237)

Waters on the landward side of the baseline of the territorial sea. Sometimes known as interior waters, internal waters as a rule include ports, harbors, bays, estuaries, and waters on the landward side of straight baselines. Under the 1982 United Nations Convention on the Law of the Sea, an archipelagic state may, within its archipelagic waters, draw closing lines for the delimitation of internal waters of individual islands. Under customary international law, the coastal state enjoys full sovereignty over its internal waters and normally no right of innocent passage exists through them. However, the 1958 Convention on the Territorial Sea and Contiguous Zone and the 1982 Convention provide that such right does exist in internal waters in cases where the establishment of a straight baseline should have the effect of enclosing as internal waters areas which had not previously been considered as such. Although asserted by some publicists, there exists in principle no general right of access of foreign ships to ports and other internal waters of the coastal state, except for ships in distress. There is, however, a presumption that ports traditionally designated for foreign trade are open to foreign shipping and arbitrary closure of ports may give rise to protests and under certain circumstances even liability for damage. The coastal state may prescribe conditions for access of foreign ships as well as for their exit. Numerous bilateral treaties, usually known as treaties of commerce, friendship, and navigation, and the multilateral Convention and Statute on the International Regime of Maritime Ports (1923) provide for reciprocal right of access to the ports of the contracting parties. Rivers and canals in national territory belong to internal waters, but it appears that, in the absence of a treaty, ships of nonriparian states have no legal right of access to them. Interoceanic canals are governed by special treaties. Foreign merchant ships in internal waters are, in principle, under complete civil and criminal jurisdiction of the coastal state but, for reasons of comity and expediency, such a state normally asserts its jurisdiction only when (1) an offense committed on board the foreign ship disturbs the peace and good order of the port; (2) its intervention is requested by the ship's master or the flag state's consul; (3) a person who is not a member of the ship's crew is involved; and (4) in general, in all cases when the coastal state believes that its national interest requires assertion of jurisdiction. Matters relating to the ship's "internal economy" are left to the jurisdiction of the flag state; but even in such cases the coastal state might assert its jurisdiction. Although a distinction is commonly made between the Anglo-American approach (which follows the above summarized rules) and the French legal position (which is said to be that the coastal state is legally barred from exercising its jurisdiction over purely internal matters of foreign ships), the actual practice of both groups of states appears to be the same. Matters such as pollution, seaworthiness, sanitary regulations, and the like are within the jurisdiction of the coastal state. Although the matter is not entirely without controversy, ships in distress are granted a certain degree of immunity. For example, the coastal state cannot exact from them payment of harbor or customs duties or make them liable to arrest. The jurisdiction over foreign warships and other public ships operated for noncommercial purposes is much more limited than that over merchant ships. *See also* BASELINE, 221; BAY, 222; CONSTANTINOPLE CONVENTION (1888), 223; FLAG OF CONVENIENCE, 229; INNOCENT PASSAGE, 236; KIEL CANAL, 240; PANAMA CANAL TREATIES (1977), 246; TERRITORIAL SEA, 249; WARSHIP, 252.

Significance   The legal status of internal waters is based almost entirely on customary law. The 1958 Convention on the Territorial Sea and Contiguous Zone and the 1982 United Nations Convention on the Law of the Sea contain hardly any provisions relating to these waters. From the very beginning of the system of international law of territorial states, customary law recognized the fundamental principle that internal waters are under complete sovereignty of the coastal state and visiting merchant vessels must, under the principle of territorial jurisdiction, comply with the laws of this state. However, it is questionable whether a port state may impose upon visiting foreign vessels obligations with which such ships would have to comply even outside the internal waters. Therefore, for example, U.S. attempts to apply its antitrust or labor legislation to foreign ships in American ports have been contested by the flag states concerned as incompatible not just with the "internal economy" comity rule but also the fundamental principles of territorial jurisdiction under general international law.

International Sea-Bed Authority (238)

The United Nations organization, with its seat in Jamaica, through which states parties to the 1982 United Nations Convention on the Law of the Sea organize and control activities in the deep seabed beyond national jurisdiction (the "Area"), particularly with a view to administering its resources. Activities on the deep seabed unconnected with administering the resources, such as laying cables and pipelines or conducting scientific research relative to the superjacent waters, are not under the control of the Authority. All states parties to the 1982 Convention are automatically members of the Authority. The Authority has three principal organs: (1) an Assembly; (2) a Council; and (3) a Secretariat. Mining operations, transporting, processing, and marketing of the minerals recovered from the Area are to be done by the "Enterprise," which is an organ of the Authority. The Assembly, composed of all the member countries, is the supreme organ of the Authority. It lays down the general policies, approves the budget, and has certain other specific powers allotted to it by the Convention. Each member of the Assembly has one vote. Procedural decisions are taken by a majority of the members present and voting; other decisions require a two-thirds majority. Special procedural devices are designed to prevent issues from being forced by bloc voting. The thirty-six-member Council is the crucial and most powerful organ of the Authority. Half of its thirty-six members are to come from four major interest groups: (1) the largest investors in seabed mining—four states, but at least one state from Eastern Europe; (2) the major consumers or importers of minerals found in the Area—four states, but in any case one state from Eastern Europe as well as the largest consumer state; (3) major land-based exporters of the minerals—four states, including at least two developing states; (4) "special interests" among the developing countries—six states (states with large populations, the landlocked or geographically disadvantaged, major mineral importers, potential producers of the minerals in question, and least developed states). The other eighteen members would be elected (taking account of an equitable geographical distribution) with at least one country to be elected from each geographical region—Africa, Asia, Eastern Europe, Latin America, and Western Europe, and Others. The Council's task would be to execute the policies set out in the Convention and defined in general terms by the Assembly. Approval of the rules, regulations, and procedures governing the seabed mining would be among the most important tasks.

The four-tier decision-making system of the Council is most complex. In general, the more important the issue, the larger majority would be needed. Some, but not all, of the most sensitive questions (especially issues of principle and approval of rules, regulations, and procedures for mining) would be decided by consensus, defined as the absence of a formal objection. Other substantive matters would be resolved by two-thirds or three-fourths majorities, but in the category subject to the latter any ten members could block the Council's action. Procedural questions would require a simple majority. In its work, the Council is to be served by the Economic Planning Commision and the Legal and Technical Commission, each with fifteen members elected by the Council with due regard to geographical balance. The international Sea-Bed Authority would be financed by assessed contributions from its members, the earnings of the Enterprise, receipts from taxes on contractors, loans, and voluntary contributions. Work on the establishment of the Authority started before the entry of the 1982 Convention into effect. Resolution I, annexed to the Final Act of UNCLOS III, established a Preparatory Commission for the International Sea-Bed Authority and for the International Tribunal for the Law of the Sea, with the task of drawing detailed rules and procedures for the Authority. The Commission was to function as the preparatory body until the end of the first session of the Assembly. *See also* THE "AREA," 220.

Significance   As devised in the detailed provisions of the 1982 Convention, the International Sea-Bed Authority constitutes a most complex regulatory system for the exploration and exploitation of the resources of the deep seabed. Although the composition, powers, and the voting system of the Authority's crucial organ—the Council—are a product of compromise between the Western countries and the Group of 77, the very creation of a unique public international organization to manage one category of the planet's resources was an important achievement for the proponents of a New International Economic Order (NIEO), with significant precedential implications for other possible categories of the "common heritage of mankind."

Island   (239)
A naturally formed area of land surrounded by marine water, which is above water at high tide. The legal status of islands was governed by rules of customary international law until it was defined in the 1958

Convention on the Territorial Sea and Contiguous Zone and the 1982 United Nations Convention on the Law of the Sea. Every island, islet, or rock, irrespective of its size, generates its territorial sea and contiguous zone. Under the 1982 Convention, islands also have their Exclusive Economic Zones (EEZs) and continental shelves, but "rocks which cannot sustain human habitation or economic life of their own shall have no exclusive economic zone or contintental shelf," a rule which probably reflects the status of customary international law on the subject. Rocks may, however, be used as basepoints in constructing a straight baseline or archipelagic baseline system. The 1982 Convention does not elaborate on the criteria of "human habitation" or "economic life." Islands forming part of archipelagos are reserved special treatment. Artificial islands are not entitled to territorial sea or to any other zone and their presence does not affect the delimitation of such zones. Construction of artificial islands in the exclusive economic zone is an exclusive right of the coastal state, but on the high seas construction of such islands is recognized as one of the freedoms of the high seas. Construction on the continental shelf (which may extend beyond the limits that apply to exclusive economic zone) is also reserved to the coastal state. *See also* ARCHIPELAGO, 219; BASELINE, 221; CONTINENTAL SHELF, 225; TERRITORIAL SEA, 249.

Significance   The legal status of an overwhelming number of islands does not cause any difficulties. Furthermore, since most rocks lie close to shore in any case, the fact that they must be discounted as basepoints for the delimitation of the exclusive economic zone and continental shelf will not greatly affect the extent of the maritime jurisdiction of the state concerned. The vague drafting of the provisions of the 1982 Convention on rocks is likely to give rise to controversies as evidenced by the case of Rockall, a rock in the North Atlantic 180 miles northwest of the Hebrides, of less than 0.01 square mile in area. This desolate place was occupied by the United Kingdom, which eventually claimed the surrounding continental shelf and an Exclusive Economic Zone (EEZ) around it against protests by Ireland and Denmark, the two countries invoking the 1982 Convention in support of their position. A number of other states have claimed exclusive economic zones around similar tiny rocks and islets in the Pacific and Indian Oceans, which probably would not pass the test of "island" in the meaning of the 1982 Convention.

Kiel Canal   (240)

The canal connecting the Baltic with the North Sea which runs entirely through German territory. The Kiel Canal (also known as the North

Sea–Baltic Canal) was constructed for strategic reasons by the German Empire before World War I. Its legal status is not entirely clear, but the Federal Republic of Germany in whose territory the Canal is located declared the Canal open to ships of all nations according to the principles laid down in the Treaty of Versailles in 1919. The Treaty provided for maintaining the Kiel Canal and its approaches free and open to the merchant vessels and warships of all nations at peace with Germany, with Germany retaining the right to collect tolls for the maintenance of the Canal. *See also* CONSTANTINOPLE CONVENTION (1888), 223; PANAMA CANAL TREATIES (1977), 246; STRAIT, 248.

Significance   In 1920, soon after the Treaty of Versailles took effect, a dispute arose between Poland and Germany over the German government's denial of passage through the Canal of the British vessel the *Wimbledon*, laden with munitions for Poland, then at war with Soviet Russia. To justify its indirect aid to Russia, Germany contended that the passage would constitute a breach of neutrality on its part. Following the defeat of Russia, the issue came before the Permanent Court of International Justice in 1923 which in its judgment in the *S.S. Wimbledon* case (United Kingdom, France, Italy, and Japan v. Germany, with Poland intervening) decided against Germany, holding that the Canal (like a natural strait) was to be open to states at peace with Germany and that even a passage of a belligerent warship would not have compromised Germany's neutrality. In 1936, Germany unilaterally denounced the articles of the Treaty of Versailles governing the status of the Kiel Canal but allowed the passage of merchant ships. The passage of warships was made subject to individual permits issued by Germany. There were no protests on the part of the majority of the signatories of the Treaty, who acquiesced in the illegal act of Nazi Germany. After World War II the Federal Republic of Germany opened the Canal according to the principles of the Treaty of Versailles.

Landlocked and Geographically Disadvantaged States   (241)

States that have no seacoast (landlocked) and states whose coastline is very short in relation to their area or which, because of the close vicinity to other states, cannot have an Exclusive Economic Zone (EEZ) or a continental shelf commensurate with the length of their coastline or their area, or whose exclusive economic zones are poor in natural resources (geographically disadvantaged). The right of landlocked countries' ships to navigate on the sea has been firmly established in the law of the sea since the 1921 League of Nations' Conference on Communications and Transit. It has been confirmed both by the 1958 Geneva Convention on the High Seas and the 1982 United Nations Convention on the Law of the Sea and can be regarded as part of customary international law. The use by a landlocked country of ports of other states is based on bilateral international agreements and—for the signatory landlocked states—on the 1923 Convention and Statute on the International Regime of Maritime Ports. Under the 1982 Convention, ships flying the flag of a landlocked state enjoy treatment equal to that accorded to other foreign ships in maritime ports. Under international law, such treatment need not necessarily be most-favored-nation treatment. It is a controversial issue whether, under customary international law, landlocked states have a right of transit to the coast through the territory of neighboring states, but this right is guaranteed under such international agreements as the 1921 Convention and Statute on Freedom of Transit and the 1947 General Agreement on Tariffs and Trade (GATT). The 1958 Convention on the High Seas provides that rights of access to sea ports and transit are to be granted to landlocked countries by agreement. The 1965 Convention on Transit Trade of Land-Locked States is an example of such agreements, as are also numerous bilateral treaties to the same effect and multilateral agreements relating to a specific mode of transportation, such as the 1923 Convention and Statute on the International Regime of Railways and the 1921 Convention and Statute on the Regime of Navigable Waterways of International Concern, the 1968 Convention on Road Traffic, and agreements dealing with specific rivers. The landlocked states' right of transit is also guaranteed in the 1982 Convention on the Law of the Sea, but must be implemented by agreements. Transit states, that is, states (with or without a seacoast) situated between a landlocked country and the sea, through whose territory traffic in transit passes, have the right to ensure that such transit in no way infringes upon their legitimate interests. Under the general principle of the freedom of the high seas, landlocked and geographically disadvantaged countries have access to high seas resources. According to the projected deep seabed regime of the 1982 Convention, developing landlocked and, to some extent, geographically disadvantaged states enjoy preferential treatment and are represented on the Council of the International Sea-Bed Authority. The Convention also grants landlocked and geographically disadvantaged states, especially the developing ones, access to the surplus of the living resources of Exclusive Economic Zones (EEZs) in the same region or subregion (terms not defined in the Convention). Such access, however, must be negotiated by agreement. *See also* EXCLUSIVE ECONOMIC ZONE (EEZ), 227; FREEDOM OF THE HIGH SEAS, 231; INTERNATIONAL SEA-BED AUTHORITY, 238.

Significance   The number of landlocked countries has greatly increased since World War II. Some thirty states (fourteen in Africa) have no seacoast. At the Third United Nations Conference on the Law of the Sea (UNCLOS III), the landlocked states were joined by more than twenty geographically disadvantaged countries, forming together (despite wide disparities in economic development and political systems) a numerically powerful group in order to assert their joint interests at the Conference. However, they were not entirely satisfied with the treatment accorded them in the Convention, both insofar as their participation in the future deep seabed regime is concerned and in the matter of access to exclusive economic zones. Their rights of transit and to the zones' surplus still depend on negotiating agreements and are formulated in a language that does not clearly safeguard them. Finally, most developing landlocked countries do not possess adequate fishing technology and industry that would allow them to take advantage of these rights even if they were granted access to exclusive economic zones of neighboring countries.

Law of the Sea   (242)

That part of public international law that governs the rights and duties of states and possibly other subjects of international law with regard to the use and utilization of the oceans. In this sense the law of the sea must be distinguished from private maritime law, which is concerned with the rights and obligations in maritime matters of private persons, such as the carriage of goods by sea, marine insurance, and the like. Furthermore, the law of the sea deals only with international law in time of peace and does not include the rules governing the conduct of naval warfare and maritime neutrality.

Significance   Although some of the rules of the law of the sea can be traced to medieval private compilations governing primarily maritime rights and obligations of merchants and shipowners in the Mediterranean (*Lex Rhodia*—the Rhodian Laws—seventh century; the *Tabula Amalfitana* of Amalfi, Italy, eleventh century; *Consolato del Mare*—The Consulate of the Sea—of Barcelona, fourteenth century); the Atlantic Ocean and the Baltic Sea (Rolls of Oléron, twelfth century); and the Baltic and North Seas (*Leges Wisbuenses*—Code of Visby on the Island of Gothland—fifteenth century); the law of the sea developed as part of the law of nations in the early centuries of the modern territorial state system. Early works on the law of the sea, among which Hugo Grotius' pamphlet *Mare Liberum* (Freedom of the Sea, 1609) is best known, originated within the context of the controversy surrounding the freedom of the seas, which eventually asserted itself in state practice as the fundamental principle of the law of the sea. The classical publicists drew on Roman (civil) law and discussed ocean problems in the natural law tradition. Gradually, however, as customary rules produced a body of law based on state practice and consensus, this development found its reflection in the writings of such publicists as Cornelius van Bynkershoek who wrote on the law of the sea in the eighteenth century. By the nineteenth century, the law of the sea, like other areas of public international law, developed into a system of customary principles and rules governing the rights and duties of states in the two major zones—the high seas and the territorial sea—but, increasingly, treaties (mostly bilateral ones) dealt with various aspects of the sea.

The first attempts to codify the customary law of the sea were made in the nineteenth century by nongovernmental organizations, such as the International Law Association (ILA) and the Institute of International Law. Another private codificatory work was initiated by Harvard Law School after World War I. The first official endeavor was the League of Nations–sponsored Hague Conference of 1930 which, however, failed to achieve its objective of codifying the law of territorial waters. After World War II, the codificatory work was resumed by the ILC whose drafts provided the basis for the Geneva Conference on the Law of the Sea of 1958 (UNCLOS I). The conference produced four conventions—on the territorial sea and contiguous zone; the high sea; the continental shelf; and on fisheries—but failed to agree on the breadth of the territorial sea, an issue taken over by the 1960 Geneva Conference on the Law of the Sea which ended in failure. The 1958 conventions were soon overtaken by revolutionary changes in state practice with regard to the oceans which had their roots in the growing trend to extend coastal states' jurisdiction in the form of a wider territorial sea, a fishing zone, and sovereign rights in the continental shelf. Continued technological progress, raising the possibility of deep seabed mining, economic pressures generated by increasing demand for protein, and last but not least, demands of Third World countries to reform the traditional law of the sea in the name of a New International Economic Order (NIEO), resulted in convoking the Third United Nations Conference on the Law of the Sea, 1973–1982 (UNCLOS III). This Conference adopted the United Nations Convention on the Law of the Sea, signed in December 1982 in Montego Bay, Jamaica, and constituting a comprehensive codification and development of contemporary international law governing the oceans. By the mid-1980s the legal regime of the oceans was not entirely clear, however. Although signed by approximately 160 countries, the 1982 Convention was not yet in force, and the 1958 conventions were still formally binding those relatively few states which had ratified them. A major controversy surrounded the legal status of the deep seabed—the "Area," in the terminology of the Convention—an issue of potential future conflict over the still untapped mineral resources (primarily manganese or polymetallic nodules) of the ocean. Still, some of the rules of the 1982 Convention (in particular—apart from some traditional rules of the law of the sea—the regime of the Exclusive Economic Zone [EEZ]) had become customary law. The Convention also had a stabilizing effect on the law of the sea by contributing to harmonization of state practice in various areas. In addition to fundamental codifications a large number of treaties, both global and regional, in such areas as control of marine pollution and safety of navigation, for example, form part of the conventional law of the sea. In general, the law of the sea of the 1980s was in a transitional stage from the traditional law founded on the principle of the freedom of the seas to a new legal order as set forth in the United Nations Convention on the Law of the Sea of 1982.

Marine Pollution, International Law of   (243)

That part of the law of the sea that governs the protection and preservation of the marine environment against pollution. The international law of marine pollution is at the same time part of international environmental law, which is concerned with preventing, reducing, and controlling pollution and with the conservation of the living resources of the planet. As defined in the 1982 United Nations Convention on the Law of the Sea, pollution of the marine environment means "the introduction by man, directly or indirectly, of substances or energy into the marine environment, including estuaries, which results or is likely to result in such deleterious effects as harm to living resources and marine life, hazards to human health, hindrance to marine activities, including fishing and other legitimate uses of the sea, impairment of quality for use of sea water and reduction of amenities."

In general, there are six sources of marine pollution: (1) waste from land-based sources (the most serious threat to the oceans); (2) pollution from offshore drilling; (3) pollution from dumping waste and toxic substances, the dumping of nuclear waste being the most hazardous procedure; (4) vessel-source pollution—in this regard, although oil spills from tankers have attracted most public attention because of dramatic accidents at sea (for example, the *Torrey Canyon*, 1967, and the *Amoco Cadiz*, 1978), the major part of pollution from ships is attributable to routine operational oil spillage; (5) pollution from or through the atmosphere—the least explored but the most potentially dangerous source of marine pollution; and (6) the projected deep seabed mining. International legal regulation of marine pollution has proceeded on global, regional, and subregional levels. Part XII of the 1982 Convention (Protection and Preservation of the Marine Environment) provides an overarching framework for all these legal regimes. There is no global regulation of pollution from land-based sources and offshore drilling, both of which are suitable for regional rather than global treatment. Pollution through the atmosphere is approached on the regional level through transboundary air pollution agreements, and prevention of pollution from deep seabed mining is a matter of future concern.

Vessel-source pollution has been the major target of international legal action on the global level. The International Convention of 1954 for the Prevention of Pollution of the Sea by Oil was the first global regulation, limited to combating deliberate discharges in certain sensitive zones of the oceans. Three other conventions deal with related problems: the 1969 Convention Relating to the Intervention on the High Seas in Cases of Pollution Casualties; the Convention of 1969 on Civil Liability for Oil Pollution Damage; and the 1971 Convention for the Establishment of an International Fund for Compensation for Oil Pollution Damage, complemented by additional shipowner's arrangements. However, the major global regulation of vessel-source pollution by oil and other substances is the International Convention for the Prevention of Pollution from Ships (1973)—the so-called MARPOL Convention—in force since 1983, drafted under the auspices of the International Maritime Organization (IMO), previously known as the Intergovernmental Maritime Consultative Organization (IMCO). Dumping is regulated globally by the 1972 Convention on the Prevention of Marine Pollution by Dumping Waste and Other Matter. Conventions designed to prevent accidents at sea indirectly strengthen the global regime for the protection of the marine environment. Among them are the Convention for the Safety of Life at Sea (1974); the Convention on the International Regulations for Preventing Collisions at Sea (1972); the International Convention on Loadlines (1966); and the International Convention on Standards of Training, Certification, and Watchkeeping for Seafarers (1978).

Much of the international law of marine pollution has resulted from regional cooperation, which takes into account the local peculiarities of the marine environment. The regional arrangements can be categorized according to their approach to the problem of marine pollution, which can be piecemeal, framework, or comprehensive. Under the piecemeal approach, initiated in the Atlantic Northeast, specific types of marine pollution are treated by special conventions such as the 1969 Bonn Agreement for Cooperation in Dealing with Pollution of the North Sea by Oil; the 1972 Oslo Convention for the Prevention of Marine Pollution by Dumping from Ships and Aircraft; the 1974 Paris Convention for the Prevention of Marine Pollution from Landbased Sources; the London Convention on Civil Liability for Oil

Pollution Damage Resulting from the Exploration for, or Exploitation of, Submarine Mineral Resources, 1977; and the 1982 Memorandum of Understanding on Port State Control in Implementing Agreements on Maritime Safety and Protection of the Marine Environment. There are also numerous subregional and bilateral agreements concerned mostly with controlling accidental vessel-source pollution; for example, the U.S.-Canadian Agreement of 1974 Relating to the Establishment of Joint Pollution Contingency Plan for Spills and Other Noxious Substances.

Under the framework approach, the coastal states of an enclosed or semienclosed sea conclude a framework "umbrella" convention that spells out general principles of pollution control, leaving the detailed regulation of specific sources of pollution to special protocols. Sponsored by the Regional Seas Programme of the United Nations Environment Programme (UNEP), this system was first adopted in the 1976 Convention for the Protection of the Mediterranean Sea against Pollution with subsequent protocols on dumping, oil pollution, and other types of hazard. The Mediterranean Action Plan served as the model for other regional seas programs: the Persian (Arabian) Gulf and the Gulf of Oman (1978); the Gulf of Guinea (1981); the Caribbean and the Gulf of Mexico (1981); the Red Sea and the Gulf of Aden (1982); and the South Pacific (1986).

Under the comprehensive approach, all sources of marine pollution are regulated in a single convention. The 1974 Helsinki Convention on the Protection of the Marine Environment of the Baltic Sea Area is a unique case of this approach. Part XII of the 1982 United Nations Convention on the Law of the Sea is not intended by itself to regulate all the issues of marine pollution but spells out some fundamental principles, such as the obligation to protect and preserve the marine environment (probably a rule of customary international law), to cooperate in combating pollution, to monitor its risks and effects, and to provide scientific and technical assistance to developing nations. It is only in the area of vessel-source pollution that the 1982 Convention contains more elaborate provisions which balance the navigational interests of the flag states against the environmental concerns of the port and coastal nations. The Convention also contains special provisions designed to protect ice-covered areas of the ocean, which apply primarily to the Arctic Ocean. *See also* ENCLOSED OR SEMIENCLOSED SEA, 226; ENVIRONMENT, PROTECTION OF, 183; LONG-RANGE TRANSBOUNDARY AIR POLLUTION, 208.

Significance   In recent decades, and especially after the United Nations Conference on the Human Environment in Stockholm in 1972, states have become increasingly aware of dangers that pollution poses to the marine environment. By the early 1980s a network of international agreements, displaying a great variety of legal regimes both in terms of functional scope and areal domain, had produced a body of international law governing the protection and preservation of the marine environment. However, certain major conventions such as MARPOL have not received a sufficient number of ratifications; there are still gaps in the coverage of certain sources of pollution; there is lack of coordination among the individual legal regimes; enforcement is not satisfactory; and scientific data on marine pollution are incomplete. Despite these drawbacks, the international law of marine pollution has, at least at the global level, contributed to reducing pollution, especially insofar as operational pollution by oil is concerned. At the regional level, the deterioration of the marine environment of such sensitive areas as the Baltic and the Northeast Atlantic seems to have been arrested. The general principles and rules of the 1982 United Nations Convention on the Law of the Sea governing the protection and preservation of the marine environment should further contribute to improving the health of the oceans.

Montreux Convention (1936) (244)

A multilateral convention governing the use of the Turkish Straits of the Bosphorus and the Dardanelles. The Montreux Convention guarantees complete freedom of transit and navigation to merchant vessels in times of peace and war, but imposes limitations upon the tonnage, size, and length of stay of foreign warships. In time of peace, the aggregate tonnage of ships of non–Black Sea powers permitted to enter the Black Sea must not exceed 30,000 tons or, under certain circumstances, 45,000 tons. The aggregate tonnage of ships allowed to transit the Straits at any one time is 15,000 tons; but the Black Sea powers may send capital ships through the Straits without any tonnage restrictions provided that they pass singly and are escorted by no more than two destroyers. There is no express authorization for the transit of aircraft carriers and, in its Annex II, the Convention specifically excludes aircraft carriers from the category of "capital ships." Light and minor surface ships and auxiliary vessels of any power are not subject to any restrictions. In time of war—but only if Turkey is not a belligerent—warships of belligerents have freedom of passage subject under the Montreux Convention to the rules of the League of Nations Covenant and presumably now of the United Nations Charter. *See also* STRAIT, 248.

Significance The Turkish Straits include the Dardanelles (41 miles long) and the Bosphorus (19 miles long and at its narrowest only 600 yards wide), separated by the Sea of Marmara (125 miles long). The Straits are entirely under Turkish sovereignty. The control of the Straits was a major issue in European diplomacy for two centuries, with Russia and then the Soviet Union making repeated bids for their control. The Montreux Convention, which at Turkey's request replaced the 1923 Lausanne Straits Convention, is a compromise reconciling the Black Sea powers' right to transit to the Mediterranean and non–Black Sea powers' right to enter the Black Sea. For the Soviet Union, which maintains naval units in the Mediterranean and has a large Black Sea fleet, the transit through the Turkish Straits is of vital importance apart from their use for commercial shipping. The case of the *Kiev*, a Soviet warship equipped with a dozen aircraft and two dozen helicopters, which since 1976—along with her sister ships—has been using the transit through the Straits, with Turkey's consent, under the guise of a "tactical aircraft carrying cruiser" (but not aircraft carrier), highlights the dilemma of the USSR with regard to the legal status of the Straits. The USSR's long-term objective is likely to be a revision of the Montreux Convention to allow free transit for bigger capital ships which, for all practical purposes, will have to be considered aircraft carriers.

Nationality of Ships   (245)

A legal institution linking a ship to a state and indicating that that state, known as the state of nationality or flag state (or state of registry), has the right to exercise jurisdiction over the ship, is responsible for it, and has the right to protect it under international law. Nationality implies that the ship has been registered in a state and has been granted the right to fly its flag. A ship may sail under the flag of one state only and may not change its flag during a voyage or while in a port of call, save in the case of a real transfer of ownership or change of registry. A ship flying the flags of two or more states may be assimilated to a ship without nationality. In practice, such ships do not normally enjoy the protection of any state unless protection is exercised by the state of the owner's nationality or by the state of which the crew or passengers are nationals. Ships may also fly the flag of an international organization. The 1982 United Nations Convention on the Law of the Sea explicitly grants this right only to the United Nations, its specialized agencies, and the International Atomic Energy Agency (IAEA). *See also* FLAG OF CONVENIENCE, 229; FLAG-STATE JURISDICTION, 230.

Significance   The institution of nationality of ships is indispensable for orderly and safe navigation on the high seas and for attribution to states of rights and obligations relative to ships in international traffic. Under traditional international law, conditions for granting nationality to ships were determined exclusively by the municipal law of each country, and such laws require registration of all but very small craft. More recently, in connection with the emergence of "flags of convenience," the 1958 Geneva Convention on the High Seas appeared to limit this national discretionary power by adding to the traditional principle a provision to the effect that there must exist a genuine link between the state of registry and the ship, and that "in particular the State must effectively exercise its jurisdiction and control in administrative, technical and social matters over ships flying its flag." The inclusion of the requirement of "genuine link" was largely influenced by the decision of the International Court of Justice (ICJ) in the *Nottebohm* case (*Liechtenstein v. Guatemala*, 1955) in which the Court, in a case concerning nationality of an individual, ruled that for Liechtenstein to have the right to protect an individual claimed to be its national there must exist a genuine link between that individual and Liechtenstein. The 1958 Convention on the High Seas did not, however, specify concrete criteria for determining whether or not a genuine link exists between a ship and its state of registry. Nor did it spell out what consequences absence of genuine link would entail under international law. Although the requirement of genuine link did not eliminate flags of convenience, the 1982 United Nations Convention on the Law of the Sea reiterated it without, however, linking the clause directly to provisions on the effective exercise of jurisdiction by the flag state. On the other hand, such duty as well as the duty to ensure safety at sea are stipulated in great detail in a special article on the duties of the flag state.

Panama Canal Treaties (1977) (246)

Two treaties between Panama and the United States governing the legal status of the Panama Canal. The Treaty Concerning the Permanent Neutrality and Operation of the Panama Canal guarantees the permanent neutrality of the Canal, and the Panama Canal Treaty governs its operation and defense until the end of 1999. Under these treaties, which entered into force in 1979, the United States has a permanent right to defend the Canal and to use areas and facilities necessary for its operation and defense, and U.S. warships have the right to transit the Canal expeditiously and without conditions. The United States continues to operate the Canal with Panamanian participation until the end of 1999, when Panama will assume control of the operations. To implement the treaties the United States Congress passed the Panama Canal Act of 1979, establishing the Panama Canal Commission, a U.S.

agency to manage and operate the Canal until the end of the century. *See also* CONSTANTINOPLE CONVENTION (1888), 223; KIEL CANAL, 240; STRAIT, 248.

Significance The 1977 Panama Canal Treaties replace the previous U.S.-Panama Agreement of 1903, concluded before the Canal opened for traffic in 1914. Under that original agreement, the United States obtained (for payment) the monopoly to construct a canal across the Panamanian territory and was granted in perpetuity the right to act as if it were sovereign in a zone ten miles wide along the Canal. Following World War II, Panama was no longer prepared to suffer limitations upon its sovereignty in the Panama Canal Zone, and a prolonged period of tension between the two countries ensued which, after years of negotiations, eventually ended in the conclusion of the 1977 Treaties granting Panama full sovereignty over the Canal Zone and spelling out the rules for the operation of the Canal. The new treaties were controversial both in Panama and the United States, but their approval— in Panama by a national referendum—and then their successful implementation made a positive contribution to improving the relations between Panama and the United States.

Piracy (247)

Any illegal acts of violence or detention, or any act of depredation, committed for private ends by the crew or the passengers of a private ship or a private aircraft and directed (1) on the high seas (or the exclusive economic zone beyond the territorial sea) against another ship or aircraft, or against persons or property on board such ships or aircraft; or (2) against a ship, aircraft, persons, or property in a place outside the jurisdiction of any state. Voluntary participation in the operation of a piratical ship or aircraft and inciting and facilitating piratical acts are also considered as piracy. A frustrated attempt to commit a piratical act also constitutes piracy. Acts of piracy by a warship or a governmental ship or aircraft whose crew has mutinied and taken control of the ship or aircraft are assimilated to acts committed by a private ship or aircraft. Ships reasonably suspected of piracy may, regardless of their nationality, be boarded and, if the suspicion proves justified, persons and property on board may be seized. The courts of the state whose ship carried out the seizure may try the pirate without being limited by any rules restricting the jurisdiction of domestic courts in criminal matters. This state may also determine the action to be taken with regard to the ships, aircraft, or property, subject to the rights of third parties acting in good faith. This means that ships and goods must be restored to their owners in accordance with the rule that a pirate cannot acquire legal ownership of his booty (*pirata non mutat dominium*; pirate does not change ownership). The piratical ship does not lose its nationality unless otherwise provided by the law of the flag state. If the seizure of an allegedly pirate ship was effected without any adequate justification, the state making the seizure is liable for any damage to the state of the ship's (or aircraft's) nationality. *See also* FLAG-STATE JURISDICTION, 230; INTERNATIONAL CRIMINAL LAW, 93.

Significance   Piracy has for centuries been a crime under customary law of nations, and a pirate has always been considered an outlaw and "enemy of mankind" (*hostis humani generis*). Piracy is the first "international crime," which means that a piratical act is a crime directly under international law and any state may bring a pirate to justice. The rules against piracy developed in the common interest of maritime states to protect their overseas trade. The customary law of piracy was codified and developed in the Geneva Convention on the High Seas (1958), whose rules on piracy were taken over virtually unchanged by the 1982 United Nations Convention on the Law of the Sea. Although piracy was, to a large extent, eradicated by the nineteenth century, sporadic cases of piracy have occurred even in recent times, as demonstrated by attacks on Vietnamese refugees ("boat people") in Southeast Asian waters. Cooperation in the repression of piracy is not just a right but a duty of all states. It must be remembered that in a layperson's terminology the term "piracy" is used loosely to include acts which are not piracy under international law. For example, attacks on ships in the territorial sea or internal waters are not piracy and, from the point of view of international law, are treated as any similar acts on land even though, under the domestic criminal law of the coastal state, they may be termed "piracy." Therefore, piracy under international law (piracy *jure gentium*) must not be confused with piracy as defined by municipal law. For example, British law considers slave trading on the high seas as piracy. It must also be kept in mind that, for piracy under international law to take place, at least two ships—pirate and victim—must be involved. Therefore, the taking over by Captain Galvao of the Portuguese vessel the *Santa Maria* in 1961 to dramatize his opposition to the Portuguese dictator Antonio Salazar did not constitute piracy since only one vessel was involved (apart from the fact that the seizure was carried out not for private ends, which alone excluded the act in question from the scope of piracy under international law). As defined in the Conventions of 1958 and 1962, piracy may also be committed against a ship, aircraft, persons, or property in a place outside the jurisdiction of any state. The unclaimed sector of the Antarctic continent might conceivably be a locale for committing this kind of piratical act.

Strait   **(248)**

A narrow natural sea passage connecting two large marine areas. Under traditional customary law of the sea, no problems arise if the waters of a strait (a term nowhere defined in the 1982 United Nations Convention on the Law of the Sea) or at least a sufficiently wide channel in it are high seas, since the freedom of the high seas guarantees free navigation. However, if a strait is totally comprised of the territorial sea of one or more states, then foreign ships (including warships) have only the right of innocent passage which, in the prevailing but not unanimous view, cannot be suspended in straits used for international navigation between one part of the high seas or exclusive economic or fishery zone and another part of such marine spaces or the territorial sea of another state. The right of passage through international straits was upheld by the International Court of Justice (ICJ) in the *Corfu Channel* case (*United Kingdom v. Albania*, 1949) and was incorporated in the 1958 Convention on the Territorial Sea and Contiguous Zone, primarily to secure Israel's access to Eilat through the Strait of Tiran. It was, however, contested by some states—particularly Arab states—none of which became party to the 1958 Convention. Overflight of international straits has also been a controversial issue.

Because of the extension by many states of their territorial waters up to twelve miles in the 1960s and 1970s, major maritime powers became concerned about securing passage (especially for their warships) through a number of strategically important straits—Dover, Hormuz, and Bab-el-Mandeb, for example. Consequently, they indicated at UNCLOS III that they would agree to the twelve-mile territorial sea limit only on the condition that a special regime be established for international straits which would be more favorable to foreign ships than a mere innocent passage. The resulting new legal institution of unimpedable and nonsuspendable "transit passage" (and also "archipelagic sea lanes passage") created by the 1982 Convention goes a long way toward meeting the needs of the maritime powers without granting international straits the status of the high seas. The regime of transit passage applies only to straits "used for international navigation between one part of the high seas or an exclusive economic zone and another part of the high seas or an exclusive economic zone." However, this definition does not cover cases in which there exists through the strait a route, through the high seas or through an exclusive economic zone, of similar convenience with respect to navigational and hydrological characteristics, and where—as in the Corfu Strait—the strait is formed by an island of a state bordering the strait and its mainland, and a route possessing such characteristics exists seaward of the island through the high seas or through an exclusive economic zone. In such a case, there exists only a nonsuspendable right of innocent passage between the island and the mainland. The same applies to straits between a part of the high seas or an exclusive economic zone and the territorial sea of a foreign state; for example, in the case of the Strait of Tiran.

Transit passage means the exercise of the freedom of navigation and overflight solely for the purpose of continuous and expeditious transit. The wording of the 1982 Convention implies that submarines may transit international straits while submerged. Although there is no requirement of "innocence," all ships and aircraft must refrain from any activity threatening a strait state. Such activity may result in denial of transit passage and even innocent passage rights. All ships and aircraft must comply with regulations concerning navigation, prevention of pollution, and research and survey activities by foreign ships. States bordering straits may design sea lanes; prescribe traffic separation schemes; and adopt laws and regulations relating to transit through straits in respect of fishing, loading or unloading any commodity, currency, or persons in contravention of the strait countries' fiscal, immigration, or sanitary regulations. Enforcement jurisdiction is limited to cases of pollution causing or threatening major damage to the marine environment of the strait. The 1982 Convention in no way affects the legal regime of straits regulated by long-standing international conventions such as the Montreux Convention of 1936 concerning the Turkish Straits of the Bosphorus and the Dardanelles. *See also* ARCHIPELAGO, 219; INNOCENT PASSAGE, 236; MONTREUX CONVENTION (1936), 244; WARSHIP, 252.

Significance   The most sensitive legal issue related to straits is the right of free navigation through international straits, which is of particular importance to major maritime powers not only for commercial but also military and strategic reasons. As demonstrated by the Corfu Channel incident of 1946 in which Great Britain sent warships into Albanian territorial waters of the Corfu Channel to carry out minesweeping operations following explosions of mines which had severely damaged some British warships, a maritime power would not hesitate to assert the right of passage through international straits by resort to self-help. In another part of the oceans, the threatened closure of the Straits of Tiran in 1967 was a major focus of one round in the Arab-Israeli military confrontation. In the mid-1980s, the extent of the right of transit through international straits by foreign warships (particularly submarines) and the right of overflight by foreign aircraft remain controversial, and the possibility of future conflicts over such rights cannot be ruled out even after the entry of the 1982 Convention into effect.

Territorial Sea   **(249)**

A belt of sea adjacent to the coast over which the coastal state has complete sovereignty, subject to the foreign ships' right of innocent passage, and which also extends to the superjacent airspace and the subjacent seabed and subsoil. The institution of the territorial sea, also known as the maritime belt or territorial waters, can be traced back to the early centuries of the European territorial states system in the sixteenth and seventeenth centuries. The distinction between the high seas, proclaimed by most as free and open to all, and the territorial waters susceptible to appropriation by the coastal state was established by the beginning of the eighteenth century as witnessed by Cornelius van Bynkershoek's *De domini maris dissertatio* (Dissertation on the Sovereignty of the Sea, 1702). Although doubts about the exact legal nature of the coastal state's rights in the territorial sea persisted long afterward, the clear trend was toward the principle of complete sovereignty of the coastal state subject to the right of innocent passage of foreign ships. This principle had been firmly established by the time of the Hague Codification Conference of 1930 and was incorporated in the 1958 Convention on the Territorial Sea and Contiguous Zone and the 1982 United Nations Convention on the Law of the Sea. Both Conventions also recognize that roadsteads (that is, places offshore where ships may ride at anchor) normally used for the loading, unloading, and anchoring of ships, which would otherwise be situated wholly or partly outside the outer limit of the territorial sea, are included in this sea.

The breadth of the territorial sea remained for a long time one of the most controversial issues in the law of the sea and was not entirely settled even in the mid-1980s. By the nineteenth century, a three-nautical-miles' continuous belt, popularly said to have originated in the "cannon shot" rule (once referring to isolated pockets of offshore waters covered by the range of coastal artillery in the eighteenth century) had been accepted by most states, including Great Britain and the United States. The Scandinavian states historically claimed one Scandinavian "league"; that is, four nautical miles, and Spain and Portugal six miles. Attempts to reach agreement on the breadth of the territorial sea at the Hague Codification Conference of 1930 failed, despite the fact that the states claiming three miles were in the majority. Following World War II this majority progressively dwindled and, at the Geneva Conference of 1958 (UNCLOS I), only 21 out of the 86 participating states represented the traditional three-mile limit. Neither UNCLOS I of 1958 nor UNCLOS II of 1960 could reach agreement on the breadth of the territorial sea. However, since under the 1958 Convention on the Territorial Sea and Contiguous Zone the contiguous zone (an area beyond the territorial sea) could not extend farther than 12 miles from the baselines of the territorial sea, it followed that the territorial sea itself could not be wider than 12 miles. The dominant and steady trend in state practice in the past two or three decades has been to claim a 12-mile territorial sea. In 1986, this breadth was claimed by some 90 states and less than 20 states still followed the three-mile limit. (Two other states claimed 4 miles and 4 states claimed 6 miles.) The 1982 United Nations Convention on the Law of the Sea adopted the maximum limit of 12 miles, but there were states which raised exorbitant claims to the territorial sea: 11 states (mostly in Africa) claimed between 15 and 150 miles, and 13 Latin American and African "territorialists" claimed a 200-mile territorial sea.

Delimitation of the territorial sea between states with adjacent or opposite coasts normally follows the equidistance (median line) principle, but by reason of special circumstances—such as the presence of offshore islands—delimitation in some cases departs from the equidistance method which consists in drawing a median line every point of which is equidistant from the nearest points on the baselines from which the breadth of the territorial sea of each of the two states is measured. The rules of the 1958 Convention on the Territorial Sea and Contiguous Zone and the 1982 United Nations Convention conform to states' practice.

There is no unanimity in states' practice concerning the coastal state's jurisdiction over foreign vessels in its territorial sea. In principle, most states claim plenary legislative jurisdiction, but for reasons of comity and expediency they normally restrain from exercising it fully. Consistent with this practice, the 1958 Convention on the Territorial Sea and Contiguous Zone imposes no limitations on such jurisdiction in clearly mandatory terms. The 1982 Convention limits the coastal state's jurisdiction to apply its laws to ships in innocent passage to such matters as safety of navigation, pollution control, fisheries, protection of cables and pipelines, and customs, fiscal, immigration, and sanitary matters (but not the design, construction, manning, or equipment of foreign ships). The coastal state may not legislate to hamper or levy charges upon foreign ships for innocent passage or discriminate against any state. Ships not in innocent passage are fully subject to the coastal state's laws. Despite some theoretical divergencies (plenary jurisdiction of the United Kingdom and the United States versus limited jurisdiction only, claimed by France, Belgium, and Norway, for example), the enforcement practice has also been fairly uniform. The coastal state reserves for itself the ultimate legal right to enforce its laws if it so wishes, but refrains from doing so on grounds of comity. Like the 1958 Convention, the 1982 United Nations Convention conforms to this customary law except that, generally speaking, it excludes (but not in the mandatory "shall" wording) from the coastal state's jurisdiction crimes committed before a foreign ship passing through its territorial sea entered that sea, and in civil matters jurisdiction to arrest a ship in respect of obligations or liabilities not incurred in the course or for the purpose of the voyage through the waters of the coastal state. Special rules apply to warships and other government ships operated for noncommercial purposes. *See also* BASELINE, 221; INNOCENT PASSAGE, 236; WARSHIP, 252.

Significance   The existence of the institution of the territorial sea is a corollary of the principle of territorial sovereignty, tempered only by the interests of third countries' ships exercising the right of innocent passage. Unless otherwise agreed upon in a treaty, the coastal state has, in addition to legislative and enforcement powers, exclusive rights to all resources of the territorial sea, its seabed and subsoil, and to the superjacent airspace, without any right of innocent passage of foreign aircraft. It also has the exclusive right to carry on cabotage; that is, coastwise navigation along its shores, and the right to demand that belligerents do not fight or capture ships in its territorial waters. However, in the interests of navigation and safety of shipping or all nations the territorial sea entails responsibilities of the coastal state as well as rights, and in this sense possession of a minimum breadth territorial sea (probably three miles) is a legal duty of the coastal states. In the transitional period in the evolution of the law of the sea in the 1980s (before the entry into effect of the 1982 United Nations Convention on the Law of the Sea), the breadth of the territorial sea was not yet a totally settled issue, as the prevailing twelve-mile claim, adopted also by the 1982 Convention, was not necessarily recognized by all countries. In particular, the United States, which claimed only three miles, continued to object to wider claims made by those states that required notification or prior authorization for the innocent passage of U.S. warships. For its part, Turkey declared that it would regard as *casus belli* (an act real or alleged which provides a reason to start a war) the extension by Greece of the territorial sea in the Aegean Sea from six to twelve miles. Exorbitant claims (above twelve miles) were not recognized except between "territorialist" countries laying such claims; that is, those whose claims were "opposable" to one another. In general, the twelve-mile rule appeared likely to become universally accepted as a general rule of the law of the sea in the 1980s.

Third United Nations Conference on the Law of the   (250)
Sea, 1973–1982 (UNCLOS III)

A United Nations–sponsored international conference, first convened for a procedural session in New York in 1973, that after eight years of substantive work (1974–1982), in the first session in Caracas and subsequently in Geneva and New York, produced a comprehensive Convention on the Law of the Sea signed at Montego Bay, Jamaica, in December 1982. The work of UNCLOS III was carried out under the presidency of Amerasinghe (Sri Lanka) and, after his death in 1980, Koh (Singapore) in three main committees: Committee One dealing with the regime of the deep seabed; Committee Two dealing with the traditional jurisdictional problems of the sea such as the territorial sea and contiguous zone, the high seas, straits, as well as fishing, continental shelf and archipelagic waters; and Committee Three dealing with the marine environment, scientific research, and transfer of technology. Special working groups within each Committee were charged with considering specific issues. Unlike the 1958 Geneva Conference, UNCLOS III did not have any International Law Commission (ILC) drafts on which to base its work and was conceived not only as a legal codificatory work but primarily a political undertaking. It dealt with a host of complex but interrelated issues in which crisscrossing interests of various groups of states made negotiations difficult and protracted. These groups included the Western nations, the Soviet bloc, and the "Group of 77" (a coalition of developing countries numbering some 120 members, which substantially influenced the outcome of the Conference, representing the perceived ideas of the "New International Economic Order" [NIEO] of the oceans). There were also other interest groups on specific issues, such as the landlocked and geographically disadvantaged countries and the archipelagic states, whose membership overlapped that of the three main groupings of participants. Unlike the two previous law of the sea conferences, UNCLOS III followed the consensus procedure in adopting its consecutive drafts, but at the request of the United States, the final product of the conference—the Convention on the Law of the Sea—was adopted by a recorded vote. The official summary record and historical background of the Conference is included in its Final Act, which was signed by all the signatories of the Convention and most other states, including the United States and other Western industrialized countries. The Final Act also established the Preparatory Commission for the International Sea-Bed Authority and for the International Tribunal for the Law of the Sea. *See also* GENEVA CONFERENCE ON THE LAW OF THE SEA, 1958 (UNCLOS I), 232; GENEVA CONFERENCE ON THE LAW OF THE SEA, 1960 (UNCLOS II), 233; LAW OF THE SEA, 242; UNITED NATIONS CONVENTION ON THE LAW OF THE SEA (1982), 251.

Significance   UNCLOS III represented a major milestone in the development of the law of the sea. It was also the largest diplomatic conference in the history of mankind, both in terms of participating nations (some 160 states and other entities such as the European Community and non-self-governing territories as well as observers from national liberation movements and international organizations) and the number of delegates. UNCLOS III had its origins in the Sea-Bed Committee set by the United Nations General Assembly in 1967 to study the question of the deep seabed beyond the limits of national jurisdiction following the "common heritage of mankind" address of Malta's United Nations Ambassador Arvid Pardo before the United Nations General Assembly's First Committee in the same year. Originally, the projected conference planned to deal only with this problem, but in 1970 the United Nations General Assembly decided on a comprehensive review of the law of the sea and to this end convened UNCLOS III. After nine years of work, and despite seemingly insurmountable obstacles, the Conference achieved its objective in 1982.

United Nations Convention on the Law of the Sea   (251) (1982)

A United Nations–sponsored multilateral convention that comprehensively codifies and develops the contemporary law of the sea in time of peace. It was adopted in April 1982 after eight years of drafting work by the Third United Nations Conference on the Law of the Sea 1973–1982 (UNCLOS III). At the request of the United States, the Convention was adopted not by consensus but by recorded vote—130 for, 4 against, and 17 abstentions. Four states were "not participating" in the vote and 13 were absent. The Convention was opened for signature for two years at a special signing ceremony at Montego Bay, Jamaica, on 10 December 1982; it is therefore sometimes known as the Montego Bay Convention. When it was closed for signature on 9 December 1984, a total of 159 signatures had been affixed to it, including 51 states from Africa, 45 from Asia, 30 from Latin America, 10 from Eastern Europe, and 21 from the "Western European and other" group of nations, as well as the European Economic Community (EEC), Cook Island, and Niue. Although closed for signature in December 1984, the Convention remained open indefinitely for accession. It was to enter into force for states and other entities party to it twelve months after the date of deposit of the sixtieth instrument of ratification. By September 1986 only thirty-one instruments of ratification had been received by the Secretary-General of the United Nations. The text of the Convention consists of 320 articles in 17 parts and 9 annexes. Among the substantive issues dealt with in the Convention are (1) territorial sea and contiguous zone; (2) straits used for international navigation; (3) archipelagic states; (4) Exclusive Economic Zone

(EEZ); (5) continental shelf; (6) high seas; (7) islands; (8) enclosed or semienclosed seas; (9) landlocked states; (10) deep seabed (the "Area"); (11) protection and preservation of the marine environment; (12) marine scientific research; and (13) development and transfer of marine technology. A special part of the Convention deals with the settlement of disputes. *See also* CODIFICATION AND PROGRESSIVE DEVELOPMENT OF INTERNATIONAL LAW, 4; THIRD UNITED NATIONS CONFERENCE ON THE LAW OF THE SEA, 1973–1982 (UNCLOS III), 250; LAW OF THE SEA, 242.

Significance   The 1982 Convention has been widely recognized as the greatest codificatory work in international law and the major milestone in the history of the law of the sea. It dealt with a highly complex and broad subject matter, covering not only jurisdictional issues but also a variety of ocean uses. Many of its provisions, and in particular those that are identical with the rules of the 1958 Conventions on the Territorial Sea and Contiguous Zone and on the High Seas, codify customary law, but in many areas the 1982 Convention contains innovative concepts negotiated in response to advancements in technology and demands of the developing nations. The regulation of the deep seabed beyond national jurisdiction is an outstanding example of such "progressive development" of international law. It is this part of the Convention that was the reason the United States, the United Kingdom, and the Federal Republic of Germany refused to sign it. Some nonsignatory states had problems with certain other provisions, such as the delimitation of maritime areas between states with opposite or adjacent coasts (Venezuela) or the breadth of the territorial sea (Ecuador). Even before its entry into effect the Convention had an impact on the attitudes of states regarding marine affairs. At the national level many states—even those that did not sign the Convention—began to adjust their policies and legislation to the rules of the Convention. This trend was particularly pronounced in the area of maritime boundaries where, for example, the rules on the maximum 12-mile territorial sea and a 200-mile EEZ adopted by the Convention may have already become part of the customary law of the sea. At the international level, international organizations engaged in maritime affairs, such as the International Maritime Organization (IMO), have begun to assess the impact of the 1982 Convention on their mandates and activities. However, some provisions of the Convention, in particular those on the regime of the deep seabed (the "Area"), are viewed by a number of Western nations as unacceptable and in this sense such provisions do not reflect international consensus. Yet they are indicative of trends in contemporary law of the sea, which may eventually lead to their general acceptance sometime in the future.

Warship (252)

A ship belonging to the armed forces of a state bearing the external marks distinguishing such ships of its nationality, under the command of an officer duly commissioned by the government of the state and whose name appears in the appropriate service list or its equivalent, and manned by a crew which is under regular armed forces discipline. Under the general rules of international law on sovereign immunity, warships and other governmental ships operated for noncommercial purposes are subject only to the state whose flag they fly and are immune from the jurisdiction of any other state irrespective of whether they are in foreign internal waters, territorial sea, or any other part of the ocean. *See also* FLAG-STATE JURISDICTION, 230; HOT PURSUIT, 235; INNOCENT PASSAGE, 236; SOVEREIGN (STATE) IMMUNITY, 143; STRAIT, 248.

Significance   Although warships are expected to comply with the coastal state's laws and regulations concerning navigation, pollution, and the like, the authorities of that state are barred from setting foot on board the ship or carrying out any act on board without the permission of its captain or other competent authority of the flag state. However, a foreign warship failing to comply with laws and regulations of the coastal state may be required by that state to leave its waters immediately and its flag state must bear international responsibility for any loss or damage to the coastal state resulting from the noncompliance. Unless the flag state waives their immunity, crew members are immune from prosecution by the coastal state for crimes committed on board the ship and even those committed on shore if they were there in uniform and in official capacity. Although the 1958 Convention on the Territorial Sea and Contiguous Zone and the 1982 United Nations Convention on the Law of the Sea grant the right of innocent passage to ships in general, the right of innocent passage of foreign warships is a highly controversial matter. The exact nature of foreign warships' rights in international straits is also controversial, but the 1982 Convention grants all ships the right of "transit passage" in such straits and the right of "archipelagic sea lanes passage" in archipelagic waters. The drafting work of UNCLOS III shows that the maritime nations insisted on foreign warships enjoying these rights. It is not clear under the 1982 Convention whether and to what extent warships can engage in naval maneuvers or weapons practice in a foreign Exclusive Economic Zone (EEZ), especially since the Convention in its Article 88 which applies to the EEZ as well provides that "the high seas shall be reserved for peaceful purposes."

9. Treaties

Accession   **(253)**

Formal acceptance of a treaty by a state which did not take part in negotiating and signing it. Accession is possible only if it is provided for in the treaty, if agreement of the negotiating states can otherwise be established, or if all the parties have subsequently agreed to a state's accession. As with ratification, acceptance, or approval (unless the treaty provides otherwise), an instrument of accession establishes a state's consent to be bound by the treaty only upon the exchange, deposit, or notification of the instrument. Although the matter was once controversial, recent practice allows a state to accede to a treaty which is not yet in force. Distinctions sometimes made between accession and "adherence" or "adhesion" are not generally supported by the practice of states. *See also* ENTRY INTO FORCE, 257; RATIFICATION, 272; SIGNATURE, 275.

Significance   The institution of accession allows states to join a treaty arrangement in whose negotiations and signature they did not participate. In this sense, it has the same legal effects as signature and ratification combined. By allowing flexibility in the procedure of becoming a party to a treaty, accession encourages wider acceptance and universality of treaty arrangements. Such expansion in participation commonly occurs in the case of multilateral but rarely bilateral treaties. Modern practice has largely blurred the distinction between accession on the one hand and signature and ratification on the other. Multilateral treaties, especially those negotiated under the auspices of the United Nations or its agencies, are often open for signature for as long as two years to states which did not participate in their drafting.

241

Adoption (254)

A formal act whereby the form and content of the text of a proposed treaty are settled. Adoption does not mean that the treaty has been signed. The adoption of the text takes place by the consent of the states participating in the drawing up of the text. However, at large international conferences the adoption of the text of the negotiated treaty takes place by a vote. The 1969 Vienna Convention on the Law of Treaties suggests a two-thirds majority, but any special rules of the international organization within which the conference was held will apply to the adoption. *See also* AUTHENTICATION, 256; RATIFICATION, 272; SIGNATURE, 275.

Significance   The adoption of a treaty does not yet mean that the negotiating parties have expressed consent to be bound by the treaty or, as is normally the case at major international codificatory conferences, even signed it. For example, the United Nations Convention on the Law of the Sea was adopted by the Third United Nations Conference on the Law of the Sea (UNCLOS III) in New York in April 1982, but signed in Montego Bay, Jamaica, in December 1982. Historically, the adoption of the text of a treaty took place by unanimous agreement, something that remains the rule (apart from bilateral treaties) in the case of the so-called restricted multilateral treaties—treaties which establish very close interdependence among the parties and whose purpose is such that application of the treaty in its entirety to all parties is an essential condition of the consent of each to be bound by the treaty. The treaties establishing the European Economic Community (EEC) are examples of this type of treaty. In the EEC, unanimity is also required for the admission of a new member.

Amendment (255)

An alteration of a treaty adopted by consent and intended to be binding upon all the parties. An amendment may involve either individual provisions or a general review of a treaty. The latter procedure is frequently referred to as "revision," but the terminology in state practice is far from uniform. The 1969 Vienna Convention on the Law of Treaties uses the term amendment to cover both situations since, from the legal point of view, there is no difference between them. The Convention does not use the term revision because of its awkward political connotations. A multilateral treaty may be changed also by "modification," a term in the Convention referring to an alteration agreed upon, in an *inter se* (between or among themselves) agreement, only by some of the parties to the multilateral treaty. *See also* PEACEFUL CHANGE, 271.

Significance   Amendment of treaties is normally a political matter. It depends upon the consent of the parties and is governed by the rules of the law of treaties in general. In recent times, the development of international organizations and the proliferation of multilateral treaties have had a considerable impact upon the process of treaty amendment. Multilateral treaties, particularly those that are constituent instruments of international organizations, normally include detailed rules for amendment, generally by approval of a qualified majority of the parties. The United Nations Charter, for example, provides that its amendments shall come into force for all members when they have been adopted and ratified by two-thirds of the members, including all permanent members of the Security Council. Three such Charter amendments, otherwise politically not controversial, have been adopted.

Amendment clauses take a great variety of forms, making it difficult to deduce detailed rules of customary international law regarding amendment of multilateral treaties. The 1969 Vienna Convention on the Law of Treaties formulated only some basic rules. All the contracting states have the right to participate in the decision to be taken on the proposal and in the negotiating and concluding of any agreement for the amendment of the treaty. Every state entitled to become a party to the treaty is also entitled to become a party to the treaty as amended. Unless it expresses a different intention, a state that becomes a party to an amended treaty becomes both a party to the treaty as amended and a party to the unamended treaty in relation to any party not bound by the amending agreement. A modification is possible (unless prohibited by the treaty) if it does not affect the enjoyment by the other parties of their rights under the treaty or the performance of their obligations and does not relate to a provision, derogation from which is incompatible with the effective execution of the treaty as a whole. Although the Vienna Conference on the Law of Treaties rejected a provision on what the International Law Commission (ILC) called "modification of treaties by subsequent practice" on the ground that such a rule would create instability in treaty relations, international practice provides examples of this type of modification. Among them are modification in relations between France and the United States with regard to the bilateral Air Transport Services Agreement of 1946 and modification of certain rules of the 1958 Geneva law of the sea conventions.

Authentication   (256)
A distinct procedural step in the conclusion of a treaty whereby the definitive text of the treaty is established as correct and authentic and not subject to alterations. The procedure governing authentication is

often fixed in the text of the treaty itself or by agreement of the negotiating states. Failing any such prescribed or agreed upon procedure, authentication takes place by signature; signature *ad referendum* (that is, a signature given provisionally and subject to confirmation by the respective governments); or initialing of the text by the representatives of the negotiating states or alternatively of the final act of the conference incorporating the text. *See also* ADOPTION, 254; ENTRY INTO FORCE, 257; RATIFICATION, 272; SIGNATURE, 275; TREATY, 279.

Significance   Authentication is necessary in order that the prospective parties to the treaty may know definitively what its content is so that there be no confusion as to its exact terms. In the past, authentication was not a distinct part of the treaty-making process and signature was the general method of authenticating a text. This is still the case with bilateral treaties. More recently, new methods of authentication have been devised in negotiating multilateral treaties. These include, for example, incorporating the unsigned text in the final act of the conference, a resolution of the international organization sponsoring the negotiations, or authentication by an act performed by competent authority of the organization such as the Director-General of the International Labor Office (ILO). The text of a treaty may sometimes be authenticated in two or more languages, but adopted only in one.

Entry into Force (257)

The beginning of the period of the binding force of a treaty; that is, its coming into operation. A treaty normally enters into force or effect; that is, becomes operative upon such date as it may provide or as the negotiating states have otherwise agreed. Many treaties provide for their entry into force on the date of signature. Where ratification, acceptance, or approval is necessary, the treaty enters into force only after the exchange or deposit of the instruments of ratification, acceptance, or approval by all or a certain minimum number of states. In the case of multilateral treaties, it would normally be unreasonable to wait for ratification, acceptance, or approval by all the signatory states, and accordingly such treaties usually provide that they will enter into force following the date of the deposit of a specified number of instruments of ratification, acceptance, approval, or accession. Treaties may provide for their entry into force on a fixed date or a specified number of days or months following the date of deposit of the specified numbers of instruments of ratification or accession. Sometimes, however, a treaty may enter into force on a precise date irrespective of the number of ratifications or upon the occurrence of a certain event. The treaty is in force only between those states that have ratified (accepted, approved, or acceded to) it. For each of such states it enters into force on the date of deposit of the appropriate instrument of consent to be bound, unless the treaty provides otherwise. For some reasons, such as the urgency of the matters dealt with in the treaty, the negotiating states may specify in the treaty itself or in some other manner agree (in a separate protocol or exchange of notes, for example) that the treaty or a part of it be applied provisionally pending its entry into force. Barring contrary agreement, such a provisional application with respect to a state terminates if that state notifies the other signatories of its intention not to become a party to the treaty. Unless a different intention appears from the treaty or is otherwise established, a treaty does not apply retroactively; that is, its provisions do not bind a party in relation to any act or fact which took place or any situation which ceased to exist before the date of the entry into force of the treaty with respect to that party. Whether legal or other concepts are to be interpreted as understood at the time when a treaty provision was drafted or at the time of their application is a difficult problem of "intertemporal" international law. A very general rule here is that any fact, action, or situation must be assessed in the light of the rules of law that are contemporaneous with it. Unless a different intention appears from the treaty or is otherwise established, a treaty is presumed to bind each party in respect of its entire territory. *See also* ACCESSION, 253; INTERTEMPORAL LAW, 17; RATIFICATION, 272.

Significance   The fixing of the date on which a treaty enters into force is essential for ascertaining the rights and obligations of the parties with regard to the treaty. Modern treaties usually specify such date. A typical formula (applying to the entry into force of the 1969 Vienna Convention on the Law of Treaties, for example) reads: "The following Convention shall enter into force on the thirtieth day following the date of the deposit of the thirty-fifth instrument of ratification or accession." In those exceptional cases where no date is specified, there is a presumption that the treaty enters into force as soon as all negotiating parties have consented to be bound by it. It is, of course, tacitly assumed that matters such as authentication, signature, ratification, depositary functions, reservations, and entry into force, which must be dealt with before the treaty is in force, apply from the very moment of adopting the text. One major problem in international treaty making is the very slow rate of joining multilateral treaty arrangements and the time gap between signature and ratification. Therefore, because of the need to act promptly in regulating urgent problems and lengthy delays in obtaining ratifications (caused not necessarily only by substantive doubts but also technical and administrative difficulties), provisional application has assumed increasing importance in recent treaty practice. It is a controversial matter whether a state, which has signed a treaty subject to ratification or ratified (accepted, approved, acceded to) a treaty in the interval prior to its entry into force, has a legal obligation not to defeat in good faith the object of the treaty. The 1969 Vienna Convention stipulates that such a state has an obligation to refrain from acts which would defeat the object and purpose of the treaty until it has made its intention clear not to become a party to the treaty.

Full Powers   (258)

A document emanating from the competent authority of a state designating a person or persons to represent the state for negotiating, adopting, or authenticating the text of a treaty, for expressing the consent of the state to be bound by a treaty, or for accomplishing any other act with respect to a treaty. Heads of state or government and foreign ministers are automatically considered as representing the state and do not have to produce any full powers. Heads of diplomatic missions do not need full powers for the purpose of adopting the text of a treaty between the accrediting state and host state. Representatives of states to an international conference or organization or one of its organs have analogous standing. Other individuals are considered as representatives of a state only if they produce appropriate full powers or if it appears from the practice of states concerned or from other circumstances that the intention of the states was to dispense with the full powers. *See also* ADOPTION, 254; AUTHENTICATION, 256; INVALIDITY OF TREATIES, 262; RATIFICATION, 272; SIGNATURE, 275.

Significance   In the era of absolute monarchies and slow communications, production of full powers by a sovereign's agent was almost invariably required. In recent times, this practice is common only in the conclusion of more formal treaties, and since many treaties are concluded in simplified form, production of full powers is not normally required. The major consequence of acting on behalf of a state without appropriate full powers is invalidity of the act relating to the conclusion of the treaty unless such act is afterwards confirmed by that state. In international practice, there have been instances of acting without authority. In 1908, for example, the U.S. Minister to Romania signed two conventions without any authority to do so.

Fundamental Change of Circumstances   (259)

A very exceptional ground for terminating or withdrawing from a treaty, which may be invoked by a party if a fundamental change of circumstances (not foreseen by the parties) has occurred with regard to those existing at the time of the conclusion of the treaty. Before the fundamental change of circumstances (commonly known as the *rebus sic stantibus* clause) can be invoked as a ground for terminating a treaty, the following prerequisites must be met under the 1969 Vienna Convention on the Law of Treaties: (1) the change must be of circumstances existing at the time of the conclusion of the treaty (for an indefinite or fixed duration); (2) the change must have been fundamental; (3) the change must have been unforeseen by the parties; (4) the circumstances that have changed must have constituted an essential basis of the consent of the parties to be bound by the treaty; (5) the effect of the change must be radically to transform the extent of obligations of the party invoking the change; and (6) the obligations must still be performed under the treaty, which means that fully executed treaties are not included. Fundamental change of circumstances may also be invoked as a ground for suspending the operation of a treaty. Under no circumstances may it be invoked if the treaty in question establishes a boundary or if the fundamental change is the result of a breach by the party invoking it of an obligation under the treaty or any other international obligation owed to any other party to the treaty. The latter exception is simply an application of a general principle of law that no one may take advantage of his own wrong. *See also* PACTA SUNT SERVANDA, 269; PEACEFUL CHANGE, 271; SUSPENSION OF OPERATION OF TREATIES, 277; TERMINATION OF TREATIES, 278.

Significance   However reluctantly, the doctrine of *rebus sic stantibus* has been admitted by a great majority of publicists. It has also been invoked in international state practice. In extreme cases it can act as a safety valve, allowing a state that has no possibility to obtain any legal relief from the existence of outmoded and burdensome treaty obligations to invoke it and terminate the treaty. On the other hand, it has been widely recognized that allowing treaties to be terminated on grounds of fundamental change of circumstances involves grave dangers for the sanctity of treaties, unless the conditions for the application of the *rebus sic stantibus* clause are most closely defined and adequate safeguards provided against its arbitrary use. For this reason, the modern doctrine and practice of international law rejects as a fiction the theory followed by the classical publicists that every treaty allegedly contained an implied clause that it should remain in force only "as long as the circumstances remained the same" (*rebus sic stantibus*) as at the time of the conclusion of the treaty. This doctrine is considered as a dangerous fiction today, but the right to invoke fundamental change of circumstances as a ground for terminating or suspending a treaty is admitted (albeit only in extreme cases) in order to prevent using or abusing this right as an excuse to evade inconvenient or onerous treaty obligations. To avoid any associations with the old doctrine of an implied *rebus sic stantibus* clause, the 1969 Vienna Convention does not use this Latin phrase in the text of the relevant article or even in its title. The right to invoke fundamental change of circumstances to terminate treaty obligations has been invoked in some cases before the Permanent Court of International Justice (1) by France in the Advisory Opinion on the *Nationality Decrees Issued in Tunis and Morocco* (1923); (2) in the *Free Zones of Upper Savoy and the District of Gex* (*France v. Switzerland*, 1932); and (3) by China in the case of the *Denunciation of the Sino-Belgian Treaty of 1865* (*Belgium v. China*, 1927). While recognizing this right, the Court generally avoided giving it effect. In the *Fisheries Jurisdiction* case (*United Kingdom v. Iceland*, 1973) the International Court of Justice (ICJ) considered the applicability of the principle of fundamental change of circumstances in light of the 1969 Convention on the Law of Treaties, holding that the Convention may in many respects be regarded as a codification of the existing customary law on this matter. The principle has also been invoked in the political organs of the United Nations, and the Secretary-General, in a study of the validity of minority treaties concluded during the League of Nations era, accepted the existence of the principle in international law while stressing the exceptional and limited character of its application.

Inconsistent Treaties   (260)

Successive treaties relating to the same subject matter whose provisions are incompatible with one another, creating conflicting obligations for one or more of the parties. Unless expressly stated in the treaty, it is not clear whether or not a treaty whose provisions conflict with the obligations contracted by a party in an earlier treaty should be invalid. Treaties often contain a clause intended to regulate the relationship of the treaty to another prior or future treaty. Preeminent among all such clauses is Article 103 of the United Nations Charter which states "in the event of a conflict between the obligations of the Members of the United Nations under the . . . Charter and their obligations under any other international agreement, their obligations under the . . . Charter shall prevail." It is also clear that a treaty overrides other treaties if it represents a peremptory norm of general international law (*jus cogens*).

Only the overriding character of the United Nations Charter is recognized by the 1969 Vienna Convention on the Law of Treaties, which otherwise approaches the problem of inconsistent treaties as one of priorities and does not deal with their validity. It governs the complexity of inconsistent treaties only in a residual way; that is, it contains rules that operate only in the absence of express treaty provisions regulating priority. Under the Convention, if a treaty specifies that it is subject to or that it is not to be considered as incompatible with, an earlier or later treaty, the provisions of that other treaty prevail. For example, the 1958 Convention on the High Seas disavows any intention of overriding existing treaties. Otherwise, as between parties to an earlier treaty which also become parties to a later, inconsistent treaty, the earlier treaty applies only to the extent that its provisions are compatible with the later treaty. As between a party to both treaties and a party to only one of them, the treaty to which both are parties is to apply. This rule is without prejudice to any agreements to modify multilateral treaties between certain of the parties only, to any question of discharge because of material breach, or to any responsibility resulting from inconsistent treaties. In all matters relating to priority between inconsistent treaties, the relevant date for the earlier and later treaty is the date of the adoption of the text of the treaty and not that of the treaty's entry into force. The phrase "relating to the same subject matter" must be interpreted strictly. *See also* ADOPTION, 254; AMENDMENT, 255; INVALIDITY OF TREATIES, 262; SUSPENSION OF OPERATION OF TREATIES, 277; TERMINATION OF TREATIES, 278.

Significance   Inconsistent treaties are an increasing problem in view of the multiplication of diverse kinds of treaties and participation in multilateral treaty making by global, regional, and functional organizations. This activity has resulted in numerous overlapping treaties that frequently created conflicting obligations for one or more parties. In the area of human rights, for example, there coexist two sets of treaties: one adopted within a regional framework, as exemplified by the 1950 European Convention for the Protection of Human Rights and Fundamental Freedoms, and the other at the global level; namely, the two 1966 United Nations Covenants on Economic, Social, and Cultural Rights and on Civil and Political Rights respectively.

Interpretation of Treaties   (261)
A rational process of clarifying and elucidating the meaning of unclear and ambiguous treaty provisions, whose purpose is to ascertain in good faith the intention of the parties in accordance with the ordinary meaning of the terms used in the treaty in their context with recourse, if necessary, to supplementary means. These might include the preparatory work of the treaty and the circumstances of its conclusion and understanding the general object and purpose of the treaty. The interpretation of treaties is governed by numerous principles, maxims, canons, and rules developed by international tribunals, publicists, organs of international organizations, and diplomatic practice. Many of

these are based upon simple logic and have been borrowed from private law of contract and adapted to the context in which international law operates in relations between independent states. There exists, however, no coherent and mandatory system of rules of interpretation in international law. Therefore, the 1969 Vienna Convention on the Law of Treaties lays down comparatively few general principles which appear to constitute fundamental rules and guidelines for interpretation.

Among the approaches to the interpretation of treaties, the school of thought emphasizing the "intention of the parties" as the primary objective of interpretation is perhaps the most prevalent, but the teleological approach (focusing on establishing the general purposes of the treaty) is common in interpreting law-making treaties in economic, social, humanitarian, and similar areas. For the "meaning of the text" school, the primary objective is to ascertain the ordinary meaning of the text. These approaches may lead to the same result but may also produce divergent interpretations of the same text. Words should be construed according to their textual and plain meaning unless this would result in absurdity or conflict with the intention of the parties. It is to the ostensible intention of the parties at the time of the conclusion of the treaty and as disclosed by the text that primary regard must be paid. In exceptional cases other materials may, however, help discover the real intention of the parties. A treaty should be interpreted in its context and in the light of its object and purpose. Another general rule posits that words and phrases should be given reasonable and consistent meaning in the light of international law. Ambiguous provisions should be construed in a way least restrictive of a party's sovereignty and—an old canon of interpretation in municipal law—a specific rule should prevail over the general one (*lex specialis derogat legi generali*). One major principle of interpretation is the so-called "principle of effectiveness," which holds that a treaty should be interpreted in a way that will render it most effective and useful—a principle sometimes referred to by the Latin maxim *ut res magis valeat quam pereat*. This principle is of particular importance in the interpretation of multilateral treaties establishing international organizations.

In addition to the context, recourse may be had to supplementary means of interpretation, including the preparatory work (*travaux préparatoires*); that is, the record of the drafting of treaty and the circumstances of its conclusion. At the 1969 Vienna Conference, the United States argued for permitting the preparatory work to be used equally with the text in determining the parties' intention. Under the 1969 Vienna Convention, supplementary means may be resorted to only to confirm the meaning resulting from the textual and "object and purpose" interpretation or to determine the meaning when such interpretation leaves the meaning ambiguous or obscure or leads to a result which is manifestly absurd or unreasonable. Subsequent agreement between the parties regarding the interpretation of the treaty or the application of its provisions, and subsequent practice in the application of the treaty which establishes the agreement of the parties regarding its interpretation as well as any relevant rules of international law applicable in the relations between the parties, must also be taken into account together with the context.

Special problems arise in the case of multilingual treaties, which are very common in international diplomacy. With the advent of the United Nations, treaties drawn up in Chinese, English, French, Russian, Spanish, and Arabic are quite numerous. Normally, such treaties contain an express provision determining the status of the different language versions. In the absence of such a provision, each version is to be considered authoritative for purposes of interpretation. Under the Vienna Convention, if a treaty is authenticated in two or more languages the text is equally authoritative in each language unless the treaty provides or the parties agree that in case of divergence a particular text is to prevail. The terms of the treaty are presumed to have the same meaning in each text and that meaning which best reconciles the texts is to be adopted, having regard to the object and purpose of the treaty. *See also* ADVISORY JURISDICTION OF THE INTERNATIONAL COURT OF JUSTICE (ICJ), 282; ERROR, 266; INCONSISTENT TREATIES, 260; INVALIDITY OF TREATIES, 262.

Significance   Interpretation of treaties is the most frequent focus of disputes arising with regard to treaties. Since language is not a perfect medium for expressing legal rules, ambiguities and uncertainties in treaty texts are a common phenomenon. Hence interpretation of treaties has been a major task of arbitral and other international tribunals. Treaties themselves may confer competence to interpret their provisions to an international court as is the case of the Treaty of Rome of 1957 establishing the European Economic Community (EEC), which grants the Court of Justice of the European Community the jurisdiction to interpret the Community's treaties. In the United Nations, each principal organ interprets the Charter in carrying on its mission. In addition each of them, except the Secretariat, and all of the specialized agencies except the Universal Postal Union, may ask the International Court of Justice (ICJ) for an advisory opinion interpreting Charter provisions. Treaties may also be interpreted by international technical organs, such as the International Labor Office which interprets treaties drafted under the auspices of the International Labor Organization (ILO). Although interpretation of treaties has been exhaustively analyzed both by judicial bodies and publicists, except for obvious logical rules there exist in international law no obligatory principles or canons governing the process of interpretation.

Invalidity of Treaties   (262)

Nullity of a treaty or some of its provisions because of the existence or absence of certain circumstances or events affecting its legal status. The customary law governing validity or invalidity of treaties is unclear and controversial. The 1969 Vienna Convention on the Law of Treaties makes an attempt to codify and develop some general principles in this matter, distinguishing (in addition to the cases where representatives lack appropriate full powers) the following grounds for invalidity of treaties: (1) manifest violation of a provision of fundamental importance of a state's internal law regarding competence to conclude treaties (a violation is manifest if it would be objectively evident to any state conducting itself in the matter in accordance with normal practice and in good faith); (2) excess of authority by the representative in cases where a representative purports finally to bind his state, but only if the specific restriction imposed by his state upon his authority to express the state's final consent was notified to the other negotiating state or states prior to his expressing such consent; (3) error; (4) fraud; (5) corruption of a representative of a state; (6) coercion of a representative of a state; (7) coercion of a state by the threat or use of force; and (8) conflict of the treaty, at the time of its conclusion, with a peremptory norm of general international law (*jus cogens*). *See also* FULL POWERS, 258; INVALIDITY OF TREATIES: COERCION OF A REPRESENTATIVE, 263; INVALIDITY OF TREATIES: COERCION OF A STATE, 264; INVALIDITY OF TREATIES: CORRUPTION, 265; INVALIDITY OF TREATIES: ERROR, 266; INVALIDITY OF TREATIES: FRAUD, 267; *JUS COGENS*, 19.

Significance   Consequences of invalidity vary depending on the nature of the ground for invalidation. A fundamental distinction must be made between void and voidable treaties. The entire treaty is void—that is, automatically without any legal effect—from the very beginning (*ab initio*) in cases of lack of full powers, coercion of a representative, or coercion of a state; and from the time of voiding, that is, without retroactive effect, in case of conflict with an existing or emergent peremptory norm of general international law (*jus cogens*). In other cases the treaty is not void *ipso facto*; it is only voidable. Grounds for invalidation may be invoked (1) in the case of excess of authority by the state disavowing the act of its representative; (2) in the case of error by any party to the treaty or; (3) in the cases of fraud and corruption by the victim state. To prevent possible abuse the Vienna Convention provides that a state is barred from claiming invalidity if it has expressly agreed that the treaty is valid or continues to operate, or by reason of its conduct must be considered to have acquiesced in the validity of the treaty or in its maintenance in force or operation. As a general rule (but always in cases of coercion and conflict with *jus cogens*), grounds for invalidating a treaty may be invoked only with respect to the entire treaty; that is, the defective clauses cannot be separated from the remainder of the treaty. There is no "separability of treaty provisions"; the entire treaty is invalid. Otherwise, only specific clauses are voided where they are separable with regard to their application, where their acceptance was not an essential basis of the other party or parties to be bound by the treaty as a whole, and continued performance of the remainder of the treaty would not be unjust. However, in case of fraud or corruption the state entitled to invoke them has a choice of invalidating the whole treaty or only the particular defective clause, subject to the conditions of separability. Under the Vienna Convention, a state challenging the validity of a treaty must notify the other party or parties so that any dispute can be resolved peacefully. If no solution is reached within twelve months, the dispute is to be submitted to a special conciliation commission or, in cases of dispute involving *jus cogens*, to the International Court of Justice (ICJ). These provisions on the procedures for conciliation and judicial settlement represent an innovative development of the law of treaties by the Vienna Convention.

Invalidity of Treaties: Coercion of a Representative (263)

Acts or threats directed personally against a representative of a state as an individual in order to procure the signature, ratification, acceptance, approval of, or accession to a treaty, which render the representative's consent to be bound by the entire treaty *ipso facto* (by the fact) and *ab initio* (from the beginning) void. *See also* INVALIDITY OF TREATIES, 262; INVALIDITY OF TREATIES: COERCION OF A STATE, 264.

Significance   There is general agreement in customary law, codified in the 1969 Vienna Convention on the Law of Treaties, that personal coercion (duress) applied to a state's representative to force a treaty upon his state renders the treaty void and without any legal effects. History reveals a number of such instances of coercion not only against negotiators but also, in case of ratification, against members of the state's legislature. The most notorious case of coercion of representatives, which also displays features of the coercion of a state, was the third-degree methods of pressure applied in 1939 by Nazi Germany against President Emil Hacha and Foreign Minister František Chvalkovsky of Czechoslovakia for the purpose of extracting by intimidation their signatures to a treaty creating a German protectorate over the remaining part of the Czechoslovak state. The concept of coercion of representatives extends not only to threats to their persons but also blackmailing and threatening members of their families.

Invalidity of Treaties: Coercion of a State   (264)

Applying threats or use of force against a state or states in violation of the principles embodied in the Charter of the United Nations to procure the conclusion of a treaty. Coercion of a state by the threat or use of force renders the entire treaty *ipso facto* (by the fact) and *ab initio* (from the beginning) void. *See also* CONQUEST, 180; FORCE, ILLEGAL THREAT OR USE OF, 308; INVALIDITY OF TREATIES, 262; INVALIDITY OF TREATIES: COERCION OF A REPRESENTATIVE, 263; UNEQUAL TREATIES DOCTRINE, 280.

Significance   Although some publicists (either sincerely concerned about the stability of treaty relations or rationalizing hard facts of international politics) hesitate to accept as a legal rule that coercion of a state by the threat or use of force renders a treaty void, the rule is generally established in contemporary international law and was codified in the 1969 Vienna Convention on the Law of Treaties. Under traditional international law when resort to force was not illegal, treaties were not affected by the fact that they were brought about by the threat or use of force. However, since the Covenant of the League of Nations (1919) and the General Treaty for the Renunciation of War (Kellogg-Briand Pact or Pact of Paris, 1928), there has been a tendency (at least in theory) to consider aggression as illegal, with the corollary that treaties imposed by armed force are void. This trend culminated in the Charter of the United Nations, which proscribes the threat or use of force in the international relations of its members. This prohibition has become a peremptory norm of general international law (*jus cogens*) whose one legal consequence for all states is invalidity of treaties procured by the threat or use of force. This rule was referred to by the International Court of Justice (ICJ) in the *Fisheries Jurisdiction* case (*United Kingdom v. Iceland*, 1973) and applies to any treaty concluded after the entry into force of the United Nations Charter on 24 October 1945. Since juridical facts must be assessed in the light of contemporaneous law—that is, the law in force at the time of the conclusion of the treaty—this rule has no retroactive effect on the validity of treaties concluded prior to the outlawry of force in international relations. The Vienna Conference on the Law of Treaties left the precise scope of illegal force prohibited by the United Nations Charter to subsequent interpretation by competent organs of the United Nations. It was a controversial issue in the International Law Commission and at the

Vienna Conference whether force included not only armed force but also economic and political pressures. This latter position has been argued by many Third World countries and seconded by the Soviet Union. Western nations have opposed this interpretation, concerned that inclusion of such imprecise terms in the Convention on the Law of Treaties as political and economic coercion might encourage arbitary and unfounded invalidation of treaties. As a compromise, it was agreed to include a "Declaration on the Prohibition of Military, Political, and Economic Coercion in the Conclusion of Treaties" in the Final Act of the Vienna Conference on the Law of Treaties. This Declaration is not a legally binding treaty; hence, it must be concluded that only the threat or use of armed force invalidates a treaty.

Invalidity of Treaties: Corruption (265)

One of the grounds for invalidating a state's consent to be bound by a treaty which may be invoked if the expression of a state's consent has been procured through the corruption of its representative by another negotiating state either directly or indirectly. Corruption does not automatically void a treaty. The treaty is only voidable; that is, it gives the injured party a right to invoke corruption as invalidating its consent. *See also* INVALIDITY OF TREATIES, 262; INVALIDITY OF TREATIES: FRAUD, 267.

Significance Like fraud, corruption is not very common in the practice of treaty making. The majority of the International Law Commission considered it desirable to include corruption in the Convention on the Law of Treaties as a separate ground for invalidating a treaty, intermediate in gravity between fraud and coercion. Only acts calculated to exercise a substantial influence on the disposition of a representative to conclude a treaty and imputable to the other (or another) negotiating state may be invoked. A small courtesy or favor shown to a representative does not necessarily imply corruption.

Invalidity of Treaties: Error (266)

One of the grounds for invalidating a state's consent to be bound by a treaty which may be invoked if it relates to a fact or situation mistakenly assumed by that state to exist at the time when the treaty was concluded and which formed an essential basis of its consent. An error does not make a treaty automatically void. The treaty is only voidable; that is, it gives the concerned party a right to invoke the error as invalidating its consent. A state that contributed by its own conduct to the error or was put on notice of a possible error is not allowed to invoke it as a ground for invalidating its consent. Errors in the treaty must be distinguished from errors in the wording of the text, which do not affect the validity of the consent. *See also* INVALIDITY OF TREATIES, 262; INVALIDITY OF TREATIES: FRAUD, 267.

Significance   Errors or mistakes do not play a great role in the treaty-making process. Almost all recorded instances in which essential errors of substance have been invoked have concerned geographical errors. Deliberately falsified maps would be qualified as "fraud." The effect of errors on treaties was discussed, for example, before the Permanent Court of International Justice in the case concerning the *Legal Status of Eastern Greenland (Denmark v. Norway,* 1933) and before the International Court of Justice (ICJ) in the *Temple of Preah Vihear* case (*Cambodia v. Thailand*, 1961, 1962).

Invalidity of Treaties: Fraud   (267)

One of the grounds for invalidating a state's consent to be bound by a treaty which may be invoked if that state has been induced to conclude a treaty by the fraudulent conduct of another negotiating state. Fraud does not automatically void a treaty. The treaty is only voidable; that is, it gives the concerned party a right to invoke fraud as invalidating its consent. *See also* INVALIDITY OF TREATIES, 262; INVALIDITY OF TREATIES: CORRUPTION, 265.

Significance   There is not sufficient international practice concerning the question of what constitutes fraudulent conduct. The 1969 Vienna Convention on the Law of Treaties does not define fraud. In the opinion of the International Law Commission, which prepared a draft of the Convention, the expression "fraudulent conduct" is designed to include any false statements, misrepresentations, or other deceitful proceedings by which a state is induced to give its consent to a treaty it would not otherwise have given.

Invalidity of Treaties: Material Breach   (268)

A repudiation of the treaty by a party, not sanctioned by international law, or a serious violation of a provision essential to the accomplishment of the object of the treaty, which entitles the other party or parties to invoke the breach as a ground for terminating the treaty or suspending its operation in whole or in part. A material breach of a treaty, however serious, does not *ipso facto* rescind it; it only gives the party or parties affected the right to invoke the breach as a ground for terminating or suspending the operation of the treaty in whole or in part ("discharge through breach"). The injured party loses this right if it agrees that the treaty continues in force or, by reason of its conduct, must be considered as having acquiesced in its maintenance in force. Only a serious "material breach" (in the language of the 1969 Vienna Convention on the Law of Treaties) justifies termination or suspension. The problem of discharge through breach poses complex questions in multilateral treaty relations since breach by one state cannot entitle another to rescind it vis-à-vis the innocent parties. Under the Vienna Convention, a material breach of a multilateral treaty by one party may, according to circumstances, result in (1) a joint reaction of the other parties, or (2) the reaction of the state specifically affected by the breach. In the first situation, the parties may, by unanimous agreement, terminate or suspend the treaty in whole or in part in relations between themselves and the defaulting party, or altogether as between all the parties. In the second case, the specially injured party is entitled to suspend the operation of the treaty in whole or in part only in relations between itself and the defaulting party. Where a material breach by one party tends to undermine the whole treaty regime (for example, in arms control treaties), any party (except of course the defaulting state), in order to protect itself against the potential threat produced by the conduct of the defaulting party, is permitted to suspend the operation of the treaty with regard to itself in relations with all the other parties without first obtaining the agreement of others. To ensure that the rules on discharge through breach should not cause rescission of treaties of a humanitarian character concluded for the benefit of individuals, the Vienna Convention makes it clear that in such cases a material breach should not entitle the other parties to terminate or suspend the operation of the treaty. *See also* PACTA SUNT SERVANDA, 269; TERMINATION OF TREATIES, 278.

Significance   It has been recognized since the time of Hugo Grotius that a breach of a treaty by one party may give rise to a right of the other party or parties to be released from the obligations of the treaty. However, the doctrine and state practice differ on the extent of this right and the conditions under which it may be exercised, particularly with respect to multilateral treaties. Support for the view that only a material breach justifies the termination or suspension of a treaty is found in such international arbitral awards as the *Tacna-Arica* arbitration (*Chile v. Peru,* 1925); the Advisory Opinion of the International Court of Justice (ICJ) in the question of the *Legal Consequences for States of the Continued Presence of South Africa in Namibia (South West Africa) Notwithstanding Security Council Res. 276 (1970)* (1971); and the *Appeal*

Relating to the Jurisdiction of the ICAO Council case (International Court of Justice, 1972). In both cases, the Court relied on the authority of the Vienna Convention even prior to its entry into force.

Pacta Sunt Servanda   (269)

A Latin phrase meaning that treaties shall be observed. *Pacta sunt servanda* is the fundamental principle of the customary law of treaties and, according to some, the very foundation of international law. It is enshrined in the Preamble to the Charter of the United Nations and is included in the 1969 Vienna Convention on the Law of Treaties in its Preamble and the operative Article 26, which states that "[e]very treaty in force is binding upon the parties to it and must be performed by them in good faith." It is also a long-standing principle of customary international law, codified in the Vienna Convention, that provisions of internal law may not be invoked as justification for failure of treaty performance. There is a presumption in favor of regularity of treaties in the sense that it is presumed that they were entered into without any violation of internal law regarding competence to conclude treaties unless violation was manifest to any state conducting itself in good faith and concerned a rule of fundamental importance. *See also* FUNDAMEN-TAL CHANGE OF CIRCUMSTANCES, 259; INVALIDITY OF TREATIES, 262; PEACEFUL CHANGE, 271; TERMINATION OF TREATIES, 278; UNEQUAL TREATIES DOCTRINE, 280.

Significance   The principle *pacta sunt servanda* underlies the whole system of legal relations among nations. Although philosophically the reasons for its existence cannot be accounted for, some consider it to be a principle of natural law, others a general principle of law, and yet others a principle of customary law. The duty to observe treaties in good faith has been recognized by publicists and state practice from time immemorial. One of its best known expressions was the Declaration of London of 1871, subscribed to by the major European powers, which stated *inter alia* that "it is an essential principle of the Law of Nations that no Power can liberate itself from the engagements of a treaty nor modify the stipulations thereof, unless with the consent of the contracting parties by means of an amicable understanding." To work successfully, however, the principle *pacta sunt servanda* must be complemented by appropriate procedures for peaceful change, allowing for revision of burdensome treaty provisions by peaceful means and by admitting the possibility of terminating treaty obligations in exceptional cases of fundamental change of circumstances.

Pacta Tertiis Nec Nocent Nec Prosunt (270)

A fundamental maxim of Roman (civil) law, which in its application to international law means that treaties do not create either obligations or rights for third states without their consent. The principle *pacta tertiis nec nocent nec prosunt* is part of customary international law and is codified in the 1969 Vienna Convention on the Law of Treaties. Two situations must be distinguished: (1) creation of obligations for, and (2) conferment of rights upon third states. A third state, that is, any state that is not a party to the treaty in question, may be bound by its provisions under two conditions. First, the parties to the treaty must have intended the provisions to be means of establishing the obligation, and second, the third state must have expressly accepted the obligation. Under the Vienna Convention the acceptance must be in writing. It could be argued, however, that in such a case the legal basis of the third state's obligation is not the treaty but the collateral agreement of that state with the parties to the treaty, especially since under the Vienna Convention the third state's obligations may be revoked or modified only with the consent of the parties and the third state (unless it is established that they have agreed otherwise). A treaty rule may become binding on nonparties if it has achieved the status of customary international law. For example, the agreement for the neutralization of Switzerland (1815) and the Hague conventions regarding the rules of land warfare (1899, 1907) have been recognized by nonparty states as customary law. The provision of the United Nations Charter to the effect that the United Nations shall ensure that states which are not members of the United Nations act in accordance with the principles of the Charter (Article 2[6]) seemingly departs from the rule that treaties do not create obilgations for third parties. But the principles involved (peaceful settlement of disputes and abstention from the threat or use of force) are in any case binding upon all states as customary international law. Conferment of rights upon third parties is more controversial than creation of obligations. Under the 1969 Vienna Convention the general rule is that a right arises for a third state from a treaty only if the parties intend the treaty provision to accord a legal right (as distinct from a mere benefit) either to the particular state in question or to a group of states to which it belongs, or to states generally, and if the third state assents to the conferment of the right. A third state's right may not be revoked or modified by the parties if it is established that it was intended not to be revoked or modified without the third state's consent. *See also* ENTRY INTO FORCE, 257; TREATY, 279.

Significance   The principle that a treaty applies only between the parties to it is a corollary of the principle of consent inherent in the system of sovereign and independent states. Many treaties expressly declare that they are to be binding upon the parties only, and this has been confirmed in arbitral awards; for example, the *Island of Palmas* award (*United States v. Netherlands*, 1928) and by international tribunals, for example, the Permanent Court of International Justice in the *Free Zones of Upper Savoy and the District of Gex* case (*France v. Switzerland*, 1932) where the Court held that Article 435 of the Treaty of Versailles was "not binding upon Switzerland, who is not a Party to that Treaty, except to the extent to which that country accepted it." As far as rights arising for a third state from a treaty are concerned, international practice provides numerous examples of treaties containing stipulations in favor of third states (*pactum in favorem tertii*). Among them are (1) a convention concluded by France, Great Britain, and Russia in 1856 concerning the nonfortification of the Aaland Islands, then under Russian rule, which was invoked by Sweden; (2) provisions of the Treaty of Versailles in favor of Denmark and Switzerland; and (3) provisions guaranteeing freedom of passage for ships through the Suez Canal under the Constantinople Convention of 1888 and through the Kiel Canal under the Treaty of Versailles. There is no consensus on the question whether the so-called "dispositive" treaties which create "objective" regimes—that is, obligations and rights valid not only for the parties but for all states, *erga omnes*—represent a special institution of the law of treaties or are simply an application of the general rule (intention of the parties plus assent or conversion into customary law). Examples include demilitarization treaties such as the Antarctic Treaty, 1959, neutralization provisions such as the Treaty of Versailles confirming the permanent neutrality of Switzerland, and treaties providing for freedom of navigation on international rivers or maritime canals. The 1969 Vienna Convention does not contain any provisions on treaties creating such objective regimes.

Peaceful Change (271)

A concept in international political doctrine of paramount importance for international law, referring to the process of substituting peaceful for forcible methods of resolving international disputes arising out of demands for alteration of the existing legally established *status quo*, including treaties in force, especially those governing territorial settlements. *See also* AMENDMENT, 255; FUNDAMENTAL CHANGE OF CIRCUMSTANCES, 259; JUSTICIABLE AND NONJUSTICIABLE DISPUTES, 293; *PACTA SUNT SERVANDA*, 269; TERMINATION OF TREATIES, 278.

Significance   Most treaties do not create permanent obligations and allow for amendment and termination procedures, but in most exceptional cases where a treaty perceived to be a serious burden for a party cannot be legally amended or terminated, the existing treaty relationship may result in a threat to international peace. Alteration of burdensome treaties is only one aspect of peaceful change in the sense of adjustment of "nonjusticiable" or "political" disputes about the existing international legal order in general. The problem of peaceful change acquired prominence in the interwar period in the context of agitation by the defeated states for changes in the territorial settlements in the treaties ending World War I. The League of Nations Covenant made an attempt to set up a procedure for revising treaties and, in general, for securing peaceful change in international relations. Article 19 of the Covenant provided for the League Assembly's right to advise the reconsideration by members of treaties which had become "inapplicable." However, attempts to make use of this right—for example, Bolivia and Peru's endeavors to secure reconsideration of treaties imposed on them by Chile after its victory in the Pacific War of 1879–1884, or China's attempts to bring the problem of "unequal treaties" before the League's Assembly—were opposed by countries satisfied with the territorial *status quo*, particularly by France which was concerned about revisionist demands of Germany. In Article 14 the United Nations Charter authorizes the General Assembly to "recommend measures for the peaceful adjustment of any situation regardless of origin, which it deems likely to impair the general welfare or friendly relations among nations. . . ." The term "situation" may be interpreted to include treaty relationships under executed treaties, as well as those still to be performed. However, even if this interpretation were correct, the General Assembly could not undertake any legally binding action in the matter of the peaceful change of treaty settlements since its powers are of recommendatory character only. Inasmuch as the 1969 Vienna Convention on the Law of Treaties provides for conciliatory and judicial procedures to be followed with respect to claims of invalidity or termination and suspension of treaties because of fundamental change of circumstances, for example, it may indirectly contribute to peaceful change if it is widely accepted and followed in good faith. In general, however, the problem of peaceful change remains a major challenge for a system of international law which forbids forcible change of treaties but does not provide for appropriate and effective peaceful mechanisms to change the *status quo* established under treaties in force.

Ratification (272)

An international act whereby a state establishes on the international plane its definitive consent to be bound by a treaty. Ratification is an indispensable act for a state to be bound by a treaty if (1) the treaty provides for consent to be expressed by means of ratification; (2) it is otherwise established that the negotiating states were agreed that ratification should be required; or (3) the intention of the states to sign the treaty subject to ratification appears from the full powers of its representatives or was expressed during the negotiation. There is no legal presumption in favor of ratification as a means of expressing consent to be bound if the treaty is silent on this point. Unless the treaty provides otherwise, instruments of ratification do not establish the consent of the states to be bound by a treaty until they are exchanged between them or deposited with the depositary, or notified to the other state or states concerned. In the case of bilateral treaties, ratification instruments are exchanged by the states parties and each instrument is filed in the archives of each state. This method would be cumbersome in the case of multilateral treaties, and therefore such treaties normally provide for the deposit of all instruments of ratification with a single state party known as the depositary. In the case of treaties under the auspices of the United Nations, the Secretary-General of the organization performs this function. Ratification in the international sense—by the exchange or deposit of instruments of ratification—must be distinguished from ratification in municipal law by the prescribed organ of state—for example, in the United States by the President with the advice and consent of two-thirds of senators present and voting. There is no legal duty to ratify a treaty or convey to other state or states the reasons for refusal to ratify. A number of bilateral treaties signed by the United States have been rejected by the Senate, for example, the treaty of 1869 with Great Britain on the *Alabama* claims, or not even submitted to the Senate for ratification. From the viewpoint of international law, the fact that under the implied powers of the executive in the United States the so-called "executive agreements" do not require advice and consent of the Senate is irrelevant. Under U.S. law, the Case Act (1972) only requires such agreements to be transmitted to the Congress within sixty days after the execution of the agreement. The procedures of acceptance and approval established in international treaty practice during the past three decades have the same legal effect as ratification or accession. If a treaty provides that it shall be open for signature "subject to acceptance," the process—from the viewpoint of international law—is like signature subject to ratification. The practice was introduced in order to provide a simplified form of ratification which would enable a state to avoid submission of the treaty to its constitutional process of ratification. If a treaty is made open to acceptance without prior signature, the process is like accession. Approval has substantially the same meaning and effect as acceptance. Multilateral treaties drawn up by international organizations are often declared open for ratification, acceptance, approval, and accession. In general, treaty practice is not consistent in its terminology. *See also* ACCESSION, 253; ENTRY INTO FORCE, 257; SIGNATURE, 275.

Significance   The institution of ratification allows states to reexamine the provisions of treaties before undertaking formal obligations and, in the period between signature and ratification, enables them to pass the necessary legislation or obtain the necessary parliamentary approval. Prior to the nineteenth century, ratification was not an approval of the treaty itself but a formal and limited act whereby a sovereign confirmed his plenipotentiary's full powers to negotiate the treaty. If they were in order, the sovereign was obliged to ratify it. In the nineteenth century ratification assumed its modern significance as a formal declaration of a state of its definitive consent to be bound by a treaty, which with progressing democratization of governments entailed submitting the executive's treaty-making power to parliamentary control. Since most treaties were of a formal nature, a rule developed that ratification was necessary to render a treaty binding. Eventually, however, with the expansion of treaty relations to all areas of international intercourse, many less formal treaties would become (with the parties' agreement) binding on signature alone. Treaties normally provide either that they are to be ratified, or dispense with ratification by laying down that they will enter into force upon signature or upon a specified date or event. Total silence on the subject is exceptional. In such cases, it is the matter of the parties' intention whether or not a treaty requires ratification as a condition of its binding operation. Performance of a treaty by a state that has not ratified it may be construed as tacit ratification.

Registration of Treaties   (273)
The public recording of treaties, usually performed by an international body. According to the Charter of the United Nations, registration is to be performed as soon as possible of every treaty and every international engagement entered into by any member of the United Nations. Treaties are registered with the United Nations Secretariat, which then publishes them in the United Nations Treaty Series. Article 102 of the United Nations Charter repeats in somewhat different terms an analogous provision of the Covenant of the League of Nations, but the difference between the two provisions is in the effects of failure to register a treaty. Whereas under the Covenant no treaty was binding until registered, under the United Nations Charter a nonregistered treaty remains valid but no party to it may invoke it before any organ of the United Nations. In the interim period before registration, a treaty

may be invoked before the United Nations subject to the duty to register it as soon as possible. Subsequent registration can cure a treaty's handicap. Under the Regulations Concerning the Registration and Publication of Treaties and International Agreements, adopted by the United Nations General Assembly in 1946, among registrable instruments are not only treaties between members but also treaties between members and nonmembers and intergovernmental organizations; treaties between such organizations; declarations accepting compulsory jurisdiction of the International Court of Justice (ICJ) under the "optional clause" of its Statute; declarations by new members of the United Nations accepting membership; and even unilateral engagements of an international character, for example, Egypt's 1957 Declaration on the Suez Canal and Arrangements for Its Operation. However, registration by the United Nations Secretariat does not imply its judgment on the nature of the instrument. The Final Act of the Helsinki Conference on Security and Cooperation in Europe of 1975 was not eligible for registration since it was not binding in law. Although treaties between nonmembers are not covered by the duty to register, in practice nonmember states have voluntarily filed and recorded their treaties, which is a form of registration. The 1969 Vienna Convention on the Law of Treaties makes obligatory registration with the Secretariat of the United Nations or filing and recording of all treaties after their entry into force, the duty to be performed by the depositary of all the instruments of ratification. *See also* TREATY, 279.

Significance   Largely as a result of President Wilson's criticism of secret diplomacy, registration of treaties under the League of Nations Covenant and subsequently under the United Nations Charter was intended to prevent states from entering into secret treaties and in general to ensure publicity for their conclusion and contents. Under the United Nations Charter, a nonregistered treaty cannot be relied upon before the International Court of Justice (ICJ) or any other United Nations organ. It can, however, be invoked before other courts and bodies. Publication of the registered instruments in the United Nations Treaty Series (UNTS), a continuation of the League of Nations Treaty Series (LNTS), provides a useful source of reference for practitioners and students of international law.

Reservation   (274)
A unilateral statement made by a state when signing, ratifying, accepting, approving, or acceding to a treaty, whereby it purports to exclude or to modify the legal effect of certain provisions of the treaty in their application to that state. In the case of a bilateral treaty, a reservation

does not cause problems since it represents a counteroffer of the reserving state the other party either accepts (thus agreeing to the treaty in its modified text) or rejects (and thereby does not become a party to the treaty). However, in the case of reservations to multilateral treaties difficult problems arise because some states may object to another state's attempt to become a party to a treaty subject to one or more reservations. The international law on the question of the validity and effects of reservations is not settled, but in general the rules of the 1969 Vienna Convention on the Law of Treaties reflect the position of a great majority of states. Under the Convention, a reservation (as well as an express acceptance of a reservation and an objection to a reservation) must be formulated in writing and communicated to the depositary of the treaty or directly to the contracting states and other states entitled to become parties to the treaty. Reservations made when signing a treaty must be formally confirmed upon ratification. The effect of a reservation is to modify certain provisions of the treaty in the reserving state's relations with the other parties without, however, modifying the provisions of the treaty for those parties *inter se*; that is, in their relations with each other. If a state objecting to a reservation has not opposed the entry into force of the treaty between itself and the reserving state, its treaty relations vis-à-vis the reserving state are modified by the reservation. Two approaches developed in international practice concerning admissibility of reservations to multilateral conventions. The Western European approach—shared by the Secretariat of the League of Nations and later the United Nations until about 1950—followed the conception of absolute integrity of the treaty as adopted. Specifically, if a party to a treaty objected to a reservation made by another state, the reserving state could not be considered a party to the treaty. On the other hand, since 1938 members of the Pan American Union (later the Organization of American States [OAS]) followed a more flexible approach which, in the name of the universality of the treaty, permitted a reserving state to become a party in relation to the nonobjecting states. The Soviet Union has always argued for complete freedom of states to make reservations, and it was the Soviet bloc's reservations to the Genocide Convention of 1948 that eventually led to the Advisory Opinion of the International Court of Justice on *Reservations to the Convention on Genocide* (1951). The Court's principal ruling held that a state that had made a reservation objected to by some parties to that Convention was to be regarded as being party to it if the reservation was compatible with the object and purpose of the Convention. This principle was eventually adopted in the practice of the United Nations Secretary-General in his capacity as depositary of multilateral treaties and by the International Law Commission in its codification of the law of treaties. The 1969 Vienna Convention recognizes the general freedom to make reservations except in three cases: (1) reservations expressly prohibited; (2) those not falling within provisions in the treaty permitting specified reservations and not other reservations; and (3) reservations incompatible with the object and purpose of the treaty. Reservations expressly authorized by a treaty do not require any subsequent acceptance by the other contracting states unless the treaty provides otherwise. One concession made to the traditional rule of the integrity of the treaty is that if it is clear from the object and purpose of a treaty negotiated by a limited number of states ("restricted treaty") that the application of the treaty in its entirety is an essential condition for the consent of each state to be bound by the treaty, then the admissibility of reservations will depend upon unanimous acceptance of reservations. Similarly, unless the treaty provides otherwise, reservations to treaties establishing an international organization require acceptance by the competent organ of the organization. In all other treaties a more flexible, relative approach applies under which a reserving state may become a party to the treaty in relation to a state accepting the reservation, while an objection to a reservation does not preclude the entry into force of the treaty as between the objecting and reserving states unless a contrary intention is expressed by the objecting state. The Vienna Convention recognizes tacit acceptance of a reservation by a state if it has raised no objections within a year of the notification of the reservation or of its ratification of the treaty, whichever occurs later. *See also* ENTRY INTO FORCE, 257; RATIFICATION, 272; SIGNATURE, 275; TREATY, 279.

Significance   The problem of reservations arises only within the context of multilateral treaty making. The right to make reservations is regarded as stemming from the principle of the sovereignty and equality of states. The institution of reservations is designed to reconcile the objective of treaty integrity with as wide a universality of participation as possible. It makes it possible for a state wishing to join an otherwise attractive treaty arrangement to be exempt from one or more provisions of the treaty it finds inconvenient. A mere declaration of national policy concerning the manner of applying the treaty in relations with the other signatories is not a true reservation. Although the institution of reservations may contribute to widening treaty participation, excessive resort to this device can introduce a certain element of chaos and uncertainty in treaty relations, as the criterion of compatibility can be interpreted differently by individual signatories, each deciding for itself whether or not a reservation is compatible with the object and purpose of a treaty. Problems relating to interpreting the legal effects of reservations can be at least partially remedied by a careful drafting of the text of the treaty to achieve genuine consensus and by making explicit provisions on the subject of reservations, such as providing for decisions on incompatibility of reservations to be made by a majority rule. Under the Convention on the Elimination of All Forms of Racial Discrimination (1966), for example, a reservation is incompatible if at least two-thirds of the contracting parties object to it.

Signature   (275)

The official affixing of names to the text of a treaty by the representatives of the negotiating states either as a means of expressing the definitive consent of a state to be bound by a treaty, or as an expression of provisional consent subject to ratification, acceptance, or approval. The initialing of a treaty text is the equivalent of a signature expressing definitive consent to be bound by a treaty when it is established that the negotiating states so agreed. Also, if a signature *ad referendum*—that is, a signature given by a representative provisionally and subject to confirmation by his government—is so confirmed, it constitutes a full signature of the treaty. Exchange of instruments constituting a treaty, the so-called "exchange of notes," expresses consent to be bound by the treaty if such instruments so provide or it is otherwise established that the states were agreed that the exchange should have that effect. *See also* ADOPTION, 254; AUTHENTICATION, 256; ENTRY INTO FORCE, 257; RATIFICATION, 272.

Significance   The effect of signature depends upon whether or not the treaty is subject to ratification, acceptance, or approval by the signing states. If it is subject, then the signature means only that the text of the treaty has been authenticated and the plenipotentiaries are willing to refer it to their respective governments for definitive acceptance or rejection as the case may be. In the absence of any express agreement, there is no obligation to submit the text of the treaty to the national legislature for action. However, even in cases where signature or exchange of instruments constituting the treaty subject to ratification does not express a definitive consent to be bound by the treaty, the signatory states are obliged to refrain in good faith from acts that would defeat the object and purpose of the treaty until they have made their intention clear not to become parties. The signatory states may also expressly agree that the treaty is to operate on a provisional basis as from the date of signature. If a treaty is not subject to ratification, acceptance, or approval, then it is binding upon signature alone. Very often treaties on minor and technical matters are simply signed, operating as from the date of signature without the necessity of ratification. This can occur in three instances: (1) when the treaty itself provides that such is to be the effect of signature, a practice common in bilateral treaties; (2) when it is otherwise established that the negotiating states were agreed that signature shall have that effect; and (3) when the intention of a state to give that effect to its signature appears from the full powers of its representative or was expressed during the negotiations.

Supervening Impossibility of Performance   (276)

A ground for terminating or withdrawing from a treaty, resulting from the permanent disappearance or destruction of an object indispensable for the execution of the treaty. It is controversial in customary law whether or not supervening impossibility of performance automatically terminates a treaty. Under the 1969 Vienna Convention on the Law of Treaties it merely gives a party the option to terminate a treaty. A temporary impossibility may be invoked only as a ground for suspending the operation of the treaty. A party that caused the impossibility by a breach of its treaty obligations or any other international obligation owed to any other party to the treaty may not invoke it as a ground for terminating, withdrawing from, or suspending the operation of the treaty. *See also* FUNDAMENTAL CHANGE OF CIRCUMSTANCES, 259; SUSPENSION OF OPERATION OF TREATIES, 277; TERMINATION OF TREATIES, 278.

Significance   There are very few examples in state practice of the termination of a treaty on the ground of supervening impossibility of performance. The International Law Commission which drafted the Vienna Convention envisaged such events as the submergence of an island, the drying up of a river, or the destruction of a dam or hydroelectric installation indispensable for the execution of a treaty. Total extinction of the international personality of one of the parties to a bilateral treaty is often cited as an instance of impossibility of performance.

Suspension of Operation of Treaties   (277)

Making a treaty temporarily inoperative in regard to either all or to a particular party. Like termination, suspension of the operation of a treaty may take place according to the provisions of the treaty or at any time by consent of all the parties after consultation with the other contracting states. Suspension of a treaty may be implied by the conclusion of a later treaty. A unilateral breach by any of the parties may entitle the other party or parties to invoke the breach as a ground for suspending the operation of the treaty in whole or in part. Subject to the provisions of the treaty in question and compatibility of the suspension with the object and purpose of the treaty, two or more parties to a multilateral treaty may suspend the operation of its provisions as between themselves alone. *See also* MATERIAL BREACH, 268; TERMINATION OF TREATIES, 278.

Significance   Treaties sometimes provide for the possibility of suspension of the entire treaty or of some of its provisions in certain circumstances or under certain conditions. Apart from that, suspension may take place by consent of all the parties with regard to all of them or if, for example, one or a group of them finds itself in temporary difficulties to a particular party or group of parties. Barring contrary agreement, suspension of the operation of a treaty releases the parties concerned from the obligation to perform the treaty during the period of suspension. Suspension does not otherwise affect the legal relations between the parties established by the treaty. In conformity with the principles of good faith and *pacta sunt servanda*, during the period of suspension the parties are required to refrain from acts tending to obstruct the resumption of the operation of the treaty.

Termination of Treaties   (278)

The end of the operation of a treaty, resulting in depriving all the parties of all the rights under the treaty and releasing them from any further obligation to perform the treaty. Under international law, the termination of a treaty or a withdrawal of a party may take place only in conformity with the treaty provisions or, at any time, by consent of all the parties after consultation with the other contracting parties. A great majority of treaties contain clauses fixing their duration or the date of their termination or a condition or event that will bring about the termination. They also normally provide for a right to denounce or withdraw from them, usually after a certain period of notice. Customary law does not require any definite period of denunciation, but the 1969 Vienna Convention requires at least twelve months' notice of intention to denounce or withdraw. Some treaties fix a comparatively limited period of duration (for example, five or ten years) providing for their continuance thereafter for a period of time or indefinitely, subject to a right of denunciation or withdrawal. Other treaties assign no period of duration, providing only for the right to denounce the treaty or withdraw from it either with or without a period of notice. In addition to terminating in conformity with its specific provisions, a treaty may terminate by the consent of all the parties, which may be explicit or implied. The latter situation occurs if it is clear from the conduct of the parties that they no longer consider the treaty to be in force and that it has grown out of use; that is, has fallen into "desuetude." A treaty may also be considered as terminated if all the parties conclude a later treaty which is intended to govern the subject matter of the earlier treaty, or if the later treaty is incompatible with the provisions of the earlier one. However, the earlier treaty may be considered as suspended only if it appears from the later one or is otherwise established that such was the intention of the parties. Emergence of a new peremptory norm of general international law (*jus cogens*) voids and terminates any existing treaty in conflict with that norm, but the voiding does not have retroactive effect. Unless it otherwise provides, a multilateral treaty does not terminate by reason of the fact that the number of the parties falls below the number necessary for its entry into force. Under the 1969 Vienna Convention on the Law of Treaties, a treaty which does not contain any provision regarding its termination, denunciation, or withdrawal (e.g., the 1961 Vienna Convention on Diplomatic Relations or the four 1958 Geneva conventions on the law of the sea) is not subject to denunciation or withdrawal unless such right may be implied from the nature of the treaty or it is established that the parties intended to admit such possibility. Treaties of peace are not normally open to unilateral denunciation. Those governing boundaries are not denounceable since by their very nature they have already been executed. In addition to cases of automatic termination of treaties, there may arise situations that give party or parties in exceptional situations an option to terminate or suspend the treaty. They include (1) a material breach by a party; (2) supervening impossibility of performance; and (3) fundamental change of circumstances (the *rebus sic stantibus* clause). Severance of diplomatic or consular relations between parties does not necessarily affect the treaty except insofar as the existence of such relations is indispensable for the application of the treaty. Under the 1969 Convention, in all cases where option to terminate a treaty is available to a party, procedures with respect to invalidation of treaties apply to termination as well. The question as to whether or not treaties are terminated by the outbreak of war between the parties is complex and controversial. No general conclusions can be drawn regarding the state of customary law in this matter. The Vienna Convention does not deal with the effect of war on treaties and no international tribunal has ever decided a case involving this issue. Although municipal courts in some countries (for example, France) have ruled that the outbreak of war automatically abrogates treaties, the more general view is that this is not the case. Also, in view of the outlawry of force, it is not clear to what extent illegal resort to armed force affects the right to regard a treaty as terminated or suspended. Because countries have been reluctant officially to admit the existence of the state of war, in post–World War II armed conflicts, treaties appear to continue in force even if the parties are in a *de facto* state of war with each other. It is obvious that treaties regulating the conduct of hostilities do not terminate but by their very nature start their operation when an armed conflict breaks out. Also, some other multilateral treaties (e.g., the 1944 Chicago Convention on International Civil Aviation) provide for their effect in time of war. In practice, however, at the outbreak of war, treaties are at least suspended and, after the end of hostilities, peace treaties (for example, the 1919 Peace Treaty of Versailles and the 1947 treaties with the European Axis allies) usually contain clauses dealing with the status of such prewar treaties between belligerents, revising some of them and declaring others not specifically named as abrogated. *See also* ENTRY INTO FORCE, 257; FUNDAMENTAL CHANGE OF CIRCUMSTANCES, 259; INCONSISTENT TREATIES, 260; INVALIDITY OF TREATIES, 262; MATERIAL BREACH, 268; *PACTA SUNT SERVANDA*, 269; PEACEFUL CHANGE, 271; SUPERVENING IMPOSSIBILITY OF PERFORMANCE, 276; SUSPENSION OF OPERATION OF TREATIES, 277; UNEQUAL TREATIES DOCTRINE, 280.

Significance The major legal consequence of the termination of a treaty is the release of parties from any further obligation to perform the treaty. Some treaties (for example, the 1962 Convention on the Liability of Operators of Nuclear Ships) contain express provisions regarding consequences which follow upon their termination or withdrawal of a party. Termination of a treaty may result in responsibility because of breach by a party. The 1969 Vienna Convention provides that a treaty's termination does not affect any rights, obligations or legal situation of the parties created through the execution of the treaty prior to its termination. In general the rules of international law on termination of treaties in force take into account the fact that, unless there is a legal possibility for termination, the law will be too rigid resulting in the insecurity of treaty relations and conflict among nations.

Treaty (279)

A written international agreement concluded between states or other subjects of international law, governed by international law, whether embodied in a single instrument or in two or more related instruments and whatever its particular designation. The term treaty is used in English as a convenient generic term for any kind of written international agreement under international law irrespective of the extraordinarily varied nomenclature that has been employed to denote this type of agreement. The appellation of the agreement does not affect its validity under international law. In addition to "treaty," international practice uses such terms as "convention," "agreement," "arrangement," "pact," "covenant," "declaration," "accord," "charter," "act," "general act," "statute," "*modus vivendi*," "protocol," "*procès-verbal*," and "concordat" (for bilateral treaties of the Holy See governing the status of the Church in the contracting state), to mention the most frequently used terms. The Statute of the International Court of Justice (ICJ) uses the term "treaty" in Article 36, but "conventions" in Article 38; yet both embrace all international agreements. The term "final act" refers to the instrument that records the winding up of an international conference; for example, the Final Act of the United Nations Conference on the Law of Treaties (1969) or the Final Act of the United Nations Conference on the Law of the Sea (1982). A final act is not a treaty unless the parties intend it to be so. Thus, the Final Act of the Helsinki Conference on Security and Cooperation in Europe (1975) creates only political and not legal obligations. The term "executive agreement" is not a term in international law; it belongs to U.S. constitutional practice. Normally it is states that are parties to treaties. Treaties may be cast in various forms: as agreements between states; between heads of state ("high contracting parties"); as intergovernmental agreements (an increasingly common form); as agreements between ministers of foreign affairs or other ministers of the countries concerned; between representatives of other government departments; or between commanders-in-chief (armistice agreements). In addition to states, other subjects of international law, such as intergovernmental organizations and national liberation movements, may have international personality allowing them to enter into treaties. Occasionally, non-self-governing territories on their way to political self-determination have been recognized as having treaty-making capacity. Component states of a federation may possess such capacity within the limits admitted by the federal constitution. For example, the *Länder* of the Federal Republic of Germany may, with the consent of the federal government, conclude treaties with foreign states. States, including unitary ones, may also agree that their border regions and municipalities make agreements with one another on matters of mutual interest, as provided, for example, under the Council of Europe's Convention of 1980 on Transfrontier Cooperation between Territorial Communities or Authorities. Individuals do not have the capacity to make treaties.

Since a treaty must be governed by international law, agreements between states that are not intended to create legal relations between the parties, and agreements such as those for the acquisition of premises for diplomatic missions, or some purely commercial transactions, are contracts governed by the municipal law of one of the parties or some other municipal system of law chosen by them. The intention of the parties seems to be the test used in determining whether or not an agreement between states is governed by international law or by municipal law. It is also possible that a state in a contract with a private person may agree to apply general principles of law to such a contract.

Although treaties are normally made in written form, oral agreements, a rare phenomenon in today's international diplomacy, are valid if concluded between authorized agents of government, a principle upheld by the Permanent Court of International Justice in the *Eastern Greenland* case (Denmark/Norway, 1933). A unilateral declaration may create international obligation if it is clear that the state making it intended to be legally bound by it. For example, Egypt's declaration of 1957 concerning the Suez Canal was such an act. However, a unilateral declaration requires acceptance by other states as a condition of validity under international law. If a unilateral declaration is directed *erga omnes* (that is, not to any specific state but to all "international community"), intention to undertake a legal, and not just political, obligation by the declaring state is not lightly to be presumed.

A typical treaty consists of a preamble; substantive clauses, sometimes known as "dispositive provisions"; and the final clauses dealing with formal matters (opening for signature, entry into force, duration, denunciation period, languages in which the treaty was drafted, amendments, depositary of instruments of ratification, and the like), followed by signatures of the plenipotentiaries. The conclusion (that is, formation of a treaty) goes through several stages: establishing the full powers of the representatives; negotiations, either directly between the states or at a diplomatic conference; adoption and authentication of the text; the negotiating states' expression of consent to be bound by the treaty (signature or exchange of instruments constituting the treaty), and—very often—ratification (acceptance, approval) or—in the case of states that did not participate in the negotiating process—accession (adhesion, adherence); and entry into force. *See also* SOURCES OF INTERNATIONAL LAW: TREATIES, 43.

Significance Treaties have been in evidence throughout recorded history and can be traced as far back as the third millennium. They have been the major instrument for the legal regulation of the mutual relations of states for centuries and, in more recent times, their role as a source of international law has become increasingly pronounced. Especially after World War I and World War II, the expanding relations of states have produced thousands of bi- and multilateral (multipartite) treaties governing not just the traditional "high politics" of nations but innumerable economic, social, cultural, technical, and other aspects of international relations. Among the multilateral treaties, the so-called "law-making treaties" which lay down rules of universal application and not just provisions of interest to two or a few states are of paramount importance as sources of general international law. Altogether, some 30,000 treaties have been registered with the United Nations since 1946. Until recently, international law governing the conclusion (formation) of treaties was based on customary rules. In 1969 the Vienna Convention on the Law of Treaties (in force since 1980) codified and developed this important area of international law. However, by the early 1980s only about one-quarter of the states had ratified the Vienna Convention, and countries such as France, China, the United States, and the Soviet Union were not parties. The Vienna Convention applies only to treaties between states. A draft Convention governing treaties concluded between states and international organizations and between such organizations has been prepared by the International Law Commission. Customary law relating to succession of states in respect of treaties was codified and developed in the 1978 Vienna Convention on the Succession of States in Respect of Treaties.

Unequal Treaties Doctrine   (280)

A controversial doctrine invoked by communist and many Third World countries, proclaiming invalidity of treaties that, as alleged by the advocates of this doctrine, were not concluded on the basis of the sovereign equality of the parties. Under the unequal treaties doctrine, treaties concluded between Western nations and developing countries under alleged economic or political pressure exercised by Western nations may be legally terminated by a developing country as invalid. *See also* AGGRESSION, 303; CAPITULATIONS, 153; COERCION OF A STATE, 264; FORCE, ILLEGAL THREAT OR USE OF, 308; INDIRECT AGGRESSION, 311; INVALIDITY OF TREATIES, 262; *PACTA SUNT SERVANDA*, 269; PEACEFUL CHANGE, 271; TERMINATION OF TREATIES, 278.

Significance   The unequal treaties doctrine is of dubious validity in international law. It is opposed by Western jurists and states as vague and subversive of the fundamental principle of *pacta sunt servanda*. Issues related to the doctrine were debated by the International Law Commission within the context of coercion by the threat or use of force as acts invalidating a treaty when it was preparing the draft for the 1969 Vienna Convention on the Law of Treaties. The communist and more militant Third World states interpreted force as covering economic and political pressures applied in the conclusion of unequal treaties, but the Vienna Convention left the matter open without defining the meaning of force, simply referring to the prohibition of force in the United Nations Charter. The proponents of the unequal treaties doctrine are at a loss to define its meaning and often use the term to denote treaties that contain burdensome terms regardless of the circumstances of their conclusion. Moreover, despite the fundamental principle that rules of law do not operate retroactively, Soviet writers include among unequal, and hence invalid, treaties the nineteenth-century capitulatory regimes, otherwise terminated by the European powers by their own consent long ago. Under these "capitulations," concluded by some European powers with a number of Asian and African states, subjects of those powers in the territory of the Asian and African state concerned were wholly under the jurisdiction of the respective European power. Another example of unequal treaty according to Soviet publicists was the Anglo-Egyptian treaty of alliance of 1936. However, the unequal treaties doctrine is invoked by the Soviet writers in an inconsistent and selective manner, as demonstrated by the nineteenth-century Russo-Chinese treaties (a classical instance of unequal treaties if the doctrine were to be applied consistently) whereby imperial Russia forced large territorial concessions upon China. These treaties are considered perfectly valid by the Soviet publicists and government and, in their view, are covered by the principle of *pacta sunt servanda*. The unequal treaties doctrine must be interpreted as a political tool rather than a principle of international law.

10. Peaceful Settlement of Disputes

Ad Hoc Judge   (281)

A judge whom a party before the International Court of Justice (ICJ) may choose when it does not have a judge of its nationality on the bench. An *ad hoc* judge takes part in the proceedings on terms of complete equality with his or her colleagues, and may be appointed by either of the parties if the Court includes no judge of their nationality. Where there are more than two parties to a dispute, however, parties acting in the same interest may choose only one *ad hoc* judge among them. If one of them already has a judge of its nationality on the bench, it is not entitled to appoint an *ad hoc* judge. A judge *ad hoc* need not necessarily be a national of the appointing country. Such a situation has occurred quite often. For example, in the *Continental Shelf* case (Libya/Malta, International Court of Justice, 1984), Libya chose an Uruguayan and Malta a Greek national as their respective *ad hoc* judges. A judge *ad hoc* may have the nationality of the same country as an elected member of the Court. Because of the provision in the Statute of the International Court of Justice for judges *ad hoc*, the normal fifteen-judge bench of the Court may be increased to seventeen. An *ad hoc* judge may also be appointed in cases where the Court sits in a chamber formed by the Court on its own initiative or at the request of the parties. Under the rules of the International Court of Justice, a judge *ad hoc* may also be appointed in advisory proceedings before the Court; namely, if an advisory opinion is requested upon a legal question pending between two or more states, each may be allowed to appoint an *ad hoc* judge, but the decision lies with the Court. The Permanent Court of International Justice agreed to the appointment of such judges in six advisory cases. Only two requests of this kind have been received by the International Court of Justice, namely in the *Legal*

Consequences for States of the Continued Presence of South Africa in Namibia (1971) and *Western Sahara* (1975) cases. In the former case the Court turned down the request, and in the latter accepted Morocco's request but rejected that of Mauritania. *See also* ADVISORY JURISDICTION OF THE INTERNATIONAL COURT OF JUSTICE, 282; INTERNATIONAL COURT OF JUSTICE (ICJ), 292.

Significance		The institution of judges *ad hoc* has been criticized as distorting the international and impartial nature of the World Court. On the other hand, this remnant of the institution of national arbitrators participating in *ad hoc* arbitration tribunals is simply a concession to the political context in which the Court operates and to the theory that the "national" judge should "represent" the party on the Court's bench. As a rule, judges *ad hoc* have voted in favor of the country selecting them, frequently the country of their nationality. They typically have appended dissenting opinions if the majority on the bench decided against their vote. There has never been a case of an *ad hoc* judge (or national judge for that matter) dissenting from a majority decision favoring that judge's country.

## Advisory Jurisdiction of the International Court of Justice		(282)

The authority of the International Court of Justice (ICJ) under Article 96 of the Charter of the United Nations to give an "advisory opinion" on "any legal question" at the request of the United Nations General Assembly, the Security Council, or other organs of the United Nations and its specialized agencies authorized by the General Assembly to make a request for an advisory opinion on legal questions arising within the scope of their activities. A request for an advisory opinion may be refused by the Court irrespective of the organ or body that made the request. The procedure in advisory matters follows, wherever applicable, the rules governing the contentious jurisdiction of the Court. This includes written request for the opinion laid before the Court, notification by the Court of states and international organizations concerned, submission by them of written and oral statements, individual opinions, and other aspects of contentious procedure. Although an advisory opinion has a strong persuasive force as a statement of the law by a prestigious tribunal and carries considerable political weight, it lacks the legal binding force of a judgment even for the organ or other body requesting it. *See also* AD HOC JUDGE, 281; CONTENTIOUS JURISDICTION OF THE INTERNATIONAL COURT OF JUSTICE, 286; INDIVIDUAL OPINION, 289; INTERNATIONAL COURT OF JUSTICE (ICJ), 292.

Significance   Comparatively little use has been made of the advisory jurisdiction of the International Court of Justice. Whereas the Permanent Court of International Justice delivered twenty-seven advisory opinions (all in the years 1922 through 1935), only seventeen opinions have been handed down by the United Nations Court in the forty years of its existence (most of the opinions dating to the period through 1956). One more request for an advisory opinion was received in 1984. The advisory jurisdiction proved important in the League of Nations' period as the Council, its main political body (in order to avoid making some decisions itself), availed itself of the power to request an advisory opinion on "any dispute or question." All advisory opinions of the Permanent Court of International Justice were requested by the Council and most related to the aftermath of World War I. Under the United Nations, twelve out of the eighteen opinions sought were requested by the General Assembly; one by the Security Council; one by the Intergovernmental Maritime Consultative Organization (now known as International Maritime Organization, [IMO]); one by the United Nations Educational, Scientific, and Cultural Organization (UNESCO); and three by the United Nations Committee on Applications for Review of Administrative Tribunal Judgments. Four requests made in the 1950s (in spite of the opposition of the Soviet bloc) concerned matters connected with the Cold War; five dealt with decolonization (four on South-West Africa and one on Western Sahara); and the remaining requests involved constitutional questions about the functioning of the requesting body and judgments on the United Nations Administrative Tribunal. Under the League of Nations, advisory opinions were in almost all cases treated with respect by the states concerned that otherwise would vote in the Council for requesting them. However, under the United Nations, requests for advisory opinions connected with the East-West conflict or the status of South-West Africa (Namibia) were made in the face of a strong opposition of the states concerned whose policies remained unaffected by the Court's opinions. A state may by treaty, however, undertake in advance to be legally bound by advisory opinions in certain questions. The Convention of 1946 on the Privileges and Immunities of the United Nations, for example, has a clause to this effect. Despite failure to use the advisory opinions of the International Court of Justice as an instrument of political pressure on states, the advisory procedure has, in strictly legal terms, contributed to clarifying and developing international law on such issues as the capacity of the United Nations to advance an international claim in respect of damage suffered (*Reparation for Injuries Suffered in the Service of the United Nations*, 1949) and reservations to multilateral conventions (*Reservations to the Convention on the Prevention and Punishment of the Crime of Genocide*, 1951).

The exercise by the Court of its advisory function may give rise to controversy in cases where request for an opinion originates in an actual international dispute. Therefore the Court has the power to, and in principle must, decline to give an advisory opinion if the main point on which an opinion is requested is decisive in a pending dispute between states and any one of them in not before the Court. To give an advisory opinion in such a case would conflict with the basic principle that without its consent no state can be compelled to submit disputes to the Court. It is for this reason that in 1923 the Permanent Court of International Justice declined to give its opinion on the status of Eastern Carelia since that question directly concerned a dispute between Finland and the Soviet Union, the latter not bound by the League of Nations' Covenant and objecting to the Court's jurisdiction. Unlike the Permanent Court of International Justice, the International Court of Justice has never refused to deliver an advisory opinion, including cases where in its opinion it had to pronounce on legal questions on which there was a divergence of views between a state and the United Nations. The Court has held that the interpretation of a treaty is essentially a judicial, not a political task. It has also consistently refused to decline to give an opinion on the ground that it might be subjected to political pressure. Advisory opinions on the review procedure concerning decisions of the United Nations Administrative Tribunal have not been considered by the Court as incompatible with the essential rules that guide its activity as a judicial body.

Arbitration   (283)

A peaceful method of legally binding settlement of international disputes by judges of the parties' choice, according to the rules set forth by them, and on the basis of voluntary submission and respect for law. Arbitration is one technique of international adjudication or judicial settlement, although it differs from judicial settlement in the strict sense of the term in that the disputing parties normally have the freedom to select arbitrators and, to some extent, determine the procedure and the law to be applied. Like judicial settlement, however, arbitration does include the element of a legally binding decision known as an "award." Consent to submit to arbitration a specific dispute or a group of disputes which have already arisen is formalized in an international agreement known as a *compromis* or *compromis d'arbitrage*. This agreement also stipulates the terms under which the tribunal will function, such as the applicable rules of law, possibly the right to decide *ex aequo et bono* the procedure to be followed, and any other provisions deemed desirable by the parties. Questions not dealt with in the *compromis*, including the tribunal's competence to determine its own jurisdiction, must be settled by the tribunal itself. As for future disputes, consent may be expressed either in a general arbitration treaty whereby the parties undertake to submit to arbitration all or any class of disputes, or in a "compromissory clause" of some other treaty which refers to disputes arising in regard to the interpretation and application of the treaty which will be settled by arbitration. However, most arbitration treaties and treaties with a compromissory clause still require the conclusion of a *compromis* as a precondition for submission to arbitration of any dispute covered by the treaty. Arbitration tribunals may consist of a single arbitrator, sometimes head of a third state who delegates his or her charge to experts, or a collegiate body. In the latter case it is usually a mixed commission of odd number, made up of arbitrators or commissioners selected in equal number by the parties (for example, two by each party under the rules of the Permanent Court of Arbitration) and an umpire named by the arbitrators or appointed by the parties.

An arbitral award is final unless otherwise agreed by the parties. Its validity may be challenged by either party, but there is little agreement in the doctrine and practice of international law concerning grounds of the challenge. Besides, instances of repudiating an arbitral award have been few. In general, the following grounds for invalidation have been invoked in arbitral practice: (1) that the undertaking to arbitrate or the *compromis* was invalid; (2) that the tribunal exceeded its power (*excès de pouvoir*), for example, by deciding on an issue not submitted to it or applying the law not authorized by the *compromis*; (3) that there has been a failure to state the reasons for the award or a serious departure from a fundamental role of procedure; and (4) that there was corruption or fraud on the part of a member of the tribunal. What constitutes an "essential" or "manifest" error warranting invalidating an award has been a highly controversial matter. *See also* CONCILIATION, 285; JUSTICIABLE AND NONJUSTICIABLE DISPUTES, 293; PERMANENT COURT OF ARBITRATION, 298.

Significance   Although arbitration was known in ancient Greece and in a certain sense in the Middle Ages, it fell into disuse in the early centuries of the modern state system although arbitration clauses were occasionally included in treaties in the seventeenth and eighteenth centuries. The history of modern arbitration is generally traced back to the Jay Treaty of 1794 between the United States and Great Britain, which provided for arbitration of various legal issues by mixed U.S.-British commissions. This precedent inaugurated a widespread practice of arbitration in the nineteenth century. State responsibility for injury to aliens was the most common subject matter of arbitration by mixed claims commissions (which, strictly speaking, were not organs of third party adjudication since they were normally set up on the parity principle by each party). A turning point in the history of arbitration was the successful settlement in the *Alabama Claims* award of 1872 of the U.S. claims against Great Britain for compensation for the losses caused the United States by the Confederate cruiser, *The Alabama*, and some other ships supplied to the southern states by British interests in violation of international law. The *Alabama* arbitration represented a departure from the mixed commission system by inaugurating a parallel institution of a truly third-party collegiate arbitral body. The next important landmark in the history of arbitration was the first Hague Peace Conference of 1899, which codified international arbitration procedure in the Convention for the Pacific Settlement of Disputes (later revised by the Second Hague Conference of 1907) and established the so-called Permanent Court of Arbitration (in reality, only a standing panel of potential arbitrators from which states could draw *ad hoc* tribunals to have their disputes arbitrated). Attempts to create a permanent tribunal or to secure acceptance by states of a firm obligation to submit their disputes to arbitration ended in failure. Moreover, since the first standing arbitration treaty was concluded between Great Britain and France in 1903, nonlegal or "political" disputes were not arbitrable in such treaties. Under special "restrictive clauses," disputes affecting "vital interests, the independence, or the honor of the two Contracting Parties" were excluded. Other reservations included such matters as interests of third states, territorial integrity, sovereign rights, and matters of domestic jurisdiction. Many of these clauses had the effect of virtually eliminating the obligation of the parties to arbitrate their disputes. Following World War I the creation of the Permanent Court of International Justice overshadowed arbitration, but was not intended to replace it altogether. Numerous arbitral tribunals, for example, were set up within the framework of Mexican Claims Commissions, and in Europe special Mixed Arbitral Tribunals were created to deal with some 70,000 claims resulting from the peace treaties. Arbitration received considerable attention from the League of Nations, which approved a multilateral treaty in 1928 known as the General Act for the Pacific Settlement of International Disputes. This act provided for dispute settlement by resort to arbitration or submission to the Permanent Court of International Justice. It was followed in 1929 in the Western Hemisphere by the General Treaty of Inter-American Arbitration. These multilateral agreements were complemented by many bilateral and subregional treaties requiring reference of legal disputes to arbitration. In practice, however, apart from the mixed commissions, not much use was made of arbitration in the interwar period. The United States–Netherlands *Island of Palmas* arbitration of 1929, decided by a sole arbitrator from Switzerland, and the Portugal-Germany arbitration in the *Naulilaa* case (1928) are two major examples of arbitration of that period.

In the contemporary period, the Charter of the United Nations includes arbitration as one method for the pacific settlement of international disputes. In 1949, the United Nations General Assembly adopted a revised version of the General Act for the Pacific Settlement of International Disputes and, in 1958, it adopted the Model Rules of Arbitral Procedure. However, the General Assembly rejected an International Law Commission draft of the Rules which, given the parties' consent to submit to arbitration, would have provided for the compulsory jurisdiction of the International Court of Justice to determine whether or not a dispute existed, to bring about a *compromis*, and even to revise and annul arbitral awards. In the post–World War II period, numerous bilateral and multilateral treaties made reference to arbitration as a preferred method of third-party settlement, but in practice not much use has been made of these provisions. There were, however, some *ad hoc* arbitrations, such as the *Rann of Kutch* case between India and Pakistan (1968) and the *Delimitation of the Continental Shelf* arbitration between the United Kingdom and France (1977). The Beagle Channel dispute between Argentina and Chile was first decided in 1977 by an arbitral award of the Queen of England as nominal arbitrator (the actual tribunal consisting of five judges of the International Court of Justice), but Argentina rejected it as null and void (a rare instance of a party repudiating an arbitral award after it has agreed to accept arbitration). Subsequently, however, the two countries agreed to papal mediation, leading to agreement on the pope's arbitration. The award, which was accepted by the parties, was delivered in 1984.

One significant trend in international arbitration in recent decades has been arbitration of international commercial disputes between states and private corporations. These have included, for example, the *Abu Dhabi* arbitration of 1951 between Abu Dhabi and Petroleum Development (Trucial Coast) Ltd.; the *Texaco-Libya* arbitration of 1977; the awards delivered within the framework of the International Center for the Settlement of Investment Disputes, set up under the Convention of 1965; and the International Chamber of Commerce Court of Arbitration awards.

Automatic Reservation (284)

A reservation to the acceptance by a state of the compulsory jurisdiction of the International Court of Justice (ICJ) under the so-called "optional clause" of Article 36(2) of the Court's Statute, whereby an accepting state unilaterally claims the right to determine the scope of its reservation. The automatic reservation may, for example, apply to a state's reservation exempting from the Court's jurisdiction all matters within the domestic jurisdiction of that state. The automatic reservation formula usually refers to matters "as determined" by the state or which the state considers essentially within its domestic jurisdiction. The automatic or "self-judging" reservation operates automatically. It is sufficient for a state to declare that a question in relation to which another state has brought proceedings before the Court falls within its domestic jurisdiction. In this way, the Court is deprived of jurisdiction over the case. Since the automatic reservation "as determined by the United States" was first introduced by the United States following its proposal by Senator Thomas Connally, it is popularly known as the Connally Amendment. *See also* CONTENTIOUS JURISDICTION OF THE IN-TERNATIONAL COURT OF JUSTICE, 286; OPTIONAL CLAUSE, 296; PEACEFUL SETTLEMENT OF INTERNATIONAL DISPUTES, 297; RESERVATION TO AC-CEPTANCE OF COMPULSORY JURISDICTION OF THE INTERNATIONAL COURT OF JUSTICE, 302.

Significance   The automatic reservation enables a state to determine subjectively and unilaterally whether or not a case falls within the scope of its acceptance of the International Court of Justice's jurisdiction. In this sense, it has a potential for limiting the Court's optional system of compulsory jurisdiction, the more so by virtue of the condition of reciprocity, explicitly or implicitly applicable to all declarations of acceptance of the International Court of Justice's compulsory jurisdiction. The automatic reservation filed by a state party to a dispute can be invoked by the other party or parties, thus depriving the Court of jurisdiction in the case. For example, the self-judging domestic jurisdiction reservation in the French declaration was invoked by the defendant state, Norway, against which France had instituted proceedings in the *Norwegian Loans* case of 1957. The Court upheld the Norwegian objection and declined jurisdiction without considering the validity of the reservation on which Norway so successfully relied. Similarly, in the *Aerial Incident* case of 1955, the defendant state, Bulgaria, invoked against the United States the notorious Connally Amendment automatic reservation, whereupon the claimant state, the United States, withdrew the case before the Court could make any ruling on its jurisdiction. Although the Court has so far refrained from pronouncing upon the legality of the automatic reservation, individual judges and the majority of publicists have condemned it as contrary to the Statute of the International Court of Justice, which provides that in the event of a dispute as to whether the Court has jurisdiction the matter shall be settled by the decision of the Court (Article 36[6]). Some judges have expressed the opinion that the automatic reservation is null and void, while others believe that since a reservation cannot be detached from the rest of the acceptance of compulsory jurisdiction, the entire declaration must be null and void. Criticism of the reservation and the application of the principle of reciprocity are primary reasons why the threat that the self-judging reservation once seemed to pose to the system of compulsory jurisdiction under the optional clause has not materialized. In relative terms, that is in relation to the number of states adhering to the optional clause, the number of such reservations has fallen significantly. Some countries—India, Pakistan, and the United Kingdom, for example—have abandoned it altogether. In 1985, of the forty-nine states subscribing to the optional clause, six— Liberia, Malawi, Mexico, the Philippines, the Sudan, and the United States—retained the self-judging automatic reservation. In the United States (when it was still bound by the optional clause declaration), efforts to have the severely criticized Connally Amendment repealed were not successful despite recommendations to do so by the Department of State, the Senate Foreign Relations Committee, and several Presidents.

Conciliation (285)

A procedure of third-party peaceful settlement of an international dispute by referring the dispute to a standing or *ad hoc* commission of conciliation, appointed with the parties' agreement, whose task is to objectively and impartially elucidate the facts and to issue a report containing a concrete proposal for a settlement which, however, the parties to the dispute are under no legal obligation to accept. Conciliation is more formal and less flexible than mediation. If a mediator's suggestion is not accepted, the mediator can still continue mediation by formulating new proposals, whereas the conciliator (a "conciliation commission" or a "commission of investigation and conciliation"), having investigated the facts and discussed the issue with the parties behind the scenes, issues a single formal report with conclusions and a proposal. Also, unlike mediation, conciliation is the task of an impartial commission, not governments. It differs from arbitration in that the conciliation report only suggests the terms of settlement, whereas the arbitral tribunal's award is legally binding upon the parties. In international practice this distinction is not always observed, and the terminology may be confusing since some agreements refer to conciliation commissions that are expected to make binding decisions. Such conciliation commissions are in fact arbitral tribunals. *See also* ARBITRATION, 283; GOOD OFFICES, 288; MEDIATION, 294; PEACEFUL SETTLEMENT OF INTERNATIONAL DISPUTES, 297.

Significance   Provided for in the Hague Pacific Settlement Conventions of 1899 and 1907, the first conciliation commissions were established by the so-called "Bryan Treaties," the first of which was concluded in 1914 between Great Britain and the United States. Altogether, the United States entered into forty-eight such treaties. Under them, disputes of any kind could be submitted to standing peace commissions for investigation and report. The commissions consisted of one national and one nonnational chosen by each party, and a fifth member, not a national of either party and chosen by agreement. In the interwar period a large number of bi- and multilateral treaties of conciliation provided for submission of disputes to be conciliated by permanent conciliation commissions. Among them were the Locarno Treaties of 1925, the General Act for the Pacific Settlement of International Disputes of 1928, and the 1929 Inter-American Conciliation Convention. In the 1920s, the League of Nations Council employed the procedure of conciliation, using its conciliators ("rapporteurs") in an imaginative and flexible way. However, only a very limited number of cases were submitted to conciliation. The Charter of the United Nations refers to conciliation as one of the peaceful procedures for the settlement of disputes. Both the Security Council and the General Assembly may recommend it among other peaceful techniques of settlement. Similar references can be found in charters of regional organizations, such as the charter of the Organization of African Unity (OAU, 1963) and the Brussels Treaty (1948). Generally speaking, conciliation has been more important in international organizations' involvement in international disputes than in direct relations between states. To encourage resort to conciliation the Institute of International Law adopted Articles on it and recommended conclusion of bilateral conciliation treaties. Some revival of the institution of concilation has occurred since the mid-1960s. A number of multilateral treaties referred to conciliation as witnessed, for example, by the Convention on the Settlement of Investment Disputes between States and Nationals of Other States (1965), the International Covenant on Civil and Political Rights (1966), and the Convention on International Liability for Damage Caused by Space Objects (1972).

Contentious Jurisdiction of the International Court of Justice   (286)

The power of the International Court of Justice (ICJ) to render, in accordance with international law, a legally binding decision in disputes of a legal nature which are submitted to it on the basis of consent by states confronting each other in adversary proceedings before the Court. The contentious jurisdiction of the World Court differs from such courts as the Court of Justice of the European Communities in Luxembourg or the Court of Justice of Human Rights in Strasbourg before which, within the respective scope of the Court's jurisdiction, persons other than states may be parties. No case can be submitted to the International Court of Justice unless both the applicant and the respondent or, generally speaking, all the parties are states. Contentious jurisdiction of the World Court must be distinguished from its advisory jurisdiction. The latter involves the power to hand down advisory opinions on any legal question at the request of the United Nations General Assembly, the Security Council, or whatever body may be authorized by the United Nations General Assembly to make such a request. Unless a case is settled by the parties at any stage of the proceedings or discontinued by the applicant, with subsequent removal of the case from the Court's list by an order of the Court or (in cases of discontinuance) of the president, contentious proceedings are brought to a conclusion by the Court's judgment. The judgment may do this either by upholding a preliminary objection or by dealing with the merits of the case. Unlike advisory opinions, judgments are legally binding decisions of the Court. As far as the parties entitled to appear before the International Court of Justice are concerned (jurisdiction *ratione personae*), the contentious jurisdiction of the Court covers (1) members of the United Nations; (2) states which are not members of the United Nations but have become parties to the Statute of the Court on conditions determined in each case by the General Assembly upon recommendation of the Security Council (Liechtenstein, San Marino, and Switzerland); and (3) any other state which has deposited with the Registry of the International Court of Justice a declaration accepting the Court's jurisdiction and undertaking to comply with its decisions.

The fact that a state belongs to one of these categories in not sufficient for the Court to have jurisdiction *ratione materiae*, which in the final resort depends upon the parties' consent. This consent may in general be manifested in three ways. First, the parties may submit an already existing dispute to adjudication by means of a special *ad hoc* agreement (*compromis*). In such cases there is neither an applicant nor a respondent state and, in the official title of the case, the names of the parties are separated by an oblique stroke, as for example, Canada/ United States of America. As ruled by the Court, a defendant state may accept, by an express statement or by implication, the jurisdiction of the Court, even after proceedings have been initiated against it (*forum prorogatum*)—a rare situation that has occurred only three times in the history of the International Court of Justice and the Permanent Court of International Justice. The second possibility is where a treaty in force contains a compromissory clause granting the International Court of

Justice jurisdiction in advance of the appearance of a particular dispute. Formally, proceedings may be instituted either through notification of a special agreement or by means of an application. In the latter case, the name of the applicant state appears first in the official title of the case and is separated from that of the respondent state by the abbreviation *v.* (*versus*) as, for example, *United States of America v. Iran*. Compromissory clauses are found in treaties dealing specifically with the peaceful settlement of disputes or with some other subject matter. The clauses that conferred jurisdiction on the Permanent Court of International Justice remain effective provided that the treaty is still in force and the states concerned are parties to the Statute of the International Court of Justice. There are some 400 bilateral treaties involving about 60 states (and numerous multilateral agreements involving even more states) conferring jurisdiction upon the Court by their compromissory clauses. However, despite the fact that the Statute of the International Court of Justice refers in Article 36(1) to "matters specially provided for in the Charter of the United Nations" as a basis of the Court's jurisdiction, it is generally accepted that there are no such matters since recommendations of the Security Council are not legally binding. This apparent contradiction is explained by the fact that the relevant article of the Statute was drafted at a time when it was expected that the United Nations Charter would provide for compulsory jurisdiction of the International Court of Justice. The third means of consenting to the Court's jurisdiction is through the "optional clause" of Article 36(2)(3) of the Court's Statute, which emerged as a compromise between countries advocating and opposing the principle of compulsory jurisdiction. Under this system of "quasi-compulsory" jurisdiction, a state may unilaterally declare its acceptance in advance, in relation to any other state accepting the same obligation, of the compulsory jurisdiction of the Court in all legal disputes concerning any question of international law, the interpretation of a treaty, the existence of a breach of an international obligations, or the nature or extent of the reparation. In formal terms, proceedings may be instituted either through notification of a special agreement or, less frequently, by means of an application. *See also* INTERNATIONAL ADJUDICATION, 291; INTERNATIONAL COURT OF JUSTICE (ICJ), 292; OPTIONAL CLAUSE, 296; PEACEFUL SETTLEMENT OF INTERNATIONAL DISPUTES, 297; PERMANENT COURT OF INTERNATIONAL JUSTICE, 299; RESERVATION TO ACCEPTANCE OF COMPULSORY JURISDICTION OF THE INTERNATIONAL COURT OF JUSTICE, 302.

Significance　　Because of the fundamental principle governing the settlement of international disputes to the effect that the jurisdiction of the International Court of Justice is founded upon the consent of states, it is their will that, in the final analysis, determines the use they make of the Court's contentious jurisdiction. In practice, this use has not been extensive. States usually prefer to resort to some other smaller or specialized tribunals if they decide to submit their disputes to international adjudication. Since 1945, approximately four times as many disputes have been brought before tribunals other than the International Court of Justice. Since the creation of the World Court after World War I, more than fifty states have been parties in proceedings before the Permanent Court of International Justice and the International Court of Justice: eight states from Africa, seven from Latin America, eight from Asia, and thirty-one from Europe and other regions. Of the more than sixty cases submitted to the Court, the greatest number were brought in pursuance of a treaty. During the forty years of its existence, the International Court of Justice has delivered judgments on the merits in seventeen cases (counting parallel proceedings and interpretative judgments in a dispute as one). Ten cases were terminated by a judgment on a preliminary objection or other jurisdictional grounds, and four by discontinuance. Although in the early period of its activities the Court's work assumed a pace comparable to that of the Permanent Court of International Justice, since 1962 the number of contentious cases brought to the Court each year has steadily diminished, averaging two or three in the 1950s and falling to one or none in the 1960s, so that from July 1962 to January 1967 no new case was brought to the Hague Court. Some signs of revived interest in the International Court of Justice could be perceived in the early 1980s (for example, merits judgments in the cases between Tunisia and Libya, Libya and Malta, Canada and the United States, and between Burkina Faso and Mali). On the other hand, the withdrawal in 1985 of the United States from the proceedings brought against it by Nicaragua in 1984 and subsequent denunciation of the acceptance of the "optional clause" in effect in 1986 did not bode well for the future of the Court which, in general, remains underused and marginal to the processes of world politics. Also the number of instruments conferring jurisdiction on the Court grew less rapidly, a development particularly true of acceptances of the optional clause jurisdiction under Article 36(2) of the Statute.

Forum Prorogatum　　　　　　　　　　　　　　　　(287)

A doctrine or principle relied upon in some cases by the International Court of Justice (ICJ), whereby the Court exercises jurisdiction over a case when consent to submit to its jurisdiction is given after the initiation of proceedings in an implied or informal way or by a succession of acts. *See also* CONTENTIOUS JURISDICTION OF THE INTERNATIONAL COURT OF JUSTICE, 286.

Significance   The doctrine of *forum prorogatum* (or "prorogated jurisdiction") can be resorted to by the International Court of Justice since ultimately the exercise of its jurisdiction depends upon the consent of the parties to the dispute. The Statute and the Rules of the International Court of Justice do not contain any specific mandatory rules concerning the form in which such consent is to be expressed. A dispute may be brought before the Court in a situation where only one of the parties recognizes the Court's jurisdiction, but the Court may declare itself competent on the basis of the other party's subsequent behavior. The doctrine of prorogated jurisdiction was relied upon by the Permanent Court of International Justice in the *Mavrommatis* case (1924) brought by Greece against the United Kingdom. In this case, the latter's reply in its written argument to an issue raised by Greece that was not within the Court's jurisdiction was sufficient to confer such jurisdiction in respect of this issue. Similarly, in the *Rights of Minorities in Polish Upper Silesia* case between Germany and Poland (Permanent Court of International Justice, 1928) the Court ruled that submission by Poland of arguments on the merits, without any reservations in regard to the question of jurisdiction, must be regarded as an indication of consent to submit to the Court's jurisdiction. In the *Corfu Channel* case (Preliminary Objection, 1948) the International Court of Justice pointed out that although Albania could have objected to the Court's jurisdiction by virtue of the unilateral initiation of proceedings by the United Kingdom, it was precluded from objecting to the jurisdiction after having accepted it in an official letter, following the initiation of the proceedings. However, assent to jurisdiction by subsequent conduct can scarcely be inferred when the respondent state consistently denies the Court's jurisdiction. Unless there is a real and not merely apparent consent, the Court will not accept jurisdiction and the case must be removed from its list—something that has happened eight times in the history of the International Court of Justice.

Good Offices   (288)
A technique of peaceful settlement of an international dispute, whereby a third party acting with the consent of the disputing states serves as a friendly intermediary in an effort to induce them to negotiate between themselves without necessarily offering the disputing states substantive suggestions of settlement. Good offices are the most modest type of third-state participation in settlement of disputes.

The person proffering good-offices may be a representative of a third state, an organ of an international organization, a nongovernmental international organization, or even a private individual. Good offices are often confused with mediation, but they differ from it in that the profferer of good offices serves as a channel of communication between the parties even after outbreak of hostilities and normally meets with them separately, whereas the mediator in the strict sense of the word actively participates with the parties in the negotiations, seeking solution to the dispute. To a large extent, however, the difference between good offices and mediation is a matter of degree. There is nothing unusual if the good-offices intermediary not only transmits messages between the disputing states but also makes suggestions which may touch upon the merits of the dispute. The state proffering good offices may be invited by the disputants to continue its friendly intercession by means of mediation. In no case may good offices be regarded as an unfriendly act, a rule declared already in the Hague Conventions for the Pacific Settlement of International Disputes of 1899 and 1907. *See also* CONCILIATION, 285; MEDIATION, 294; PEACEFUL SETTLEMENT OF INTERNATIONAL DISPUTES, 297; PERMANENT COURT OF ARBITRATION, 298.

Significance   Recourse to good offices was codified in the Hague Conventions of 1899 and 1907 and has become a standard feature of numerous treaties, such as the Inter-American Treaty on Good Offices and Mediation (1936) and the Charter of the Organization of American States (the Bogotá Pact, 1948). Although Article 33(1) of the United Nations Charter has no express reference to good offices, the competence of the General Assembly and the Security Council to recommend them is implied in the Charter's provisions dealing with the functions and powers of the General Assembly (Articles 10 and 14) and the Pacific Settlement of International Disputes (Chapter VI) respectively. The General Assembly, for example, recommended establishment of a permanent commission of good offices during the Korean War in 1950. The United Nations Secretary-General may also exercise good offices at the recommendation of the Security Council, if the parties to a dispute invited him to do so, or even on his own initiative. There have been numerous instances of United Nations organs engaged in good offices that in practice would often assume features of mediation, inquiry, or conciliation. Among many examples of good offices offered by states are those performed by President Theodore Roosevelt of the United States, which brought about the termination of the Russo-Japanese War in 1905; the U.S. action in persuading Egypt and Israel in 1973 to agree to meet to negotiate the terms of cease-fire; and the Algerian good offices in the U.S.-Iranian hostages crisis 1979–1981. It is in the nature of good offices that their scope as a method to settle international disputes is rather limited. To be effective they must be complemented by a more specialized third-party involvement, such as conciliation or adjudication.

Individual Opinion   (289)

An opinion that an individual judge of the International Court of Justice (ICJ) may append to the Court's judgments, orders, and advisory opinions in which he states and explains his position in regard to certain points in the Court's decision. Individual opinions may take the form of a dissenting opinion, a separate opinion, or a declaration. A dissenting opinion is one given by a judge who disagrees with the view of the majority. It states the reasons for the disagreement in one or more points with the Court's decision, and why in consequence it was voted against. A separate opinion is one given by a judge who, although voting in favor of the Court's decision, disagrees with some or all of the Court's reasoning. This means that a separate opinion may be given even if the Court's decision is unanimous. This rare situation occurred, for example, in the *Minquiers and Ecrehos* case (International Court of Justice, 1953). Two or more judges may write a joint dissenting or separate opinion. A declaration is a brief indication of concurrence or dissent by the declaring judge. *See also* ADVISORY JURISDICTION OF THE INTERNATIONAL COURT OF JUSTICE, 282; INTERNATIONAL COURT OF JUS-TICE (ICJ), 292.

Significance   The Statute of the World Court has always recognized the right of individual judges to append their individual opinions if they so desire. Since under the old Rules of the International Court of Justice, the decisions provided only the number of judges voting for and against each point of the operative provisions of the decision without stating who voted which way, it was impossible to discern which judge voted with the majority. The revised Rules of the Court, which entered into force on 1 July 1978, provide that each decision shall also indicate the names of the judges constituting the majority. On an average, the individual opinions number seven; but there have been decisions in which thirteen such opinions were appended. The right to append individual opinions, unknown in the continental judicial systems but frequently used in common law jurisdictions, has been a controversial issue within the context of the International Court of Justice. In one view, this right may weaken the authority and cohesion of the Court. In another view, the judges' right to express their opinions freely is an essential safeguard of their independence in the interest of international justice. Moreover, individual opinions have always demanded attention and have been frequently quoted because of the prestige of their authors, and in this sense they occupy the position midway between judicial decisions and opinions of publicists.

Inquiry (290)

Elucidation of the facts surrounding an international dispute by an impartial investigative body for the purpose of a successful adjustment of the dispute. Inquiry may be either an independent procedure terminating in the issuance of a report (in which case the disputing parties are free to determine the use they will make of the findings), or it may be a preliminary but integral stage in the procedure of dispute settlement by means of mediation, conciliation, arbitration, or adjudication in the strict sense of the term. Inquiry as a procedure designed merely to ascertain and clarify disputed facts has not been common and usually involves incidental clarification of points of law as well. *See also* CONCILIATION, 285; PEACEFUL SETTLEMENT OF INTERNATIONAL DISPUTES, 297.

Significance Inquiry was institutionalized in the Hague Convention of 1899 which provided for the maintenance of a standing panel of names from which parties could select fact-finding experts for specific cases, each party selecting two commissioners, the fifth to be named by the other four. Only one of the party's nominees could be its own appointee on the panel. The 1907 Convention for the Pacific Settlement of International Disputes required each commission of inquiry to have three neutrals. The commissions of inquiry set up under the Hague Conventions proved useful in several instances, the best known of which was the first case of the use of a Hague commission of inquiry in the Anglo-Russian dispute (the *Dogger Bank* incident), concerning the accidental sinking of and damage to British fishing boats by Russian warships during the Russo-Japanese war in 1904. In treaty law prior to World War I, each of the "Bryan treaties" and a number of treaties of Latin American states provided for the establishment of permanent commissions of inquiry. In the interwar period the League of Nations, whose Covenant included reference to inquiry as a useful technique for settlement of disputes, employed inquiry in six international disputes. The report of the Lytton Commission investigating the facts surrounding the Manchurian Crisis of 1931 is one major example. The United Nations Charter includes inquiry among the peaceful means of settlement of disputes and the organization itself, and regional organizations have on numerous occasions employed commissions of inquiry (fact-finding missions) within the framework of their respective institutional arrangements. In 1967, the United Nations General Assembly adopted a resolution upholding the institution of impartial fact-finding and requested the Secretary-General to set up a register of experts whose services could be used by states in specific disputes.

International Adjudication (291)

The settlement of international disputes according to international law by permanent international tribunals. Although in its strictest meaning adjudication implies the existence of a standing international court, the term is also loosely used to cover all forms of legally binding third-party settlement, including not only judicial settlement by a standing tribunal but also arbitration by various kinds of *ad hoc* bodies. In either case, jurisdiction depends upon the consent of the parties which are legally bound to comply with the decision handed down on the basis of respect for international law (or on the basis agreed upon by the parties) by an impartial judge (arbitrator) or judges (arbitrators), and following a procedure which enables the parties to submit their views on the basis of full equality. Moreover, adjudication in the form of institutionalized permanent courts historically developed from the much longer experience of arbitration. Apart from the abortive Central American Court of Justice (1908–1918), whose jurisdiction included cases between individuals and foreign states, the Permanent Court of International Justice, functioning in the League of Nations period, was the first permanent international tribunal to decide disputes between states. Its successor, the International Court of Justice (ICJ), is essentially a continuation of the old Court.

In the post–World War II era, new institutions of international adjudication emerged on the regional level. In Western Europe, the Court of Justice of the European Communities (created in 1952) has a broad jurisdiction to ensure the observance of the law in the interpretation and application of the treaties governing the Communities. Unlike the International Court of Justice, where only states may be parties, disputes before the Court of Justice of the European Communities may be brought by European Communities (EC) institutions, member states, national tribunals, and even individuals. Like the International Court of Justice, the European Communities Court can in certain instances deliver advisory opinions at the request of EC organs or member states. Due to the unique nature of the EC, its Court has not only features of an international tribunal but also performs functions of a constitutional, administrative, and appeals court. An institution similar to the EC Court was established in 1979 by the Andean countries Bolivia, Colombia, Ecuador, Peru, and Venezuela. This Court of Justice of the Cartagena Agreement (or Andean Court of Justice) has a general authority to define the community law of the Andean Group, resolve the controversies arising under it, and to interpret it uniformly. The Organization of Arab Petroleum Exporting Countries (OAPEC) inaugurated its judicial tribunal in 1984. A different type of international tribunal is represented by the regional courts of human rights; namely, the European Court of Human Rights, established by the European Convention for the Protection of Human Rights and Fundamental Freedoms (1950) under the auspices of the Council of Europe and the Inter-American Court of Human Rights, created by the American Convention on Human Rights of 1969, and elected in 1979. Also, the United Nations and International Labor Organization (ILO) maintain permanent administrative tribunals whose function is to adjudicate labor disputes between the United Nations and its agencies on the one hand and their employees on the other. Although these tribunals do not deal with international disputes, they have made a significant contribution to international administrative law. *See also* ARBITRATION, 283; CONTENTIOUS JURISDICTION OF THE INTERNATIONAL COURT OF JUSTICE (ICJ), 292; JUSTICIABLE AND NONJUSTICIABLE DISPUTES, 293; PEACEFUL SETTLEMENT OF INTERNATIONAL DISPUTES, 297; PERMANENT COURT OF ARBITRATION, 298; PERMANENT COURT OF INTERNATIONAL JUSTICE, 299.

Significance   Adjudication is a recognized technique of settling international disputes, and judicial settlement is specifically named in Article 33 of the United Nations Charter along with other peaceful means of settlement. However, its actual contribution to resolving conflict and the part that it should play within the general framework of a progressive world order remain controversial issues. Adjudication has not played a significant part in resolving major political conflicts among nations. Since jurisdiction of international courts remains voluntary (except for certain regional adjudicatory systems in Western Europe), sovereign states are reluctant to submit to adjudication political (nonjusticiable) disputes when their perceived vital interests are at stake, particularly if their legal case rests on shaky grounds. As a rule, states prefer to resort to more familiar techniques, such as diplomatic negotiations, rather than to less flexible and usually final judicial determination. Uncertainty of the law, lack of legislative institutions with the power to adjust legal rules to the changing international environment, and the lack of organized judicial procedures for the enforcement of judgments further contribute to the precarious state of international adjudication. Various proposals for extending the compulsory jurisdiction of the International Court of Justice and resolutions of the United Nations General Assembly to make greater use of this Court have so far had little impact on national attitudes regarding the use of adjudication in international disputes.

International Court of Justice (ICJ) (292)

One of the six principal organs of the United Nations and its principal judicial organ. The International Court of Justice is the successor to the Permanent Court of International Justice, which was formally dissolved in 1946. Popularly known as the World Court, the International Court of Justice functions on the legal basis of Chapter XIV of the United Nations Charter and the Court's Statute which forms an integral part of the Charter. The Rules of Court of 1946, largely based on the Rules of the predecessor Permanent Court of International Justice, supplement the provisions of the Statute. The Rules were amended in 1972 and thoroughly revised in 1978 in order to simplify the proceedings and increase their flexibility. All members of the United Nations are *ipso facto* parties to the Statute of the International Court of Justice, but nonmember states may become parties to the Statute on conditions to be determined in each case by the General Assembly upon the recommendation of the Security Council. Switzerland, Liechtenstein, and San Marino are parties to the Court's Statute on this basis. In addition, any other state may appear as a party before the Court after depositing with the Registry a declaration accepting the Court's jurisdiction and undertaking to comply with its decisions in respect of all or a particular class of decisions.

The Court is composed of fifteen judges elected for nine years (five being elected every three years), with the possibility of reelection by the majority of the General Assembly and by the Security Council (without the right of veto) from a list of persons nominated by the national groups in the Permanent Court of Arbitration or, if the United Nations member is not represented in this Court, by national groups appointed for this purpose by the government. It is therefore clear that governments have influence upon the selection of the nominees, and political alliances in the two organs of the United Nations play a role in the elections of the judges. The judges of the Court are elected as individuals regardless of their nationality, but no two of them can be nationals of the same state.

Under its Statute, the Court must assure the representation of the main forms of civilization and of the principal legal systems of the world. The permanent members of the Security Council normally have judges elected to the Court, but China had no judge in the period 1960–1984. Prior to that, a judge from nationalist China had been sitting on the Court. It was not until 1984 that the first judge from the

People's Republic of China was elected to the Court and took office in 1985. In that year, in addition to the five judges from the permanent members of the Security Council, the Court included judges from Italy, Norway, Poland, India, Japan, Algeria, Nigeria, Senegal, Argentina, and Brazil. The Court elects its President and Vice President for three years with the possibility of reelection, and appoints its Registrar who heads the Registry, the administrative organ of the International Court of Justice with a staff of some thirty officials. Much of the Registry's activity involves the publication of the Court's documents and linguistic matters in view of the fact that English and French are the official languages of the Court. The International Court of Justice has its seat at the Hague in the Peace Palace funded by Andrew Carnegie before World War I, but it may sit elsewhere whenever it considers it desirable.

As a rule, decisions are made by the full Court, with a quorum of nine being sufficient to constitute the Court. There is, however, a possibility that the parties may ask that their dispute be decided not by the full Court but by a chamber composed of certain judges elected by ballot by the Court and applying a simplified procedure. There are three kinds of chambers; (1) the Chamber of Summary Procedure, comprising five judges and constituted annually; (2) any chamber of three judges that the Court may form to deal with a given category of cases; and (3) any chamber that the Court may form to deal with a particular case, after consulting the parties regarding the number and names of its members. The case of *Delimitation of the Maritime Boundary in the Gulf of Maine Area* (Canada/United States of America, 1984) was the first time that use was made of the possibility of referring a dispute to a special chamber. As a concession to the politics of the Court (reminiscent of national commissioners in *ad hoc* arbitral bodies), judges of the nationality of each of the parties retain their right to sit in the case. Furthermore, if there is no judge of a party's nationality, a judge *ad hoc* may be appointed by the party concerned who may be of some other nationality than that of the party. Only states may be parties before the Court. It is the fundamental principle of the Court that its jurisdiction depends on the consent of the parties which may take, in general, three forms: (1) *ad hoc* submission of a specific dispute; (2) conferring jurisdiction in advance on the basis of a treaty; and (3) optional declaration of accepting the Court's jurisdiction in certain legal disputes under the so-called "optional clause" of Article 36(2)(3) of the Statute of the International Court of Justice. The Court is a judicial organ and must decide disputes in accordance with international law, applying treaties, customary law, general principles of law recognized by civilized nations and—as subsidiary means for the determination of rules of law—judicial decisions (subject to the rule that the decisions of the Court have no binding force except between the parties and in respect of the particular case) and teachings of publicists. Decisions *ex aequo et bono* (on an equitable basis or other extralegal considerations) are possible only with the parties' consent; but the Court has never decided any case on the basis of *ex aequo et bono*.

The proceedings before the Court consist of written pleadings (memorials, countermemorials, and—if authorized by the Court—replies and rejoinders) and oral hearings which are public unless the Court decides otherwise or the parties request the proceedings to be *in camera* (in closed session). All questions are decided by a majority of the judges present. In the event of an equality of votes the president has a casting vote. The judgment must state the reasons behind the decision, and the names of the judges voting for and against the majority must be stated. Individual opinions and declarations are allowed. Proceedings before the Court are frequently affected by "preliminary objections," requiring a special judgment of the Court. The Court may order "provisional measures" or joinder of proceedings. Nonappearance of the respondent state does not affect the proceedings. The Court's judgment is final and without appeal, but requests for an interpretative judgment are possible as are applications for revision of a judgment in case of discovery of new decisive facts. In 1984 the Court was for the first time in its history requested to revise its judgment and for the second time to interpret it. The application came from Tunisia, which requested revision and interpretation of the Court's judgment of 1982 in the case concerning the Continental Shelf (Libya/Tunisia). The Court may permit intervention in the proceedings by the state that has an interest of a legal nature which may be affected by the decision in the case.

Under an express provision of the United Nations Charter (Article 94[1]) parties must comply with the Court's decision. The Court itself has no procedures for enforcement, but if any party fails to perform its obligation incumbent upon it under a judgment of the Court, the other party may have recourse to the Security Council which may make recommendations or decide upon measures to be taken to give effect to the judgment. The Security Council has never used these powers, although in the *Anglo-Iranian Oil Co.* case (*United Kingdom v. Iran*, 1951) the United Kingdom did have recourse to the Security Council to enforce provisional measures indicated by the Court which, however, eventually held that it had no jurisdiction in the case. In practice, the enforcement of the Court's judgment has not caused any serious problems except in the *Corfu Channel* case (*United Kingdom v. Albania*, 1949) and the *Fisheries Jurisdiction* cases (*United Kingdom v. Iceland* and *Federal Republic of Germany v. Iceland*, 1974) where the establishment of the Court's jurisdiction was a matter of controversy. Unlike judgments, advisory opinions of the Court are not binding, but carry political weight and in some cases have contributed to the development of international law. *See also* ADVISORY JURISDICTION OF THE INTERNATIONAL COURT OF JUSTICE, 282; AUTOMATIC RESERVATION, 284; CONTENTIOUS JURISDICTION OF THE INTERNATIONAL COURT OF JUSTICE (ICJ), 286; *FORUM PROROGATUM*, 287; INTERNATIONAL ADJUDICATION, 291; OPTIONAL CLAUSE, 296; RESERVATION TO ACCEPTANCE OF COMPULSORY JURISDICTION OF THE INTERNATIONAL COURT OF JUSTICE, 302.

Significance   Although the International Court of Justice represents the most progressive institution in securing the rule of law in the settlement of international disputes, its value and achievements remain a matter of controversy. Some sixty cases were filed before the Court in the years 1946–1985. The Court handed down eighteen judgments on the merits, ten on preliminary objections, and delivered seventeen advisory opinions. The major handicap of the Court is that it lacks compulsory jurisdiction. Even though such jurisdiction in legal matters is possible under the optional clause, many types of crippling reservations render it illusory, apart from the fact that its acceptance has dwindled in relation to the increased number of the parties to the Statute of the Court. No communist state has ever appeared before the Court in contentious proceedings (unless one considers Nicaragua as such) or made a declaration under the optional clause, and very few Third World countries have subscribed to it. Morover, even some Western countries that traditionally supported resort to international adjudication have shown disregard for the World Court's role in promoting the rule of law in international affairs. France, for example (which in the years 1920–1971 had been a party in more proceedings before the Court than any other state), refused to appear before the Court in the *Nuclear Tests* cases (*Australia v. France; New Zealand v. France*, 1974) and subsequently withdrew its declaration of acceptance. The conduct of the United States has not departed much from the general pattern of reluctance to submit to the Court's jurisdiction. Quite apart from the notorious Connally Amendment of 1946, the more recent U.S. attempt to deprive the World Court of jurisdiction in the case brought against it by Nicaragua in 1984 and the subsequent U.S. refusal to participate in the merits phase of the proceedings followed by the denunciation of the acceptance of the optional clause in 1985 show how the narrowly conceived national interest can frustrate the rule of law that the World Court represents.

With very few exceptions (*Nicaragua v. United States*, and the more recent cases of *Nicaragua v. Costa Rica* and *Nicaragua v. Honduras*, for example), the contentious cases before the Court have not dealt with major international issues of the day. The Court's judgments and advisory opinions have made, however, a contribution to developing international law in certain limited areas. Some of the reasons for the underuse of the Court are common to those which account for states' hesitancy to submit to adjudication in general. Apart from reluctance to accept adjudication in settling disputes that a state's decisionmakers believe they simply cannot afford to lose and the natural tendency not to let the dispute out of the grip of the state's diplomacy, the major reasons for this underuse are distrust of sometimes unfamiliar rules of law and judicial proceedings and concern about the unpredictability of the Court's decision (something that the frequency of dissenting opinions seems to confirm). Doubts about the judges' impartiality also play a role, as does the reserved attitude of new states toward the Court (reflecting their distrust of some traditional rules of international law and the Western judges who interpret it in support of the *status quo*). On the other hand, some Western states may distrust the Court for the opposite reason; namely, concern that instead of applying the law the Court is changing it to the detriment of their perceived interests. The Court's time-consuming and expensive procedure may be an additional reason why states sometimes prefer the flexibility of arbitration and its more specialized tribunals. Still, given the condition of the international society within which it operates, the International Court of Justice must be considered mankind's highest effort to date in upholding the rule of international law in world affairs.

Justiciable and Nonjusticiable Disputes   (293)

A distinction based on the assumption that only some international disputes lend themselves to legal settlement by arbitration or adjudication and hence are "justiciable" or "legal," whereas other disputes are "nonjusticiable" or "political" and can be settled only by political and diplomatic techniques of negotiation, good offices, mediation, inquiry, or conciliation. The question of the distinction between justiciable and nonjusticiable disputes has long preoccupied the doctrine of international law, but what criteria should govern this distinction is a controversial matter. Moreover, the distinction itself is considered by some to be of dubious and questionable validity. At least three approaches to the problem have emerged. In one view, justiciable disputes are those differences between states capable of judicial settlement because there exist rules of international law that can be applied in order to settle the dispute in question. In another view, they are minor disputes which do not involve vital national interests, specifically those interests that are usually included in the "restrictive clauses" of arbitration agreements. The third and most common view adopts a less vague criterion: a dispute is legal and justiciable if it concerns an existing legal right, the parties accepting the existing law as the basis for settlement. If, on the other hand, a party seeks to change this law, the dispute is political and nonjusticiable.

Some publicists believe that the distinction between justiciable and nonjusticiable disputes is unsustainable and maintain that justiciability is determined by the parties' attitude toward the dispute. If both parties are willing to accept a judicial settlement, then the dispute is justiciable regardless of its subject matter. Furthermore, it is contended that there is always some rule of international law that can be applied to a dispute and that the parties may always agree to a decision *ex aequo et bono* if they believe that the legal rules are not satisfactory under the circumstances. Finally, there always remains the possibility of adjusting the existing rules of international law by peaceful change, a procedure which in certain cases may be more suitable in settling international conflict than adjudication itself. *See also* ARBITRATION, 283; CONTENTIOUS JURISDIC-TION OF THE INTERNATIONAL COURT OF JUSTICE, 286; *EX AEQUO ET BONO*, 13; INTERNATIONAL ADJUDICATION, 291; INTERNATIONAL COURT OF JUS-TICE (ICJ), 292; PEACEFUL SETTLEMENT OF INTERNATIONAL DISPUTES, 297; RESERVATION TO ACCEPTANCE OF COMPULSORY JURISDICTION OF THE INTERNATIONAL COURT OF JUSTICE, 302.

Significance   International practice has always made a distinction between "legal" disputes which states are willing to submit to adjudica-tion and those disputes perceived to affect a state's vital interests (in-cluding disputes on legal issues related to them) which states will not regard as justiciable. Thus, for example, disputes affecting vital inter-ests and the independence or the honor of the contracting parties were excluded from arbitration before World War I, and after it arbitration agreements frequently limited their scope to differences which are justiciable by reason of being susceptible of decision by the application of the principles of law. The General Act for the Pacific Settlement of Disputes (1928) made a distinction between legal and nonlegal disputes and Article 36(2) of the Statute of the Permanent Court of Interna-tional Justice, and later International Court of Justice, limited the application of the declarations under the optional clause to specified categories of "legal" disputes. Also, in Article 36(3), the United Nations Charter itself distinguishes "legal" disputes which should as a general rule be referred to the Court—the implication being that there are other "nonlegal" disputes to be settled as a rule by other methods, including diplomatic techniques of adjustment.

Mediation   (294)
A technique of third-party peaceful settlement of an international dispute whereby that party, acting with the agreement of the disputing

states, actively participates in the negotiating process by offering substantive suggestions concerning terms of settlement and, in general, trying to reconcile the opposite claims and appeasing any feelings of resentment between the parties. Mediation differs from good offices in that a mediator, instead of serving only as a channel of communication between the parties, assists them directly by offering concrete proposals either in joint or separate meetings. The parties are under no legal obligation whatever to accept these proposals. Like good offices, mediation may not be regarded as an unfriendly act or interference in the affairs of another country, a rule declared in the Hague Conventions on the Pacific Settlement of International Disputes of 1899 and 1907. The mediating party may be a third state or a group of states, an organ of an international organization, or even an individual. *See also* GOOD OFFICES, 288; PEACEFUL SETTLEMENT OF INTERNATIONAL DISPUTES, 297.

Significance   Like good offices, recourse to mediation as a method of settling international disputes was codified in the Hague Conventions of 1899 and 1907 whose rules on the subject have been followed by numerous treaties. These include, for example, the Inter-American Treaty of Good Offices and Mediation of 1936 and the Charter of the Organization of American States (Bogotá Pact of 1948). The Charter of the United Nations expressly includes mediation among other peaceful means of settling disputes likely to endanger the maintenance of international peace and security. There have been a number of instances where mediation helped settle an international dispute. The Soviet Tashkent mediation in the Indo-Pakistani conflict of 1966 and the U.S. Camp David mediation to end the state of war between Egypt and Israel (1979) are among the more recent successful instances of mediation by individual states. However, like good offices, most mediation activity has taken place under the auspices of the United Nations or regional organizations. The record of mediation has been rather mixed. Although in some cases it has contributed to settling a dispute, it has failed to do so in many other cases. These failures include critical situations such as attempts at United Nations mediation in the war in Vietnam. Mediation does go beyond mere good offices by allowing the mediator to initiate suggestions for solution, but it is still only a mild third-party intercession in international disputes.

Negotiation   (295)
A diplomatic procedure in which representatives of states, in direct personal contact or through correspondence, engage in discussing matters of mutual concern and attempt to resolve disputes that have arisen in their relations with one another. Diplomatic negotiations,

bilateral or multilateral, are the oldest and most common technique of peaceful settlement of international disputes. The obligation to negotiate before resorting to force has been a well-established rule of common international law for centuries and today is enshrined in many treaties, the foremost of which is the United Nations Charter. In Article 33(1) the Charter prescribes that the parties to any dispute (the continuance of which is likely to endanger the maintenance of international peace and security) should, first of all, seek a solution through negotiation or some other peaceful means of their choice. The legal obligation to negotiate can also be implied from numerous treaties on pacific settlement of disputes which refer to conciliation, arbitration, or adjudication of disputes that could not be settled by negotiation. Various resolutions of the United Nations General Assembly, including the 1982 resolution approving the Manila Declaration on the Pacific Settlement of Disputes, emphasize the importance of negotiation as a flexible and effective means of peaceful settlement. The obligation to negotiate, however, does not entail an obligation to reach agreement; but states should negotiate meaningfully in order to arrive at an early settlement. There are no clear standards for determining the point in time at which the inability to reach agreement begins. In any case, as noted by the Permanent Court of International Justice in the *Mavrommatis Palestine Concessions* case (*Greece v. Great Britain*, 1924), the subject matter of a dispute should be clearly defined before the dispute can be submitted to adjudication—something that must be decided in each case. It is not certain whether or not the requirement of preliminary negotiation can be implied if it is not expressly stated in an agreement providing for a third-party settlement, but the Permanent Court of International Justice once rejected a contention to this effect in the *Case of German Interests in Polish Upper Silesia* (*Germany v. Poland*, 1924). *See also* PEACEFUL SETTLEMENT OF INTERNATIONAL DISPUTES, 297.

Significance   The bulk of international disputes are settled by negotiation. Thousands of treaties testify to the success of negotiation as a technique of resolving problems arising between and among states. Furthermore a large number of disputes are resolved every day by routine diplomatic procedures without being formalized in written agreements. Whether negotiation should be accorded special legal emphasis as against the other peaceful means of settlement is debatable. Advocates of this position have emphasized the advantages of negotiation as a flexible instrument more suited to deal with disputes, promoting compromise, and conducive to peaceful change of the legal *status quo*. On the other hand, it has been contended that the constant trend in international law in this century has been to transcend negotiation and establish institutionalized means of settlement based on participation of third parties, including international tribunals. In this view negotiations have disadvantages in that they do not allow the facts to be ascertained objectively, lack the moderating influence of third parties, and cannot prevent putting forward exaggerating claims, especially when one party's bargaining power is superior to the other's. These valid arguments notwithstanding, international practice continues to testify to negotiations being the most appropriate method of resolving international disputes.

Optional Clause (296)

One of the three principal means whereby a state may consent to compulsory jurisdiction of the International Court of Justice (ICJ). The so-called optional clause is contained in Article 36(2) of the Statute of the International Court of Justice under which parties to the Statute may at any time declare that they recognize as compulsory *ipso facto* and without special agreement, in relation to any other state accepting the same obligation, the jurisdiction of the Court in all legal disputes concerning (1) the interpretation of a treaty; (2) any question of international law; (3) the existence of any fact which, if established, would constitute a breach of an international obligation; and (4) the nature or extent of the reparation to be made for the breach of an international obligation. The acceptance of the Court's jurisdiction is effected by depositing a unilateral declaration with the Secretary-General of the United Nations. The declaration is registered under Article 102 of the United Nations Charter as an international agreement. As is the case of treaties that provide the basis of the Court's jurisdiction, declarations referring to the Permanent Court of International Justice are regarded as applying to the International Court of Justice. Declarations may be made unconditionally, on conditions of reciprocity, or for a certain time. The "optional clause" acceptance of compulsory jurisdiction is governed by the principle of reciprocity, which either expressly or by implication applies to all declarations. Under this principle, the Court's jurisdiction is limited to matters common in the declarations of both the applicant and respondent state, with the corollary that each party may take advantage of any reservation in the other party's declaration and invoke it if it wants to exclude the Court's jurisdiction in the case. As a result, the Court's jurisdiction over a case is restricted to these classes of disputes not excluded by any of the parties. However, under Article 36(6), only the Court has the power to decide whether or not it possesses jurisdiction in a given case (*compétence de la compétence*). *See also* AUTOMATIC RESERVATION, 284; CONTENTIOUS JURISDICTION OF THE INTERNATIONAL COURT OF JUSTICE, 286; RESERVATION TO ACCEPTANCE OF

COMPULSORY JURISDICTION OF THE INTERNATIONAL COURT OF JUSTICE, 302.

Significance   The optional clause emerged as a compromise achieved in the Statute of the Permanent Court of International Justice in 1920, and maintained in the new Court's Statute in 1946, between states advocating and those opposing a true compulsory jurisdiction. The expectation that a more widespread acceptance of the optional clause would in practice lead to compulsory jurisdiction has not been fulfilled despite solemn appeals by the United Nations General Assembly, the United Nations Secretary-General, and the Institute of International Law. In general, two developments point to a decline of the World Court's compulsory jurisdiction under the optional clause. First, the number of acceptances has diminished in relative terms. In 1955, the 32 acceptances represented 50 percent of the 64 states parties; but at the beginning of 1985, 47 declarations amounted to only about 30 percent of the more than 160 signatories of the Statute. In terms of regional distribution, some 40 percent of the declarations were by Western European nations, the United States, Canada, Australia, and New Zealand. Fewer than half of the Latin American states and less than a quarter of the Afro-Asian states, and only two Arab states have accepted the optional clause. None of the communist states have subscribed to it. The other development pointing to the decline of the optional clause has been a marked narrowing of the terms of acceptance. In particular, unqualified acceptances have diminished both in relative and in absolute terms. Commitments of uncertain duration (for example, declarations terminable immediately or on six months' notice) have multiplied, and although the automatic, Connally-type reservation appears to be losing ground, many crippling reservations of an amazing variety have had a damaging effect upon the otherwise shrinking compulsory jurisdiction of the World Court under the optional clause of Article 36(2) of the Statute of the International Court of justice. In 1985, a serious blow to the optional clause jurisdiction was the denunciation of the acceptance of this jurisdiction by the United States—arising from U.S. dissatisfaction with the World Court's decision in the U.S. dispute with Nicaragua. The denunciation entered into effect in 1986.

Peaceful Settlement of International Disputes (297)

Resolution of disputes without recourse to force or threat of force and in such a manner that international peace and security and justice are not endangered. International law is primarily concerned with international disputes to which states are parties, but wherever appropriate and applicable the procedures for settling disputes between states apply also to disputes of states with international organizations and those between international organizations. Occasionally even disputes between states and private persons may be governed by these procedures. The term "dispute" has no precise connotation in international law but, as defined by the Permanent Court of International Justice in the *Mavrommatis Palestine Concessions* case (*Greece v. Great Britain*, 1924), it generally means "a disagreement on a point of law or fact, a conflict of legal views or of interests between [the parties]." However, this definition does not answer the fundamental question of what is meant by "international" disputes. Under international law, as laid down in Article 2(3) of the United Nations Charter and other numerous treaties, only such disputes must be settled by peaceful means—a principle which has become a peremptory rule of general international law in any case. Noninternational disputes—that is, disputes whose subject matter is essentially within the domestic jurisdiction of a state—need not be settled by peaceful means. Hence a state may invoke the plea of domestic jurisdiction against any other state wishing to raise a matter to the level of an "international" dispute. Consequently there is a logical connection between the issue of the delimitation of "international" from "domestic" disputes and the borderline between the legal scope of the principle of peaceful settlement and the principle of nonintervention in the domestic affairs of states. There is no general answer to this question and, as held by the Permanent Court of International Justice in the *Tunis-Morocco Nationality Decrees* Advisory Opinion (1923), the scope of a state's domestic jurisdiction is essentially relative and depends upon the development of international law. If a state has accepted obligations under international law, the matters relating to such obligations may become a subject of an international dispute. Consent to mediation by an international organization implies that the dispute in question is of international character.

Procedures of peaceful settlement may be diplomatic (nonadjudicative) where the parties agree on terms of settlement themselves or adjudicative where a third party resolves the dispute by means of a legally binding decision. The settlement of an international dispute by diplomatic procedures may be either via negotiation between the parties without any intercession of third parties or by other diplomatic procedures, in all of which a third party intercedes in the dispute. In the latter type of procedure, participation of a third party varies in influence from the weakest involvement in the form of good offices through mediation and inquiry to conciliation, the highest degree of diplomatic third-party participation. Very often these procedures cannot be rigidly separated and merge into one process of friendly third-party attempts to facilitate a solution of the dispute. International organizations have on numerous occasions engaged in this kind of settlement. Adjudicative procedures may be in the form of arbitration or judicial settlement by an international court in the strict sense of the word. In substance, there is little difference between these two forms since both involve judicial determination of facts and application of international law and both are legally binding upon the parties, except that in the case of arbitration the parties select the court and agree upon the procedure to be applied by it. As far as judicial settlement in the strict sense of the term is concerned, the International Court of Justice is the main judicial organ available to resolve legal disputes between states. *See also* ARBITRATION, 382; CONCILIATION, 285; GOOD OFFICES, 288; INQUIRY, 290; INTERNATIONAL ADJUDICATION, 291; IN-TERNATIONAL COURT OF JUSTICE (ICJ), 292; JUSTICIABLE AND NONJUSTIC-IABLE DISPUTES, 293; MEDIATION, 294; NEGOTIATION, 295; PERMANENT COURT OF ARBITRATION, 298; PERMANENT COURT OF INTERNATIONAL JUSTICE, 299.

Significance   Negotiation and some other techniques of peaceful settlement including arbitration have long been known in international practice, but until the turn of the century there were virtually no legal restraints upon resort to force as a means of resolving international disputes. The Hague Peace Conferences of 1899 and 1907 were the first significant multilateral efforts to limit resort to force in settling international disputes. Of interest here is the Convention of 1907 Respecting the Limitation of the Employment of Force for the Recovery of Contract Debts and the Conventions for the Pacific Settlement of International Disputes of 1899 and 1907 which codified and progressively developed various techniques of settling disputes, including arbitration. The work of the Hague Conventions was supplemented by numerous international agreements referring to various techniques of resolving international differences in a peaceful manner. However, it was the League of Nations that, despite its failure, represented a major turning point in the history of peaceful settlement, primarily because of the Permanent Court of International Justice—the first permanent global international tribunal. The Pact of Paris (Kellogg-Briand Pact) of 1928 brought further legal restraints on resort to war and reemphasized the duty to settle international disputes by peaceful means.

The current position of international law on the question of peaceful settlement is embodied in the United Nations Charter. One of the major purposes of this organization is to maintain international peace and security and to this end take collective measures and "bring about by peaceful means, and in conformity with the principles of justice and international law, adjustment or settlement of international disputes or situations which might lead to a breach of peace" (Article 1 of the Charter). One of the seven principles of the United Nations is the duty of all members to settle their international disputes by peaceful means—a principle which has become part of general (customary) international law. In the opinion of the United Nations and majority of publicists this principle represents not just a "negative" duty simply not to resort to force in composing differences but a positive obligation of the parties actively and perseveringly to strive for pacific settlement of disputes by means of their own choice. In this respect, the Charter of the United Nations refers in Article 33(1) to "negotiation, inquiry, mediation, conciliation, arbitration, judicial settlement, resort to regional agencies or arrangements, or other peaceful means." "Legal" disputes should as a general rule be referred to the International Court of Justice (ICJ) which, however, is handicapped by lack of compulsory jurisdiction. Rededication to the principle of peaceful settlement has been a frequent theme of United Nations General Assembly resolutions. Despite many setbacks, attributable primarily to the international political environment within which the United Nations operates, the organization has made some modest contributions to peaceful settlement of international disputes by formally dealing with specific conflicts, encouraging peaceful means of settlement and providing informal channels of bilateral and multilateral communication available through the "parliamentary" diplomacy of the United Nations.

Apart from the International Court of Justice, three principal United Nations organs deal with peaceful settlement: (1) the Security Council; (2) the General Assembly, and (3) the Secretariat acting through the Secretary-General. Chapter VI of the United Nations Charter governs the role of the Security Council in the settlement of disputes or situations which might lead to international friction or give rise to a dispute. But the distinction between disputes and situations has been blurred in the practice of the Security Council. Both may be brought before the Council by the General Assembly, the Secretary-General, or any state. It is for the Council to decide by a procedural (and hence nonvetoable) vote whether or not to place a dispute or a situation on its agenda or to remove it. It is the duty of the parties to a dispute, the continuance of which is likely to endanger the maintenance of international peace and security, to refer it to the Security Council. The Council may itself determine that a dispute or a situation belongs in this category and may make all sorts of recommendations under Chapter VI which, however, do not create legal obligations but are of nonprocedural character and therefore subject to veto. Disputes may also be brought before the General Assembly, which can make legally nonbinding recommendations; however no recommendations may be made with regard to a dispute or situation that is being dealt with by the Security Council unless the Council so requests.

The contribution of the Secretary-General to the pacific settlement of disputes has been more significant than that of the other United Nations organs. He has the right to bring to the attention of the Security Council any matter which in his opinion may threaten the maintenance of international peace and security (Article 99 of the United Nations Charter). There is no unanimity of view on the issue as to whether or not the Secretary-General is legally competent to act independently if the Security Council or the General Assembly has failed in producing a peaceful settlement. In particular, the Soviet Union contends that his intervention in international disputes requires a specific mandate of the Security Council under Article 99 of the Charter. The right of regional arrangements and agencies to develop and achieve pacific settlement of local disputes is recognized by the United Nations and the development of regional mechanisms for such settlement is encouraged by the Security Council.

Permanent Court of Arbitration (298)

A standing panel of jurists established in 1900 under the 1899 Hague Convention for the Pacific Settlement of International Disputes (revised in 1907), from among whom states can select arbitrators to resolve their disputes. The name "Permanent Court of Arbitration" is misleading since in reality (apart from a permanent Bureau at the Hague) the 1899 Convention did not create a court but rather a machinery for facilitating the creation of arbitral tribunals as necessary. Each "Party participating in the Permanent Court of Arbitration" selects up to four persons to serve as potential arbitrators for a renewable period of six years as so-called "members of the Permanent Court of Arbitration." States agreeing to refer their dispute to the Court can select arbitrators from the Court's panel. If they cannot agree upon the composition of their tribunal, each party appoints two arbitrators of whom only one can be its national or chosen from among the persons it designated as "members" of the Court. The four arbitrators then select an umpire. A special selection procedure deals with cases where there is no agreement on the person of the umpire. *See also* ARBITRATION, 283; INTERNATIONAL COURT OF JUSTICE(ICJ), 292; PEACEFUL SETTLEMENT OF INTERNATIONAL DISPUTES, 297.

Significance The simple machinery of the Permanent Court of Arbitration proved useful in several important cases, including the *North Atlantic Fisheries* case (1910) between Great Britain and the United

States and the *Island of Palmas* case (1928) between the Netherlands and the United States. Altogether, only twenty-five cases (two after World War II) have been decided by arbitral tribunals established through the recourse to the machinery of the Permanent Court of Arbitration. The Court still exists, independent of any international organization, and there are some seventy-four participating parties. While demonstrating that arbitration under the auspices of the Permanent Court of Arbitration can work, the system established in 1899 has also demonstrated its limitations, such as the lack of the duty to follow the rules of procedure of the Convention which first established the Court. Still the existence of the Permanent Court of Arbitration inspired various plans and proposals for the establishment of an international tribunal, which culminated in the creation of the Permanent Court of International Justice after World War I and the International Court of Justice under the Charter of the United Nations. There is also a linkage between the Permanent Court of Arbitration and the International Court of Justice since the members of the latter are elected from a list of persons nominated by the national groups in the Permanent Court of Arbitration.

Permanent Court of International Justice   (299)

The first permanent international global tribunal which was brought into being by the League of Nations to settle legal disputes between states and give advisory opinions upon any dispute or question referred to it by the Council or the Assembly of the League. The Permanent Court of International Justice was created pursuant to Article 14 of the League's Covenant by a treaty known as the Statute of the Permanent Court of International Justice, drafted by an Advisory Commission of Jurists and adopted by the Assembly of the League in 1920. The Statute entered into effect in 1921, following signatures and ratifications of a Protocol of Signature adopting it by a majority of the League's members. The first session of the Court was held in 1922. It was formally dissolved in 1946 when its functions were taken over by the International Court of Justice (ICJ) whose Statute is virtually the same as that of its predecessor. One major difference between the two Courts is that the International Court of Justice is an organ of the United Nations, and therefore all the United Nations members are automatically parties to the Statute; whereas the Permanent Court of International Justice was not an integral part of the League of Nations, and only those states that ratified the Protocol of Signature were bound by the Statute. Neither the United States nor the Soviet Union became parties to the Statute of the Permanent Court of International Justice.

See also INTERNATIONAL COURT OF JUSTICE (ICJ), 292; PEACEFUL SETTLEMENT OF INTERNATIONAL DISPUTES, 297.

Significance   The founding of the Permanent Court of International Justice was a turning point in the history of international legal institutions. Unlike arbitral tribunals whose experience otherwise contributed to its creation, the Court was a permanently constituted judicial body with a permanent Registry, largely public proceedings, and published records of pleadings and other documentary evidence. It was accessible to all states, but the principle of compulsory jurisdiction proposed in the draft Statute was rejected by the states in favor of a weak compromise in the form of the "optional clause" inherited by the International Court of Justice. In the years 1922 through 1940 the Permanent Court of International Justice dealt with twenty-nine contentious cases and delivered twenty-seven advisory opinions. At one time (in 1935), as many as forty-two out of the forty-nine states parties to the Statute accepted compulsory jurisdiction of the Court under the optional clause. At the same time, hundreds of treaties conferred jurisdiction upon it over specified classes of disputes. The Court demonstrated its value in the life of the League of Nations' period in a number of ways; in particular, it developed true judicial techniques which provided a blueprint for its successor, the International Court of Justice. It helped to resolve some serious international disputes, many of which were related to the interpretation of the 1919 peace settlements, and clarified some areas of international law. For example, the principle that "domestic jurisdiction" is an essentially relative concept whose content depends upon the development of international relations (Advisory Opinion on the *Nationality Decrees Issued in Tunis and Morocco*, 1923) did much to shape the development of international law following World War II. In this and other cases, the Permanent Court of International Justice built up a judicial tradition which has continued in the work of the International Court of Justice.

Preliminary Objection (300)

An objection raised before the International Court of Justice, as a rule by the respondent state, after the application instituting proceedings have been filed, with the purpose of preventing the Court from delivering judgment on the merits of the case. Preliminary objections fall into three general categories. One category is based on the allegation that the title of jurisdiction invoked by the applicant state simply does not exist. The respondent state may, for example, contend that the treaty or the declaration accepting compulsory jurisdiction of the Court is no longer in force or is null and void or that a reservation attached to the declaration excludes the dispute in question. In a second category of objections, the respondent state may, without contesting the title to jurisdiction as such, argue that the dispute does not come within the scope of the title. The third category of preliminary objections does not contest the Court's jurisdiction as such, but argues that the application is inadmissible on more general grounds such as noncompliance with essential provisions of the Statute or the Rules of the International Court of Justice, lack of capacity to act or—in claims on behalf of nationals—nonexhaustion of local remedies or lack of the link of nationality between the injured private person and the applicant state. The question of whether or not the Court has jurisdiction in a case is dealt with in a special distinct phase of proceedings, terminating in the Court's judgment in the usual way. However, the parties may, by agreement, ask the Court to join the preliminary objections to the merits; that is, to deal with them in the merits judgment. Until the 1972 revision of the Rules of Court, the World Court could decide on this course itself and indeed did on several occasions. The Statute of the International Court of Justice in Article 36(6) provides that, in the case of a dispute as to whether or not the Court has jurisdiction, the matter shall be settled by the decision of the Court, which means that insofar as this jurisdiction is concerned there exists true compulsory jurisdiction of the International Court of Justice. In its preliminary objections judgment, the Court may either uphold at least one of the objections (and the case will thereby come to an end), reject the preliminary objection or objections and resume the proceedings on the merits, or declare that the objections are not just preliminary and will deal with all the issues of the case. Preliminary objections may be raised by the applicant state itself, something that occurred only once in the history of the International Court of Justice in the *Monetary Gold Removed from Rome in 1943* case (*Italy v. France, the United Kingdom, and the United States of America,* 1954). In a few cases, the Court considered a preliminary issue on its own intiative, for example, the *Nuclear Tests* cases (*Australia v. France* and *New Zealand v. France,* 1953, 1954). The respondent state may withdraw its preliminary objections at any time of the proceedings. *See also* CONTENTIOUS JURISDICTION OF THE INTERNATIONAL COURT OF JUSTICE, 286; INTERNATIONAL COURT OF JUSTICE (ICJ), 292.

Significance   Preliminary objections have been frequently raised before the World Court. In the Permanent Court of International Justice they were raised thirteen times—upheld in three and rejected in eight. In two cases, proceedings had ended before the Court could decide on the objections. In the International Court of Justice, preliminary objections have been a more prominent feature and in only eleven cases has the jurisdiction of the Court gone uncontested. Preliminary objections have been more successful in relative terms in the International Court of Justice than in the Permanent Court of International Justice, a fact which prompted some critics to accuse the Court of formalism and timidity in accepting jurisdiction. On the other hand, as long as the Court's jurisdiction is not compulsory, it must exercise prudence and caution not to overstep the limits set by states and to insure that the preliminary objection procedure provides an essential safeguard for the system of voluntary submission of disputes before the International Court of Justice.

Provisional Measures   (301)
Measures which the International Court of Justice may, under Article 41 of its Statute, indicate in the course of contentious proceedings and that pending the Court's final decision, ought to be taken to preserve the respective rights of either party. Also known as interim measures of protection, provisional measures are roughly equivalent to the interim injunction which a domestic court may issue pending the final determination of a case. Although the International Court of Justice may indicate provisional measures at the request of the respondent state or of its own initiative, it has never done so. Request for provisional measures is considered an urgent matter and constitutes a separate phase of the case leading, in general, to a decision within three weeks, which is handed down in the form of an order read by the president of the Court at a public sitting. Already at the phase of provisional measures the respondent state may contest the Court's jurisdiction as was done, for example, by the United States in the proceedings brought against it by Nicaragua in 1984; or it may fail to appear, as did Iran in the case concerning *United States Diplomatic and Consular Staff in Tehran* (*United States of America v. Iran*, 1979). In such cases, the Court will indicate provisional measures only if it does not manifestly lack jurisdiction as to the merits of the case, but the order indicating the measures in no way prejudges the question of such jurisdiction and leaves unaffected the right of the parties to submit arguments in respect of such jurisdiction. *See also* CONTENTIOUS JURISDICTION OF THE INTERNATIONAL COURT OF JUSTICE, 286; INTERNATIONAL COURT OF JUSTICE (ICJ), 292.

Significance   Provisional measures are designed to safeguard the rights of the applicant state pending the final decision of the Court on the merits of the case and to prevent any aggravation or extension of the dispute. Since the matter of provisional measures very often has political implications, the Court must give notice of the measures not only to the parties but also to the Security Council. The Court does not have direct responsibility for the maintenance of international peace, but has the right to rely on the good faith of the parties not to aggravate the dispute with which it is dealing. The Court has dealt with eight requests for provisional measures. It "indicated" such measures in five cases: (1) the *Anglo-Iranian Oil Co.* (*United Kingdom v. Iran*, 1951); (2) the *Fisheries Jurisdiction* (*United Kingdom v. Iceland*; *Federal Republic of Germany v. Iceland*, 1972); (3) *Nuclear Tests* (*Australia v. France*; *New Zealand v. France*, 1973); (4) *United States Diplomatic and Consular Staff in Tehran* (*United States of America v. Iran*, 1979); and (5) the *Military and Paramilitary Activities in and against Nicaragua* (*Nicaragua v. United States of America*, 1984). In the *Interhandel* case (*Switzerland v. United States of America*, 1957), the Court found that there was no need for provisional measures at the time. In the *Trial of Pakistani Prisoners of War* case (*Pakistan v. India*, 1973), no measures were indicated since the request was withdrawn after hearing. In the *Aegean Sea Continental Shelf* case (*Greece v. Turkey*, 1976), the Court refused to indicate any measures.

Reservation to Acceptance of Compulsory   (302)
Jurisdiction of the International Court of Justice

A reservation which a state, accepting the compulsory jurisdiction of the International Court of Justice (ICJ) under the optional clause of Article 36(2)(3) of the Court's Statute, attaches to its declaration of acceptance, excluding from the Court's jurisdiction a specific kind of dispute. Article 36(3) of the Statutes allows reservations relating to reciprocity "on the part of several or certain States" (meaning that until some other states have accepted the optional clause, the state making the reservation cannot be respondent in any proceedings before the Court) and reservations relating to time. Whereas no state has ever made a reservation of reciprocity in the meaning of Article 36(3), many states have made reservations concerning time. Thus, out of forty-nine declarations in force in 1985, fourteen were made for a specific period (generally for five years) with tacit renewal. Also, declarations usually provide for termination by simple notice, taking effect after a specified time (eleven declarations) or immediately (twenty-one declarations). However, expiry of a declaration of one of the parties subsequent to the Court's seizure of a case does not affect the Court's jurisdiction in that case. In addition to the reservations explicitly allowed by the Statute, many other reservations have been made by accepting states and have been recognized as valid by the Court, subject to the proviso that they should not be repugnant to the Statute. *See also* AUTOMATIC RESERVATION, 284; CONTENTIOUS JURISDICTION OF THE INTERNATIONAL COURT OF

JUSTICE, 286; INTERNATIONAL COURT OF JUSTICE (ICJ), 292; OPTIONAL
CLAUSE, 296.

Significance   In 1985, thirty-three out of the forty-nine acceptances
of compulsory jurisdiction of the International Court of Justice had
some kind of reservation or reservations. This trend started in 1921
when the Netherlands excluded disputes with regard to which the
parties had agreed to use some other means of pacific settlement. On
the whole, however, there were not many reservations under the Permanent Court of International Justice. On the other hand, they have
proliferated in amazing varieties in the present Court's era. The most
frequently employed reservations exclude disputes subject to other
means of pacific settlement (twenty-five states). Other reservations
concern disputes arising before a particular date (23); disputes relating
to matters falling within the domestic jurisdiction of the declaring state,
as determined by international law (12) or by the state making the
declaration itself (6)—the last mentioned subcategory being known as
an "automatic" reservation or, more popularly, the Connally Amendment; disputes arising during or out of hostilities (8); disputes for the
specific purpose of which the other party appears to have made its
declaration (7); those relating to certain aspects of the law of the sea (7);
disputes between Commonwealth countries (7); disputes with states
with which the accepting country has no diplomatic relations (2); and
some other more exotic exclusions. One recent addition to this long
inventory was the reservation made in 1984 by the United States
whereby this country excluded from the scope of its 1946 Declaration
of acceptance of the optional clause, for two years and with immediate
effect, disputes with any Central American state or arising out of or
related to events in Central America. This modification of the 1946
Declaration was one legal basis on which the United States contested
the Court's jurisdiction in the proceeding instituted against it by
Nicaragua a few days following the deposition of the U.S. reservation.
Disregarding this challenge, the Court ruled in its judgment of 1984
that it had jurisdiction to entertain Nicaragua's application, one of the
grounds being the fact that the United States had disregarded the six
months' notice clause appended to its 1946 acceptance Declaration.
(The United States then denounced its 1946 declaration of acceptance
of the optional clause.)

Reservations by themselves have considerably weakened the optional clause compulsory jurisdiction of the World Court, but their
adverse effect is multiplied by the condition of reciprocity which
applies to all declarations of acceptance. Specifically, a reservation
made by any party to a dispute between two or more states can be

invoked against it by all the others. Thus a defendant state is allowed to invoke a reservation of the applicant state to deprive the Court of jurisdiction, as shown, for example, by the *Certain Norwegian Loans* case (*France v. Norway*, 1957).

11. Coercive Measures, Including Resort to Force and War

Aggression (303)

The use of armed force by a state against the sovereignty, territorial integrity or political independence of another state, or in any other manner inconsistent with the Charter of the United Nations. This definition of aggression was adopted by consensus by the United Nations General Assembly in 1974 at the recommendation of the Report of the Special Committee on the Question of Defining Aggression (which had also adopted the same definition by consensus) following six years of work, preceded in turn by years of labor by other United Nations General Assembly committees. Among acts qualifying as aggression (regardless of a declaration of war) are (1) invasion of the territory of another state or military occupation resulting from it, or any annexation by the use of force; (2) bombardment of foreign territory; (3) blockade of ports or coast; (4) use of armed forces staying in foreign territory with the agreement of the receiving state, in contravention of the agreement; (5) allowing a state's territory to be used by another state for perpetrating acts of aggression against a third state; and (6) sending by or on behalf of a state armed bands or mercenaries which carry out acts of aggression against another state. This is not an exhaustive enumeration, and any other act may constitute aggression if so determined by the United Nations Security Council which, in any case, is not bound by the definition of the General Assembly. No consideration of any nature may serve as justification for aggression.

Following the law of the Nuremberg Tribunal, the 1954 Draft Code of Offenses against the Peace and Security of Mankind drafted by the International Law Commission, and the 1970 General Assembly Declaration of Principles of International Law Concerning Friendly Relations and Cooperation among States in accordance with the Charter of the United Nations, a "war of aggression" is labeled as a most reprehensible act of aggression. It is branded as a crime against international peace, which means that it results in individual criminal responsibility under international law, whereas lesser forms of aggression give rise only to international responsibility—that is, state responsibility of a "civil" kind with an obligation to make reparation. Aggression is the major form of illegal use of force and constitutes one kind of what Article 39 of the United Nations Charter calls (without defining the term) "a breach of the peace." Like the fundamental Article 2(4) of the Charter which outlaws force, the 1974 definition of aggression is limited to "force," which a majority of opinion understands to mean "armed force"; hence, it excludes what sometimes (especially in Third World countries) is referred to as "economic aggression." Unlike the Charter's prohibition, the 1974 definition does not include "threat of force" in the concept of aggression and also protects the sovereignty of a state. Except for the case of sending armed bands and the like, the definition does not cover or mention the concept of "indirect aggression." No territorial acquisition or special advantage resulting from aggression can be recognized as lawful. The first illegal use of armed force constitutes *prima facie* evidence of an act of aggression ("priority principle"), although the Security Council may conclude otherwise in the light of other relevant circumstances, including the gravity of consequences of the act. *See also* COERCIVE MEASURES SHORT OF WAR, 304; COLLECTIVE SECURITY SYSTEM, 305; FORCE, ILLEGAL THREAT OR USE OF, 308; INDIRECT AGGRESSION, 311; INTERVENTION, 312; SELF-DEFENSE, RIGHT OF, 317; SELF-DEFENSE, RIGHT OF COLLECTIVE, 318; WAR, 320.

Significance   What constitutes aggression is one of the most controversial questions of international law. As emanating from the United Nations General Assembly, the 1974 definition of aggression does not represent an authoritative and legally binding understanding of this intractable and highly political phenomenon. At the San Francisco Conference in 1945, the United States successfully opposed attempts to insert a definition of aggression in the United Nations Charter. Such a definition in its view could never be comprehensive enough to encompass all cases of aggression or take into account all circumstances of individual cases. In the words of President Harry Truman, a definition of aggression would be "a trap to the innocent and an invitation to the guilty." Since aggression is not defined in the United Nations Charter, the Security Council must determine whether or not aggression has taken place in each particular case. Still, the question of the definition of aggression had been on the agenda of the United Nations since

1952, and the League of Nations had also grappled with the subject. Two approaches to the definition emerged: (1) the enumerative approach whereby all the acts constituting aggression are listed; and (2) the general definition approach of one general and comprehensive formula. The Special Committee followed a "mixed" approach in which a general formula precedes an enumeration of specific acts of aggression by way of illustration and without claim to being exhaustive. The 1974 definition did not solve the problem of defining aggression but at least provided some tests and criteria for qualifying certain acts as aggressive. However, in the absence of common international standards and in a world of political and ideological cleavages, it was impossible to arrive at a legally binding definition. The 1974 definition itself adopted a dual standard by leaving the door open to the lawfulness of the use of armed force in the name of the otherwise ambiguous and undefinable and inconsistently applied right of self-determination of "peoples" as well as recognizing that the intention of a state resorting to armed force might also be to exercise its legitimate right of self-defense. In the final analysis, only specific actions of states can be qualified as aggression by the Security Council provided that this political organ has the will to do so and is not frustrated by discord among its permanent members.

Coercive Measures Short of War   (304)

Unilateral measures of compulsion of various forms and degrees of intensity, including the use of armed force, undertaken by a state without belligerent intent against another state for the purpose of retaliating for injury suffered, enforcing legal rights, or attaining political or other advantages. Under traditional international law, coercive or "hostile" measures short of war, sometimes known as "self-help" measures, vary in form and intensity and their terminology lacks precision and consistency in use. Severance of diplomatic relations often precedes the application of specific measures short of war. Retorsion is still a relatively mild action in that an act of retorsion is legal in itself and retorsion does not involve resort to armed force. An act of reprisal, illegal in itself, is undertaken in response to an equally illegal act of the other state. Reprisals may be either short of force or by means of armed force. Pacific blockade was once resorted to by major European powers. As a measure short of war, "intervention" (a vague, political rather than legal term) covers a variety of interference in the affairs of a state, ranging from subtle diplomatic pressures to open dictatorial interference with or without the use of force. Where diplomacy ends and intervention as a "measure short of war" begins is often difficult to tell. Also, the boundary line between "measures short of war" and "war" may easily be blurred in cases of armed intervention resulting in *de facto* hostilities between the states concerned. A legitimate humanitarian intervention cannot be considered a dictatorial interference but still remains one form of measures short of war. *See also* CUBAN QUARANTINE, 1962, 306; FORCE, ILLEGAL THREAT OR USE OF, 308; HUMANITARIAN INTERVENTION, 310; INTERVENTION, 312; PACIFIC BLOCKADE, 314; REPRISALS, 315; RETORSION, 316; WAR, 320.

Significance   In the nineteenth century, great powers resorted to measures short of war, including the use of armed force, against weaker states in retaliation for real or alleged delinquencies committed by the target states. In view of the preponderance of force on the side of great powers, such measures usually remained short of war, which served as a rationale for their use as "pacific" tools of statecraft of a great power restraining itself from exercising its legitimate right to go to war. Still, international law developed rules governing the conditions of resorting to some measures short of war, for example, reprisals. The Covenant of the League of Nations (1919) and the General Treaty for the Renunciation of War (1928, Kellogg-Briand Pact) expressly limited resort to or prohibited war only. Their effect on the legality of measures short of war by means of armed force, and especially reprisals, was not clear. A committee of jurists appointed by the League's Council to report whether or not the Italian bombardment of the Greek island of Corfu in 1923 in reprisal for the murder by Greek extremists of an Italian general who was a member of the Greek-Albanian boundary commission violated the Covenant, expressed the opinion that such reprisals, even if not regarded as war, were incompatible with the obligation to settle by peaceful means disputes likely to lead to a rupture between states. Under the Charter of the United Nations, which banned the use of force in international relations, measures short of war involving threat or use of armed force became illegal. Other coercive measures, if applied proportionately to the injury suffered, appear to be legal. Despite the Charter's prohibition, states continue to resort even to armed measures short of war as the United Nations' mechanisms intended to substitute collective measures for unilateral action remain inadequate.

Collective Security System   (305)

The centralized system of international rules, embodied in the Charter of the United Nations, which governs the collective resort to force under the authority of the United Nations for the purpose of maintaining or restoring international peace and security. The legal framework of the collective security system is a logical consequence of the outlawry of force in international relations. The system is centralized in the United Nations Security Council, which is charged with primary responsibility for the maintenance of international peace and security. Enforcement action under regional arrangements or by regional agencies also requires prior authorization of the Security Council. Whereas in the pacific settlement of disputes (Chapter VI of the Charter) the Security Council may only make recommendations, in matters involving "threats to the peace, breaches of the peace, and acts of aggression" (Chapter VII of the Charter) it also has the power of making legally binding decisions. Since these three concepts are not defined in the Charter, the first task of the Council is to determine the existence of a threat to the peace, breach of the peace, or an act of aggression in each case brought to its attention by a state, the United Nations Secretary-General, or presumably also the General Assembly. The concept "threat to the peace" includes not only the threat of force under Article 2(4) of the Charter but, under the circumstances, also other phenomena such as civil war or even violation of human rights. A "breach of the peace" need not necessarily entail the use of armed force, and an "act of aggression" is not entirely coterminous with the use of armed force falling under Article 2(4) or an "armed attack" under Article 51 entitling a state to self-defense. Once the Security Council determines that there is a threat to the peace, breach of the peace, or act of aggression, it has the power to "call upon" (interpreted as meaning to "order") the parties concerned to comply with certain provisional measures (Article 40); make recommendations; decide on employment of measures not involving the use of armed force; or—if these would be inadequate or proved inadequate—to use force. Provisional measures might include calling upon the parties to cease fighting or to withdraw. The substance of recommendations (which are not mandatory) depends upon the discretion of the Security Council.

Enforcement action may be of two kinds: (1) measures against the delinquent state not involving the use of armed force (Article 41); and (2) military measures (Article 42) including demonstrations, blockade, and other operations. The former may include interruption of economic relations and means of communication, and the severance of diplomatic relations. The Council may either order or merely recommend such measures. Unlike the case of nonmilitary enforcement measures, no state is legally obliged to take part in military action against an aggressor unless it has concluded with the Security Council a "special agreement" under Article 43 of the Charter on making available to the Council specific numbers and types of forces, their degree of readiness and general location, and the nature of facilities and assistance to be provided. Since no agreement has ever been concluded because of the political split among the Council's permanent members, these provisions remain inoperative. There seems to be no legal way whereby the United Nations could undertake a military enforcement action mandatory for its members unless the Security Council should order them to take such action outside the special agreements procedure of Article 43 which—apart from being controversial legally— does not seem politically realistic because of an almost certain veto by at least one permanent member of the Council. The Military Staff Committee, a subsidiary organ of the Security Council consisting of the Chiefs of Staff of the five permanent members of the Security Council (China, France, USSR, United Kingdom, and the United States) has, for all practical purposes, been inactive. Although the matter is somewhat controversial, the Security Council may authorize a state to use force as it did in 1966 when it authorized the United Kingdom to search ships on the high seas to check whether or not they were carrying oil destined for Southern Rhodesia.

The Security Council has the power to make collective security decisions but, for political reasons, its decisions on nonprocedural matters (which include those under Chapter VII) require an affirmative vote of nine members, including the concurrent votes of the permanent members. Moreover, if the state against which enforcement measures are proposed happens to be a member of the Council, it also has the right to vote in its own case. In practice, and contrary to the wording of Article 27(3) of the United Nations Charter, abstention has not been regarded as a veto. Whether or not absence of a permanent member is to be treated as abstention is not clear. The General Assembly has no legal power to order mandatory collective security enforcement measures, but may make recommendations relating to the maintenance of international peace and security. However, whenever there is a question on which action is necessary or if a dispute or situation is before the Security Council, the General Assembly can only discuss it and must refer it to the Security Council. During the Korean War, when eventually the Security Council's decision making was blocked by the Soviet veto in the fall of 1950, in order to assert what it considered to be its "secondary responsibility" for the maintenance of international peace and security, the General Assembly adopted the so-called "Uniting for Peace" Resolution under which it resolved that if the Security Council failed to exercise its primary responsibility (in practice because of a veto), the Assembly shall consider the matter immediately with a view to making recommendations for collective measures. The Soviet Union opposed this Resolution as illegal, but in subsequent practice took advantage of it when expedience dictated it. *See also* AGGRESSION, 303; FORCE, ILLEGAL THREAT OR USE OF, 308; WAR, 320.

Significance   The legal framework of the United Nations collective security system is an improvement over the League of Nations' system. It is centralized in the Security Council, which has the power of making legally binding decisions, acts on behalf of all its members, and has the legal power to take enforcement action against the delinquent state. Still, the United Nations system has proved to be a failure like that of its predecessor. The ideological and political conflict involving the permanent members of the Security Council has prevented implementation of the vital provisions of the collective security system and made it a foregone conclusion that because of the veto the system would not operate against a permanent member or its protégé. The only cases where the Security Council has been able to order enforcement action were the comprehensive nonmilitary measures against Southern Rhodesia in 1966 and the ban on export of arms to South Africa in 1977. Compliance by United Nations members with these measures was not entirely satisfactory, however. No military enforcement action according to the Charter has ever been undertaken. The action in Korea (1950–1953) was legally an exercise of the right of collective self-defense under Article 51 of the Charter under the Security Council's authorization, rather than United Nations military action under Article 42 of the Charter. The Council recommended that member states assist the Republic of Korea in its defense against aggression from North Korea and place forces in a unified command under a U.S. commander. It is doubtful whether these forces were legally United Nations forces, although they were authorized by the Security Council to fly the United Nations flag. Where the Security Council dealt with threats to the peace, breaches of the peace, or acts of aggression, it has been reluctant to make a clear determination under Article 39. The reason for this posture has been either the desire to reach at least some kind of compromise decision or pure political expediency, particularly in cases of conflicts between Third World countries. Most provisional measures decided upon by the Council were phrased as recommendations and not orders.

The improvised United Nations actions on sending military observers and "peacekeeping forces" in areas of conflict in the Third World were not enforcement actions of the collective security system, although they were compatible with the purposes and principles of the Charter and in a general sense part of the collective security system. It is not clear which exact provisions of the Charter provided the legal basis for their creation. One possibility is that they were provisional measures under Article 40 and another that they were set up under Chapter VI of the Charter on "Pacific Settlement of Disputes." Concerning the competence to create peacekeeping forces, the Soviet Union and

France have followed the view that only the Security Council has such competence. Although the first peacekeeping force—UNEF I (United Nations Emergency Force I) patrolling the Egypt-Israel border (1956–1967)—was set up by the General Assembly (the Soviet Union abstaining in the vote), subsequent forces were created under resolutions of the Security Council: ONUC (*Opération des Nations Unies au Congo*) in the Congo (1960–1964), set up unanimously but subsequently opposed by the Soviet Union; UNFICYP (United Nations Force in Cyprus), (1964–); UNEF II, patrolling the Egypt-Israel cease-fire line, (1973–1979); UNDOF (United Nations Disengagement Observer Force) patrolling the Syria-Israel cease-fire line (1974–); and UNIFIL (United Nations Interim Force for Southern Lebanon) (1978–). All these peacekeeping operations reflected the determination of the United Nations to make at least some contribution to maintaining security in an international system in which its collective security system had only limited application.

Cuban Quarantine, 1962 (306)

The coercive measure short of war applied by the U.S. naval and air forces for four weeks during the so-called Cuban missile crisis in 1962. The Cuban quarantine was based on a resolution of the Council of the Organization of American States (OAS) acting as the Provisional Organ of Consultation. It was designed to interdict on the high seas the delivery to Cuba of specified offensive weapons carried by ships and craft of whatever nationality. *See also* BELLIGERENT BLOCKADE, 327; COERCIVE MEASURES SHORT OF WAR, 304; FORCE, ILLEGAL THREAT OR USE OF, 308; PACIFIC BLOCKADE, 314; WAR, 320.

Significance   The Cuban quarantine was a completely new type of maritime blockade the legality of which, however, is highly controversial. The measure was described by the United States deliberately as a "quarantine" and not a "blockade" since, under traditional international law, interference with shipping of third states would imply that it was a belligerent blockade. Yet the quarantine had features of both a pacific and belligerent blockade and displayed, in addition, some unique characteristics of its own. It was pacific since a state of war did not exist between the United States and Cuba, neither side manifested any belligerent intent (*animus belligerendi*), and no third state considered the incident as war. On the other hand, the application of the quarantine to vessels of third states exhibited features of belligerent blockade. Unlike a traditional blockade, the Cuban quarantine was not intended to blockade the coast of a state as such but only to interdict the supply of certain specific weapons to Cuba. Entry of other cargo and exit of all cargo and ships were not barred. Furthermore, vessels en route to Cuba were subject to visit and search, with possible exercise of force, but were subject only to "custody" and not to capture for any breach of the quarantine. Finally, the quarantine was proclaimed pursuant to a resolution of a regional arrangement (the 1947 Inter-American Treaty of Reciprocal Assistance, also known as the Rio Treaty), purporting to act in conformity with Chapter VIII of the United Nations Charter on regional arrangements. In order to justify the quarantine, the United States did not invoke the right of self-defense under Article 51 of the United Nations Charter, since reliance upon it would have created a dangerous precedent that might subsequently be abused by other countries and turned against the United States in some future crisis. The U.S. action in the Cuban quarantine has been criticized as inconsistent with the purposes of the United Nations, as a threat of force in breach of the United Nations Charter, and as a violation of the principle of freedom of the high seas. It has also been pointed out that there was no justification for the quarantine as a regional enforcement action since no authorization was obtained from the Security Council as required under Article 53(1) of the Charter, although the Security Council did discuss the quarantine without condemning it or adopting any resolution on the subject.

Enemy States Clauses   (307)

Article 107 and part of Article 53 of the United Nations Charter which provide, as an exception to the general prohibition of force, for the legality of action in relation to any state which, during World War II, was an enemy of any state signatory of the Charter. The enemy states clauses remain in the Charter despite their obsolete rationale. Article 107 sanctions as legal action taken or authorized as a result of war by the governments having responsibility for such action. Although under the general rule of Article 53 enforcement action by regional arrangements or agencies requires the authorization of the Security Council, no such authorization is required for measures taken against any former enemy state provided for pursuant to Article 107 or in regional arrangements directed against renewal of "aggressive policy" on the part of any such state until, on request of the governments concerned, the United Nations may be charged with the responsibility for preventing further aggression by such a state. *See also* AGGRESSION, 303; COLLECTIVE SECURITY SYSTEM, 305; FORCE, ILLEGAL THREAT OR USE OF, 308; INTERVENTION, 312.

Significance   The legal implications of the enemy state clauses, of particular interest to the Federal Republic of Germany (and possibly the German Democratic Republic), are controversial. In the Western view these clauses are clearly obsolete, since Article 107 is part of the Charter's chapter on "Transitional Security Arrangements" and the clauses were intended to cover the immediate postwar period, making no sense in a situation where all the former enemies are now signatories of the Charter (apart from the fact that there exists no single Germany, but two German states). Furthermore, in this interpretation, any discrimination against a member state would violate the United Nations principle of sovereign equality of the members of the United Nations. In any case, admission into the organization of the former enemy states (in the case of Germany its two successor states) automatically removed the enemy character of the states concerned since only peace-loving states can become members of the United Nations. On the other hand, the Soviet Union has never relinquished the right to invoke the clauses and made reference to them in justification of the invasion of Czechoslovakia in 1968—the country allegedly threatened by the "aggressive policy" of the Federal Republic of Germany. Although in 1970 the Soviet Union concluded a nonaggression treaty with the Federal Republic of Germany, it had made it clear that any such treaty was without prejudice to the special rights, including the right of intervention, derived from the enemy states clauses for the Soviet Union itself and for the regional arrangements of which it was a party. The enemy states clauses of the United Nations Charter may be used by the Soviet Union as a convenient legal escape clause for any future use of force against the Federal Republic of Germany.

Force, Illegal Threat or Use of   (308)

The threat or use of force in international relations against the territorial integrity or political independence of any state or in any other manner inconsistent with the purposes of the United Nations. Illegal threat or use of force, as defined above according to Article 2(4) of United Nations Charter, is recognized as a rule of customary international law binding all states, both members and nonmembers. Unlike previous attempts to deal with international violence (such as the League of Nations and the Kellogg-Briand Pact), the ban in the Charter covers not only war but the "threat or use of force" regardless of whether or not it is "war" in the technical legal sense, "nonwar" hostilities, or any other illegal acts of resort to force. It should be noted that the terms "war" and "aggression" are not mentioned in Article 2(4) and the sweeping ban of force encompasses even such theoretical cases as war as a "duel" by mutual consent, where neither side would commit aggression. Under the Charter, there are four exceptions to the prohibition of the threat or use of force in international relations: (1) collective security enforcement action ordered by the Security Council under Article 42; (2) enforcement action by regional arrangements or agencies with prior authorization of the Security Council; (3) self-defense; and (4) action against former enemy states under the "enemy states clauses." In addition, there may exist special circumstances where the use of force is permitted under general international law: by a warship on the high seas against a vessel suspected of piracy or slave trade and offering resistance; in response to intrusion into territorial domain (e.g., by a foreign military aircraft); against foreign troops in a state's territory, refusing to withdraw after that state has revoked its consent to their presence; or in case of a natural catastrophe in a foreign territory if the sovereign of that territory is not able or willing to contain the danger threatening a neighboring state. Although the proscription of force under article 2(4) is interpreted by some to mean that force used for purposes other than "against the territorial integrity or political independence of any State" (for example, to enforce international law) is legal, the prevailing view interprets the provision broadly as prohibition of any force, in the light of the phrase "or in any other manner inconsistent with the purposes of the United Nations," including the overriding purpose to maintain international peace and security. This interpretation was also supported by the International Court of Justice (ICJ), in the *Corfu Channel* case (*United Kingdom v. Albania*, 1949), in which the Court, rejecting Great Britain's argument that its action of minesweeping in the Albanian territorial sea had threatened neither the territorial integrity nor the political independence of Albania, held that the British operation had violated the fundamental rule of the Charter on the prohibition of force. The rule of Article 2(4) was further elaborated in the 1970 Declaration on Principles of International Law Concerning Friendly Relations and Cooperation among States in Accordance with the Charter of the United Nations, adopted without vote by the United Nations General Assembly. This Declaration specifies such categories of the threat or use of force as (1) wars of aggression; (2) propaganda for wars of aggression; (3) threat or use of force to violate international boundaries or international lines of demarcation; (4) acts of reprisal involving the use of force; (5) forcible action to deprive peoples of self-determination, freedom, and independence; (6) organizing armed bands for incursion into another state's territory; (7) organizing, instigating, assisting, or participating in acts of civil strife or terrorist acts in another state, or acquiescing in organized activities within its territory directed towards the commission of such acts of force; and (8) acquisition of foreign territory by the threat or use of force. Article 2(4) bans force only in international relations, which means that force may be used against insurgents or otherwise in a situation of civil war. The Third World countries, however, supported by the communist states and some Western nations, assert that a "war of national liberation" is an international war in which only the colonial people use force legally. There is some uncertainty and controversy concerning the question whether illegal force means armed force only or includes economic and political pressures as claimed by many Third World countries, but the view prevails that economic and political forms of coercion do not come under the prohibition of force in Article 2(4) which is understood as referring to the threat or use of armed force only. Yet in an extreme (perhaps only academic) case of economic strangulation of a state, such restrictive interpretation of the Charter's prohibition of force would clearly conflict with the basic purposes and principles of the United Nations.

The United Nations Charter's ban on force covers not only the use but also the threat of force, but the Charter does not provide guidelines clarifying the concept of threat. In international relations, threat of force occurs when a state expressly or in implied ways communicates its determination to resort to force conditional on nonacceptance by the threatened state of certain demands of the threatening state. The most typical explicit form of threat is an ultimatum; that is, a formal communication addressed by a state to another state requiring the latter to accept within a given time limit (usually very short, such as 24 hours) the demands made upon it or be prepared to face war or other acts of armed force. Under Article 2(4) the existence of implied threat of force depends upon the specific circumstances and must be assessed on its own merits. It may take the form of armaments, military buildup, a demonstration of force, an ultimatum, and the like. The purpose and intent of the threatening state must be a decisive factor in qualifying a behavior as threat. Whether action in self-defense is allowed against the threat of force is a controversial issue related to the question of the legality of anticipatory self-defense. *See also* AGGRESSION, 303; COERCIVE MEASURES SHORT OF WAR, 304; COLLECTIVE SECURITY SYSTEM, 305; GENERAL TREATY FOR THE RENUNCIATION OF WAR (1928), 309; SELF-DEFENSE, RIGHT OF, 317; SELF-PRESERVATION, DOCTRINE OF, 319; WAR, 320.

Significance   The introduction in 1945 of a sweeping ban on the threat or use of force in international relations was the culmination of efforts to limit resort to force beginning with the Hague Convention II on the Limitation of the Employment of Force for the Recovery of Contract Debts (1907) and a landmark in the history of international law. The outlawry of force has undoubtedly had some restraining influence on states desiring to undertake unilateral military action; but, in general, there has been a serious gap between the letter of the law and actual international practice, which has provided numerous instances of resort to violence in relations between states. Apart from the fundamental extralegal considerations on the causes of violence and specific situations in an era of overseas decolonization where the Third World countries—without any legal basis in the United Nations Charter—assert the legality of force against a colonial state (e.g. India's assertion of the legality of its invasion of Portuguese Goa in 1960), there are some inherent weaknesses in the system of international law governing force which have contributed to continued violence in international relations. One problem is that the law governing force employs imprecise and ambiguous terms such as "force," "aggression," "self-defense," and the like, which lend themselves to unilateral interpretation in rationalizing a legally doubtful or dubious conduct. Even organs of the United Nations called upon to make a determination on the legality of an act of force have sometimes been divided in their opinion, let alone blocked in their decision making by political conflict. Another fundamental weakness of contemporary international law is that although it proscribes violence it has developed no orderly procedures and institutions for compulsory settlement of disputes unresolved by negotiation. As a result, a state may violate another state's rights with impunity by means other than armed force, and the injured state remains helpless since it is not allowed to respond by armed force even to the most grievous violations. In such situations, temptation to resort to armed force may prevail over respect for the law. One paradoxical effect of the transformation of the international law governing resort to force in an international political system in which violence is still endemic is the fact that traditional rules must still be applied to assess the conditions of legality of such phenomena as self-defense and reprisals and to regulate the conduct of armed conflict, which must be subject to some moderating influence of international law even insofar as the states violating the law of the Charter are concerned.

General Treaty for the Renunciation of War (1928)   (309)

A multilateral treaty of indefinite duration, commonly known as the Kellogg-Briand Pact or Pact of Paris, in which the parties condemn recourse to war for the solution of international controversies, renounce it as an instrument of national policy in their relations with one another, and agree to settle all disputes or conflicts solely by pacific means. The Kellogg-Briand Pact entered into force in 1929, and sixty-three states were parties to it when World War II started in 1939. As of 1 January 1984 sixty-four states were parties, including the United States, the Soviet Union, and even some newly independent states. It has never been terminated although, for all practical purposes, it has been superseded by the United Nations Charter, specifically its Article

2(3)(4). *See also* AGGRESSION, 303; COERCIVE MEASURES SHORT OF WAR, 304; JUST WAR DOCTRINE, 313; FORCE, ILLEGAL THREAT OR USE OF, 308; WAR, 320.

Significance   Although it turned out to be a futile bar to war, the Kellogg-Briand Pact (named after the U.S. Secretary of State and French Foreign Minister who negotiated the treaty) is a historical landmark in international law, because for the first time aggressive war was outlawed in international relations. The customary right of self-defense is not restricted or impaired in any way, however. The Pact is an advance over the Covenant of the League of Nations which had gaps allowing resort to war under certain circumstances. In addition, the Pact enabled the United States (which was not a member of the League) to join in a general outlawry of war. Initially the Pact of Paris did not apply to relations between parties and nonparties (several Latin American states were among them), but eventually this distinction ceased to apply since the basic principles of the Pact became part of customary international law. After World War II, the Pact was invoked by international tribunals and municipal courts in the trials of war criminals charged with the crimes against peace. While the Kellogg-Briand Pact is a major legal achievement in comparison to the Covenant of the League of Nations, it is not without some defects of its own. It does not make clear, for example, whether or not and to what extent armed measures short of war such as reprisals are prohibited, and it does not establish any machinery for enforcement of its rules. In general, the Kellogg-Briand Pact is an idealistic instrument which still remains far ahead of the actual state of international politics it purports to regulate.

Humanitarian Intervention   (310)

Forcible intervention by one state in another state's territory for the purpose of protecting individuals from threats to their lives, inhumane and cruel treatment, or persecution. A distinction is frequently made between humanitarian intervention to protect the intervening state's own nationals and intervention to protect foreign nationals (including those of the state in which intervention takes place). The latter type of intervention is sometimes referred to as "humanitarian intervention" in the strict sense of the term. Both kinds of intervention are a most controversial issue in international law. The Third World countries, supported by the Soviet Union and other communist states, consider all humanitarian intervention as a violation of the principle of territorial sovereignty. In the West, opinions are divided among publicists and governments. In one view, intervention by force to protect nationals is allowed in exceptional cases where there is imminent threat of irreparable injury to them, the territorial sovereign fails to protect them in conformity with generally accepted standards or morality and decency, and the intervention is strictly confined to protecting nationals against injury. The opposing view holds that, although intervention to protect nationals was lawful before the United Nations Charter, it is illegal as a violation of the ban on force in international relations under Article 2(4) of the Charter. Furthermore, it is claimed that such intervention may provide a legal pretext for the pursuit of national rather than humanitarian interests of the intervening state. Although the matter is not entirely without controversy, there is more consensus on the view that humanitarian intervention to protect foreign nationals is illegal. *See also* AGGRESSION, 303; FORCE, ILLEGAL THREAT OR USE OF, 308; INTERVENTION, 312.

Significance   Although some claim that the doctrine of humanitarian intervention was never part of international law, the opinion prevails that traditional international law recognized the lawfulness of such intervention to protect individuals (both nationals and nonnationals) from an imminent threat of injury or death in a situation where the local sovereign was either unwilling or unable to protect them, or when the government itself was guilty of treating them in a way shocking the conscience of mankind. Humanitarian intervention was resorted to by European powers in Turkey and in China in the nineteenth century. In the post–World War II era, interventions by Western powers in Third World countries were criticized by the latter and in some cases condemned by the United Nations. For example, the Belgian intervention in the Congo in 1960—ostensibly on purely humanitarian grounds—was condemned by the Security Council. While it is true that—as evidenced by the British and French intervention in Egypt in 1956 and the U.S. interventions in the Dominican Republic in 1965 and in Grenada in 1983—humanitarian intervention may be a pretext for intervention for political reasons, the fact is that in situations of legitimate humanitarian emergency the manifest inability of the United Nations to set up an effective international machinery for protecting innocent lives simply leaves no alternative other than unilateral humanitarian intervention. The case of the U.S. humanitarian intervention to save several hundred white residents in the eastern Congo during the civil war in 1964 and the Israeli Entebbe raid into Uganda in 1976 to rescue about one hundred Jewish passengers of a hijacked Air France airliner are examples of such intervention.

Indirect Aggression   (311)

Hostile acts against a state whereby the aggressor state, without itself committing the acts as a state (1) organizes, encourages, or tolerates the organization of irregular forces or armed bands—including mercenaries—for incursion into the territory of another state; or (2) organizes, assists, foments, finances, incites, or tolerates subversive, terrorist, or armed activities directed toward the violent overthrow of the regime of another state, or interferes in civil strife in another state. According to the prevailing doctrine and the United Nations General Assembly, the first type of activity [(1)] is an illegal use of armed force. It constitutes aggression and is listed, without mentioning the term "indirect aggression," among acts of aggression illustrating the definition of aggression adopted by the General Assembly in 1974. In this definition only sending of bands and similar groups is considered as one of the listed acts of aggression. The alternative type of activity [(2)] is generally subject to the prohibition of intervention in the internal affairs of a state, but has also been described as "indirect aggression," a concept which in the opinion of some countries and publicists should also encompass such acts as hostile or ideological propaganda or aggression. Whether or not economic coercion—in the sense of unilateral action to deprive a state of economic resources or to endanger its basic economy—can be included within the concept of aggression is a controversial matter, depending upon whether or not the prohibition of force under the United Nations Charter is interpreted restrictively as only armed force or broadly as including other forms of coercion, such as economic coercion. *See also* AGGRESSION, 303; FORCE, ILLEGAL THREAT OR USE OF, 308; INTERVENTION, 312.

Significance   The concept of indirect aggression poses an even greater challenge to the theory of international law than that of aggression in its more traditional meaning. The elusive threats to a state's integrity that arise from "indirect aggression" are compounded by the fact that they often occur within the context of civil strife. This raises questions related to admissibility of intervention in a civil conflict as well as the question of aggression. Indirect aggression is not a precise term in international law, and its interpretation in international practice is far from being consistent, depending very much on changing national interests and the political ideology of the states involved. For example, the Western nations oppose the Third World's idea that economic coercion is an act of indirect aggression against which the legitimate right of self-defense may be exercised by the target state. Although the Third World states failed to include economic aggression in the 1974 definition of aggression, several United Nations General Assembly resolutions have denounced economic and political coercion as subverting sovereign rights of states. Among these resolutions are, for example, the Declaration of the Inadmissibility of Intervention in Domestic Affairs of States and the Protection of Their Independence and Sovereignty (1965), the Declaration on Principles of International Law Concerning Friendly Relations and Cooperation among States in Accordance with the Charter of the United Nations (1970), and the Charter of Economic Rights and Duties of States (1974). The Charter of the Organization of American States (OAS) includes an explicit duty of nonintervention. Ironically, following the application of the Arab oil embargo against some Western states in 1973 (with the approval of most of the Third World countries), the Third World's position was undermined by its use of previously condemned economic coercion as a legal tool in international law. On the other hand, a number of publicists in the West, particularly in the United States, criticized the alleged illegality of the embargo, thereby endorsing the antieconomic aggression injunctions of the Third World–inspired General Assembly resolutions.

Intervention   (312)

Dictatorial interference by a state or group of states in the affairs (internal or external) of another state or states, frequently involving the threat or use of force, for the purpose of maintaining or altering existing conditions. Although wide consensus exists among publicists and states that intervention is, in principle, unlawful, the definition and scope of this prohibition as well as the legality of the target state's response are highly controversial. Also the practice of states, following as it does the pragmatic considerations of the moment, is inconsistent and confusing, with the resulting gap between the doctrine of absolute prohibition of intervention and actual international behavior of states. Intervention is a highly political concept which has been used indiscriminately to cover all kinds of interference in the affairs of states, from hardly discernible diplomatic pressure to full-scale armed intervention. International consensus on the prohibition of intervention has been voiced in numerous resolutions of the United Nations General Assembly, of which the 1965 Declaration of the Inadmissibility of Intervention in the Domestic Affairs of States and the Protection of Their Independence and Sovereignty (adopted by 109 votes to 0 with 1 abstention), is an outstanding example. Failure to define the terms used in this Declaration was the reason for the abstention by the United Kingdom in the vote on this instrument. The Declaration on Principles of International Law Concerning Friendly Relations and Cooperation among States in Accordance with the Charter of the United Nations, adopted without vote by the General Assembly in 1970, reiterates and develops the prohibition of intervention "for any reason whatever." Under this Declaration "armed intervention and all other forms of interference or attempted threats against the personality of the State or against its political, economic, and cultural elements, are in violation of international law." Armed intervention violates the United Nations Charter's ban on resort to force and each state's right to territorial integrity and political independence. Other more subtle forms of intervention, also named in the Declarations of 1965 and 1970 and sometimes encompassed in the concept of "indirect aggression," include support of activities directed toward the violent overthrow of the regime of another state or interference in civil strife in another state.

International practice is not consistent in the matter of intervention in civil war. The legality of such intervention, especially at the request of the incumbent government (awkwardly referred to as intervention by invitation or invitational intervention), is a matter of debate; and under some definitions sending armed forces at the genuine request of a government to assist it in a civil war is not regarded as intervention at all. For the Third World countries (supported by the communist states), the only exception to the prohibition of support of insurgents in a civil war concerns "wars of national liberation," by which only those wars to end a Western power's overseas rule are meant. In the matter of humanitarian intervention, especially one to protect nationals, the Western doctrine and states in general admit the legality of intervention under certain circumstances while the Third World countries categorically reject it. Enforcement action under the authority of the United Nations Security Council and stationing peacekeeping forces by the United Nations or a regional organization with the permission of the state concerned are not considered an unlawful intervention. Intervention by virtue of the enemy states clauses of the United Nations Charter would also be lawful except that these clauses are obsolete, at least in the Western view. *See also* AGGRESSION, 303; ENEMY STATES CLAUSES, 307; FORCE, ILLEGAL THREAT OR USE OF, 308; HUMANITARIAN INTERVENTION, 310; INDIRECT AGGRESSION, 311; WAR, 320.

Significance   Historically, states (especially great powers) have resorted to armed intervention to protect their interests and those of their nationals in weaker states. Since World War I ideological motivation has been added to others, as evidenced by the example of the Spanish Civil War, 1936–1939. After World War II, there has been a sharp contrast between the doctrine of nonintervention and the actual practice of states. Innumerable cases of intervention have been recorded in most regions of the world by states of all ranks for ideological or power politics reasons, or nationalist grounds, and for other reasons such as humanitarian considerations. In their respective spheres of influence, both superpowers have resorted to armed intervention. The Soviet Union intervened in Hungary (1956), Czechoslovakia (1968), and Afghanistan (1979–), as well as in Poland, where intervention occurred in the form of dictatorial interference in the domestic affairs of that country by means of the threat of armed force (1981). The United States intervened in the Dominican Republic (1965) and in Grenada (1983). There have also been numerous cases of armed intervention at the request of the state concerned. The U.S. interventions in Lebanon (1958) and in South Vietnam in the 1960s and early 1970s; British intervention in Jordan (1958); similar actions of France in a number of African countries; of Cuba in Angola and Ethiopia in the 1970s and 1980s; and the U.S., British, French, and Italian armed presence in Lebanon (1983) are only a few examples. In each case, the intervening state rationalized its intervention in terms of international law, taking advantage of ambiguities in the law governing resort to force and intervention. Uncertainties in the text of a treaty may also serve as a pretext for armed intervention, as evidenced by the Turkish military action in Cyprus (1974–). Covert intervention directed at subverting a foreign government poses additional problems of proof which are equally—if not more—intractable than resort to open armed intervention. In an international system divided by ideological and political conflicts, interventions are likely to continue, especially in politically unstable regions of the world, until international law and organizations succeed in substituting effective collective measures for unilateral resort to military force and other forms of interference in the affairs of states.

Just War Doctrine   (313)

A doctrine of early classical publicists, adopted from Christian theologians of the Middle Ages, which distinguished between just war (*bellum justum*) and unjust war (*bellum injustum*). Under the just war doctrine, to be just, a war must have a just cause and righteous intention. There were differences in formulating the tests of a war being just, however. In general, a just war was one waged in self-defense, to avenge injuries and punish wrongs, or to obtain reparation for a prior illegal act committed by the other side. A war against pagans or heretics, being commanded by God, was also regarded by some to be just. *See also* AGGRESSION, 303; FORCE, ILLEGAL THREAT OR USE OF, 308; SELF-DEFENSE, RIGHT OF, 317; SELF-DEFENSE, RIGHT OF COLLECTIVE, 318; WAR, 320.

Significance   The just war doctrine can be traced to the writings of Cicero in the first century B.C., whose ideas were developed by Christian theologians beginning with St. Augustine at the turn of the fifth century. Conditions of just war were first formulated on the foundations of canon law by Raymond Peñaforte in the thirteenth century, followed by St. Thomas Aquinas among others. The teachings of these church scholars on distinguishing between just and unjust wars were eventually adopted by the early classical writers on the law of nations such as Alberico Gentili and his successor Hugo Grotius. All of them, however, approached the question of just war from a purely subjective point of view, admitting the possibility of both sides having a just cause and in good conscience believing in being in the right even though one of them might have been "objectively" wrong. As a result, the just war doctrine could not be objectively applied to determine whether or not a war was legal and, strictly speaking, the distinction between just and unjust war never became part of the actual law of nations although each state resorting to war would invoke the "justice" of its cause. Eventually, in the eighteenth century, the distinction was virtually abandoned by the doctrine of the law of nations. In international practice, a war fought to defend a "vital" interest was believed to be justified but, since each sovereign state remained the sole judge of what that interest actually was, wars could be fought for practically any arbitrary reason, and international jurists of the nineteenth century abandoned attempts to regulate recourse to war, concentrating on the legality of methods of the conduct of war (*jus in bello*) rather than on the legality of war as such (*jus ad bellum*). It was not until after World War I that the doctrine of just war was in a sense revived, providing an ideological underpinning to the limitations placed by the Covenant of the League of Nations (1919) upon resort to war and to the condemnation of aggressive war by the Kellogg-Briand Pact of 1928. The trend culminated in the Charter of the United Nations (1945) which, by establishing a fundamental distinction between illegal and legal resort to force, has in a way reestablished on the legal plane the old distinction between unjust and just war. However, in an international system of sovereign states with clashing national interests and conflicting ideologies, the Charter's distinction is as difficult to apply in practice as the classical distinction between just and unjust wars.

Pacific Blockade   (314)

A coercive measure short of war whereby a state or a group of states bars access to the coast of a state or part of it for the purpose of preventing entry and exit of ships of the blocked state (as well as those ships of the blockading state or states). In view of the prohibition of force by the Charter of the United Nations, pacific blockade is unlawful and is listed among acts qualifying as aggression as defined and adopted by the United Nations General Assembly in 1974. However, pacific blockade is lawful if ordered by the United Nations Security Council as an enforcement measure executed on behalf of the United Nations. *See also* AGGRESSION, 303; BLOCKADE, BELLIGERENT, 327; COER-CIVE MEASURES SHORT OF WAR, 304; CUBAN QUARANTINE, 326; FORCE, ILLEGAL THREAT OR USE OF, 308.

Significance   Under traditional international law, pacific blockade was resorted to by great powers against weaker states to obtain repara-tion for alleged wrongs. Sometimes the powers would act in concert to coerce the blockaded state into complying with their demands. Since 1814, more than twenty instances of blockade have been recorded, most of them by Great Britain and France. The best known was the 1902 joint blockade of Venezuela by Great Britain, Germany, and Italy to coerce that country to honor claims filed against it by the three powers' nationals. Whether or not the blockading power could apply its coercive measures to the vessels of third states was not entirely clear. It was due to the protest against the blockade of Venezuela in 1902 that the blockading powers proclaimed their measures to be a belligerent blockade so that technically a state of war existed for a period of time between them and Venezuela (which under the laws of war entitled them to search neutral shipping). Eventually the view prevailed that, in the case of pacific blockade, the blockading state had no right to apply the blockade to vessels of third countries. Since World War II, no instances of pacific blockade conforming to the requirements of tradi-tional international law have occurred. The 1949 blockade by Nationalist China of ports held by the Chinese People's Republic was more of a belligerent blockade since it applied also to vessels of third countries (against their protests), and the 1962 Cuban "quarantine" was a unique case in the records of coercive measures short of war. The blockade by the United Kingdom of the then Portuguese port of Beira was authorized by the Security Council in 1966 as part of the United Nations enforcement measures against Southern Rhodesia.

Reprisals   (315)

Coercive measures short of war, directed by a state against another state in retaliation for alleged acts of the latter and as a means for obtaining reparation or satisfaction for such acts. Reprisals differ from retorsion in that retorsion is retaliation by means of legal acts, whereas reprisals are retaliatiory acts which, by themselves, would be illegal. Reprisals as a measure short of war must be distinguished from reprisals in time of war designed to compel the other belligerent to comply with the laws of war. Reprisals may take the form of action not involving armed force, or they may be in the form of armed action against the offending state.

Whereas under traditional international law both forms of reprisals were lawful under certain conditions, armed reprisals are illegal in contemporary international law as violating the United Nations Charter's prohibition of the use of force. The 1970 Declaration on Principles of International Law Concerning Friendly Relations and Cooperation among States in Accordance with the Charter of the United Nations explicitly prohibits acts of reprisal involving the use of force. Reprisals short of the use of armed force are still allowed and may assume a variety of forms—nonperformance of treaty obligations, seizure of the offending state's property, or taking into custody its nationals. In former times other measures were also used, such as seizure of the offending state's ships found in the waters of the injured state, known as "embargo." (This measure must be distinguished from two other concepts: embargo in the law of war and neutrality; and embargo in the meaning of a ban on exports and/or imports from and to a country which is a legal measure unless in violation of treaty obligations.) Seizure of the offending state's ships or property on the high seas and pacific blockade were also among acts of reprisals resorted to in the past. The practice of the so-called "special reprisal," whereby a state authorized a private individual by its "letters of marque" to redress, by an act of reprisal against the offending state or its citizens, the wrong inflicted upon him by that state, had become obsolete by the end of the eighteenth century. Before the United Nations Charter banned resort to force, the only restriction on forcible reprisals had been the Hague Convention No. II (the Porter Convention), which prohibited such reprisals for the purpose of recovering contract debts unless the debtor state refused arbitration or did not comply with the arbitration award. To be legitimate, the allowable reprisals must meet three conditions, as laid down in the *Naulilaa* arbitration (*Portugal v. Germany*, 1928): (1) there must have been an illegal act on the part of the offending state; (2) an unsatisfied demand for redress must have been made; and (3) the reprisals must be reasonably proportionate to the injury suffered. *See also* COERCIVE MEASURES SHORT OF WAR, 304; FORCE, ILLEGAL THREAT OR USE OF, 308; RETORSION, 316.

Significance   Historically, reprisals were resorted to by more powerful states as retaliatory measures against weaker states. The United States employed reprisals on several occasions; for example, against Nicaragua in 1854 by shelling one of its ports and against Mexico in 1914 by occupying Veracruz. In more recent times, armed reprisals have been a common occurrence in the context of the Israeli-Arab relations. These have involved Israel's punitive raids in Lebanon, such as the attack on the Beirut airport in 1968 and many subsequent incursions into Lebanon to destroy anti-Israeli guerrilla bases located in that country, sometimes on the legally dubious grounds of "hot pursuit." In conditions of frequent violence and counterviolence, the line between illegal punitive reprisals and possibly legal anticipatory self-defense tends to be blurred as demonstrated also by the U.S. air raids on Libya in 1986. Another area where armed reprisals have been used is the South-West Africa (Namibia)-Angola border where South African incursions into Angola against SWAPO (South West Africa People's Organization) bases created problems similar to those on the Israeli-Lebanese border. All these and other cases of reprisals point to the inadequacy of the contemporary international law of armed reprisals based on the sweeping prohibition of resort to force found in the United Nations Charter. In international practice, the offended state often has no legal possibility of remedy and leaves its leaders with the perception of having no choice but to respond with force against violations of its legitimate rights.

Retorsion (316)
A legal but deliberately unfriendly act directed by a state against another state in retaliation for an equally unfriendly though legal act, for the purpose of compelling that state to alter its unfriendly conduct. Unlike reprisals, the acts of both sides are within the bounds of international law, although a lawful response to an unlawful act would also be categorized as retorsion. Retorsion is never undertaken in the form of armed force, since it then would be an act of illegal reprisal. Retorsion need not be retaliation in kind, although it frequently assumes the form of acts of the same kind as the original unfriendly act. Examples of retorsion include the severance of diplomatic relations; limiting the freedom of movement of foreign diplomats or nationals or their expulsion; retricting foreign nationals' rights to exercise professions; discriminatory tariffs; banning exports; and curbing the fishing rights of an offending state in the retaliating state's waters. *See also* COERCIVE MEASURES SHORT OF WAR, 304; REPRISALS, 315.

Significance Retorsion has been a common method of retaliation in international relations. Since it does not involve the application of armed force, it remains, in principle, lawful in contemporary international law. However, depending upon the circumstances, an otherwise lawful act of retorsion might become unlawful if it endangered international peace and security, since under Article 2(3) of the United Nations Charter and general international law disputes between states must be settled by peaceful means in a manner that does not endanger peace and security.

Self-defense, Right of   (317)

The inherent right of individual or collective self-defense if an armed attack occurs against a state, until the Security Council has taken the measures necessary to restore and maintain international peace and security. This definition of the right of self-defense is based on Article 51 of the United Nations Charter, which constitutes a major exception from the general ban on resort to force in international relations. Although the Charter refers to "a Member" and not "a State," there is general agreement that it simply means "any state." As formulated in the Charter, the scope of the right of self-defense is a subject of fundamental controversy. There are two conflicting interpretations: (1) restrictive and (2) extensive. In the prevailing restrictive view, the right of self-defense (including self-defense by means of armed force) exists if and only if an armed attack occurs. This means that no right of self-defense by armed force exists against hostile action which does not constitute an armed attack however lethal such action might be for the existence of the state, and only nonarmed force coercive measures can in such cases be used in self-defense. Secondly, this interpretation implies that anticipatory (preemptive or preventive) self-defense—that is, defense against an impending attack—is not allowed since the Charter limits self-defense to cases where the armed attack "occurs," (although the French text is rather ambiguous, reading "dans un cas où un Membre des Nations Unies est l'object d'une agression armée ["in a case where a member of the United Nations is the object of armed attack"]). According to the extensive interpretation, the right of self-defense (including armed self-defense) is allowed against an armed attack and against other violations of a state's fundamental rights which do not amount to an armed attack. In this interpretation, anticipatory self-defense is allowed. In the broad construction, the phrase "if an armed attack occurs" is merely one (albeit major) illustration of the broader, natural right of self-defense, an illustration worthy of being emphasized by the Charter. The supporters of this view claim that the Charter does not impair the scope of the "inherent" (natural) right of self-defense under customary international law. It is contended that while less than the pure instinct of self-preservation, this right still allows self-defense by armed force not only against an armed attack but also in the defense of rights other than the right to be free from armed attack. However, no clear roster of such other essential rights has ever been established in traditional law. Despite the controversy concerning the scope of the right to resort to armed self-defense, there is general agreement that armed self-defense need not be limited to defense against attacks on a state's territory; it is allowed to repulse attacks on ships on the high seas and ships exercising a legitimate right of innocent passage. The peacekeeping forces of the United Nations or a regional organization also have the right or self-defense against an armed attack. The right to resort to armed force to protect nationals abroad on grounds of self-defense is controversial, however.

There appears to be consensus that the exercise of the right of self-defense under the United Nations Charter is subject to the minimum conditions developed still under customary international law. Specifically, the necessity for self-defense must be "instant, over-whelming, leaving no choice of means, and no moment for delibera-tion," the criteria formulated in 1841 by U.S. Secretary of State Daniel Webster in the *Caroline* incident of 1837 between the United States and Great Britain and adopted by the International Military Tribunal at Nuremberg in its 1946 judgment. In addition, acts of self-defense must be proportionate to the severity of the attack and justified by the seriousness of the danger. Under no circumstances can they turn into armed reprisals. Under Article 51 of the United Nations Charter, measures taken in the exercise of the right of self-defense must be immediately reported to the Security Council. *See also* AGGRESSION, 303; COLLECTIVE SECURITY SYSTEM, 305; FORCE, ILLEGAL THREAT OR USE OF, 308; INDIRECT AGGRESSION, 311; REPRISALS, 315; SELF-DEFENSE, RIGHT OF COLLECTIVE, 318; SELF-PRESERVATION, DOCTRINE OF, 319.

Significance   The exact scope of the right of self-defense is un-certain, allowing states to invoke it depending upon their perceived national interest even in those situations where the legitimacy of self-defense is rather dubious. For example, in 1951 and 1954 Egypt invoked this right in justification of its interference with the passage of ships through the Suez Canal with cargo destined for Israel, and in 1956 Israel and the United Kingdom referred to the same right when attacking Egypt. Also, in 1986 the United States rationalized its bomb-ing of Libya in terms of self-defense. In these and other cases, the United Nations Security Council (and the General Assembly) followed the restrictive interpretation of Article 51 of the Charter, rejecting the argument that armed self-defense was lawful in response to acts other than armed attack. Yet even the United Nations has not been entirely consistent—especially in the matter of anticipatory self-defense—since, following the preemptive strike by Israel against its Arab neighbors in 1967, it failed to condemn that country as an aggressor. This allows the conclusion that at least some members of the United Nations regarded the Israeli attack as an act of legitimate self-defense. It is also of interest to note that, in 1946, in its report to the Security Council, the United Nations Atomic Energy Commission admitted the possibility of a preventive self-defense strike against a country which would commit a grave violation of the treaty banning the manufacture of atomic weapons, then under consideration by the Commission.

Self-defense, Right of Collective   (318)

An inherent right of a state or group of states to come to the defense of another state against which an armed attack occurs, until the Security Council has taken the measures necessary to restore and maintain international peace and security. The right of collective self-defense under Article 51 of the United Nations Charter is interpreted by a great majority of publicists and by state practice as the right of states to come to the defense of a state whose situation meets the conditions of legitimate individual self-defense under the Charter. Contrary to some commentators, there is no requirement that the state or states coming to the aid of the victim of armed attack should also be in a situation entitling it or them respectively to individual self-defense. The legal conditions of self-defense in general, and controversies relating to the interpretation of the right of self-defense, apply to the exercise of the right of collective self-defense as well. *See also* SELF-DEFENSE, RIGHT OF, 317.

Significance The use of the term collective self-defense in article 51 of the United Nations Charter is somewhat misleading and has nothing to do with "collective security." The term "collective defense" or "defense of another state" would be more appropriate. The lawfulness of collective defense in this sense is confirmed by the *travaux préparatoires* of the 1945 San Francisco Conference on International Organization and subsequent practice of states which, in view of the paralysis of the collective security system of the United Nations, concluded a number of bi- and multilateral treaties stipulating, with explicit reference to Article 51, that one party would come to the aid of another if the latter was an object of an armed attack. Both the North Atlantic Treaty (1949) and the Soviet-sponsored Treaty of Friendship and Cooperation and Mutual Assistance (the Warsaw Pact) of 1955 are explicitly based on Article 51. The right to conclude collective defense alliances has never been questioned by the United Nations, and the concept of collective self-defense itself was originally introduced into the Charter to fit regional arrangements (in particular the Pan American System) into the global security system of the United Nations.

Self-preservation, Doctrine of   (319)

A doctrine of traditional international law, rejected under the law of the United Nations Charter, under which a state was allowed to use force if its vital interests were at stake. The doctrine of self-preservation, or (as it was also known) necessity or self-help, was invoked in the period of international law when resort to force was considered legal. What interests and rights could be covered by this plea was not clear, and in the name of survival states claimed to have the right to resort to forcible self-help even against an innocent state on the assumption that their legal duties were subordinated to the supreme right (or rather instinct) of self-preservation. *See also* CUBAN QUARANTINE, 1962, 306; FORCE, ILLEGAL THREAT OR USE OF, 308; REPRISALS, 315; SELF-DEFENSE, RIGHT OF, 317; WAR, 320.

Significance   The history of international relations provides numerous examples of states resorting to armed force in the name of self-preservation or necessity. Among the most quoted cases are the bombardment of Copenhagen and seizure of the Danish fleet by Great Britain in 1807; the German violation of the permanent neutrality of Belgium and Luxembourg in 1914; the German occupation of Denmark in 1940 with the subsequent occupation of the then Danish Iceland by Great Britain; the British attack on the French naval units in Oran in 1940; and the Soviet-British occupation of Iran in 1941. Under the United Nations Charter, the plea of self-preservation or necessity is no longer admissible even if a state should take forcible measures to vindicate its legal rights, as ruled by the International Court of Justice (ICJ) in the *Corfu Channel* case (*United Kingdom v. Albania*, 1949). In this case, the Court rejected the British plea of self-protection in justification of the British minesweeping operation in the Albanian waters. Despite the Charter's prohibition, the behavior of states in some cases was reminiscent of the time when the doctrine of self-preservation could be invoked. Cases of resort to force by superpowers were among the most prominent examples of such behavior, otherwise rationalized as lawful under ambiguous rules of international law.

War   **(320)**
A status or condition of armed hostility between two or more states. War comes into existence either (1) by a formal declaration; (2) by acts of armed force committed by a state or group of states against another state or group of states with implied belligerent intent (or without such intent but treated as war by that other state or group of states); or (3) by acts of armed force between the two sides sufficiently serious and prolonged to warrant the status of war, even if both sides disclaim any belligerent intent. There is no agreement among international lawyers on the definition of war, and various tests can be applied to determine whether or not a state of war exists in any given case. If war has been declared, legally war exists even if no armed force has been employed by the contestants. For example, during World War II most states formally at war with the Axis powers did not actively participate in hostilities (e.g., some Latin American countries and Turkey). If the test

of war is objective, war exists irrespective of what the intentions are of the states engaged in conflict if fighting has assumed dimensions of regular warfare. If the test is subjective, war exists only if both sides, or at least one, intend it to exist. In recent times, the problem of defining war has been compounded by the existence of various levels and shades of international violence, obscuring the traditional distinction between war and peace to such an extent that some publicists have proposed the recognition of a third state between war and peace—the "intermediacy" concept—or even a continuum of coercive measures without any dichotomy between war and peace. *See also* AGGRESSION, 303; COERCIVE MEASURES SHORT OF WAR, 304; FORCE, ILLEGAL THREAT OR USE OF, 308; INDIRECT AGGRESSION, 311; JUST WAR DOCTRINE, 313.

Significance   Historically, a declaration of war by at least one party was evidence that a state of war existed between the contestants. In more recent times, however (before World War II and especially thereafter), numerous armed conflicts involving widespread hostilities have taken place without any declaration of war or even belligerent intent (*animus belligerendi*) of one or both sides. For example, Japan never declared war on China when it started its aggression in the 1930s, and no declarations of war preceded the large-scale hostilities between Japan and the Soviet Union in 1938. Among many *de facto* wars where no declaration of war occurred and, in some cases, diplomatic relations were not even severed, the Korean War (1950–1953); the Suez conflict of 1956; the Sino-Indian border war in 1962; the Indo-Pakistani conflicts in 1965 and 1971; the Sino-Vietnamese border war in 1979; the Falkland War between Argentina and the United Kingdom in 1982; and the Iran-Iraq war of the 1980s can be cited as examples. It appears that if an armed conflict assumes large-scale dimensions, even if both sides disclaim any belligerent intent, third states are justified to treat such a *de facto* war as war in the legal sense of the term and are entitled to declare neutrality. However, the contestants could still have a technically nonwar status in their mutual relations. An examination of state practice following World War II shows that in an overwhelming number of cases of armed conflict states have preferred not to consider themselves to be engaged in war in the legal sense of the term. One might even say that the practice of formally recognizing a state of belligerency had fallen into disuse. The emergence of these "nonwar" armed conflicts has been taken into account by the law governing the conduct of hostilities and other treaties and by United Nations General Assembly resolutions which refer to "armed conflict" in general, irrespective of whether or not war in the legal sense has been declared.

   There are a number of reasons why states are reluctant to openly declare war. Declaration of war is a grave and solemn act with far-reaching political and legal repercussions both internationally and domestically. It brings about automatic severance of diplomatic relations, terminates or suspends most treaties, normally results in third states' declarations of neutrality with all the inconveniences for the belligerents, and has serious implications for the municipal law systems of the states involved. Another reason for the emergence of "nonwar" conflicts has been the desire of the contestants to localize the conflict, signal their unwillingness to become engaged in a general war, and leave the door open for possible negotiations. Finally, states have been concerned with avoiding any charges of violating treaty obligations not to resort to war for the solution of controversies.

Prior to the Covenant of the League of Nations (1919), war was a legitimate instrument of sovereign states to which they were entitled to resort either as means of self-help to enforce an existing or alleged legal claim or as a legally admissible tool for altering existing rights in the name of national interest. The old "just war" doctrine had been discarded even by the doctrine of international law by the end of the eighteenth century. It was not until the twentieth century that the legality of war underwent a fundamental change. The Covenant of the League of Nations did not prohibit war altogether. The League's members undertook not to resort to war against a member which complied with an arbitral award or judicial decision or with the recommendation of a unanimous report by the League's Council. However, they could go to war in other situations, but not until a cooling-off period of three months after the award of arbitrators, the judicial decision, or the report by the Council. The award or the judicial decision had to be made "within a reasonable time" and the report of the Council within six months after the submission of the dispute. The Kellogg-Briand Pact (1928) widened the League's partial ban on war into total prohibition of recourse to war for the solution of international controversies and renunciation of war as as instrument of national policy. Finally, the Charter of the United Nations (1945) went beyond the Pact since it formulated the international law governing resort to violence in terms of prohibiting not only war but, more generally, the threat or use of force inconsistent with the purposes of the United Nations. At the same time, "aggressive war"—the gravest category of illegal use of force— was declared a supreme international crime (crime against peace) by the Nuremberg International Military Tribunal in 1946.

The International Law Commission, in its Principles of International Law Recognized in the Charter and Judgment of the Nuremberg Tribunal (1950), declared as crimes against peace (1) planning, preparation, initiation, or waging of a war of aggression or war in violation of international treaties, agreements, or assurances; and (2) participation in a common plan or conspiracy for the accomplishment of these acts.

These rules were later incorporated in the Draft Code of Offenses against the Peace and Security of Mankind (1954) prepared by the International Law Commission and subsequently reaffirmed in a number of resolutions of the United Nations General Assembly, for example, in the 1970 Declaration of Principles of International Law Concerning Friendly Relations and Cooperation among States in Accordance with the Charter of the United Nations. Prohibition of aggressive war as an international crime has become a peremptory norm of general international law (*jus cogens*). There is no prohibition in international law against civil wars, however bloody they may be, except that the Third World countries, supported by the communist states and some Western nations, would like to make illegal civil war in the meaning of the use of force against "peoples" exercising their right of self-determination. As far as international wars are concerned, despite the sweeping condemnation of the right to go to war (*jus ad bellum*), numerous wars have occurred and even the United Nations recognizes that their conduct must be governed by rules of warfare (*jus in bello*), which originated in the period when all wars were legal.

12. The Laws of War and Neutrality

Air Warfare (321)

Hostilities between parties engaged in armed conflict carried out in their airspace or above the high seas, and hostile acts directed from the air against the territory or ships of the adversary, including participation in belligerent blockade and the exercise of the right of capture. Speculation concerning air warfare began before the invention of aircraft when a Hague Declaration of 1899, renewed in 1907, prohibited the discharge of projectiles and explosives from balloons and by other new methods of a similar nature. In 1984 this Declaration was still formally in force for twenty-eight states. Article 25 of Hague Regulations of Convention IV (and the corresponding 1899 Convention) prohibited the attack or bombardment of undefended towns, villages, etc. by "any means whatever," and attempts were made to apply it by analogy to aerial warfare. Unlike hostilities on land, however, air warfare is not governed by any comprehensive treaty or treaties, and only a limited number of rules of land warfare can be applied to aerial warfare. Such rules as do exist are reflected in the U.S. Air Force manual of 1976, *International Law: The Conduct of Armed Conflict and Air Operations. See also* PROHIBITED METHODS OF WARFARE, 356.

Significance Aerial bombardment causing injury to the civilian population and destruction and damage to nonmilitary targets produced the primary legal problem concerning air warfare. The use of air in warfare was pioneered by Italy, who used balloons for spotting the enemy and dropping bombs in its war with Turkey in 1911–1912. During World War I, aircraft were used on an increasing scale in warfare, including bombarding civilian localities. Article 25 of Hague Regulations was disregarded. Following World War I, a codification effort by a commission of jurists drew up a Code of Air Warfare (1923), which abandoned the Hague Regulations distinction between defended and undefended localities and differentiated between legitimate air bombardment of specified military objectives, including munitions factories, and unlawful bombardment in situations where it could not take place without indiscriminate injury to the civilian population. The Code was never ratified, however, and its distinctions proved to be virtually meaningless even prior to World War II, as demonstrated by the deliberate bombing of towns by the German *Luftwaffe* in the Spanish Civil War and by the Japanese in China. Unrestricted air bombardment, initiated by Germany, became a routine military operation in World War II, whose total nature made it hardly possible to define which targets were not military, particularly since aerial warfare was increasingly and deliberately directed at undermining the morale of the enemy's civilian population. In view of the practice of states, it appears that it would be difficult to make a case for the illegality of aerial bombing. Even the International Military Tribunal at Nuremberg did not charge the major war criminals with indiscriminate use of this method of warfare. Thus, air warfare remains an unregulated area of armed conflict. Moreover, recent technological advances have raised the prospect of expanding the region of warfare beyond the airspace into outer space itself.

Angary (322)

The right of a belligerent state—in cases of urgent necessity—to destroy or use neutral property on its own or enemy's territory or on the high seas. The right of angary, which is a kind of wartime embargo, extends in particular to neutral vessels and other means of transportation. Hague Convention V of 1907 recognizes a special case of the right of angary envisaging the possibility of requisitioning, in cases of absolute necessity, neutral railway material; but the neutral state affected may, to a corresponding extent, retain railway material of the belligerent. Under customary law, a belligerent state must pay compensation for any damage done to the neutral owner. *See also* NEUTRALITY, 351.

Significance   The right of angary has its historical origins in the medieval right of belligerents to seize vessels and crews of third states, known as *jus angariae*. This practice was discontinued in the seventeenth century but reappeared in a modified form during World War I when it was resorted to by some belligerents seizing neutral vessels in their ports. For example, the United States seized seventy-seven Dutch ships against protests by the Netherlands government, but subsequently either returned them or indemnified the owners. The extent of the right of angary on the high seas is a controversial matter, as illustrated by the case of the *Zamora* (Great Britain, Judicial Committee of the Privy Council, 1916), a Swedish vessel seized by the British navy in 1915. In this case, the (British) Privy Council ruled that the seizure was illegal in the absence of urgent military necessity.

Armed Conflict: International   (323)
A concept adopted for purposes of international humanitarian law which, in addition to traditional war in the legal sense, includes any clash of armed forces between states or other subjects of international law as well as occupation of foreign territory by armed forces even if it meets with no armed resistance. Whereas early codifications of the law of war referred to "war," such as the Hague Conventions of 1899 and 1907, the more recent international humanitarian law conventions (the four Geneva Conventions of 1949, Protocol I of 1977, and the 1954 Hague Convention for the Protection of Cultural Property in Time of War) apply not only to cases of declared war but also to any other international armed conflict even if the state of war is not recognized by the parties. *See also* AGGRESSION, 303; ARMED CONFLICT: NONINTERNA-TIONAL, 324; COLLECTIVE SECURITY SYSTEM, 305; DECLARATION OF WAR, 336; INTERVENTION, 312; PACIFIC BLOCKADE, 314; REPRISALS, 315; WAR, 320.

Significance   The adoption of the concept of international armed conflict can be attributed on the one hand to the fact that the international law of the United Nations Charter is based on the outlawry of force and not merely war, and on the other by the proliferation in state practice of armed conflicts—frequently within the context of civil strife or decolonization—with no formal state of declared war. Such international conflicts include *de facto* wars, armed reprisals, military interventions, pacific blockades, and a whole range of activities included as examples of acts of aggression in the definition of aggression adopted by the United Nations General Assembly in 1974. In addition to conflicts between states, the concept of international armed conflict includes two categories of situations where at least one party is not a state: (1) military enforcement action undertaken by the United Nations under Article 42 of the United Nations Charter (something that so far has remained only a theory) and any armed clashes in which the United Nations or regional peacekeeping forces may become involved; and (2) a by far more relevant but controversial situation of "armed conflicts in which peoples are fighting against colonial domination and alien occupation and against racist regimes in the exercise of their right of self-determination," a formulation of Protocol I of 1977. Whereas the Third World countries, supported by the Soviet Union and other communist states, assert that such conflicts are international even under customary law, most Western countries contend that only conflicts between traditional subjects of international law are international, and point to the legally meaningless, politically vague, and sociologically elusive concept of "people," the ambiguity of the concept of "self-determination" and double standards in its application, and the virtual impossibility of determining when resort to violence ceases to be a mere act of terror and a "national liberation war" begins. The inclusion of wars of national liberation, as conceived by the Third World countries, within the concept of international armed conflict, was a major reason for the refusal of the United States and some other Western countries to become parties to Protocol I of 1977.

Armed Conflict: Noninternational   (324)

An armed conflict taking place in the territory of a state between its armed forces and dissident armed forces or other organized armed groups which, under responsible command, exercise such control over a part of its territory as to enable them to carry out sustained and concerted military operations and to observe a certain minimum of humanitarian rules of warfare. Whether or not or to what extent the traditional law of war applied also to civil wars, national liberation struggles, and other internal armed conflicts was uncertain in customary international law. The fanaticism with which such conflicts are frequently waged caused inclusion in each of the four Geneva Conventions of 1949 of an identical Article 3 which stipulated a minimum of humane treatment to noncombatants in civil wars, including members of armed forces who had laid down arms and those placed *hors de combat* by sickness, wounds, detention, or any other cause. Although Article 3 was observed in some civil wars and similar conflicts and the presence of the International Committee of the Red Cross was, as required by this Article, admitted on the spot, the protection offered the victims proved inadequate in other internal conflicts. Therefore, in 1977 the Diplomatic Conference on Reaffirmation and Development of International Humanitarian Law Applicable in Armed Conflict adopted Protocol II, which develops and supplements Article 3 and deals exclusively with "noninternational armed conflicts." However, under Protocol I, wars of national liberation are qualified as international armed conflict.

Protocol II grants noncombatants certain fundamental guarantees, prohibiting *inter alia* collective punishment, terrorism, the taking of hostages, and pillage. It offers a minimum of protection to interned and detained persons and spells out provisions designed to protect the civilian population against the dangers arising from military operations. Attacks on works and installations containing "dangerous forces" (for example, nuclear power stations, dams, and dikes) are prohibited if they should cause severe loss in civilian life. All wounded, sick, and shipwrecked must be protected, and the emblems of the red cross (red crescent or red lion and sun respectively) must be displayed by medical and religious personnel. Protocol II entered into force in 1978, but only some thirty states (excluding the United States and most Western nations) are parties to it. *See also* ARMED CONFLICT: INTERNATIONAL, 323; BELLIGERENCY, RECOGNITION OF, 64; INSURGENCY, RECOGNITION OF, 71; IRREGULAR FORCE, 345; PROTOCOLS I AND II (1967), 359.

Significance　　　The regulation of noninternational armed conflict by Protocol II of 1977 was a major achievement of international humanitarian law, despite the fact that the application of the Protocol encounters serious problems resulting from the nature of internal armed conflict. Civil wars are often fought by irregular forces which are frequently difficult to distinguish from the civilian population. Internationalization of a noninternational armed conflict by a foreign armed intervention does not necessarily improve the protection of the victims of war. A major problem with applying the rules in international humanitarian law to noninternational armed conflicts is the difficulty of distinguishing them from other acts of internal violence. Protocol II explicitly stipulates that it does not apply to "situations of internal disturbances and tensions, such as riots, isolated and sporadic acts of violence and other acts of a similar nature" which are not "armed conflict." Since governments are reluctant to admit the existence of a real "armed conflict" in their countries, as defined by the rather high threshold of violence in Protocol II, the chances are that the Protocol will not often be recognized as applying to armed strife within the territory of a signatory country. In practice, rules of humanity and Article 3 of the widely ratified Geneva Conventions of 1949 will provide a legal basis for the conduct of internal armed conflicts.

Armistice　　　　　　　　　　　　　　　　　　　　　　(325)
The cessation of active hostilities for a period agreed upon by the belligerents. As regulated by the Hague Regulations of Hague Convention IV of 1907 (or the corresponding 1899 Convention), an armistice may be general—suspending the military operations everywhere and frequently preceding negotiations for peace, or local—also known as "truce" or "cease-fire," only between certain factions of the belligerent armies and within a fixed radius. A "suspension of arms" is a form of armistice concluded between commanders for some local military pur-

poses, such as to bury the dead, collect the wounded, or to arrange for the exchange of prisoners. Although no form is prescribed for an armistice agreement, it should be in writing and should, in general, stipulate at least the precise day and hours of its commencement, duration, principal lines, and other signs necessary to determine the location of the belligerent troops; relations of the armies with the local inhabitants; acts prohibited during the armistice; disposition of prisoners of war; and provisions on consultative machinery. Any serious violation of the armistice by a party gives the other party the right to denounce it and even, in cases of urgency, to recommence hostilities. In naval warfare, a blockade may continue unless the armistice agreement specifically provides for cessation of the blockade. See also PEACE TREATY, 353.

Significance   The conclusion of an armistice does not mean the end of war. Although in practice in World War I, for example, the armistice represented a *de facto* termination of the conflict. In the Korean War (1950–1953), the armistice put an end to the conflict, but no peace treaty was concluded. The United Nations Security Council has used the terms "truce" or "cease-fire" for suspension of hostilities. For example, a truce was established in Palestine in 1948, and various decisions and recommendations were made by the Security Council concerning cease-fires in the Congo between the United Nations peacekeeping forces and the armed forces of Katanga in 1961 and in the Indo-Pakistani conflict in 1965. The term "disengagement" was used in the agreement between Israel and Egypt in 1973. Other modes of terminating hostilities analogous to armistice include agreement on "cessation" or "suspension" of hostilities; for example, the Geneva Agreement of 1954 relating to the war in Indochina.

Belligerent Occupation (326)

A type of military occupation whereby a part or all of the territory of a state at war with the occupying power is, without any transfer of sovereignty, actually placed under the authority of a hostile army exercising military authority subject to rights and duties under international law. Belligerent occupation must be distinguished from invasion—a stage of military operations prior to establishing complete control—and from subjugation followed by annexation or transfer of sovereignty by means of a treaty of cession. Belligerent occupation also differs from the occupation of nonenemy territory as a measure against a common enemy; for example, the Allied occupation of Iceland during World War II. The law of belligerent occupation is codified and developed in the Regulations of Hague Convention IV of 1907 (or the corresponding Convention of 1899), supplemented by Geneva Convention IV of 1949 and Protocol I of 1977, which apply not only to belligerent occupation in the strict sence of the term but also to occupation following cessation of hostilities. Manuals of the armed forces of major powers, dating back to the U.S. *Instructions for the Government of the Armies of the United States in the Field* issued to the Union Army during the Civil War in 1863 and based on a draft by Francis Lieber, deal at length with the rules governing belligerent occupation.

Belligerent occupation establishes a complex system of legal relations involving the occupying power, the inhabitants, and the absent sovereign of the occupied territory. This territory is temporarily administered by the occupant who may issue laws and regulations, but the legitimate government retains its sovereignty and its laws still apply unless superseded by those imposed by the occupying power. Incorporation of occupied territory into the occupying state during the course of war and its division or turning into an independent state are illegal. Hence, occupation does not result in any change of nationality of the inhabitants. The rights and duties of the occupant are conditioned by the necessity to maintain order and administer the territory in the interest of the inhabitants and for the occupant's military needs. Protection and humane treatment of the population in the occupied territory are the fundamental principles of the international law of belligerent occupation. A long list of guarantees of rights of the inhabitants is spelled out in Geneva Convention IV and Protocol I. Among them are respect for their honor, family rights, religious practices, private property, and customs. The taking of hostages; collective punishment; discrimination on racial, religious, and political grounds; transfer or deportation; and requisitioning of food and medical supplies to the detriment of the ordinary needs of the population are prohibited. Settlement of occupied territory by the occupant's own civilian population is also illegal. Requisition of services must be for fair wages, must not involve the inhabitants in operations against their own country, and a minumum age of eighteen is set for requisitioned labor. The occupant's rights with regard to education in the occupied territory are controversial, although Geneva Convention IV stipulates that the occupant should facilitate the proper operation of educational institutions. Guarantees of humane treatment apply also in noninternational armed conflict and are developed in detail in Protocol II of 1977.

The population in the occupied territory has certain duties toward the enemy occupying the territory. The scope of the duty of obedience is not clear, but in practice the occupant has the power to dictate its limits subject to any restrictions imposed by conventional law. In any case the occupant has the right to punish individuals for armed resistance, but the scope of the right to impose the death penalty is a controversial matter. The occupant is expected to allow the functioning of the legal, judicial, and administrative systems of the occupied territory, but at the occupant's discretion these systems may be replaced with institutions and officials of military nature. Some activities of the population under belligerent occupation may be regulated or even forbidden by the occupant as, for example, public meetings, displaying the flag of the lawful sovereign, and the singing of the national anthem. Operations of news media are normally restricted.

Complex, but not entirely comprehensive, rules govern the economic sphere. The occupant is entitled to collect taxes and customs revenues but, in the prevailing view, not debts owed to the lawful sovereign. Money contributions may be levied, but not as collective reprisals for acts of individuals. War supplies may be seized without limits, but requisition of other supplies must be in reasonable proportion to the resources of the occupied territory. It is also unclear whether or not the occupying power has the right to exploit the natural resources of the territory, a question that arose during the occupation of Egyptian territory (Sinai) by Israel. In any case, wanton spoliation of the resources is illegal. The belligerent occupant is only the administrator and usufructuary (that is, a person entitled to utilize property) of the immovable public property of the sovereign of the occupied territory and is not allowed to appropriate it. It is not entirely clear, however, what is included within the concept of public property. Confiscation, destruction, or damaging of cultural property is prohibited. Like private property, it is beyond the reach of the occupant. The 1954 Hague Convention for the Protection of Cultural Property in Time of War regulates the matter in detail. Movable public property that can be used for military operations by the occupant can be appropriated. "War booty," that is, public enemy property captured on the battlefield, can be taken by the occupant irrespective of its nature. Private property cannot be confiscated, except for movable property useful for military purposes, but indemnity must be paid for it upon conclusion of peace. In contrast to the protection of enemy private property in land warfare, the law of maritime warfare allows capture of private vessels and cargo, subject to certain conditions. *See also* CONTRABAND, 333; ENEMY CHARACTER, 339; GENEVA CONVENTIONS (1949), 342; PROTOCOLS I AND II (1977), 359; WAR CRIMES, 367.

Significance   The Hague rules concerning belligerent occupation were subject to a severe test in World War I, but it was in World War II that Nazi Germany became guilty, especially in the territories occupied in Eastern Europe, of unprecedented violations of all rules of belligerent occupation, subjecting the occupied territories to wholesale spoliation and the conquered populations to a systematic rule of terror, brutality, and violence culminating in the policy of genocide against the Jews and other racial groups. Most of the major war criminals before the International Military Tribunal at Nuremberg were sentenced for war crimes connected with the violation of the law of belligerent occupation. Serious breaches of this law were also committed by other belligerents, specifically Japan and the Soviet Union. The occupation of Germany following World War II was a unique type of military occupation which was not belligerent occupation, since the enemy state and government had been destroyed and hostilities were terminated. The experiences of World War II resulted in expanding the Hague law of belligerent occupation with respect to the treatment of the civilian population by Geneva Convention IV and subsequently Protocol I. If the detailed rules of these treaties were to be observed in practice, they would greatly contribute to humanization of warfare in occupied territories. In recent years, issues related to belligerent occupation reemerged within the context of the occupation of Arab territories by Israel, with charges of violations of the laws of war leveled against that country, by deportation of inhabitants, collective punishment, establishing settlements, and *de facto* annexation of occupied territories. These actions were condemned as illegal by the United Nations General Assembly, and their illegality was pointed out by the United States and other states but was denied by Israel.

Blockade: Belligerent   (327)
The blocking by a belligerent's warships of the access to the enemy coast, or part of it, for the purpose of preventing entry and exit of vessels and aircraft of all states. A belligerent or hostile (wartime) blockade is distinguished from a pacific blockade in that it applies to vessels and cargo of all nations. Under the Declaration of Paris of 1856, in order to be legal and binding on neutrals, a blockade must be declared (that is, notified to all states) and effective (that is, maintained by a naval force capable of carrying out the purpose of the blockade). For example, the blockade of the Confederate coast by the Union in the American Civil War was not effective until the latter part of the war. A neutral blockade runner does not violate any laws of neutrality, nor does the blockade runner's state permitting such conduct. On the other hand, a neutral merchant vessel trying to break through a blockade is liable to capture and condemnation by the captor's prize court. Whether or not insurgents in a noninternational war can lawfully blockade the coast of the *de jure* government is a controversial issue, but the prevailing opinion is that they do have such right if possessed of the status of belligerency. *See also* BELLIGERENCY, RECOGNITION OF, 64;

BLOCKADE: LONG-DISTANCE, 328; CONTINUOUS VOYAGE, DOCTRINE OF, 332; CONTRABAND, 333; CUBAN QUARANTINE, 1962, 306; DECLARATION OF PARIS (1856), 335; NAVICERT SYSTEM, 350; NEUTRALITY, 351; PACIFIC BLOCKADE, 314; PRIZE COURT, 355.

Significance   The institution of belligerent blockade can be traced to the sixteenth century. Originally it was directed only at ports and fortified towns along a coast; but by the time of the Napoleonic wars it was extended to include the entire enemy coast. With profound changes in the conditions and means of modern naval warfare in the two world wars, the traditional blockade maintained close to the coast ("close" blockade) lost its importance and was largely replaced by a long-distance blockade of all seaborne commerce of the enemy.

Blockade: Long-Distance   (328)

A belligerent blockade of the enemy's coast which unlike an ordinary ("close") blockade, is not maintained in the immediate vicinity of the enemy ports but covers large, virtually unlimited areas of the high seas and is designed to cut off the enemy's territory completely and force economic isolation of the enemy. In a total war, the long-distance blockade represents a major tool for waging economic warfare by covering commerce with the enemy, passing not only directly to and from ports but also indirectly through neutral ports. Although in World War I neutral states questioned the legality of the long-distance blockade on the grounds that it extended to their coastlines and was in many respects ineffective, eventually opinion prevailed that such a blockade is lawful in modern conditions of warfare. *See also* BLOCKADE: BELLIGERENT, 327; CONTINUOUS VOYAGE, DOCTRINE OF, 332; CONTRABAND, 333; DECLARATION OF PARIS (1856), 335; DEFENSE (WAR) ZONES, 337; NAVICERT SYSTEM, 350; NEUTRALITY, 351; PACIFIC BLOCKADE, 314; PRIZE COURT, 355; UNNEUTRAL SERVICE, 366.

Significance   The long-distance blockade was first instituted by Great Britain and its allies in 1915 by blockading Germany through ships operating more than one hundred nautical miles from German ports. Originally, this blockade was declared to be only a reprisal in response to the German declaration that the waters around Great Britain were an operational war zone in which all enemy shipping would be attacked and even neutral vessels exposed to risks. However, the blockade soon became an explicit policy designed to prevent all passage to and from Germany by sea. Similar action was taken by France. The long-distance blockade was also instituted by the Allies against Germany in World War II. It resulted in a complex system of arrangements by the blockading nations, especially Great Britain, to discriminate between *bona fide* neutral commerce and commerce ultimately destined for, and originating in, Germany. It involved the introduction of the system of navicerts, certificates of origin and interest, "blacklists" of suspect neutral traders, and other elaborate devices to control neutral shipping.

Capitulation   (329)

An agreement between commanders of belligerent forces for the surrender of a body of troops, a fortress, or other defended locality, or of a district of the theater of operations. A capitulation must be distinguished from "unconditional surrender," which need not be effected on the basis of an instrument signed by both parties and is not an agreement. A capitulation may also be arranged by the political authorities of the belligerents, in which case it may contain other than military stipulations *See also* UNCONDITIONAL SURRENDER, 365.

Significance   A capitulation is not a treaty of peace and therefore does not end the state of war between the belligerents. The validity of a capitulation is not impaired if a commander surrenders in violation of orders or the law of his own state. Normally, surrendered troops become prisoners of war, and the surrendering party has no right to destroy or damage installations or material under its control. Violation of the terms of capitulation by individuals is punishable as a war crime and, if it is directed by the commander who capitulated or by a higher authority, the other belligerent may resume hostilities. The same action may be taken if the capitulation was obtained through a breach of faith.

Cartel   (330)

An agreement entered into by parties to an armed conflict for the exchange of prisoners of war. In its broader sense, a cartel is any agreement between belligerents for the purpose of arranging and regulating certain kinds of nonhostile relations otherwise barred by reason of the existence of the conflict. Both parties are bound to observe its provisions, but a cartel is voidable by either party upon proof that it has been deliberately violated in an important part by the other party. *See also* SAFE-CONDUCT, 362; TREATY, 279.

Significance   Historically, the first cartels were concluded to fix the amount of ransom to redeem prisoners of war from captivity. The last instance of such a cartel took place between Great Britain and France in 1780. In the nineteenth century, cartels were arranged for maintaining communications by post, telegraph, telephone, and railway between belligerents. In the two World Wars, cartel ships were used by belligerents to carry exchanged prisoners of war and internees.

Combatants and Noncombatants   (331)

A distinction of international humanitarian law between individuals who are members of the armed forces of a party to an armed conflict and have the right to participate directly in hostilities, and other individuals, civilians, and noncombatant members of armed forces who normally have no such right and are not to be willfully attacked or injured. The distinction between combatants and noncombatants is a basic principle of international humanitarian law. Combatants include the regular armed forces of a party to a conflict, whose composition and structure is primarily a matter of municipal law (for example, this law determines whether or not militias or volunteer corps form part of the regular armed forces). However, international law (Hague Regulations annexed to Convention IV of 1907, Geneva Convention III of 1949, and Protocol I of 1977) determines categories of individuals who have the right to engage in hostilities and are entitled to be treated as prisoners of war upon capture. In general, the combatant armed forces consist of (1) all organized regular forces including paramilitary and armed law enforcement agencies under a command responsible to the party to a conflict, even if that party is represented by a government or authority not recognized by an adverse party (as was, for example, the case of the armed forces of those allies in World War II whose countries were overrun by Germany; and (2) irregular forces (guerrillas, resistance groups, partisans, etc.) and *levée en masse*. Noncombatants include (1) the "noncombatant" categories of armed forces such as medical personnel, chaplains, war correspondents, contractors, and the like who, however, are entitled to treatment as prisoners of war; and (2) civilians, who normally fall under the protection of international humanitarian law unless they happen to be unlawful combatants, in which case they are liable to punishment by military tribunal after a fair trial. Spies are a unique category of combatants. The legal status of mercenaries and foreign volunteers is a matter of controversy. A person owing allegiance to one belligerent country who joins the armed forces of the adverse party cannot claim the status of lawful combatant if subsequently captured by that country. *See also* BELLIGERENT OCCUPATION, 326; IRREGULAR FORCES, 345; *LEVÉE EN MASSE*, 346; MERCENARY, 348; PROHIBITED WEAPONS, 357; SPY, 363.

Significance   The distinction between combatants and noncombatants became an established principle of the law of war by 1914 and was implied in the Regulations of Hague Convention IV (1907). During World War I, this distinction came to be disregarded under the impact of new technology and modes of warfare and, in the conditions of total warfare in World War II, it was virtually obliterated. Artillery and naval bombardment, sieges, blockade, extensive interpretation of the concept of contraband, and finally indiscriminate aerial warfare were the typical situations in which noncombatants (while not necessarily the primary targets) were in fact denied international protection from injuries and damage resulting from acts of war. In view of these adverse developments Geneva Convention IV (1949), supplemented by Protocol I (1977), attempted to strengthen the protection of civilian noncombatants from risks and injuries of war under the basic assumption that parties to an armed conflict must at all times distinguish between civilians and combatants and between nonmilitary and military targets. The general principles of international law relative to the protection of noncombatant civilian population are developed in detail in the Hague Regulations of Convention IV, Geneva Convention IV (1949), and Protocol I (1977) and reaffirmed by a Resolution of the United Nations General Assembly in 1968. Indiscriminate attacks upon a civilian population are prohibited, but the realities of modern warfare make it impossible to avoid adverse effects upon civilians of attacks against military targets. Therefore Protocol I stipulates that the civilian population "as such" shall not be object of attack. The experiences of World War II and the local wars of the postwar period demonstrated the futility of any prohibition of indiscriminate attacks. Geneva Convention IV and Protocols I and II prohibit such attacks, with the implication that the use of weapons of mass destruction (such as nuclear weapons) was illegal; but no clear rule exists that explicitly restricts or bans their employment. Special provisions of these treaties as well as the Hague Regulations and Hague Convention IX provide for special protection of nondefended localities and neutral and demilitarized zones. In addition, cultural objects are protected under the 1954 Hague Convention for the Protection of Cultural Property in Time of War.

Apart from the rules concerning the protection of civilian noncombatants irrespective of their nationality, numerous provisions of Geneva Convention IV (1949) and Protocol I (1977) protect civilian individuals in the power of a party to the conflict who are not its nationals; that is, are nationals either of the adversary or of third states. Detailed provisions, prompted largely by Nazi atrocities, guarantee such noncombatant "protected persons" humane treatment and nondiscrimination and, among other measures, prohibit reprisals, taking hostages, and collective punishment. However, a party to the conflict may apply such measures of control and security in regard to protected persons as may be necessary as a result of the war. Assigned residence and internment, regulated in detail in Geneva Convention IV, are the most severe measures allowed. The treatment of the civilian population under belligerent occupation is governed by the Hague Regulations and developed and supplemented by Geneva Convention IV and Protocol I. The protection of the wounded, sick, and shipwrecked members of armed forces and the status of prisoners of war are governed in detail by Geneva Conventions I, II, and III.

Continuous Voyage, Doctrine of   (332)

A doctrine applied in maritime warfare whereby a belligerent has the right to seize and condemn neutral goods, judged to be contraband, going from one neutral port ostensibly to another, if it can be proven that the particular goods had in reality an ultimate enemy destination by sea or by land. The doctrine of continuous voyage (or, more generally, of continuous transportation) provides a theoretical basis for tightening the economic isolation of an enemy but represents a restriction on the freedom of neutral states to trade with belligerents and even to trade in general since, under the doctrine of continuous transportation, goods are also liable to seizure if the vessel is not aware of any arrangements for the goods to be sent afterwards by land or by sea to the captor's enemy. Nevertheless, there is general consensus on the lawfulness of the doctrine of continuous voyage or continuous transportation. *See also* BLOCKADE: BELLIGERENT, 327; BLOCKADE: LONG-DISTANCE, 328; CONTRABAND, 333; DECLARATION OF LONDON (1909), 334; DECLARATION OF PARIS (1856), 335; MARITIME WARFARE, THE LAW OF, 347; NAVICERT SYSTEM, 350; NEUTRALITY, 351; PRIZE COURT, 355.

Significance   The doctrine of continuous voyage can be traced back at least to the mid-eighteenth century when, during the war between France and Great Britain, neutral Dutch vessels carried on (with France's permission) trade between French colonies and metropolitan France via the Netherlands' ports. Applying the test of ultimate destination of goods, the British prize courts approved seizure and condemnation of such vessels and cargo—the "rule of 1756." This rule was eventually enforced against all neutral ships carrying contraband in subsequent wars of Great Britain with France. The doctrine of continuous voyage was also applied by the U.S. Supreme Court in almost all cases of contraband or breach of blockade in the American Civil War. The British practice in the Boer War pointed to the same position, as demonstrated by the case of the German vessel *Bundesrath* and other vessels seized by the British navy under the suspicion of carrying contraband to the Boers via the neutral Portuguese port of Lourenço Marques in Mozambique (1900). The unratified Declaration of London of 1909 provided that the doctrine of continuous voyage should apply to absolute contraband and to conditional contraband only in a war against a landlocked enemy. However, the practice of both World Wars rejected this compromise, and the doctrine was applied to all kinds of goods deemed to be, in the captor's judgment, absolute or conditional contraband.

Contraband　　　　　　　　　　　　　　　　　　　　(333)

Such goods as are prohibited by a belligerent to reach the enemy on the grounds that they assist the enemy in the conduct of war. Contraband is a crucial concept in the law of neutrality and economic warfare at sea. Under the Declaration of Paris (1856), the neutral flag protects non-contraband enemy goods and noncontraband neutral goods under an enemy flag. Although there exists the general consensus that contraband has two essential characteristics—first, the nature of the goods and, second, an enemy destination—there is no agreement on what articles are to be considered contraband and subject to seizure. As far as the nature of goods is concerned, a traditional distinction is drawn between "absolute" contraband—that is, articles clearly of military character (weapons, munitions, and the like)—and "conditional" or "relative" contraband—that is, articles that can be used both for peaceful purposes and in the war effort (for example, food, fuel, and the like). Noncontraband goods comprise the third category. No agreement has ever existed on the question of which articles belong to each of the three categories of goods except for certain obvious instruments of war or other warlike materials belonging to absolute contraband. In practice, therefore, the right to determine which particular articles are to be included in which category of contraband has been exercised by each belligerent. *See also* BLOCKADE: BELLIGERENT, 327; BLOCKADE: LONG-DISTANCE, 328; CONTINUOUS VOYAGE, DOCTRINE OF, 332; DECLARATION OF PARIS (1856), 335; MARITIME WARFARE, THE LAW OF, 347; NAVICERT SYSTEM, 350; NEUTRALITY, 351; PRIZE COURT, 355.

Significance　　It is obvious that, with the increasing impact of science and technology upon the conduct of warfare and the total involvement of "nations at arms" in the war effort, ever more items were added to the list of absolute contraband. Many articles were also shifted from the "free" list to the rank of conditional contraband; so that by the end of World War I, the distinction between absolute and conditional contraband broke down as did the rapidly disappearing distinction between combatants and noncombatants. In World War II, hardly any article was not considered of warlike use, and the official contraband lists covered every conceivable kind of article and material.

Declaration of London (1909)   (334)

An unratified treaty attempting to codify the law of maritime (naval) warfare. The Declaration of London was signed by the states participating in the London Naval Conference (1908–1909) which met to find a basis of generally acceptable prize law for the jurisdiction of the International Prize Court under the unratified Hague Convention XII of 1907. See also MARITIME WARFARE, THE LAW OF, 347; PRIZE COURT, 355.

Significance   Although not ratified by any power, the Declaration of London was complied with by the belligerents in the Italo-Turkish war of 1911–1912. When World War I broke out in 1914, Germany and Austria-Hungary agreed to adopt it on condition of reciprocity, but other major powers were ready to do so only under certain additional conditions. By 1916 the Declaration was no longer applied even in part. The failure of the Declaration of London demonstrated the difficulties inherent in reconciling the conflicting naval and commercial interests of the major powers engaged in maritime warfare.

Declaration of Paris (1856)   (335)

The first multilateral treaty in the area of the laws of war and neutrality, establishing certain fundamental principles concerning warfare at sea and neutrality. The Declaration of Paris provided for the prohibition of "privateering," that is, naval warfare by private vessels under a commission ("letters of marque") from a state; recognized the principle that the neutral flag protects noncontraband enemy goods and that noncontraband neutral goods under an enemy flag are not liable to capture; and enacted the rule that in order to be legally binding a blockade must be effective, that is, maintained by forces sufficient to prevent access to the enemy coastline. The rule on blockades was reiterated in the Declaration of London (1909), which never entered into force. See also BLOCKADE: BELLIGERENT, 327; BLOCKADE: LONG-DISTANCE, 328; CONTINUOUS VOYAGE, DOCTRINE OF, 332; CONTRABAND, 333; DECLARATION OF LONDON (1909), 334; NAVICERT SYSTEM, 350; NEUTRALITY, 351; PRIZE COURT, 355; UNNEUTRAL SERVICE, 366.

Significance   The Declaration of Paris was adopted by the Congress of Paris following the Crimean War and was attended by representatives of the leading European powers. After being signed by Austria,

France, Great Britain, Prussia, Russia, Sardinia, and Turkey, it was eventually adhered to by almost all other maritime powers except the United States, which stood for complete abolition of capture at sea, and a few South American states. Since, however, even nonsignatory powers have, by and large, acted in accordance with the Declaration, it may be considered a law-making treaty declaratory of general international law. Yet, the rule that the neutral flag covers noncontraband enemy goods was, to a large extent, disregarded during the two world wars.

Declaration of War (336)

A communication by one state to another that the condition of peace between them has come to an end and that a state of war exists between them. Under Hague Convention III (1907), a declaration of war or an ultimatum with conditional declaration of war is required before the commencement of hostilities, but surprise is still possible since no particular length of time must elapse between the declaration of war and the commencement of hostilities. Although municipal courts in some countries (for example, in the United States) have held that a state of war exists upon the outbreak of hostilities, there seems to be consensus among publicists that if a declaration of war follows such outbreak, the war has its legal beginning on the date of the declaration of war. The declaration of war must be "reasoned," which means that a written document handed over to the other party is required. *See also* WAR, 320.

Significance   Although Hague Convention III (1907) Relative to the Opening of Hostilities (adopted under the impact of the Japanese attack on Russia without warning in 1904) requires that hostilities be preceded by previous and explicit warning in the form of a declaration of war or an ultimatum, the practice of states even prior to 1907 and thereafter (especially in the post–World War II period) has witnessed numerous wars fought without a declaration of war, even in cases where the parties involved were bound by Hague Convention III (for example, the U.S. conflict with North Vietnam or the Iraq-Iran war of the 1980s). The abandonment of the practice to declare war has prompted suggestions by some publicists that declaration of war is an obsolete institution which perhaps never developed into a rule of customary international law. This is claimed to be especially true since the outlawry of war and, more generally, force by the United Nations Charter has made the form in which hostilities are to commence less relevant. However, the International Military Tribunal of Nuremberg cited violation of Hague Convention III by Germany among other breaches of treaty obligations by that state. Strictly speaking, therefore, at least for states parties to Hague Convention III, a declaration of war or an ultimatum with conditional declaration is necessary before such a state may engage in hostilities. In 1984, forty-two states (mostly European and American), including the United States and the Soviet Union, were parties to the Convention. The U.S. Department of the Army *Field Manual on the Law of Land Warfare* cites Hague Convention III as legally binding upon the United States. The problem of the declaration of war illustrates the conflict between the traditional law governing resort to war and the new law of the United Nations Charter. The very declaration of war or ultimatum, in accordance with a legally binding treaty, would violate the United Nations Charter's prohibition of the threat or use of force unless the state issuing it was a victim of aggression acting in legitimate self-defense under Article 51 of the Charter.

Defense (War) Zones   (337)

Zones at sea proclaimed by belligerents in maritime warfare in which they restrict or completely ban neutral shipping as reprisals for purposes of economic warfare against the enemy. The legal basis for creating various "defense," "war," or "operations" zones is rather controversial since such zones impose limitations upon the traditional freedom of the high seas, which are open to neutral shipping in war as well as in the peacetime. The zones in question must be distinguished from the 300-nautical-mile security zone established by twenty-two American republics (including the United States) under the Panama Declaration of 1939. This zone was established around America (except for Canada) as a measure of self-protection and defense of neutrality. The legal validity of the zone was contested by the belligerents, including Great Britain, France, and Germany. *See also* FREEDOM OF THE HIGH SEAS, 231; MARITIME WARFARE, THE LAW OF, 347.

Significance   Historically the first defense zones at sea were established up to 10 nautical miles from the coastline by Japan in 1904. During World War I, zones of the same nature and width were proclaimed by the United States upon its entry into the war. Much more extensive war zones were introduced by other belligerents, first Great Britain, and then Germany, whose zone eventually encompassed all waters around Great Britain, France, Italy, and the Eastern Mediterranean. During World War II, after Great Britain instituted a long-distance blockade against Germany in retaliation against the German mining of the waters around Great Britain, Germany proclaimed a total blockade of Great Britain in an operational zone extending far west of Ireland. Various zones were also established in conflicts after World War II. Thus, a war zone was proclaimed in the Persian Gulf by Iraq in its war against Iran, which started in 1980. In response to this,

Iran proclaimed its own, even wider, zone in the Gulf. A special kind of zone made its appearance during the Falklands War of 1982 between Argentina and the United Kingdom. In that conflict, the United Kingdom first established a 200-nautical-mile "maritime exclusion zone" around the Falkland Islands from which all Argentinian warships and naval auxiliaries were barred. Subsequently, this zone was replaced by a "total exclusion zone" of the same width, applying not only to the Argentinian warships but to any other ship and aircraft, including merchant vessels and civilian aircraft that were operating in support of the illegal occupation of the Falkland Islands by Argentina. Any such ships and aircraft were liable to be attacked by British forces. After the termination of hostilities, the zone was again replaced by a 150-nautical-mile "protection zone" from which Argentinian ships and aircraft were barred without the permission of the U.K. government.

Enemy Alien   **(338)**
A national of an enemy state who happens to be in the belligerent's territory at the outbreak of war. The legal status of enemy aliens is governed by customary law and—as far as parties to these treaties are concerned—Geneva Convention IV (1949) and Protocol I (1977). Under customary international law, enemy aliens (except for the actual and potential members of the enemy armed forces) must be granted a reasonable time to leave the belligerent's territory. All or some of the enemy aliens remaining there may be interned or left at liberty, subject to the duty of registration and other measures of control. In international practice, especially as ruled by courts in the United Kingdom and the United States, enemy aliens remaining in the belligerent's territory do not automatically acquire enemy character; a belligerent's nationals may do business with them, and they can sue and be sued in the courts of the belligerent. The protection of resident enemy aliens has been strengthened by Geneva Convention IV (1949) on the Protection of Civilian Population in Time of War, in which such aliens are classified as one category of "protected persons." They are assured extensive humanitarian safeguards concerning their departure, residence, employment, transfer to another state, and the like. Elaborate provisions govern the conditions of internment of enemy aliens. *See also* ALIEN, 150; ENEMY CHARACTER, 339.

Significance   In general, international practice confirms the view that enemy aliens may be permitted to remain in the belligerent's territory, although instances of expulsion have occurred. For example, France expelled all Prussian and other enemy subjects in 1870, and Russia expelled all Japanese from its far eastern territories in 1904.

Internment of enemy aliens was practiced on a large scale during the two world wars. Some exchanges of aliens took place through the intermediary of the International Committee of the Red Cross.

Enemy Character   (339)

A concept in the law of war whereby the qualification of enemy is not limited to enemy combatants but also includes nationals (individuals and legal entities) of the enemy state, its vessels and goods and, under certain circumstances, nationals, ships, and goods of neutral states. International law on enemy character is, to a large extent, unsettled. In general, enemy nationals residing in enemy territory bear enemy character. For the purposes of trading, enemy nationals residing in a neutral territory are deemed to have enemy character. Nationals of neutral countries can acquire enemy character if they reside in enemy territory or carry on business there; if they enlist in the enemy's armed force; of if they commit hostile acts against the belligerent. Even nationals of a belligerent may acquire enemy character if they find themselves in enemy-controlled territory. Corporations incorporated or carrying on business in enemy territory or controlled by enemy nationals are vested with enemy character. The enemy character of vessels is determined *prima facie* ("at first sight," pending final judicial determination) by their flag, but enemy-owned or controlled vessels under a neutral flag also have enemy character if they take a direct part in hostilities on behalf of the enemy or forcibly resist the legitimate exercise of the right of visit and search. For purposes of determining whether or not a vessel's flag is a "lawful flag" (that is, does not provide a cover for enemy interests) a prewar transfer of registry from the enemy to a neutral flag may be disregarded by the belligerent if the transfer agreement includes clauses on repurchase of the vessel by the former owners upon the termination of war. Transfer of title to a warship (or some other public ship) from the enemy to a neutral state, like the transfer by Germany to the then still neutral Turkey of the cruisers *Breslau* and *Goeben* during World War I, is void in the eyes of the belligerent.

Ownership is the basic test for establishing the enemy character of goods aboard a vessel, but the trade relationship of the neutral owner with the enemy or the enemy origin of goods have also been applied as tests of enemy character. All goods found aboard enemy vessels are presumed to have enemy character unless the contrary is proved by neutral owners. The enemy character of goods depends upon the enemy character of their owners, but as the rules on the enemy character of individuals and entities are not entirely clear, there are no universally recognized rules as to the enemy character of goods. There is no unanimity of view on the question whether or not transfer of enemy goods at sea (*in transitu*) to a neutral vessel divests such goods of their enemy character. *See also* CONTRABAND, 333; ENEMY PROPERTY, 340; NATIONALITY OF SHIPS, 245; NEUTRALITY, 351.

Significance   State practice on the subject of enemy character varied considerably in World Wars I and II. Hague Convention V of 1907 Respecting the Rights and Duties of Neutral Powers and Persons in Case of War on Land had only a few minor provisions on the matter, and the London Declaration (1909), which had offered some common basis for international practice of maritime powers, never entered into force. Investment with enemy character is important in that municipal law imposes either a complete ban or severe restrictions on contracts with persons possessing enemy character, especially in the area of commercial relations. In general, the trend toward the totalization of war effort in the two world wars resulted in widening the scope of the concept of enemy character.

Enemy Property   (340)

Property owned by an enemy state or its nationals in the belligerent state upon the outbreak of hostilities. Enemy property in this sense must be distinguished from enemy property found in occupied territory whose legal status is governed by the law of belligerent occupation. The treatment of enemy property varies depending upon whether it is public or private. While public property can be seized, buildings belonging to the enemy's diplomatic representation are excluded from seizure. Although, until the early nineteenth century, belligerents were permitted to confiscate property belonging to private enemy subjects, this practice was eventually reversed. Enemy property in the form of stock held by enemy aliens in business enterprises is administered under the custodianship of the belligerent state which, as demonstrated by the practice of the two world wars, would even dispose of the property if needed. Whether or not the seized enemy property is to be returned to the owners if the peace treaty does not call for it remains a controversial issue. Prior to World War I, enemy private merchant vessels in the belligerents' waters were, by comity, granted a limited period of time—so-called "days of grace" (*délai de faveur*)—during which they were allowed to leave. However, when war was imminent, the potential belligerents would sometimes lay an embargo upon each other's vessels. Hague Convention VI of 1907 Relative to the Status of Enemy Merchant Ships at the Outbreak of Hostilities stated that it was desirable that private enemy vessels in a belligerent's ports should be allowed to depart and were not subject to confiscation. However, in the practice of the two world wars, these rules were disregarded. There are no rules governing the status of enemy civil aircraft, but confiscation does not appear contrary to international law. *See also* ALIEN, 150; ENEMY ALIEN, 338; ENEMY CHARACTER, 339.

Significance   International law governing enemy property located in the belligerent's territory is not adequately developed and is based primarily on state practice in the two world wars. Most states which initially avoided confiscation of enemy aliens' property eventually adopted measures which, albeit not confiscatory, would result in the aliens' loss of property. The peace treaties provided for compensation only for the nationals of the victorious power. The United States followed this practice by ordering registration with the Alien Property Custodian of all enemy-controlled business enterprises located in the United States. The U.S. War Claims Act of 1948 provided that owners of alien property seized during World War II would not be compensated. One case of alien property, involving the General Aniline and Film Corporation, incorporated in the United States but owned by a Swiss company, Interhandel (itself ultimately controlled by a German firm), became the object of the celebrated case before the International Court of Justice (ICJ)—the *Interhandel* case (*Switzerland v. the United States*, 1959). The Swiss claim was held inadmissible because of nonexhaustion of local remedies.

General Participation Clause   (341)

A clause found in the Hague Conventions of 1899 and 1907 governing the conduct of hostilities, stating that the Conventions shall be binding upon the belligerents only as long as all are parties to them. A general participation clause was also included in other pre–World War I conventions, such as the Geneva Convention of 1906. *See also* HAGUE CONVENTIONS (1907), 343; INTERNATIONAL HUMANITARIAN LAW, 344.

Significance   The general participation clause considerably weakened the effectiveness of the conventions containing it, since as soon as a nonsignatory state (however insignificant) joined the war, the convention ceased to be binding if the clause was invoked by a belligerent. During World War I, for example, Germany availed itself of this possibility. However, as affirmed by some municipal courts (for example, the British courts), the conventions with a general participation clause applied in any case since for the most part, they were declaratory of the existing customary international law. The same position was taken by the Nuremberg International Military Tribunal in 1946, which ruled that the fact that the Soviet Union was not a party to the

1929 Geneva Convention Relative to the Treatment of Prisoners of War did not permit Germany in its war with the Soviet Union to violate the generally accepted principles of international law on the subject. The general participation clause is rejected in contemporary international humanitarian law. The 1949 Geneva Conventions uniformly provide that even if a party to an armed conflict is not a party to the Convention the states parties must remain bound by its provisions in their mutual relations and even in relation to a nonparty belligerent if the latter accepts and applies the Convention. The principle of reciprocity, which allows a belligerent not to abide by the rules of warfare in relations with an adversary who patently and deliberately violates such rules, must be distinguished from the now abandoned general participation clause.

Geneva Conventions (1949) (342)

Four conventions revising, developing, and codifying the international humanitarian law on the protection of the victims of war. The Geneva Conventions, sometimes known as the Red Cross Conventions, were drafted under the aegis of the International Committee of the Red Cross and approved by the representatives of fifty-eight states at a diplomatic conference in Geneva in 1949. Virtually all the states of the world are parties to these four Conventions. Convention I for the Amelioration of the Condition of the Wounded and Sick in Armed Forces in the Field is a further improvement of the orginal Geneva Conventions of 1864 (revised in 1906) and 1929. Convention II for the Amelioration of the Condition of the Wounded, Sick, and Shipwrecked Members of Armed Forces at Sea updates similar Conventions of 1899 and 1907. Convention III Relative to the Treatment of Prisoners of War updates the Geneva Convention of 1929 which, in turn, was preceded by provisions on prisoners of war of the Hague Regulations annexed to Hague Convention IV of 1907 and a similar Convention of 1899 respectively. Geneva Convention IV Relative to the Protection of Civilian Persons in Time of War was to a large extent prompted by the atrocities committed against populations primarily by Nazi Germany in World War II. *See also* BELLIGERENT OCCUPATION, 326; INTERNATIONAL HUMANITARIAN LAW, 344; PRISONERS OF WAR, 354; PROTECTING POWER, 358; PROTOCOLS I AND II (1977), 359; WOUNDED, SICK, AND SHIPWRECKED, 368.

Significance The Geneva Conventions of 1949 represent the most important codification of international humanitarian law protecting the victims of armed conflict, both members of armed forces and civilians (protected persons). To a large extent, many of the provisions of the Conventions are the result of the tragic experiences of World

War II. However, soon after the adoption of the Geneva Conventions, new kinds of warfare and armed conflict as well as new types of weapons made it necessary to revise and adjust them to new technological and political contexts. The two Protocols of 1977 were designed to achieve this objective.

Hague Conventions (1907)   (343)

Eleven conventions adopted at the second Hague Peace Conference, regulating various aspects of the laws of war and neutrality. Of the eleven Hague Conventions of 1907, ten were ratified and are still in force. Convention XII on the Establishment of an International Prize Court never entered into force. The other ten instruments are (1) Convention III Relative to the Opening of Hostilities; (2) Convention IV Respecting the Laws and Customs of War on Land, with Annex and Regulations (the most important of the Hague Conventions, in force for forty-three states and replacing as between the contracting parties the 1899 Convention which is still in force for seventeen states); (3) Convention V Respecting the Rights and Duties of Neutral Powers and Persons in Case of War on Land; (4) Convention VI Relative to the Status of Enemy Merchant Ships at the Outbreak of Hostilities; (5) Convention VII Relative to the Conversion of Merchant Ships into Warships; (6) Convention VIII Relative to the Laying of Automatic Submarine Contact Mines; (7) Convention IX Respecting Bombardment by Naval Forces in Time of War; (8) Convention X (a revision of Convention III of 1899) for the Adaptation to Maritime Warfare of the Principles of the Geneva Convention (of 1864); (9) Convention XI Relative to Certain Restrictions with Regard to the Exercise of the Right of Capture in Naval War; and (10) Convention XIII Concerning the Rights and Duties of Neutral Powers in Naval War. (Conventions I and II did not deal with the laws of war and neutrality.) *See also* DECLARATION OF WAR, 336; INTERNATIONAL HUMANITARIAN LAW, 344; MARITIME WARFARE, LAW OF, 347; NEUTRALITY, 351.

Significance   The Hague Conventions of 1907 were a major codification of the laws of war and neutrality adopted at a conference attended by representatives of forty-four countries. Among the Hague Conventions, Convention IV is the best known since it deals with the conduct of hostilities on land, regulated in detail in the Regulations (Hague Regulations) annexed to the Convention. The Hague Conventions are still legally binding, although many of their provisions lie far behind the modern conditions of warfare and have otherwise been overtaken by political and economic conditions. The number of states for which the conventions are in force is relatively small, amounting to not more than forty-odd parties. The United States is a party to all of the Conventions except Conventions VI, VII, and X; but, generally speaking, to the extent that the Hague Conventions are declaratory of customary international law, they bind all parties to an armed conflict, although in the past their effectiveness was considerably impaired by the "general participation clause" invoked by some belligerents.

International Humanitarian Law   (344)

The part of public international law governing the use of armed force and the treatment of individuals in the course of armed conflict. International humanitarian law is designed to reduce and limit the suffering of individuals in war and other armed conflict, and in this sense it is an extension of the principles of the protection of human rights to the international law governing armed conflict. The concept of international humanitarian law has, in general, replaced the concept of the law of war or, more inclusively, the law of international armed conflict. A distinction is still sometimes made, however, between international humanitarian law in the strict sense of the word (the Geneva law) and the law of war in a more general meaning, encompassing also matters not directly related to humanitarian considerations. International humanitarian law applies in international armed conflicts and— stipulated in general terms in the 1949 Geneva Conventions and regulated in more detail in Protocol II of 1977—in noninternational armed conflicts. States, individuals, the United Nations, and possibly other intergovernmental organizations, national liberation movements, insurgents, and the International Committee of the Red Cross in its capacity of protecting power can be subjects of international humanitarian law. There is general agreement that, since international humanitarian law is designed to protect individuals, its benefits cannot be withheld from a state on the grounds that it has violated the United Nations principle prohibiting resort to force. International humanitarian law binds all parties to an armed conflict. The so-called "general participations clause" of the old Hague law of war is rejected in modern international law. Although general principles of humanity apply to warfare on land, at sea, and in the air (and potentially in outer space), a distinction is usually made between the law of land warfare and the law of maritime (naval) warfare. The law of air warfare is the least developed branch of the law of armed conflict.

In the second half of the nineteenth century and in the early twentieth century the laws of war, heretofore customary except for occasional agreements regarding exchange of prisoners and tending each other's wounded, began to be codified in a series of treaties beginning with the Declaration of Paris of 1856 dealing with certain aspects of naval warfare. The next treaty was the Geneva Convention of 1864 (later replaced by the Geneva Convention of 1906) for the Amelioration of the Condition of Soldiers Wounded in Armies in the Field, adopted under the aegis of Switzerland at the initiative of Henri Dunant, the founder of the International Committee of the Red Cross (ICRC). This was followed by the Declaration of St. Petersburg of 1868 prohibiting the use of certain projectiles. The Hague Peace Conferences of 1899 and especially 1907 are a major landmark in the history of the law of war. The first Conference produced a Convention with Respect to the Laws and Customs of War on Land, subsequently revised in 1907 and known in its new version as Hague Convention IV Respecting the Laws and Customs of War on Land whose annex in the form of detailed and fundamental Regulations became the main source of the law of land warfare in both world wars. The Convention was based on instructions issued by the United States to its armed forces during the American Civil War, prepared from a draft by Francis Lieber, a German-born professor of history and political science at Columbia College in New York. Eventually other major powers prepared manuals of land warfare for their respective forces. The First Hague Conference (1899) also adopted a Convention (No. III of 1899) for the Adaptation to Sea Warfare of the Principles of the Geneva Convention of 1864, subsequently revised as Hague Convention X in 1907, and three Declarations: (1) Concerning Expanding (Dum-dum) Bullets; (2) Concerning Projectiles and Explosives Launched from Balloons; and (3) Concerning Projectiles Diffusing Asphyxiating or Deleterious Gases. The Second Hague Peace Conference (1907) produced, in addition to Convention IV, ten other Conventions dealing with opening of hostilities, neutrality, and various aspects of war at sea. Only one of these instruments (Convention XII on International Prize Court) failed to enter into force. To a large extent, these early treaties represented rules that were already part of customary law or were subsequently recognized as such. Some of the rules (particularly those protecting the victims of war) have become peremptory norms of general international law (*jus cogens*). Following the experiences of World War I, the law of war was further developed by the 1925 Protocol for the Prohibition of the Use in War of Asphyxiating, Poisonous, or Other Gases, and of Bacteriological Methods of Warfare; two Geneva Conventions of 1929, one on the Treatment of Prisoners of War and the other for the Amelioration of the Condition of the Wounded and Sick Armies in the Field (replacing as between the signatories the Conventions of 1864 and 1906); and the 1936 London Protocol Relating to the Use of Submarines against Merchant Vessels. At the regional level, some American states signed a Convention on Maritime Neutrality in Havana (1928) of which eight states, including the United States, are still parties. The lessons of World War II brought about reaffirmation and expansion of the 1929 Geneva Conventions by four Geneva Conventions of 1949 on (1) the wounded and sick in the field; (2) the wounded, sick, and shipwrecked at sea; (3) prisoners of war; and (4) the protection of civilian persons. These Red Cross conventions have been ratified by virtually all the countries of the world. In 1977, they were supplemented by two Protocols: (1) on the International Armed Conflict; and (2) on the Noninternational Armed Conflict, adopted by the Diplomatic Conference on Reaffirmation and Development of International Humanitarian Law Applicable in Armed Conflict (1974–1977). However, the Protocols have been ratified by only a limited number of states, mostly from the Third World. Other post–World War II treaties relating to the conduct of war include the Hague Convention of 1954 for the Protection of Cultural Property in Time of War; the Convention of 1977 on the Prohibition of Military or Any Other Hostile Use of Environmental Modification Techniques; and the Convention of 1980 (open for signature in 1981) on Prohibitions and Restrictions on the Use of Certain Conventional Weapons Which May Be Deemed to Be Excessively Injurious or to Have Indiscriminate Effects, with three Protocols (on nondetectable fragments; on mines, booby traps and other devices; and on incendiary weapons); and one Resolution on small-caliber weapon systems. As part of arms control measures, the United Nations sponsored the Conventions of 1972 on the Prohibition of the Development, Production, and Stockpiling of Bacteriological (Biological) and Toxin Weapons. It is generally admitted that, beyond all the conventional law, parties to an armed conflict are bound by laws of humanity and the dictates of public conscience, especially in the areas not regulated by any treaty provision. This principle dates back to a clause in the Preamble to Hague Convention IV of 1907 (the so-called "Martens clause"). *See also* AIR WARFARE, 321; ARMED CONFLICT: INTERNATIONAL, 323; ARMED CONFLICT: NONINTERNATIONAL, 324; DECLARATION OF LONDON (1909), 334; DECLARATION OF PARIS (1856), 335; GENERAL PARTICIPATION CLAUSE, 341; GENEVA CONVENTIONS (1949), 342; HAGUE CONVENTIONS (1907), 343; MARITIME WARFARE, LAW OF, 347; NEUTRALITY, 351; PROTOCOLS I AND II (1977), 359; WAR CRIMES, 367.

Significance   While rules commanding humane treatment of individuals during war can be traced to the teachings of the Church in the Middle Ages, customary "law of war" (an important part of the doctrine of the law of nations already in its classical period from the sixteenth to the eighteenth century) continued to grow in the practice of states in the eighteenth and nineteenth centuries when absence of ideological fervor and the balance of power system of flexible alliances exercised a restraining influence upon the brutality of armed conflict. War was basically a contest between armed forces of sovereign states, and armed action had the objective of destroying the military capability of the enemy by applying the necessary force without inflicting unnecessary suffering for no military advantage. The traditional law of war, from which the modern international humanitarian law is derived, was based upon these fundamental principles: (1) that even during the war the conduct of the belligerents is subject to the commands of international law, the violation of which is not justified even by military necessity; (2) that unnecessary suffering and superfluous injury must be avoided; (3) that a distinction must be maintained between belligerent and neutral states, between combatants and noncombatants, and between military and nonmilitary targets; and (4) that laws of humanity and the "dictates of the public conscience" also apply in cases not regulated by the conventional law. However, since World War I (1914–1918) these principles have been subjected to serious challenges brought about by developments in weapons technology, the advent of total warfare, and (particularly during and following World War II [1939–1945]) bitter ideological conflict leading to a life-and-death struggle in which many traditional rules of war were disregarded or made obsolete. The undermining of the traditional rules started during World War I, with resort to total economic warfare, unrestricted submarine warfare, and inclusion of the airspace in the hostilities by the use of air power, the developments which made the distinction between armed forces and the civilian population virtually meaningless, a process culminating in the unprecedented destruction and atrocities of World War II, fought for virtually unlimited objectives and until the total surrender of the enemy. The post–World War II era has witnessed, on the one hand, further rapid technological advances in the art of war and, on the other, the proliferation of partly civil and partly international armed conflicts waged in a ruthless ideological and nationalistic climate and conditions which did not fit the relatively simple war-peace dichotomy of the traditional international war. Finally, the prospect of a push-button "dehumanized" nuclear war, in which all the traditional distinctions would have little if any relevance, has brought into question the very existence of international humanitarian law. Yet, despite all the obstacles in the way of applying its rules, this branch of international law has brought at least some restraints on the inhumanity of war in the numerous regional armed conflicts that have occurred in the period following World War II.

Irregular Forces (345)

Members of the armed forces of a party to an armed conflict (other than its regular forces) operating in or outside their own territory, even if this territory is occupied, who under certain conditions have rights and duties under the laws of war. Under both Hague Regulations (Convention IV of 1907 or the corresponding Convention of 1899) and the Geneva Convention III of 1949, irregular forces, commonly known as guerrillas (partisans and resistance movements in World War II), meet these conditions if (1) they are commanded by a person responsible for his subordinates; (2) have a fixed distinctive sign recognizable at a distance; (3) carry arms openly; and (4) conduct their operations in accordance with the laws and customs of war. These requirements are completely unrealistic and incompatible with the modes of guerrilla warfare, which means that in most cases, members of irregular forces would have to be treated like common criminals. In recognition of this, apart from including wars of national liberation among international conflicts, Protocol I of 1977 has changed the legal status of irregular forces by which most states participating in the Diplomatic Conference of 1974–1977 understood guerrillas fighting such wars. In particular, while establishing a general duty of combatants to distinguish themselves from the civilian population, in exceptional situations Protocol I allows irregular forces to appear as civilians provided they carry their arms openly during each military engagement and during such time as they are visible to the adversary at the stage of military deployment preceding the attack. *See also* ARMED CONFLICT: INTERNATIONAL, 323; ARMED CONFLICT: NONINTERNATIONAL, 324; COMBATANTS AND NONCOMBATANTS, 331; PRISONERS OF WAR, 354.

Significance Participation of irregular forces in war had been known long before the term guerrilla (in Spanish "little war") became widely known, having originated in the Spanish guerrilla against Napoleonic France. Partisan warfare against Nazi Germany during World War II (especially in Poland, Yugoslavia, and the Soviet Union) was the most famous chapter in the history of irregular forces. For all practical purposes, such forces were denied any rights of lawful combatants by Germany. After World War II, irregular forces have been usually associated with participants in anticolonial nationalist armed struggle, such as in Algeria, in Kenya (the Mau-Mau uprising), and in Indochina, and with leftist insurgencies such as El Salvador. However, nationalist, "separatist" guerrilla irregular forces, such as the Eritreans in Ethiopia, should not be overlooked.

Levée en masse   (346)

Spontaneous taking up of arms on the approach of an enemy by inhabitants of an unoccupied territory who had no time to form themselves into regular armed units. In order to be considered lawful combatants entitled to the status of prisoners of war in case of capture, the inhabitants participating in a *levée en masse* must, under Geneva Convention IV of 1949, carry arms openly and respect the laws and customs of war. *See also* COMBATANTS AND NONCOMBATANTS, 331; IR-REGULAR FORCES, 345; PRISONERS OF WAR, 354.

Significance   One essential element of the *levée en masse* is that the mass rising of the inhabitants should take place when the enemy approaches, not after the enemy has occupied the territory. Members of a *levée en masse* are considered lawful combatants even though they wear no distinctive signs. When a mass rising of citizenry takes place, all the inhabitants of the area may be considered legitimate enemies until the area is taken. Thereafter, the enemy may treat all males of military age as prisoners of war even if they may have laid down arms and returned to their homes.

Maritime Warfare, Law of   (347)

The rules of the law of war governing hostilities at sea. There is no instrument designed (such as the Hague Regulations governing the law of land warfare) that would comprehensively deal with the law of maritime warfare. The Declaration of London (1909), which otherwise never entered into force, dealt only with the economic aspects of the problem. The rules of warfare at sea are to be sought partly in customary law and considerations of humanity and partly in various treaties beginning with the Declaration of Paris (1856).

   The bulk of the law of naval warfare is constituted by seven Hague Conventions of 1907: (1) Convention VI Relating to the Status of Enemy Merchant Ships at the Outbreak of Hostilities; (2) Convention VII Relative to the Conversion of Merchant Ships into Warships; (3) Convention VIII Relative to the Laying of Automatic Submarine Contact Mines; (4) Convention IX Respecting Bombardment by Naval Forces in Time of War; (5) Convention X (replacing a Convention of 1899) for the Adaptation to Maritime Warfare of the Principles of the Geneva (1906) Convention (6) Convention XI Relative to Certain Restrictions with Regard to the Exercise of the Right of Capture in Naval War; and—of indirect interest—Convention XIII Concerning the Rights and Duties of Neutral Powers in Naval War. Convention X was revised and substantially enlarged by Geneva Convention II of 1949 for the Amelioration of the Condition of Wounded, Sick, and Ship-

wrecked Members of Armed Forces at Sea, subsequently complemented by some provisions of Protocol I (1977). Submarine warfare
is still subject to the 1936 London Protocol relating to the use of
submarines against merchant vessels, which forms Part IV of the London Treaty (1930) for the limitation and reduction of naval armaments,
terminated in 1936.

Unlike land warfare, whose aim is to defeat the enemy army and
occupy the enemy territory, the objective of naval warfare is not only to
overpower the enemy's armed forces at sea but also to weaken him
economically by means of such acts of economic warfare as capture of
merchant vessels and property of the enemy and (under certain circumstances) also of the neutrals. Naval warfare is normally conducted
by warships of the belligerents, among which submarines occupy a
special position from the point of view of the rules of naval warfare.
Privateering—that is, commissioning by a state of private merchant
vessels to fight by issuance of "letters of marque"—was made illegal by
the Declaration of Paris (1856). However, a merchant vessel may refuse
to submit to visit and search by an enemy man-of-war and is allowed to
defend herself against an attack. Under Hague Convention VII of
1907 (not signed by the United States), merchant vessels may be lawfully converted into warships in which case they must observe the laws
and usages of war and be under the authority of the flag state and
command of a duly commissioned officer. The question of where
conversion may be performed is controversial, but the British practice
during the two world wars required that it be effected in a home port
and not at sea or in a neutral port.

The general rules of international humanitarian law apply to
maritime warfare as well. Only military targets such as enemy warships,
military aircraft, and military coastal installations may be lawfully attacked. Merchant vessels may be attacked only if they refuse to submit
themselves to visit and search by enemy warships. Submarine warfare
against merchant vessels is a controversial issue. Small craft and coastal
fishing boats are exempt from attack and capture under customary law
(as thoroughly analyzed by the U.S. Supreme Court in the Case of the
Paquete Habana and the *Lola* in 1900) and Hague Convention XI.
Hospital ships are immune under Hague Convention X and Geneva
Convention II (1949). Correspondence in mail bags (but not parcel
post) is immune from capture under Hague Convention XI but may be
subject to censorship. International practice seems to allow the cutting
of submarine cables by belligerents. Naval bombardment of undefended ports and towns is prohibited under Hague Convention IX
unless the local authority refuses to comply with a formal requisitioning demand for provisions and supplies. Automatic submarine contact
mines belong to weapons prohibited under Hague Convention VIII.

The protection of wounded, sick, and shipwrecked is governed by Geneva Convention II of 1949, complemented by Protocol I of 1977. Hostile acts relating to economic warfare at sea include condemnation of captured merchant vessels and goods as lawful prize by a prize court of the captor state and belligerent blockade, including the long-distance blockade. The law of neutrality is closely related to the law of maritime warfare. *See also* ANGARY, RIGHT OF, 322; BLOCKADE: BELLIGERENT, 327; BLOCKADE: LONG-DISTANCE, 328; CONTINUOUS VOYAGE, DOCTRINE OF, 332; CONTRABAND, 333; DECLARATION OF LONDON (1909), 334; DECLARATION OF PARIS (1856), 335; DEFENSE (WAR) ZONES, 337; HAGUE CONVENTIONS (1907), 348; NAVICERT SYSTEM, 350; PRIZE COURT, 355; PROHIBITED WEAPONS, 357; SUBMARINE WARFARE (UNRESTRICTED), 364.

Significance   The laws and usages of war at sea experienced serious challenges in the two world wars and frequently proved to be unrealistic in the face of technological advances and the nature of warfare in the twentieth century. A case in point was unrestricted warfare by submarines against merchant vessels. Technically, sinking such vessels was a war crime; but it was practiced on a large scale by all maritime belligerent powers whose submarines found it difficult for technical reasons to abide by the rules governing the treatment of merchant vessels. Other rules of maritime warfare, disregarded in both world wars (and by the United States off the North Vietnamese coast), included prohibitions relating to the laying of automatic submarine contact mines and bombardment of undefended enemy coast. Germany was accused of sinking coastal fishing vessels and hospital ships and killing shipwrecked at sea in both wars. Since the rules concerning the treatment of enemy merchant vessels and war at sea in general have not been reviewed since the early twentieth century, the status of the law of maritime warfare continues to be uncertain.

Mercenary   (348)
A national of a third state recruited to fight in an armed conflict, who is motivated by the desire of private gain and does in fact take a direct part in hostilities. Under general customary law and the Hague Regulations of Convention IV of 1907 (and the corresponding Convention of 1899) and Geneva Convention II (1949), mercenaries as well as foreign volunteers are treated as any other combatants (regular or irregular as the case may be) provided that they obey the laws and customs of war. However, under Protocol I (1977), a mercenary (but not a foreign volunteer) has no right to be a combatant and, therefore, is not entitled

to the status of prisoner of war on capture. Under this treaty, to be a mercenary an individual (in addition to meeting the essentials of the above definition) must meet the following conditions: (1) he must be promised material compensation substantially in excess of that promised or paid to combatants of similar ranks and functions in the armed forces of the party that hires him; (2) he must not be a national, resident, or member of the armed forces of a party to the conflict; and (3) he must not have been sent by a third state on official duty as a member of its armed forces. *See also* COMBATANTS AND NONCOMBATANTS, 331; IRREGULAR FORCES, 345; PRISONERS OF WAR, 354.

Significance   The issue of mercenaries acquired notoriety in connection with civil strife in countries of black Africa as, for example, in the Congo (now Zaire). Since mercenaries were normally hired by parties to an armed conflict on the opposite side of the political preferences of the majority of Third World countries, the United Nations General Assembly condemned the practice of hiring mercenaries, and Protocol I denied them any rights as combatants. Therefore, state parties to the Protocol are allowed to treat mercenaries as common criminals.

Military Necessity, Doctrine of   (349)

A doctrine asserted by some German publicists before World War I and adopted on occasion by Germany and other states, according to which in cases of extreme military necessity the laws of war lose their binding force. The doctrine of military necessity is rejected by international law as illegal. The Hague Regulations (Convention IV [1907] and the 1899 Convention respectively) expressly state that the belligerent's right to adopt means of injuring the enemy is not unlimited and that this rule does not lose its binding force in cases of military necessity. Furthermore, the laws of war themselves have been framed in a way that already takes into account the concept of military necessity. *See also* INTERNATIONAL HUMANITARIAN LAW, 344; PROHIBITED METHODS OF WARFARE, 356; REPRISALS IN WAR, 361; WAR CRIMES, 367.

Significance   Historically, the doctrine of military necessity— *Kriegsraeson*—originated at a time when warfare was not regulated by international law, but lost its relevance with the emergence of customary and then conventional rules regulating the conduct of hostilities. In 1945 in the case of the *Peleus*, a British military court ruled that killing survivors at sea by the commander of a German U-boat in order to destroy any traces of sinking and make the pursuit of the submarine improbable was a violation of the laws of war, and the more proper course would have been to leave the locale of the sinking as soon as possible. The plea of military necessity was also rejected by other courts trying war criminals after World War II.

Navicert System   (350)

A system of certificates issued by a representative of the belligerent in a neutral country to a neutral shipper, testifying that the cargo aboard his neutral vessel was not liable to seizure as contraband and allowing the vessel and its cargo to proceed to its neutral destination. The navicert system, applied by Great Britain in the two world wars, was a device allowing a relatively unhindered trade between neutrals themselves and between neutrals and belligerents. Vessels provided with navicerts were exempt from search and capture, but a navicert did not offer a complete guarantee against them. *See also* CONTINUOUS VOYAGE, DOC- TRINE OF, 332; CONTRABAND, 333; NEUTRALITY, 351.

Significance   Documents in the nature of navicerts were first intro- duced by England under Queen Elizabeth I in 1590, but were not much used until the first and especially second world wars. Navicerts were issued in the form of ship navicerts, cargo navicerts, and certificates of origin and interest, the latter document referring to a pass issued in neutral territory by the belligerent, certifying that a declaration of the nonenemy origin and ownership of goods has been made by the ship- owner. "Aircerts" and "mailcerts" for goods sent from neutral countries were also introduced. Since 1940, Great Britain followed a legal pre- sumption that neutral vessels without navicerts had an enemy destina- tion, thus shifting to the shipper the burden of proof of innocence. Navicerts and similar documents were all part of arrangements by the Allies, especially Great Britain and the United States, in order to more effectively pursue the economic warfare at sea.

Neutrality   (351)

The legal status of a state during a war between third states whereby that state adopts an attitude of impartiality toward the belligerents which they recognize and which creates rights and duties under inter- national law between the neutral state and the belligerents. Neutrality can also exist in the case of a civil war where both sides are recognized as belligerents. One must distinguish a "permanently neutral" or "neu- tralized" state such as Switzerland (neutralized in 1815), Austria (in 1955), and, technically, Laos (in 1962) from a state that is neutral only in relation to a particular war that is being waged. Neutrality in the traditional sense, as it developed in the modern international system and became codifed in 1907 in Hague Conventions V (neutrality in case of war on land) and XIII (neutrality in naval war) and the never ratified Declaration of London of 1909 (elaborating prize law as part of the law of neutrality), was repeatedly violated in the two world wars.

In today's changed economic, political, and legal circumstances, neutrality has become a partially obsolete institution of international law, although under certain circumstances it can still be applied in modern war. Under the rules of traditional neutrality in war on land (Hague Convention V of 1907), a neutral state has the basic right of the inviolability of its territory and freedom from belligerent acts. Belligerents are not permitted to open recruitment offices or form military courts on neutral territory. However, since the neutral rights and obligations are vested in the neutral state and not its nationals, a neutral state has no obligation to prevent its nationals or residents from going abroad and offering their services to a belligerent. For example, Sweden allowed several thousand volunteers to join Finland in its war against the Soviet Union in 1939–1940. However, Sweden violated its neutral duties when subsequently, albeit for a brief period, it allowed recruitment of volunteers in its territory. Although a neutral state as such is prohibited from furnishing war material and services to a belligerent, its nationals are allowed to engage in such trade. A neutral state has the right—and a permanently neutral state the duty—to defend its neutrality by force of arms. If it fails to do so, the other belligerent may attack the enemy forces on the neutral territory. The sick and wounded of a belligerent may transit neutral territory. Troops of any belligerent crossing the border into a neutral state's territory must be interned.

The neutral rights and duties in naval warfare are regulated in Hague Convention XIII, and for eight American states (including the United States) in the 1928 Havana Convention on Maritime Neutrality. Neutral waters are inviolable and belligerents are prohibited from engaging in any hostilities there, but a mere passage of a belligerent warship and its prizes does not compromise neutrality. On the other hand, a neutral state may grant temporary asylum to belligerents' warships, but in the practice of the two world wars most neutrals closed their waters to belligerents' submarines. If a neutral permits belligerents' warships (a maximum of three) to use its port or waters, their length of stay is limited to twenty-four hours. Reprovisioning and refueling are allowed up to the peacetime standards of the ship in question. Only such repairs are permissible as are absolutely necessary to render the ship seaworthy without adding in any manner to its fighting capacity. The case of the German pocket battleship *Admiral Graf Spee*, granted seventy-two hours' time by Uruguay to carry out repairs in Montevideo at the beginning of World War II in 1939 but subsequently scuttled in Uruguayan territorial waters, dramatically illustrates the rights and duties of neutrals in naval warfare. Armed merchant vessels are, in principle, treated as ordinary merchant ships; but under the circumstances the neutral state may treat them as warships. A neutral state has the duty to use "the means at its disposal" to prevent the fitting out or arming of a ship which might be used by a belligerent—a rule of Hague Convention XIII, modifying the "due diligence" clause of the U.S.–Great Britain Treaty of Washington of 1870 concerning claims related to the operations of the Confederate cruiser *Alabama* and some other ships built in Great Britain. A belligerent may bring captured prizes into a neutral port only because of lack of seaworthiness, weather, or shortage of fuel or provisions. Angary, belligerent blockade, and contraband create special rights and duties for belligerents and neutrals alike.

Neutrality in air warfare is not regulated by any special conventions although an attempt was made to include this matter in the unratified Hague Code of Air Warfare of 1923. It is clear, however, that under international law the airspace of a neutral state may not be violated by belligerents' aircraft, and any crew of such aircraft, if forced to land, must be interned. For humanitarian reasons Geveva Conventions I and II of 1949 allow medical aircraft of belligerents to overfly and land in neutral territory after prior notification of the neutral state. *See also* ANGARY, RIGHT OF, 322; BLOCKADE: BELLIGERENT, 327; BLOCKADE: LONG-DISTANCE, 328; CONTINUOUS VOYAGE, DOCTRINE OF, 332; CONTRABAND, 333; DECLARATION OF PARIS (1856), 335; MARITIME WARFARE, LAW OF, 347; NAVICERT SYSTEM, 350; NEUTRALIZED STATE, 58; PRIZE COURT, 355; UNNEUTRAL SERVICE, 316.

Significance   Although the concept of neutrality was referred to as early as the fourteenth century, the institution of neutrality (a term derived from the Latin word "neuter," meaning "neither") did not become a part of the law of nations until the sixteenth and seventeenth centuries, and its rules did not fully develop until the nineteenth century. Neutralization of Switzerland (1815), Belgium (1831 and 1839), and Luxembourg (1867); the Declaration of Paris (1856); the policy of the United States in its Civil War; and in particular the continued growth of international trade have contributed to the development of the rules governing neutrality and their codification in 1907. However, the twentieth century brought the decline of the institution of neutrality. Although in the two world wars states not participating in the conflict proclaimed neutrality, this status was repeatedly violated by belligerents both on land and at sea, and violations of neutral duties also took place. Violation of Belgium's permanent neutrality by Germany in World War I was the first major breach of neutrality by a belligerent country. At sea, neutrals were soon harassed by belligerents of both sides. Among some better known cases of violation of neutrality at sea during World War I were the case of the German cruiser *Dresden*, which refused to leave neutral Chilean waters and the subsequent violation of Chilean sovereignty by British warships with the resulting scuttling of the *Dresden*, and the capture by the British navy of the German merchant ship the *Düsseldorf* in neutral Norwegian waters, subsequently declared illegal by the British Privy Council. Other violations of neutral rights involved destruction of captured neutral vessels, sinking neutral vessels without warning, blockading of neutral ports and coasts and other interference with neutral commerce, and abuse of the right of angary in the name of military necessity. The adoption of the League of Nations Covenant (1919) and the outlawry of war by the Kellogg-Briand Pact (1928) did not, in actual practice, eliminate the institution of neutrality, and at the outbreak of World War II many states officially proclaimed neutrality.

Even more than World War I, the Second World War witnessed wholesale violations of neutrality by belligerents both at sea and on land and in the air. Invasions of neutral countries by Germany, violation of the Swiss airspace by both sides to the conflict, German violation of Sweden's neutrality by pressuring that country to allow transit privileges to unarmed German troops and supplies to Norway in 1940–1943, and again in 1941 to allow an armed German division to transit Sweden from Norway to Finland, are some of the examples of breach of neutrality in World War II. Whether or not Great Britain violated Norway's neutrality in 1940 by forcibly removing British prisoners of war from the German auxiliary vessel the *Altmark* sailing in Norwegian waters is a controversial issue, in view of the fact that Norway was delinquent in enforcing certain provisions of Hague Convention XIII and its own neutrality legislation. As far as violation by neutrals of their duties is concerned, the supplying by the United States of Great Britain with warships and other war material from U.S.-owned arsenals is considered by some as a breach of neutrality. On the other hand, this bias in favor of Great Britain, clearly violating the traditional duty of strict impartiality, could be justified by the fact that Germany had unlawfully resorted to war in violation of the Kellogg-Briand Pact and thereby exempted the neutral states parties to the Pact from this duty. In fact, until it joined the war in December 1941 the U.S. position was not that of classical neutrality but of what became known as "nonbelligerency"—the status of a nonbelligerent state which, while not participating in a war, does not observe impartiality, favoring one side in the conflict. A position of nonbelligerency favoring the Axis powers was assumed by Franco's Spain.

The prohibition of force by the Charter of the United Nations raised the question of the relevance of the institution of neutrality in a collective security system in which, strictly speaking, an attitude of impartiality toward the belligerents (some of whom are aggressors while others act in self-defense) would be impermissible. In practice, however, the collective security system did not prove feasible and the Security Council was not able to designate aggressors. As a result, the assumption of the status of traditional neutrality by individual states remained a possibility.

In the post–world wars armed conflicts, states have been reluctant to proclaim neutrality for a number of reasons. First, formal proclamation of neutrality would somehow recognize legitimacy of war in international relations. Second, even the parties to an armed conflict would not recognize it legally as a war, hence no neutrality status was legally possible. Third, proclaiming neutrality would be detrimental to the economic and commercial relations of nonbelligerents and would otherwise hamper their legal and political standing. Additionally, the distiction between neutral state and neutral trader and the corresponding difference in their rights and duties are clearly obsolete in today's world when the arms trade and frequently foreign trade in general are a state monopoly or at least under strict governmental control. Yet, in a world characterized by the contradiction between ideal legal norms denying the *raison d'être* of neutrality and the reality of frequent armed conflicts, the institution of neutrality could not become altogether obsolete. Thus, the Geneva Conventions of 1949 and other international instruments refer to neutral states and in general accept neutrality as a fact of international life.

Parlementaire (352)

An agent employed by a commander of belligerent forces in the field to go in person within the enemy lines for the purpose of communicating or negotiating openly and directly with the enemy commander. Under the Hague Regulations of Convention IV (or the corresponding 1899 Convention), a parlementaire advances bearing a white flag. The parlementaire, the trumpeter (bugler or drummer), the flag bearer, and the interpreter who may accompany the parlementaire have the right to inviolability, which they subsequently lose if it is proven that their privileged position was used to commit an act of treachery. Firing at a parlementaire or his party and misuse of the white flag by the parlementaire's party represent an abuse of the flag of truce. ARMISTICE, 325; CAPITULATION, 329; PROHIBITED METHODS OF WARFARE, 356.

Significance　Parlementaires have been used for centuries as agents used to communicate with the enemy in the field. Although it is prohibited to fire at an advancing parlementaire, the commander to whom he is sent is under no legal obligation to receive him.

Peace Treaty (353)

A treaty legally terminating the state of war between states. It is the normal mode of restoring a condition of peace between warring parties. Armistice and other measures of suspending hostilities do not have this effect unless, despite their name, they state that they end the conflict or the war and not just cease active hostilities; for example, the Indo-Pakistani Cease-Fire Agreement of 1965 or the Cease-Fire Agreement of 1973 concerning Vietnam which indicated that it was ending the war and restoring peace in Vietnam. In addition to stipulating termination of the state of war and the restoration of peace, a peace treaty contains provisions on liquidating the effects of war, such as restitution of property, repatriation of the prisoners of war, reparations, the validity of prewar treaties, territorial and military clauses, and the like. *See also* ARMISTICE, 325; TREATY, 279.

Significance A peace treaty restores normal peacetime rights and duties between the parties. Unless the treaty provides to the contrary, the status of movable public property is governed by the principle of *uti possidetis*, that is, retaining such property as was in possession of each party on the day of cessation of hostilities. Rights other than property are restored, hence all disabilities affecting nationals of the former belligerents during the war are removed under the principle known under Roman law as *jus postliminii*. Release of the prisoners of war and internees has been traditionally an important effect of peace treaties.

Although a peace treaty is the normal method of terminating the state of war, other methods have also been used such as cessation of hostilities followed by a gradual resumption of peaceful relations, for example, between France and Mexico in 1867 and in relations between Latin American countries in the nineteenth century. Another way of ending war has been by a unilateral declaration of termination of the state of war accepted by the other party. For example, World War II was terminated by peace treaties (1947) only with Italy, Bulgaria, Hungary, Romania, and Finland, whereas no treaty has been concluded with Germany whose existence as a state was otherwise destroyed by the war. Hence the state of war with Germany had to be formally terminated by unilateral declarations of the states concerned, for example, by the United States and the United Kingdom in 1951. A similar declaration was issued with regard to Austria in 1947. The peace treaty with Japan (1951) was not signed by the Soviet Union, Poland, Czechoslovakia, India, and China. Each of these countries eventually entered into

various bilateral arrangements with Japan whereby conditions of peace
were restored between them.

Prisoners of War   (354)

Individuals belonging to the armed forces of a party to an armed
conflict who have fallen into the power of the enemy. The legal status of
prisoners of war, dealt with already in the Hague Regulations of Convention IV (and the corresponding Convention of 1899), is regulated
in detail by Geneva Convention III of 1949 Relative to the Treatment of
Prisoners of War (superseding the Convention of 1929), further developed by some provisions of Protocols I and II of 1977. The status of
prisoners of war applies to members of regular and irregular armed
forces, including those who profess allegiance to a government or an
authority not recognized by the detaining power; persons accompanying the armed forces such as civilian personnel, labor units, war correspondents and the like; members of crews of merchant ships and civil
aircraft who otherwise, under international law, do not enjoy more
favorable treatment; individuals belonging to a *levée en masse*; potential
members of the armed forces of the adversary; and high civil government personnel. Medical personnel and chaplains receive all the protection under Geneva Convention III, but are not to be considered as
prisoners of war except for members of the armed forces temporarily
performing medical functions. Spies, saboteurs, and other unlawful
combatants are not entitled to the status of prisoners of war, but are still
protected persons to be treated with humanity and afforded a fair trial.

The Convention imposes strict duties upon the detaining power of
treating prisoners of war in a humane way. When questioned on the
subject, a prisoner of war is bound to give only his surname, first names
and rank, date of birth and serial number, and must not be forced to
give information useful to his captors. Prisoners of war may retain their
personal effects and are entitled to the same maintenance and payment
as the equivalent troops of the captor state. The detaining power may
utilize the labor of prisoners of war in specific economic fields, but
noncommissioned officers may only do supervisory work. Officers may
in no circumstances be compelled to work but may ask for suitable work
which should be found for them insofar as possible. Compelling a
prisoner of war to serve in the hostile forces is a serious breach of the
Convention. Prisoners of war must be granted the right to contact their
families and correspondence privileges. Like the 1929 Convention,
Geneva Convention III provides for a protecting power which has the
duty to determine whether or not the provisions of the Convention are
being observed. The Convention regulates in detail many other matters such as quarters; food; clothing; medical attention; religious, intel-

lectual, and physical activities; discipline; transfer of prisoners of war; penal and disciplinary sanctions; and escapes. Escaped prisoners who rejoin their own forces and are recaptured cannot be punished. Geneva Convention III also regulates the activities of information bureaus and relief societies for prisoners of war, including the crucial role of the most important international nongovernmental organization, the Geneva-based International Committee of the Red Cross (ICRC). On the important question of termination of captivity, the Convention stipulates the duty of the detaining power to release and repatriate prisoners of war without delay after the cessation of active hostilities and not, like the 1929 Convention, after the conclusion of peace. Sick and wounded prisoners of war must be repatriated earlier. *See also* COMBATANTS AND NONCOMBATANTS, 331; GENERAL PARTICIPATION CLAUSE, 341; GENEVA CONVENTIONS (1949), 342; PROTECTING POWER, 358; WAR CRIMES, 367; WOUNDED, SICK, AND SHIPWRECKED, 368.

Significance   In antiquity, prisoners of war were normally killed or sold into slavery. The latter practice continued until about the Thirty Years' War (1618–1648), but noble prisoners of war were often released for ransom. By the eighteenth century, the treatment of prisoners of war became more humane and civilized, and in the nineteenth century customary international law required prisoners of war to be treated according to standards comparable to those accorded the armed forces of the detaining power. The provisions of the *Instructions* issued for the U.S. army during the Civil War in 1863, based on Francis Lieber's draft, reflected this progress in the humane treatment of prisoners of war. (Lieber was a German-born professor of history and political science at Columbia College in New York.) In World War I, this treatment was governed by customary rules and provisions of the Hague Regulations of Convention IV of 1907 (or the corresponding Convention of 1899). After the war, more elaborate rules were adopted in the 1929 Convention which were in effect during World War II, except in relations between Germany and the Soviet Union. The war witnessed some serious violations of the Convention by Germany, but in general the prisoners of war of the Western powers were treated relatively humanely by that country. On the other hand—in violation of the most fundamental rules of international law based on the usages of civilized peoples, laws of humanity, and dictates of public conscience— Germany treated the Soviet prisoners of war with extreme brutality and ruthlessness, as a result of which hundreds of thousands of them died of starvation, ill treatment, or executions. War crimes trials after the war disclosed many cases of inhumane treatment of prisoners of war by Germany and, also, by Japan. However, the Soviet Union also committed grave violations of the laws of war protecting prisoners of war. The mass murder of thousands of Polish prisoners of war at Katyn by the Soviet Union in 1940 was the gravest of war crimes in this respect. Another breach of the laws of war was the failure by the Soviet Union to repatriate millions of German and Japanese prisoners of war after the end of World War II.

Following the war, problems again emerged in connection with the Korean War when many North Korean and Chinese "volunteer" prisoners of war refused to return to their homes with the resulting protracted stalemate in the armistice negotiations. In the Vietnam War, repatriation of prisoners of war went relatively smoothly, but in the Indo-Pakistani war of 1971 it was delayed for several years by India which threatened to transfer some Pakistani prisoners of war to Bangladesh for trial on charges of genocide. The matter was submitted by Pakistan to the International Court of Justice (ICJ), but was subsequently removed from the Court's list after the settlement of the dispute by negotiations. The experiences of the armed conflicts in the post–World War II period led to developing and refining the law on prisoners of war in Protocol I of 1977 which more clearly defined the role of the protecting power with respect to prisoners of war.

Prize Court   (355)

A municipal (domestic) court established by a belligerent state to adjudicate according to the rules of international law the lawfulness of prizes, that is, captured enemy or neutral vessels suspected of carrying contraband or running the blockade. Under customary international law the maritime belligerents are obliged to set up prize courts whose function is to decide whether or not a vessel and/or its cargo are liable to capture and condemnation as lawful prize. Belligerent warships are authorized under international law to exercise the right of visit and search with regard to merchant ships at sea except in neutral waters. If there is any reason to believe that a vessel is carrying contraband or is trying to run the blockade, it is taken into the belligerent's port for adjudication by a prize court. If the court upholds the legitimacy of the prize, the vessel and/or its cargo are declared a good or lawful prize and confiscated by the captor's state. The condemned vessel and cargo may be sold and the purchaser acquires an internationally valid title. Certain vessels, such as small craft and coastal fishing boats, can never be lawful prizes under customary law and relevant treaty provisions, in particular Hague Conventions VI and XI of 1907. Hospital and cartel ships and ships protected by the 1954 Hague Convention for the Protection of Cultural Property in Time of War are also immune from capture. A prize may be destroyed by its captor only if sending it into the captor's port is impossible or incompatible with military necessity, but the passengers and crew and the ship's papers must be put in a safe place. *See also* BLOCKADE: BELLIGERENT, 327; BLOCKADE: LONG-DISTANCE, 328; CONTINUOUS VOYAGE, DOCTRINE OF, 332; CONTRABAND, 333; DECLARATION OF LONDON (1909), 334; DECLARATION OF PARIS (1856), 335; MARITIME WARFARE, LAW OF, 347; NAVICERT SYSTEM, 350; NEUTRALITY, 351; SUBMARINE WARFARE (UNRESTRICTED), 364.

Significance   The origins of prize law and prize courts can be traced back to the Middle Ages. For example, in England the Court of Admiralty would perform certain functions of a modern prize court. Eventually the English practice became a recognized rule of customary international law. Although the prize courts often showed objectivity in their adjudication, there were also cases of bias in favor of the prize court's state. Hence proposals were put forward for the creation of an international prize court to which appeals could be made from decisions of national prize courts. However, Hague Convention XII of 1907 on the Establishment of an International Prize Court never entered into force. Prize courts functioned during both the world wars but unrestricted submarine warfare greatly reduced the role of these courts since merchant ships were frequently sunk instead of being captured and brought for adjudication before a prize court.

Prohibited Methods of Warfare   (356)

Methods of warfare of a nature to cause superfluous injury or unnecessary suffering, even though the weapons used may otherwise be lawful, or involving perfidy or breach of established rules of fairness in relations with the enemy. Prohibition of certain methods of warfare is based on the following principles: (1) that in any armed conflict the rights of the parties to choose methods of warfare is not unlimited; (2) that only as much force may be used as is required to overpower the enemy; (3) that superfluous injury and unnecessary suffering must be avoided; and (4) that a certain amount of chivalry, fairness, and respect should prevail even in the relations between hostile parties. The methods of combat and the conduct of hostilities are governed by Regulations of Hague Convention IV of 1907 (or the corresponding Convention of 1899), other relevant Hague Conventions, the Geneva Conventions of 1949, and Protocols I and II of 1977.

Resort to perfidy is one major unlawful method of conducting hostilities. Perfidy means acts inviting the confidence of an adversary to lead him to believe that he is entitled to, or is obliged to accord, protection under the rules of international law applicable in armed conflict, with intent to betray that confidence. Acts of perfidy include (1) the feigning of an intent to negotiate under a flag of truce or of a surrender; (2) the feigning of an incapacitation by wounds or sickness, or of civilian status; or (3) the feigning of protected status by the use of signs, emblems, or uniforms of the United Nations or of states not participating in the conflict. Ruses of war such as, for example, the use of camouflage, decoys, mock operations, misinformation, and other stratagems are not proscribed. In general, a ruse is an act intended to mislead an adversary or to induce him to act recklessly, which does not infringe upon any rule of international law and which is not perfidious. In addition to acts of perfidy, prohibited methods of warfare include making improper use of the emblem of the red cross, red crescent, or red lion and sun (the last mentioned adopted by Iran), or other internationally recognized emblems and signs, including the emblem of the United Nations, the flag of truce, and the protective emblem of cultural property. It is also prohibited to make use of the flags or emblems, insignia, or uniforms of states not parties to the conflict when engaging in attack or in order to shield, favor, protect, or impede military operations. Denial of quarter and attacking an enemy *hors de combat*— that is, when the enemy is in the power of the adverse party or clearly intends to surrender or is incapacitated—are violations of the laws of war. Airborne or parachute troops are not protected, but parachutists in distress cannot be made the object of attack and should be given an opportunity to surrender unless it is apparent that they are engaging in hostile acts. In practice, however, it is difficult to determine this with certainty. Nondefended towns ("open cities") and buildings cannot be attacked or bombarded, a rule that while technically still in force seems to have become obsolete in many instances of modern international and noninternational armed conflict. Defended localities must be warned by the attacking force before the commencement of bombardment, except in the case of an assault. Distinctly marked hospitals, churches, and similar buildings must be spared. There is no rule compelling the commander of the investing (besieging) force to permit evacuation of noncombatants from the besieged locality, but endeavors must be undertaken to conclude an agreement for removal of sick and wounded, children, maternity cases, and medical and religious personnel. Cultural, religious, and similar buildings must be spared, and pillage is prohibited. Taking hostages by the invading army is illegal. Warfare at sea is governed by additional rules. The regulation of air warfare has serious gaps. *See also* AIR WARFARE, 321; DEFENSE (WAR) ZONES, 337; MARITIME WARFARE, LAW OF, 347; PROHIBITED WEAPONS, 357; REPRISALS IN WAR, 361; SUBMARINE WARFARE (UNRESTRICTED), 364; WAR CRIMES, 367.

Significance   Experiences of the two world wars, and especially the second, demonstrated that the most frequently violated rules governing the methods of warfare pertained to the fundamental distinction of international humanitarian law between combatants and the civilian population and the principle that the amount of force to be used must be proportionate to the military necessity. Prohibition of attacking and bombarding nondefended localities was rendered illusory by the end of World War I, and World War II witnessed large-scale destruction of towns and property with high civilian casualties. The systematic and wanton destruction of Warsaw by Nazi Germany during and after the uprising in 1944 was the most striking example of this development, but hundreds of other undefended towns and other nonmilitary objectives were totally or partially destroyed. Some cities, however—Paris in 1940 and Rome in 1943, for example—were declared "open cities" and largely escaped damage. World War II also witnessed other violations of Hague Regulations. Taking hostages by the invading Nazi German army became routine. There were also isolated cases of perfidy in the form of wearing the uniforms of the adversary. The most notorious case occurred in 1944 during the Battle of the Bulge when German SS troops in U.S. uniforms infiltrated behind the Allied lines. However, a U.S. war crimes tribunal acquitted eight of these soldiers in 1947 since they had not been captured in the act of violating the law of war and were arraigned only after the cessation of hostilities.

Prohibited Weapons (357)

Weapons, projectiles, and material of a nature to cause superfluous injury or unnecessary suffering. Prohibited weapons are of two general categories: (1) those prohibited under the general definition without any specific ban of the particular weapon; and (2) specifically banned weapons. Prohibition of certain types of weapons is based on two general principles of international humanitarian law: first, that in any armed conflict the right of the parties to choose means of warfare is not unlimited; and second, that only as much force may be used in warfare as is required to overpower the enemy. There is no agreement on the specific kinds of weapons whose effect is superfluous injury or unnecessary suffering and, in the absence of specific prohibition, each party to an armed conflict must decide whether or not a particular weapon belongs to this category. Some weapons, such as lances with barbed heads, irregular-shaped bullets, or bullets with substances that would tend unnecessarily to inflame a wound have been traditionally recognized as illegal because of their effects. Whether the so-called "cluster bombs" belong to this category is controversial. Protocol I (1977) added a prohibition of weapons which are intended or may be expected to cause widespread, long-term and severe damage to the natural environment. This prohibition is further developed in the 1977 Convention on the Prohibition of Military or Any Other Hostile Use of Environmental Modification Techniques. The fact that a weapon is not expressly prohibited does not signify its legality, and in acquiring a new weapon each state is obliged to determine whether or not it is compatible with the general principles of international humanitarian law.

The legality of nuclear weapons is a most controversial matter. The U.S. and most other Western nations' position is that in the absence of any customary rule of international law or a convention restricting their employment, the use in warfare of atomic and nuclear weapons is not a violation of international law. The very posture of the two superpowers (the United States and the Soviet Union) confronting each other in the mutual nuclear "balance of terror" seems to be predicated on the assumption that they accept the possibility of resort to nuclear weapons. However, when the United Nations General Assembly in 1961 declared the use of nuclear weapons illegal, the Soviet Union was among the fifty-five states supporting this point of view, whereas twenty states (the United States and most Western nations) voted against the Resolution and twenty-six states (mostly Latin American) abstained. Publicists opposing the lawfulness of the use in warfare of nuclear weapons invoke a number of rules of international law that indirectly and by analogy point to the illegality of such use, including the Hague Regulations' (Convention of 1907 or the corresponding Convention of 1899) ban on poisonous and poisoned weapons; the Geneva Protocol of 1925 prohibiting not only chemical weapons but also all "analogous liquids, materials, or devices"; and the fact that the use of nuclear weapons would cause unnecessary suffering, produce uncontrollable effects, and would make completely irrelevant the traditional international law distinction between combatants and noncombatants. One might add that such weapons would be likely to cause widespread long-term and severe damage to the natural environment ("nuclear winter") in the meaning of Protocol I.

A number of specific weapons are banned by conventional law. Chronologically, first was the now practically obsolete Declaration of St. Petersburg of 1868 banning the use of projectiles weighing less than 400 grams (14 ounces), which are either explosive or charged with inflammable substance. Next, the Hague Declaration of 1899 Concerning Expanding (Dum-dum) Bullets prohibited the use of bullets (named after an arsenal near Calcutta) that expand or flatten easily in the human body. Another Hague Declaration of 1899 (Concerning Projectiles Diffusing Asphyxiating or Deleterious Gases) was replaced by the Geneva Protocol of 1925, which banned the use of asphyxiating, poisonous, or other gases; analogous liquids, materials, or devices; and of bacteriological methods of warfare. The Geneva Protocol of 1925 represents the most important ban on any weapons, and its comprehensive outlawry of chemical and biological methods of warfare has become a rule of customary international law. Following the entry into force of the 1972 Convention on the Development, Production, and Stockpiling of Bacteriological (Biological) and Toxin Weapons and Their Destruction, such weapons are the only type of means of warfare whose production, possession, and use are illegal in international law. The use of poison and poisonous weapons is illegal under general international law and the Hague Regulations. The latest addition to the inventory of prohibited weapons is based on the Convention of 1980 (open for signature in 1981) on Prohibitions and Restrictions on the Use of Certain Conventional Weapons Which May Be Deemed to Be Excessively Injurious or to Have Indiscriminate Effects. The three Protocols annexed to this Convention prohibit (1) the use of any weapon the primary effect of which is to injure by fragments which in the human body escape detection by X rays; (2) indiscriminate use of land mines, booby traps, and remote control devices or time bombs; and (3) the use of incendiary weapons (for example, napalm) against the civilian population. A resolution annexed to the Convention appeals to the signatory states to exercise the utmost care in the development of small-caliber weapons. Finally, in the area of maritime warfare, the Hague Convention VIII of 1907 Relating to the Laying of Automatic Contact Mines prohibits laying unanchored contact mines which do not become harmless upon breaking loose from their moorings, and torpedoes which do not become harmless after missing their target. The laying of automatic contact mines off ports and coasts for the sole purpose of stopping commercial navigation is also banned. *See also* AIR WARFARE, 321; GENEVA CONVENTIONS (1949), 342; HAGUE CONVENTIONS (1907), 343; INTERNATIONAL HUMANITARIAN LAW, 344; MARITIME WARFARE, LAW OF, 347; PROHIBITED METHODS OF WARFARE, 356; PROTOCOLS I AND II (1977), 359; SUBMARINE WARFARE (UNRESTRICTED), 364.

Significance   The laws of war banning the use of various types of weapons have been only partially successful but, in general, they have been more observed than other rules of international humanitarian law and especially the rules governing the treatment of the civilian population. The Declaration of St. Petersburg (1868), still in force for seventeen states, has been rendered virtually meaningless by new developments in weapons technology, particularly antiaircraft projectiles. The ban on Dum-dum bullets has been generally complied with; but the Hague Declaration of 1899 on asphyxiating and other poisonous gases was violated on a large scale in World War I in which Germany first resorted to chemical warfare with consequent reprisals by the Allied forces. Hague Convention VIII (1907) on automatic mines was disregarded in both world wars. On the other hand, the Geneva Protocol (1925) was, by a sort of tacit agreement, observed by all the belligerents in World War II who did not resort to chemical (gas) or bacteriological warfare. In the postwar period of the 1980s, however, charges of the use of chemical warfare (nerve gas) in Indochina were leveled against Vietnam and against the Soviet Union for alleged resort to chemical and even bacteriological warfare in Afghanistan. Iraq, also a party to the 1925 Protocol, was charged by Iran with the use of poison gas in its war with Iran in the 1980s. The United States had used herbicides in the Vietnam War, claiming that they were permitted under international law, but subsequently, in 1975, renounced first use of such chemical agents both in war and in riot control, and in 1980 became a party to the 1977 environmental modification convention.

Atomic or nuclear weapons have not been used in war since 1945 when the United States dropped two atomic bombs on Japan at the end of World War II. There are treaties limiting nuclear tests (the Partial Test Ban Treaty of 1963); stipulating nuclear weapons nonproliferation (the Nonproliferation Treaty of 1968); banning nuclear and other weapons of mass destruction from outer space (the Outer Space Treaty of 1967), the seabed (the Sea-bed Treaty of 1971), and from some geographical regions (the Antarctica, 1959, the 1967 Treaty for the Prohibition of Nuclear Weapons in Latin America, and the 1985 Treaty of Rarotonga denuclearizing the Southern Pacific region). But any possible use of nuclear weapons in an armed conflict is likely to remain a matter of high politics and military strategy rather than international law.

Protecting Power   (358)

A neutral or other state not a party to the conflict, which has been designated by a party to the conflict and accepted by the adverse party and has agreed to carry out the functions of determining whether or not the provisions of the Geneva Conventions of 1949, Protocols I and II of 1977, and other rules of international humanitarian law are being observed. The specific function of a protecting power, which can also be entrusted to an impartial organization such as the International Committee of the Red Cross (ICRC), is to protect the respective powers' nationals (prisoners of war and "protected persons") under the control of the enemy. If no protecting powers have been designated, their functions are assumed by a humanitarian organization, normally the ICRC. See also GENEVA CONVENTIONS (1949), 342; PROTOCOLS I AND II (1977), 359; PRISONERS OF WAR, 354; WOUNDED, SICK, AND SHIPWRECKED, 368.

Significance The institution of protecting power was introduced in 1929 by the Convention Relating to the Treatment of Prisoners of War, and subsequently developed after World War II in the Geneva Conventions (1949) and Protocol I (1977). In practice, the tasks of protecting powers, including substitute organizations such as the International Committee of the Red Cross, have been more extensive in relation to prisoners of war than with regard to the wounded, sick, and shipwrecked members of armed forces. The effectiveness of a protecting power, especially in such matters as visits to prisoner-of-war camps and interned and detained protected persons, depends to a large extent on the readiness to cooperate and sincerity of the state in whose power such persons are held. In the armed conflicts of the post–World War II era, as before, the International Committee of the Red Cross made a significant contribution to ameliorating the conditions of prisoners of war and other victims of armed conflict.

Protocols I and II (1977)   (359)

Two treaties additional to the Geneva Conventions of 1949 that relate to the protection of the victims of international and noninternational armed conflict respectively. The first treaty—Protocol Additional to the Geneva Conventions of 12 August 1949—relates to the protection of victims of international armed conflicts (Protocol I). It develops in detail the rules of the international humanitarian law of the 1949 Geneva Conventions and the rules of the Hague Conventions concerning the methods and means of warfare. Among the matters dealt with in Protocol I are protection of the wounded, sick, and shipwrecked, including detailed regulations of evacuation and medical transportation; new weapons and other means and methods of warfare; combatant and prisoner-of-war status; protection of civilian population and civilian objects, including protection of works and installations containing dangerous forces (for example, dams and nuclear power stations); nondefended localities and demilitarized zones; civil defense; relief action; measures in favor of women and children; protection for journalists; and execution of the 1949 Geneva Conventions and the Protocol and repression of their breaches. Protocol II is a much shorter instrument than Protocol I. It develops and supplements Article 3 of the 1949 Geneva Conventions dealing with noninternational armed conflicts, the only conventional rule on such conflicts prior to Protocol II. The two Protocols entered into force in 1978, but fewer than forty states, mostly from the Third World, were parties to them in 1984. The United States and a number of other major countries were not signatories. *See also* ARMED CONFLICT: INTERNATIONAL, 323; ARMED CON-

FLICT: NONINTERNATIONAL, 324; GENEVA CONVENTIONS (1949), 342;
IRREGULAR FORCES, 345; PROHIBITED METHODS OF WARFARE, 356;
PROHIBITED WEAPONS, 357; PROTECTING POWER, 358; WOUNDED, SICK,
AND SHIPWRECKED, 368.

Significance   Protocols I and II (1977) resulted from drafts prepared
by the International Committee of the Red Cross, which provided the
basis for discussion at the Diplomatic Conference on Reaffirmation
and Development of International Humanitarian Law Applicable in
Armed Conflicts in Geneva, 1974–1977. The Protocols were adopted
by consensus. Apart from developing in more detail and in stronger
terms the rules of international humanitarian law of the Geneva Conventions of 1949, the Conference was important in that it made a
distinction between international and noninternational armed conflicts, the definition of the latter category being one of the most controversial issues at the Conference.

Region of War and Theater of War   (360)
A distinction in the law of war concerning the geographical limits of
acts of war. The region of war means that part of the earth in which the
belligerents may prepare and execute hostilities against each other, and
the theater of war refers to that part of the region of war where
hostilities are actually taking place. The region of war includes the
territories of the belligerents and those areas of the high seas which do
not constitute the territorial sea and internal waters of the third states.
The latter areas, as well as any part of the globe that is permanently
neutralized or demilitarized, fall outside of the region of war. Neutralization may be based either on a treaty concluded in peacetime or
may result from a special agreement between the belligerents. Geneva
Convention IV of 1949 and Protocol I of 1977 envision the possibility
of creating neutralized or demilitarized zones as well as special hospital
and safety zones intended to shelter from the effects of war the
wounded and sick and civilians in which no military activities may take
place. *See also* ANTARCTIC TREATY SYSTEM, 174; CONSTANTINOPLE CON-
VENTION (1888), 223; OUTER SPACE TREATY (1967), 212.

Significance   The practice of the two world wars demonstrated that
the distinction between region of war and theater of war virtually
disappears in a total and global war when the two zones are almost
coextensive. Also, as witnessed by the hostilities in the Suez Canal zone
in 1956, 1967, and 1973, the rules on demilitarized zones may be
violated by the states engaged in an armed conflict. Among the neutralized and inviolable areas which may not become regions of war are

Antarctica, demilitarized under the Antarctic Treaty of 1959; the Norwegian archipelago of Svalbard (Spitsbergen) under a Treaty of 1920; the Finnish archipelago of the Aaland Islands, neutralized and demilitarized under a Convention of 1921; the Suez Canal Zone under the Constantinople Convention of 1888; and the Vatican City under the Lateran Treaty of 1929 between Italy and the Holy See. At one time, some other areas were also declared demilitarized or neutralized, such as the Tangier Zone (1923–1956) and the Free Territory of Trieste (1947–1954). Although it is sometimes claimed that the Baltic Sea is closed to hostilities of extralittoral powers, international practice shows that no part of the high seas is demilitarized except for the Antartic waters south of 60° latitude.

Reprisals in War   (361)

Acts of retaliation in the form of conduct which would otherwise be unlawful, resorted to by one party to an armed conflict against enemy personnel or property for acts of warfare committed by the other party in violation of the law of war, for the purpose of enforcing future compliance with the recognized rules of civilized warfare. Reprisals in war or belligerent reprisals must be distinguished from reprisals in time of peace. Before belligerent reprisals may be resorted to, other remedies must normally be applied to secure compliance with the rules of the law of war. Certain kinds of reprisals such as collective punishment, the taking of hostages, and reprisals against prisoners of war and protected civilians are forbidden. Geneva Convention III (1949) does not admit of any exceptions to the rule that reprisals against prisoners of war are prohibited, which means that, strictly speaking, such reprisals are inadmissible even as a measure of retaliation against a violation of Geneva Convention III itself. Reprisals should not be arbitrary or exceed the degree of violation committed by the enemy. Normally only the commander-in-chief has the right to order reprisals. *See also* REPRISALS, 315.

Significance   Reprisals in time of war are admissible for any illegitimate acts of warfare irrespective of whether or not they constitute an international delinquency. Many instances of reprisals in war have been recorded. For example, during World War I, reprisals and counter-reprisals were applied by Great Britain and Germany in the form of solitary confinement of prisoners of war, something that would be illegal under Geneva Convention III of 1949. An example of excessive reprisals was the burning of the University of Leuven (Louvain) by the Germans in that war, alleging that Belgian civilians had fired upon German soldiers. In general, the experiences of the two world wars revealed that, instead of being a means of securing legitimate conduct of hostilities, reprisals may degenerate into atrocities and cynical violations of fundamental principles of the law of war.

Safe-Conduct (362)

A written permission issued by a belligerent to enemy nationals or others, allowing them to enter and remain within or pass through an occupied area. A safe-conduct may also be issued to persons residing within or without the occupied area to allow them to engage in trade that is otherwise prohibited. A safe-conduct must be distinguished from the so-called safeguard. One kind of safeguard is a written order issued to an enemy national (or left posted upon enemy property), addressed by the belligerent to his commander, charging him to protect the national or the enemy property. Another kind of safeguard is a detachment of soldiers posted by a commander for the protection of persons, places, or property of the enemy or of a neutral. *See also* ENEMY ALIEN, 338; ENEMY PROPERTY, 340.

Significance   Safe-conducts and safeguards are mandatory under international law only if arranged by belligerents under Geneva Conventions of 1949. Historically, safe-conducts have been issued to allow enemy aliens to return home across the sea or to neutral diplomats. For example, in 1917 Count Bernstorff, the retiring German ambassador to the United States, received a safe-conduct for returning home on a neutral vessel calling at an enemy (British) port. There is no legal requirement, however, to issue safe-conducts to neutral diplomats.

Spy (363)

A person who, acting clandestinely or on false pretenses, obtains or endeavors to obtain information in a zone of operations of a belligerent with the intention of communicating it to the hostile party. If apprehended, a spy has no right to a prisoner-of-war status. He is, however, entitled to a fair and regular trial and is granted the rights and privileges possessed of a protected person; that is, a person finding himself of herself in case of an armed conflict or occupation in the hands of a party to the conflict or occupying power of which he or she is not a national. The regular penalty for espionage in time of war is death, irrespective of whether or not the spy succeeds in obtaining information or conveying it to the enemy. Clandestine action is the essential feature of spying. Therefore soldiers, not wearing a disguise, who have penetrated into the zone of operations of the hostile army for the purpose of obtaining information are not considered spies. Similarly, soldiers and civilians carrying out their mission openly, entrusted with delivering dispatches, are not spies under the laws of war. Espionage in peacetime is not governed by international law and is subject to the rules of municipal law of individual countries. *See also* COMBATANTS AND NONCOMBATANTS, 331; PROHIBITED METHODS OF WARFARE, 356.

Significance   The Hague Regulations (Convention IV of 1907 or the corresponding Convention of 1899) and Protocol I of 1977 tacitly recognized the well-established right of belligerents to employ spies for obtaining information of the enemy. Espionage involves no breach of international law; spies are punished not as violators of the laws of war but in order to deter spying by rendering it as dangerous, difficult, and ineffective as possible.

Submarine Warfare (Unrestricted)   (364)

Attacking and sinking enemy and (under certain circumstances) neutral merchant ships, without warning and in disregard of the laws and customs of naval warfare. Under London Protocol of 1936, which *verbatim* incorporated Part IV of London Naval Treaty of 1930, submarines are subject to the same rules that govern surface ships in their operations against merchant vessels, and in particular they may attack a merchant vessel only if it resists visit and search. If such attack becomes necessary, passengers, crew, and ship's papers must first be rescued. The London Protocol remains in force for forty-nine countries, including the United States and the Soviet Union, but as it is deemed to be declaratory of customary international law its rules are of general validity. Merchant vessels sailing under a convoy of warships or military aircraft may be attacked without warning, however. *See also* MARITIME WARFARE, LAW OF, 347.

Significance   The experiences of the two world wars demonstrated that the prohibitions relative to submarine warfare against merchant shipping were unrealistic considering the nature of submarines which, if surfaced to signal an enemy merchant vessel to stop for visit and search, would normally expose themselves to danger of being destroyed as relatively defenseless targets. As long as merchant vessels were not armed and no other hazards were present, the submarines could follow the traditional rules. Otherwise they would sink a merchant vessel on sight without warning, thus technically committing a war crime. In World War I, Germany initially waged a limited submarine warfare in the years 1915–1917, the best-known case being the controversial sinking of the British liner *Lusitania* in 1915 with a loss of 1,198 lives. In 1917, Germany began an unrestricted submarine warfare against merchant shipping. In World War II, despite the rules of the London Protocol of 1936, unrestricted submarine warfare was waged first by Germany and then by the Allies whose submarines operated with particular efficiency against Japanese merchant shipping in the Pacific Ocean. The sinking of merchant vessels without warning figured prominently in the indictment of some of the major war criminals before the International Military Tribunal at Nuremberg in 1946. The Tribunal partly acquitted the accused German admirals Karl Doenitz and Erich Raeder on the grounds that the British merchant vessels were armed and had been ordered to ram U-boats if possible. On the other hand, the Tribunal ruled that sinking by Germany of neutral vessels without warning in the so-called "operational zones" was a war crime in violation of the London Protocol of 1936. The Tribunal did not find any convincing evidence that the accused had deliberately ordered the killing of survivors, but strongly censured their conduct. In 1945, in the case of the *Peleus*, a British military court found the commander of a German U-boat guilty of killing survivors of a Greek merchant vessel chartered by Great Britain. In the conditions of modern warfare, when merchant shipping increasingly forms part of integrated defense effort, the rules of the London Protocol would not realistically have a chance of being observed by belligerents in a major confrontation at sea.

Unconditional Surrender   (365)

A method of terminating hostilities whereby no limits are set upon the victor's freedom of action with regard to the fate of the defeated enemy. Unconditional surrender does not have the nature of an agreement and, therefore, must be distinguished from capitulation and armistice, both of which are agreements between representatives of belligerents. Legally, unconditional surrender does not terminate the war unless so desired by the victor. *See also* ARMISTICE, 325; CAPITULATION, 329; PEACE TREATY, 353.

Significance   Unconditional surrender, applied by the victors in World War II, was a new concept in the law of war. In relations with Germany it was resorted to in order to avoid any dealings with the defeated Nazi regime, which was totally eliminated by the order of the victorious powers. Unconditional surrender of Germany was signed at Reims, on 8 May 1945 on behalf of the German High Command, and was subsequently proclaimed by the Declaration of the United Nations on 5 June 1945. Unconditional surrender was also signed by the representatives of Japan on 1 September 1945, but was not fully made use of by the Allies. Italy signed only regular armistice agreements.

Unneutral Service (366)

Any act or conduct on the part of a neutral vessel or aircraft which furthers the interests of the enemy. The traditional concept of unneutral service or "hostile assistance" (from the French term *assistance hostile*) has expanded to include not only such activities as taking direct part in hostilities, operation under charter to the enemy, carrying enemy dispatches, and transport of members of the enemy armed forces, but also carrying enemy nationals of military age (reservists) and other persons such as scientists essential to the war effort. Carrying diplomatic agents of the enemy or communications between them and their government is not regarded as unneutral service. Contraband is a separate concept subject to special rules. *See also* NEUTRALITY, 351; PRIZE COURT, 355.

Significance A belligerent may stop a neutral vessel or aircraft suspected of unneutral service and remove persons improperly carried. Among examples illustrating this rule are the case of the French vessel *Manouba* taken by an Italian warship to Italy during the Italo-Turkish War in 1912 from which twenty-nine Turkish nationals were removed, and the seizure by a British warship in 1940 of a number of German nationals of military age from the Japanese steamer *Asama Maru*. In serious cases, the neutral vessel and its cargo may be captured and condemned according to the rules of the prize law.

War Crimes (367)

Violations of the laws and customs of war entailing individual criminal responsibility directly under international law. As specified in Article 6 of the Charter of the International Military Tribunal of 1945 and reaffirmed by the International Law Commission and the United Nations General Assembly in the Principles of International Law Recognized in the Charter and Judgment of the Nuremberg Tribunal (1950), war crimes "include, but are not limited to, murder, ill-treatment or deportation to slave labor or for any other purpose of civilian population of or in occupied territory; murder or ill-treatment of prisoners of war or persons on the seas; killing of hostages; plunder of public or private property; wanton destruction of cities, towns, or villages, or devastation not justified by military necessity." Among other violations qualifying as war crimes are the abuse of a flag of truce or of the Red Cross or similar emblems; wearing civilian clothes or enemy uniform while in combat; poisoning of streams or wells; the killing of an enemy who laid down arms; assassination; violation of surrender terms; breach of parole; and wanton destruction of enemy prize. Hostile acts committed by unlawful combatants are also, strictly speaking, war crimes which, realistically, are punishable only by the courts of such combatants' enemy. Espionage is not a war crime. As defined by the Nuremberg Tribunal, "crimes against humanity" (genocide) are wider than war crimes since they can be committed before the war as well as during the war and can be directed against any population. The definition implies that crimes against humanity committed against enemy nationals in execution of or in connection with a war crime must be also considered as one category of war crime. Complicity in the commission of war crimes is also a crime under international law. Defense of "act of State," that is, the plea that the person who committed a war crime acted as head of state or responsible government official, does not relieve that person from responsibility. A "superior order" plea—that is, the fact that the offender acted pursuant to order of his government or a superior is no defense—but may be considered in mitigation of punishment. The test is whether or not a moral choice was possible for the defendant. In the prevailing opinion, war crimes (as well as crimes against humanity) are not subject to any statute of limitations; that is, preclusion or barring of prosecution after the lapse of a specified period of time following the commission of the crime. This is certainly the case of any trial by a state party to the Convention of the Non-Applicability of Statutory Limitations to War Crimes and Crimes against Humanity, adopted by the United Nations General Assembly in 1968. The United States was among the several countries opposing this Convention. Members of the Council of Europe are bound by the European Convention of 1974 on the Non-Applicability of Statutory Limitations to Crimes against Humanity and War Crimes. The Federal Republic of Germany is one of the states in which such crimes are not subject to any statute of limitations also under domestic legislation. War crimes do not qualify as political offenses for purposes of extradition. *See also* CRIMES AGAINST PEACE, 82; EXTRADITION, 120; GENOCIDE CONVENTION (1948), 86; INDIVIDUALS AS SUBJECTS OF INTERNATIONAL LAW, 88; PIRACY, 247; WAR CRIMES TRIALS, 103.

Significance   The legal nature and punishment of war crimes has undergone a revolutionary change since World War II and, in particular, since the adoption of the London Agreement of 1945 for the Prosecution and Punishment of the Major War Criminals of the European Axis. Under its Charter, an International Military Tribunal was set up which handed down the Nuremberg Judgment in 1946. Traditionally, only piracy had been regarded as a crime against the law of nations, punishable in any state that seizes the offender, but as individuals were not otherwise considered subjects of international law, offenses against the laws of war were punishable as crimes against the municipal law of the belligerent that tried the offender, including offenders belonging to the armed forces of the enemy. In addition (except for Article 3 of Hague Convention IV of 1907 which provided for payment of compensation in responsibility for all acts committed by members of the armed forces) none of the conventions on the laws of war envisaged any punishment of individuals or states for violating such laws. The first modest steps toward a wider concept of international criminal responsibility were made with the (generally unsuccessful) attempts to try Germans accused of war crimes committed during World War I. The German ex-Emperor was to be tried not for war crimes but for offenses against "international morality and the sanctity of treaties." It was not until after the unprecedented violations of virtually all laws and customs of war by Nazi Germany that the Nuremberg Tribunal instituted the rule of law whereby responsibility under international law can be imputed directly to the individual. The International Military Tribunal, set up under the London Agreement of 1945 to which twenty-three states were parties in 1984, found all but two of the major war criminals guilty of war crimes under international law. Similarly, the International Military Tribunal for the Far East, established in Tokyo in 1946, tried Japanese major war criminals and delivered its judgment in 1948. Thousands of lesser World War II war criminals were tried by national military courts for violations of the laws and customs of war or by ordinary criminal courts for violations of local criminal law. However, the victorious powers did not investigate war crimes committed by their nationals. Following World War II, attempts to create a permanent International Criminal Court ended in failure. Although charges of war crimes were leveled in a number of local conflicts (for example in the Korean War by both sides, by Bangladesh against members of Pakistani armed forces in 1971, and in the Vietnam War by both North and South Vietnam and the United States), no offenders were tried for direct violations of international law. In the My Lai massacre trial (1971), the accused members of U.S. armed forces were tried by a U.S. court for killing Vietnamese civilians on grounds of violating U.S. law (Uniform Code of Military Justice) and not international law. No superior officers of the two accused were ever tried. Under the Geneva Conventions (1949), states have the duty to enact appropriate legislation providing for effective penal sanctions for persons committing or ordering to be committed grave breaches of the Convention and to bring offenders, regardless of their nationality, before its courts for trial or hand them over for trial to another state if the latter has made a *prima facie* case.

Wounded, Sick, and Shipwrecked   (368)

Military or civilian persons who, refraining from any act of hostility, are in need of medical assistance or care during an armed conflict because of a physical or mental disorder or disability, or who are in peril at sea or in other waters as a result of misfortune affecting them or the vessel or aircraft carrying them. The status of the wounded and sick in land warfare is governed by Geneva Convention I of 1949 for the Amelioration of the Condition of the Wounded and Sick in Armed Forces in the Field. Geneva Convention II of 1949 for the Amelioration of the Condition of the Wounded, Sick, and Shipwrecked Members of Armed Forces at Sea, replacing, as between the parties, Hague Convention X of 1907, is similar to Geneva Convention I and includes additional provisions dealing with the special problems arising in naval warfare, such as the immunity of hospital ships from attack and seizure. The provisions of Geneva Conventions I and II are further developed in Protocol I of 1977. Once captured, wounded or sick soldiers must be treated as prisoners of war. They may not be left on the field without medical attention and must be provided with all necessary care. Members of the enemy medical personnel are exempt from capture and are to be used for the care of the captured wounded and sick. Geneva Conventions I and II established a distinctive emblem and sign of the medical service of the armed forces. As a compliment to Switzerland, it is a red cross on a white ground (reverse of Switzerland's colors), the red crescent (for Islamic states), or the red lion and sun (for Iran) on a white ground. Israel signed the Conventions subject to the reservation that it would choose a red shield of David as its distinctive sign. Abuse of the red cross and similar emblems is a violation of the law of war. Detailed provisions of the two relevant Geneva Conventions and Protocol I govern the protection of military and civilian medical units and medical transportation—vehicles, hospital ships, coastal rescue craft, and medical aircraft. Although hospital ships are immune from capture, wounded, sick, and shipwrecked members of armed forces may be captured provided they are fit to be moved and the enemy warship can provide adequate medical facilities. Convention I contains special provisions on honorable interment of the dead and registration and protection of grave sites. *See also* PRISONERS OF WAR, 354; PROTECTING POWER, 358.

Significance   Although many bilateral agreements on tending each other's wounded had been concluded since the seventeenth century, no general rules of international law existed regulating the status of the wounded and sick until the second half of the nineteenth century. The humanitarian activities of Henri Dunant, the Swiss founder of the Red Cross who witnessed the suffering of the wounded in the battle of

Solferino in 1859, led indirectly to the Red Cross Convention of 1864 for the Amelioration of the Condition of the Wounded in Time of War. In 1906 a new Convention was signed, revised in 1929 as a result of the lessons of World War I. In 1949, Geneva Conventions I and II incorporated the experiences gained in World War II. The Conventions were supplemented by a number of provisions included in Protocol I of 1977. The condition of the wounded, sick, and shipwrecked in maritime warfare was first regulated by Hague Convention X of 1907 for the Adaptation of the Principles of the Geneva Convention (of 1906) to Maritime Warfare, which was subsequently revised and substantially enlarged by Geneva Convention II of 1949. In general, great progress has been made in humanitarian law on the condition of the wounded, sick, and shipwrecked, but violations of this law have also been registered in the wars of the twentieth century.

INDEX

Within the text, cross-references to dictionary entries are located at the end of each definition paragraph. In this index, references in BOLD type indicate the entry numbers where that particular term is defined within the text. Numbers in roman type refer to entries containing additional information about a term that the reader may wish to consult for further information, e.g., Mediation, 288, **294,** 297.